DOING MORE WITH LESS

DOING MORE WITH LESS

USING LONG-TERM SKILLS IN SHORT-TERM TREATMENT

Edited by

Barbara Dane, Ph.D.,
Carol Tosone, Ph.D.,
and
Alice Wolson, D.S.W.

JASON ARONSON INC.
Northvale, New Jersey
London

This book was set in 12 pt. Centaur by Alabama Book Composition of Deatsville, AL, and printed and bound by Book-mart Press of North Bergen, NJ.

Library of Congress Cataloging-in-Publication Data

Doing more with less : using long-term skills in short-term treatment / edited by
   Barbara Dane, Carol Tosone, Alice Wolson.
         p.   cm.
   Includes bibliographical references.
   ISBN 0-7657-0296-7
   1. Brief psychotherapy.   2. Psychodynamic psychotherapy.   I. Dane, Barbara.
II. Tosone, Carol.   III. Wolson, Alice.
   RC480.55 .D64   2001
   616.89'14—dc21

                                                        00-056938

Printed in the United States of America on acid-free paper. For information and catalog write to Jason Aronson Inc., 230 Livingston Street, Northvale, NJ 07647-1726, or visit our website: www.aronson.com

To my father, Albert Joseph Tosone, and to my husband,
Richard Connor Lutzy.

C.A.T.

To my husband, Milton, for his love and support,
and in loving memory of my father and my mother,
Aaron and Esther Kane.

A.K.W.

To all my mentors and especially
my husband, Sidney Paul Dane—

B.O.D.

CONTENTS

ACKNOWLEDGMENTS

A number of people provided support during the preparation and publication of this book. We are especially indebted to our colleagues at New York University Ehrenkranz School of Social Work and wish to make special mention of faculty members who participated with us in a study group on short-term treatment: Dr. Eda Goldstein, chairperson of the study group and director of the Ph.D. program, Dr. Judith Mishne, chairperson of Practice, Dr. Lala Straussner, Dr. Maryellen Noonan, Professor Roberta Kabat, and Professor Joan Klein.

We thank Kristen Denney for her patience, her invaluable administrative assistance, and her expertise in bringing this to fruition.

Many thanks are also due to Jason Aronson, our publisher, for his generosity, and the staff at Jason Aronson Inc., especially Norma Pomerantz, director of author relations, for her attention and kindness, and Judy Cohen, for her expert editorial assistance.

Alice Wolson would like to acknowledge the love and support of her children Aaron, Dina, and Frank. She would also like to thank her friends and colleagues Judith Berenson and Marjorie Zimmerman for their thoughtful comments.

Barbara Dane thanks her mother and her aunt, Julia Gucwa, who has been a special guide and mentor throughout her life, and her friends Barbara Deitz, Corinne LoBrutto, Monique Lores, and Sondra Stein, for their endless support and love.

Carol Tosone thanks her loving and supportive husband, Richard Connor Lutzy, and the other equally special members of her family. She is very proud of her father, Albert Tosone, and grateful to him for paving the way for her education. She also wishes to thank her sister, Barbara Ambroselli, her brother-in-law, Nicky Ambroselli, and her three "favorite" nephews, Nick Ambroselli, Paul Ambroselli, and Mike Ambroselli. She thanks her three outstanding stepdaughters, Jill Lutzy, Jenn Lutzy, and Rebecca Lutzy, for their ongoing patience and understanding.

CONTRIBUTORS

Ellen Agoos, Ph.D., is a supervisor at the Postgraduate Center for Mental Health and a staff therapist at the Eating Disorder Resource Center (EDRC). She is also a supervisor at WS Institute Affiliate and the Center for the Study of Anorexia and Bulimia. She has been in private practice in New York City for seventeen years, specializing in the treatment of eating disorders.

Patricia Rose Attia, M.S.W., is the vice president of Liberty Management, a national provider of behavioral health care services. For the past seventeen years, she has implemented psychiatric and addiction programs across the country. She is an adjunct professor at Yeshiva University.

May Benatar, Ph.D., is a clinical social worker in private practice in Montclair, New Jersey. She teaches at the New York University Ehrenkranz School of Social Work and supervises and lectures on the subjects of sexual abuse and the treatment of dissociative disorders. Her current research interest is in the area of countertransference reactions of clinicians working with adult survivors of sexual abuse and sexual violence.

Grace Hyslop Christ, D.S.W., is an associate professor at Columbia University School of Social Work. Prior to joining the faculty at Columbia she was the director of the Department of Social Work at Memorial Sloan-Kettering Cancer Center. She has also worked with severe and persistent mental illness. Her research has focused on psychosocial consequences of and interventions with cancer, AIDS, the dying and the bereaved, for both children and adults.

Barbara T. Dane, Ph.D., is a licensed clinical social worker and professional educator who has more than thirty years of experience in agency work, university teaching, private clinical practice, consulting, and training. She has written extensively on issues in social work. She is currently associate professor of social work at the New York University Ehrenkranz School of Social Work, where she directs the post-master's certificate program. Dr. Dane received the faculty scholars' award in 1999 from the Soros Foundation's program on death in America. Dr. Dane maintains a private practice in New York City.

Eda G. Goldstein, D.S.W., is a professor in and director of the Ph.D. program in clinical social work at the New York University Ehrenkranz School of Social Work. She is a consulting editor for *Psychoanalytic Social Work* and *Clinical Social Work Journal.* She has authored over forty publications including *Ego Psychology and Social Work Practice, Borderline Disorders: Clinical Models,* and *Short-Term Treatment and Social Work Practice* (with Dr. Maryellen Noonan). Dr. Goldstein maintains a private practice in New York City.

Joan L. Klein, C.S.W., Ph.D., is an adjunct associate professor at the New York University Ehrenkranz School of Social Work. She is also a psychotherapist in private practice in New York City. A former director of facilities for the psychiatric and developmentally disabled population, she was selected by the New York State Office of Mental Health to develop residential programs to treat the mentally ill and mildly mentally retarded, which were subsequently designated as the model programs. She is a former deputy director of a psychiatric facility providing comprehensive residential and outpatient services to a multidisabled population.

Ellen P. Lukens, Ph.D., M.S.W., is an assistant professor of social work at the School of Social Work, Columbia University, and a research scientist at New York State Psychiatric Institute. As both a researcher and a clinician, she has had a long-standing interest in the impact of schizophrenia on family members and the value of collaboration among family members and professionals in the care of severely ill persons. She has collaborated with Helle Thorning clinically and in conducting research.

James I. Martin, Ph.D., is an associate professor at the New York University Ehrenkranz School of Social Work, where he teaches in the practice and research curriculum areas. He also provides clinical and research consultation, primarily to agencies working with lesbian, gay, bisexual, and transgender clients.

Judith Mishne, D.S.W., is a professor and chairperson of the practice curriculum area at the New York University Ehrenkranz School of Social Work. She teaches in the master's and Ph.D. programs, and is coordinator of specialization in treatment of children and adolescents in the Ph.D. program. A recipient of the Distinguished Practitioner in Social Work Award, she received her D.S.W. in social welfare from the Hunter College School of Social Work and is a graduate of the child therapy program of the Chicago Institute for Psychoanalysis. She has published extensively in professional journals and has authored four books and edited two books.

Maryellen Noonan, Ph.D., is an assistant professor at New York University Ehrenkranz School of Social Work and is coordinator for the NYU-CSS Brooklyn Women's Shelter. She has presented and published numerous articles on working with difficult patients. Dr. Noonan co-authored the book, *Short-Term Treatment and Social Work Practice*, with Dr. Eda Goldstein.

Susan Oppenheim, D.S.W., is an associate director of field instruction at the Columbia University School of Social Work. She also teaches in the area of clinical practice. She has many years of practice in health and mental health, focusing especially on family therapy and interventions with chronic mental illness. Dr. Oppenheim maintains a private practice in New York City.

Harriet Rzetelny, M.S.W., is a psychotherapist in private practice. She is on the faculty of the Brookdale Center on Aging of Hunter College and is an adjunct associate professor at the New York University Ehrenkranz School of Social Work, where she teaches clinical practice with the elderly and their families.

Mary Sormanti, Ph.D., is an assistant professor at the Columbia University School of Social Work. Prior to joining the faculty at Columbia, she was an oncology social work supervisor and senior pediatric oncology social worker at the Dana Farber Cancer Institute in Boston. There she specialized in bone marrow transplantation and bereavement. Her current research focuses on interventions with cancer and AIDS, substance abuse, care of the dying and the bereaved, and domestic violence.

Shulamith Lala Ashenberg Straussner, D.S.W., BCSW, CAS, CEAP, is a professor at the New York University Ehrenkranz School of Social Work and coordinator of its post-master's program in the Treatment of Alcohol and Drug Abusing Clients (TADAC). She is the past chair of the National Association of Social Workers Section on Alcohol, Tobacco, and Other Drugs, and chairs the New York City Women's Issues Committee of Employee Assistance Professionals Association. She is the author or editor of numerous publications, including six books. Her most recent was *Gender and Addictions: Men and Women in Treatment* (co-edited with E. Zelvin, published by Jason Aronson). She is the founder and editor of the *Journal of Social Work Practice in the Addictions* (Haworth Press). Dr. Straussner has a private practice in New York City in therapy and supervision.

Helle Thorning, M.S., is the director of social work at New York State Psychiatric Institute, an assistant professor of psychiatric social work at the College of Physicians and Surgeons, Columbia University, and a doctoral candidate in clinical social work at the New York University Ehrenkranz School of Social Work. Her long-standing commitment is to the study of the impact that severe mental illness has on patients and their families. She has collaborated with Ellen P. Lukens for many years, conducting both clinical work and research in this area.

Carol Tosone, Ph.D., is an associate professor and coordinator of the clinical group work area at the New York University Ehrenkranz School of Social Work. She is also a member of the residency training faculty at NYU School of Medicine. Prior to joining the faculty of NYU, she was an assistant professor of psychiatry (social work) at the Temple University School of Medicine in Philadelphia. She is co-editor of *Love and Attachment: Contemporary Issues and Treatment Considerations,* and has written on the topics of countertransference, short-term treatment, and women's issues. Dr. Tosone serves as editor-in-chief of *Psychoanalysis and Psychotherapy,* and also serves on the editorial boards of *Psychoanalytic Social Work* and *Social Work in Health Care.* She is a member of the executive board of the New York State Society for Clinical Social Work, and has been appointed to the National Study Group of the National Membership Committee on Psychoanalysis. Dr. Tosone maintains a private practice in New York City.

Alice Wolson, D.S.W., is a clinical assistant professor at the New York University Ehrenkranz School of Social Work. She is a graduate of Yeshiva University, and earned an analytic certificate from the Westchester Center for the Study of Psychoanalysis and Psychotherapy and a certificate in supervision of the psychoanalytic process from the Postgraduate Center for Mental Health. She has led numerous seminars and workshops on supervision at NYU, dealing with diversity in the supervisory relationship, and helping practitioners sharpen their supervisory skills and enhance their theoretical knowledge about the supervisory process and the supervisor–supervisee relationship. Dr. Wolson provides professional consultation to agencies, and maintains a private practice in Westchester.

INTRODUCTION

For skeptics of the approach, the term *short-term treatment* may bring to mind the image of a strident therapist rapidly firing interpretations at an anxiety-ridden patient who is ill-prepared to receive them and on the verge of decompensation. The therapist, in an effort to attack defenses and uncover hidden affect, ends up displaying his or her own unneutralized aggression.

Does this depiction resonate with your fears? Do you believe, as do many talented and capable clinicians, that short-term treatment is harmful to your patients or clients? Do you believe that short-term treatment was conceived solely as an answer to the pressures of a managed care environment? If you answer yes to any of these questions, then *Doing More with Less: Using Long-Term Skills in Short-Term Treatment* will be an important addition to your professional library.

Not commonly known is that both modern brief treatment and contemporary psychoanalysis are derived from the early cases of Freud and his followers. In fact, as early as 1895 in "Studies on Hysteria," Freud reported he cured Lucy R. of her olfactory hallucinations after nine weekly sessions. He treated other cases that were of even shorter duration, including the composer Gustav Mahler, who was reportedly cured of his impotency after a four-hour stroll with Freud (Jones 1955).

Despite short-term treatment's legitimate heritage, clinician reluctance to conduct it is commonplace. Many clinicians, well versed in long-term practice and techniques, report feeling coerced into practicing short-term treatment by the constraints of managed care companies. Many managed care firms permit their patients only twenty outpatient psychotherapy sessions each year. Psychotherapists on their provider lists are encouraged to treat patients in as few sessions as possible. If clinicians do, they may be rewarded with additional referrals and, if not, they may be removed from the companies' lists of mental health providers, thereby reducing the size and range of their private practices. Clinicians trained in the practice of short-term therapy, particularly in regard to the treatment of Axis I disorders, are at a distinct advantage compared to practitioners of long-term psychoanalytic treatment.

The primary objective of this book is to level the playing field, that is, to provide clinicians with the skills necessary to conduct psychoanalytically informed short-term treatment. Actually, practitioners of the psychoanalytic persuasion, whether in private practice or in an outpatient treatment setting, already possess the requisite skills, and our goal is to help them recognize the adaptability of their skills to a time-limited approach. Our goal for beginning clinicians, including graduate students, is to help them acquire the fundamental therapeutic tools necessary to conduct psychodynamically informed short-term treatment with a broad range of patients commonly encountered in agency-based practice.

Given the managed care emphasis on symptom reduction and their tendency to pay primarily for short-term treatment of Axis I disorders only, this book is designed and arranged according to the *DSM-IV* (APA 1994) diagnostic categories. That is, after providing a general orientation to contemporary short-term practice and a comprehensive theoretical framework, each chapter addresses the short-term treatment of a specific condition or patient population. Each chapter outlines the theoretical, clinical, and research approaches to the topic; discusses diagnostic issues; and provides an extensive discussion of a case, from assessment to termination. The contributors are leading social work scholars and master clinicians who are experts in their areas of practice.

Chapters 1 and 2 are interrelated; they serve as an introduction to managed care and provide a theoretical foundation for treating patients. This framework is used as a guide to conceptualize the process of psychoanalytic short-term treatment. In Chapter 1, Alice Wolson presents an orientation to the requirements and constraints of managed care from the clinician's perspective. She outlines the effectiveness of treatment models that are likely to provide a sustained impetus for patient satisfaction and sustained therapeutic outcome. Treatment cases illustrate the provision of a cost-effective and worthwhile service. The clinician's interaction with the managed care system is outlined as well as the potentially intense transference and countertransference affect of the encounter. In Chapter 2, Eda Goldstein and Maryellen Noonan provide an overview of the theoretical underpinnings and major characteristics of the short-term treatment framework used throughout the book. After reviewing the contributions of classical Freudian theory, ego psychology, object relations theory, self psychology, intersubjectivity and relational theory, and trauma theory to the short-term treatment process, the chapter describes the distinguishing features of an integrated short-term treatment (ISTT) framework. Goldstein and Noonan elaborate on the fourteen core components of ISTT: problem identification, biopsychosocial assessment, engagement, planning treatment, contracting, implementing the treatment plan, maintaining or altering the focus, monitoring progress, dealing with resistance, managing transference/countertransference, addressing termination issues, reviewing progress, resolving the therapist–patient relationship, and referral and follow-up.

In Chapter 3, Judith Mishne elaborates on her work with children and adolescents. She posits that the more vulnerable the child or adolescent, the more active the clinician must be to compensate, by providing structure, modeling, mirroring, and new ways of thinking, feeling, and perceiving oneself, one's significant others, as well as the critical impinging life events that often constitute a crisis and prompt one to seek help. Concurrent with recognizing the substantial gains that can be achieved in short-term treatment of children, adolescents, and their parents, she stresses that criteria and suitability, based on assessment, are key factors in the selection of a short-term intervention.

In Chapter 4, Harriet Rzetelny discusses brief treatment approaches in work with dementia patients and their families at two points in the disease process: pre- and postdiagnosis. She stresses the need for accurate assessment and identifies *DSM-IV* diagnostic criteria that enable clinicians to educate the family about the disease and the resultant need for long-term planning. Case examples illustrate the use of short-term interventions to help families work through their denial, cope with grief and loss, and improve their communication in order to plan an appropriate level of care for the patient.

In Chapter 5, Lala Straussner and Patricia Rose Attia offer a state-of-the-art approach to working with the substance-abusing client. They provide a basic understanding of substance-related disorders, and help clinicians utilize brief interventions to motivate and to treat individuals who abuse alcohol and other drugs. A case vignette illustrates some of the issues and dynamics in short-term treatment of a substance-abusing patient that can help prevent clinicians from getting entangled in power struggles, which are detrimental for both the patient and the therapist.

Schizophrenia is a long-term chronic illness with severe psychosocial implications for the patient and his family. In today's mental health treatment system, patients often move from different levels of care, encountering different therapists in different treatment settings for short periods of time. How to focus one's treatment efforts, given the complicated variables associated with schizophrenia and the time limitations of short-term therapy, is the focus of Chapter 6. Helle Thorning and Ellen Lukens draw on current research with schizophrenics and share their perspectives on intervening with this population. Through case illustrations, they describe some of the challenges in working with patients whose lives have been negatively impacted by the illness. Thorning and Lukens note that addressing the everyday problems in living from a strengths-based perspective can yield optimism and hope.

In Chapter 7, James Martin discusses the short-term treatment of depression. He focuses on the alleviation of depressive episodes rather than on the resolution of the underlying dynamics that might cause patients to be vulnerable to depression. To accomplish this goal, clinicians need to structure their efforts around supporting and strengthening the patient's coping capacities, and resolving problems in the patient's social and physical environment. The use of a standardized measure of depression can help therapists evaluate the patient's progress. Because of the limited time available for the middle phase of treatment, Martin suggests that therapists minimize attention to transference material. He offers the reader a variety of therapeutic techniques to achieve treatment goals.

In Chapter 8, Carol Tosone offers a comprehensive approach to working with patients with anxiety disorder. She describes the distinguishing features of panic and anxiety, and examines the common cultural syndromes that are anxiety-based. She also provides a review of the theoretical literature on anxiety and considers the history of the concept from a pluralistic psychoanalytic perspective. Further, she outlines an effective psychodynamic treatment approach and provides a detailed case illustration for the reader.

In Chapter 9, Ellen Agoos presents the short-term treatment of an eating-disordered patient who retreats from the world of people to a world of food, where she has prematurely established a fragile identity, replete with rules, structures, and inflexible laws as to how she should be. A treatment approach that attempts to minimize the focus on food and allows for a real relationship in which the patient has an effect on and is affected by another person is illustrated. The techniques described in this chapter can be modified to apply to bulimics, anorexics, and compulsive overeaters as well.

Influenced in her earlier work with mildly retarded, mentally ill adults, Joan Klein in Chapter 10 provides a rich example of clinical work with this population to debunk the most insidious myth that mentally retarded individuals are not treatable and are unresponsive to modern therapeutic interventions. Mentally ill, mentally retarded individuals tend to exhibit poor self-esteem and have little self-confidence, a result of both inadequate internal resources for coping and the external reinforcements of their inadequacy. The therapist must be knowledgeable about mental illness and mental retardation to know how to effectively address these deficits in brief work. Klein works from a strengths perspective, teaching patients to recognize their emotions, especially in regard to the precipitating conditions. She also helps patients, when necessary, to replace aggressive behavioral responses with more self-managed, socially appropriate behaviors. In short-term work with this population, the themes of separation and abandonment predominate. Patients can be helped by ventilating and problem solving with a therapist who understands their sadness about their experience.

In Chapter 11, Grace Christ, Mary Sormanti, and Susan Oppenheim, who work in the field of acute, chronic, and terminal illness, discuss the psychosocial aspects of working with patients suffering from a chronic illness. Through extensive case illustrations, the authors describe how brief treatment can be powerfully effective in therapeutic work with patients and their families who confront the stresses of chronic and terminal conditions and their treatments.

Although treatment of posttraumatic conditions are frequently of longer duration, in Chapter 12 May Benatar outlines an approach that is suitable to the constraints of a setting where patient resources are limited but where important goals can be reasonably met. A wide array of interventions such as cognitive-behavioral procedures, variations on Eriksonian hypnotic methods, and the use of twelve-step programs are discussed. Short-term treatment of posttraumatic conditions may not address the developmental and personality deformations of the individuals and allow for in-depth processing of traumatic memory and its meanings; however, many important tasks can be dealt with successfully. Guided by core principles of trauma treatment and the integrative short-term therapy (ISTT) model, goals of this approach include consolidation and stabilization of the patient, psychoeducation, focus on solutions to the patient's presenting concerns, and helping the patient develop a sense of mastery over internal states as well as reality situations.

Many patients with Axis I conditions also present with an Axis II diagnosis as well. In Chapter 13, Maryellen Noonan discusses the short-term treatment of borderline patients, who present special challenges for the short-term treatment provider. Noonan presents the various perspectives on the etiology, treatment approaches, and clinical picture of borderline patients. An in-depth case presentation demonstrates an integrative short-term treatment (ISTT) framework. The chapter discusses such issues as engagement, handling transference—countertransference reactions, setting goals, and working through resistances.

In Chapter 14, Barbara Dane discusses the experience of death and a widow's mastery of the loss experience, based on her work with bereaved families. Clinicians who work with mourners often report a heightened sensitivity to life and human relationships paralleling the process of the patient's heightened experience of pain as well as an opportunity for growth.

Each author's specific approach to short-term treatment can be used in both agency and private practice work. Influenced by multiple theoretical paradigms, the authors illustrate how the patient must demonstrate some capacity for basic trust and an ability to respond to interpretations, reflections, and suggestions. Additional patient characteristics that are helpful in brief therapy treatment are ego strengths, affect tolerance, and some degree of psychological mindedness.

Our field is confronting a crucial challenge to provide sound clinical practice using a brief treatment model. We hope this timely book will serve to advance the literature on short-term treatment and assist our mental health colleagues in treating their patients.

REFERENCES

American Psychiatric Association. (1994). *Diagnostic and Statistical Manual of Mental Disorders*, 4th ed. Washington, DC: APA.

Freud, S. (1895). Studies on hysteria. *Standard Edition* 2:106–134.

Jones, E. (1955). *The Life and Work of Sigmund Freud*. New York: Basic Books.

CHAPTER ONE

The Impact of Managed Care on the Therapeutic Process

ALICE WOLSON

In the last twenty-five years managed care has had a dramatic impact on the administration and provision of health care services in the United States. The term *managed care* refers to a variety of organizational and financial structures, processes, and strategies designed to monitor and influence treatment decisions, thus providing health care in more cost-effective ways (Winegar 1997). Essentially, managed care clients' needs are matched to appropriate treatment resources, and then the delivery and outcome of these resources are monitored. In mental health care, the implications of an outside party or parties monitoring the treatment process (whether inpatient or outpatient) has often had negative ramifications. In addition to the alteration of the therapeutic frame, the mental health clinician's foundation of theoretical and practice beliefs has been shaken.

This chapter provides a brief review of the history of managed health care and discusses its impact on the therapeutic process. Although many of the issues presented here relate to the clinician in private practice, the implications of limited sessions and accountability to a third party are also applicable to mental health providers who work in hospitals, social agencies, and substance abuse clinics. They, too, face the strictures of limited sessions and utilization reviews, albeit sometimes in a more indirect way. A case example is provided to illustrate the transference and countertransference issues that arise in the beginning, middle, and end phases of treatment. The dynamics that must be dealt with by both patient and clinician are discussed, and suggestions are offered as to how they can best be worked through in a positive, therapeutic manner. Finally, issues relating to confidentiality and ethics are explored through the use of case vignettes to illustrate the dilemmas the clinician confronts in working within the constraints of managed care.

THE HISTORY OF MANAGED CARE

A number of factors have contributed to the emergence of managed health care, some of which have to do with efforts to contain growing health care costs and to provide services to a growing population that previously did not have access to insurance. In the last two decades, health maintenance organizations (HMOs) have been recognized as a logical way to arrange and pay for medical care. The goal of group practice prepayment plans is to contain costs and ensure comprehensive care. In recent years, HMOs have developed as alternatives to traditional fee-for-service health insurance. The HMO Act of 1973 gave impetus to HMO growth through legislation that "federally qualified" an HMO and mandated its offering to employees in the geographic area it served, and required that employers of twenty-five or more employees offer an HMO option if an HMO is in operation in their location and if they are requested by the HMO to do so (Winegar 1997). This act also allowed profit-making corporations to enter what had been essentially a non-profit, consumer driven, prepaid group practice arena, and helped change the direction of the private health care delivery system to one based on what we now know as managed care. Enrollment in HMOs has increased substantially as a result of this legislation. For example, in 1976, there were 174 plans with 6 million enrollees (3 percent of the United States population); in 1993, HMOs covered 38.4 million subscribers (15.1 percent of the population). Hoyt (1995c) reported that in 1995 more than 100 million Americans were covered by some organized form of health care. The number continues to increase.

Managed care has been proposed as a way to save money by reducing escalating hospital costs and physicians' bills. In addition, managed care offers insurance companies an opportunity to reduce costs to employers, thus saving money on employee benefits. In recent years much has been written about the development of managed care and its impact on consumers and health care providers (Alperin and Phillips 1997, Bloom 1997, Chambliss 2000, Hoyt 1995c, Mechanic 1999, Sauber 1997, Winegar 1997). Strong sentiments have been voiced on both sides as physicians and other health care providers often feel its constraints when trying to provide what they consider to be the optimal level of care for patients. Patients, in turn, often express ambivalent feelings when they discover that accessing a medical benefit is more complicated than in the past. Approval for many medical tests and consultations now resides not with the patient's physician but with a case manager representing an insurance company.

Four basic mechanisms underlie managed care structures: capitation, incentives/risks, gate keeping, and utilization management. The mechanisms are combined in varying ways in different structures (Alperin and Phillips 1997, Hoyt 1995a, Mechanic 1999, Winegar 1997).

Capitation is a form of payment involving fixed, predetermined payment per person for a fixed period of time and for a specified range of services (Chambliss 2000, Mechanic 1999, Winegar 1997). The capitation received by a provider organization is the same regardless of patient utilization of services. Some provision can be made to adjust capitation to take into account differences in age, sex, illness history, or other characteristics, but such prospective payment induces providers to carefully consider how they use expensive resources.

Incentives/risks are in the form of withholds and bonuses. For example: if a general physician is overwhelmed with referrals he may choose to refer a depressed patient to a mental health service rather than take responsibility for treating the patient himself. The primary care doctor may be put at risk for the cost of the referrals when they exceed a certain threshold. Often a part of their income is withheld and the amount returned depends on whether they stay within expected targets. Doctors who stay within utilization requirements may receive bonuses that reflect the extent to which they practice in economical ways (Mechanic 1999).

Brief gate keeping is a process that limits direct access to specialists, hospitals, and expensive procedures. In many plans, enrollees are required to select a primary care physician who manages everyday care and becomes a gatekeeper for referral to specialists, hospital care, and various procedures. The organization generally does not pay for services accessed directly except in an emergency, or if the enrollee is in a special point of service plan that permits outside use of services with larger out-of-pocket costs (Chambliss 2000, Mechanic 1999, Winegar 1997).

Utilization management consists of a number of mechanisms including precertification, concurrent review, high cost management, and second-opinion programs. Precertification requires a therapist to seek permission from a reviewer. Increasingly, it is common for managed care companies to administer mental health services on a risk basis, in which they utilize a variety of cost-containing strategies. Mental health services are carved out from the entire array of health benefits, and the company assumes responsibility and risk for managing the mental health care for the population covered in the contract (Chambliss 2000, Mechanic 1999).

MANAGED CARE AND MENTAL HEALTH

Although all health care costs are high, spending for mental health skyrocketed in the 1980s (Bloom 1997, Chambliss 2000, Hoyt 1995c,

Winegar 1997). Not surprisingly, therefore, managed care has had a significant impact on mental health treatment. Chambliss (2000) reported that employers faced a 50 percent increase in expenditures for psychiatric inpatient services between 1986 and 1990. The increase in insurance costs made many policies unaffordable for small businesses, and left employers searching for less expensive insurance plans.

The factors that have contributed to the development of managed mental health benefits are excessive spending on inappropriate hospitalizations, especially with certain target populations such as adolescents and substance abusers, and suspected overutilization of unmonitored long-term psychotherapy treatment. Additionally, in an effort to limit costs, many state legislatures licensed more mental health professionals in the 1980s. Many insurance companies reimburse these master's-level mental health professionals, who offer a cheaper alternative to treatment than Ph.D. psychologists or psychiatrists. Rather than restrain costs, the expansion of the pool of providers resulted in further cost increases (Chambliss 2000).

At present, most managed mental health care organizations' contracts include behavioral health or mental health services. The responsibility for overseeing mental health services has often been separated out of the health insurance plans and delegated to specialized managed behavioral health firms. Depending on the patient's policy, outpatient mental health visits are usually capped at twenty or thirty sessions per year (although recently some companies, such as Aetna and Blue Cross Blue Shield, have offered more sessions). These visits often must be precertified before a patient can make an appointment to see a psychiatrist, psychologist, or social worker. As noted above, all insurance companies require some type of utilization review. For example, outpatient treatment reports are due on a regular basis and/or a new referral must be made by the primary care physician at six-month intervals. To ensure the full financial benefit, the patient's therapist is required to be a provider on the insurance company's panel. Although most companies do offer an out-of-network benefit, it is customarily based on a yearly dollar amount and the patient receives a percentage of the practitioner's fee as reimbursement. If the provider is on the insurance company's panel, patients pay a small co-payment and the insurance carrier pays the remainder directly to the provider. Another form of payment authorized by managed care companies is capitation. In this system, providers receive a lump sum per patient per calendar year. For example, a $600 payment will cover all mental health visits for the year. The providers receive the $600 if they see the patient one or twenty times.

Although there are restrictions inherent in managed mental health care, there are positive results associated with these plans as well. Managed mental health care has made mental health benefits available and affordable to more people than in the past. Also, the fact that these benefits can be accessed in such a straightforward way reduces the stigma of therapy. Thus, many individuals are more willing to telephone a provider sanctioned by their insurance company to help them to deal with a range of problems that otherwise might have been ignored until a later date. The following vignettes illustrate the types of call made to the clinician who participates in an HMO.

> Ms. P., a 22-two-year-old recently married woman, contacted the clinician because she was having difficulty separating emotionally from her domineering mother. Her husband was not understanding of her conflict. She feared that she would hurt and lose her mother or hurt and lose her husband. She needed help in sorting out her feelings in order to decide how to best proceed. Ms. P. was seen individually for three sessions and then with her husband for three sessions. Ultimately they gained a solid understanding of what each needed and were able to work out an insightful resolution to the problem. Ms. P., always somewhat dependent, realized that she had to separate in order to understand herself better before coming together in a more mature way with her husband and mother. Significantly, her husband and mother had similar personality styles and were locked in a power struggle over possession of this young woman. Behind their need to control was their mutually shared fear

that they would not have the love of the young woman if they did not control her. A thorough understanding of the dynamics of the three individuals was crucial to the resolution of the problem. In treatment, both Ms. P. and her husband were helped to reflect on and subsequently understand the underlying conflicts and separation issues that were interfering with the establishment of their marriage. The couple then moved ahead in a more adaptive manner.

Mr. and Mrs. D. were having difficulty caring for their precocious, very active, and often provocative 10-year-old son. They were interested in learning parenting techniques, and at the same time shared concerns about the possible impact of their parenting styles on the child's behavior. After reviewing the results of a battery of psychological and neurological tests, it was ascertained that the child, although very bright, had areas in which he was developmentally delayed. His judgment was poor, and he had to be constantly supervised. Added to this was the child's tendency to provoke and test his mother in a threatening manner. Treatment for the parents consisted of a combination of psychoeducation, cognitive-behavioral techniques, and psychodynamic understanding. They learned how their perceptions of themselves and the child were having impact on their parenting abilities. It became clear that the mother's timidity and lack of confidence were perceived by the child as weakness, which enabled him to test the limits whenever he had the opportunity. The father, a passive and silently angry individual, was unknowingly colluding with his son by not maintaining the rules that were established for the child's behavior. His unconscious agenda was that the child be aligned with him against the mother. The emerging family dynamic was the mother's dislike of the child, which was compensated for by letting him do whatever he pleased. The father, angry at his wife about other issues, dealt with his unexpressed hostility toward her and his feelings of isolation by subtly reinforcing an alliance with the child, which enabled the child to continue acting out. When the parents began to gain insight into their behavior, they modified their handling of the youngster and cooperated more with each other. The child's behavior began to change when he was faced with a united front.

THE DEVELOPMENT OF BRIEF PSYCHOTHERAPY TREATMENT

Managed care requirements with respect to the number of sessions allotted to consumers for outpatient mental health care has stimulated the widespread use of brief treatment. According to Budman (1981), the continued development of brief treatment has been tied to the evolution of the overall mental health system in this country. In the 1940s there were few treatments for severe mental disorders. Although there were electric and insulin shock treatments and psychosurgical techniques, little was known about how they worked and their use engendered much controversy. In contrast to the long-term psychoanalysis available for healthier patients, the more severely ill were treated with long-term stays in mental hospitals.

Following World War II, developments occurred that focused attention on mental health care. During the war, a large number of men were turned down for armed service because of mental illness. Of the almost 5 million turned down by the selective service, 40 percent were excluded because of psychiatric problems (Budman 1981). An important factor contributing to the development of brief treatment methods was the observation that servicemen in battle could return to active functioning after a few sessions with a mental health professional. It was at this point that new, effective techniques for crisis treatment were developed and subsequently used successfully with a variety of other populations.

Additional factors contributing to the widespread use of brief treatment included (1) acceptance of more limited therapeutic goals, (2) increasing development of an array of treatments, (3) advances in the classification of mental disorders, (4) growing realization that lengthy treatments often do not meet the needs of a particular population, (5) increasing concern with the cost of treatment combined with increasing difficulty accessing treatment, and (6) growth of prepaid health plans with limited psychiatric benefits (Budman 1981).

Brief treatment is not new to psychoanalytically oriented psychotherapy. In fact, Freud and his followers utilized the brief treatment approaches in their early work. Freud practiced what would now be considered brief psychotherapy. He treated many patients in short periods of time. The cases of Katharina and Gustav Mahler are examples of successful analyses performed by Freud in just a single session spanning several hours (Crits-Christoph et al. 1991).

Sandor Ferenczi, Otto Rank, Franz Alexander, and Thomas French were contemporaries of Freud who did not abandon the concept of brief treatment and, in fact, continued to refine psychoanalytic principles (Breuer and Freud 1895, Ferenczi and Rank 1925, Jones 1955). For example, Ferenczi and Rank (1925) asserted that present-day events warranted more attention than the details of childhood. Rank (1947) developed key ideas that have become an integral part of contemporary brief psychodynamic psychotherapy. Crits-Christoph and Barber (1991) note that although Rank's theory of birth trauma did not gain acceptance, it was through this theory that the importance of the separation issues in therapy was recognized. By setting a termination date, Rank created a therapeutic atmosphere in which working on the issue of separation from the analyst became central. This approach was the forerunner of Mann's (1973) therapy, which also set a firm limit of twelve sessions, thus emphasizing separation and loss. Rank also realized that the patient's motivation to change affects the therapeutic outcome (Crits-Christoph and Barber 1991).

In the 1940s, Alexander and French (1946) developed the concept of the corrective emotional experience. They believed that patients must have a corrective emotional experience if any progress is to be made. A corrective emotional experience occurs when the therapist helps the patient overcome a past traumatic experience. The therapist facilitates the corrective emotional experience by re-creating previously intolerable situations under the more favorable circumstances of the therapeutic relationship. Alexander and French also believed that weekly sessions were sufficient and often preferable. In some cases, they maintained that daily sessions could even be detrimental by helping the patient avoid everyday life and creating a dependency. By decreasing sessions, they believed that the patient could have the opportunity to become aware of these needs and analyze them with his therapist. Interruptions were also seen as positive, as they provided patients with time to see how well they could do on their own and in what areas further work might be needed.

By the early 1950s, therapists were utilizing psychodynamic principles in more active and shorter treatment (Hoyt 1995b). In London, Balint, Ornstein, and Malan (1963, 1976a,b, as cited in Crits-Christoph et al. 1991) were developing what they referred to as "focal therapy"; in Boston, Sifneos (1972) was beginning to experiment with "short-term anxiety provoking psychotherapy"; in New York, Wolberg (1965a, as cited in Crits-Christoph and Barber 1991) was investigating various ways of shortening the length of treatment including using hypnotherapy to work through patient resistances more quickly.

Faced with long waiting lists for mental health treatment and with the experience that many patients will stay in treatment for years if given the opportunity, a number of psychoanalytically oriented therapists developed brief treatment models. Malan (1976), Mann (1973), Sifneos (1972), Davanloo (1992), and Luborsky (1984) refined and implemented effective short-term psychodynamic approaches. Strong emphasis was placed on the careful selection of patients, dynamic evaluations, and trial interpretations. Delineation of a circumscribed focus of treatment has become the hallmark of the brief treatment models of today (Bloom 1997, Budman 1981, Crits-Christoph et al. 1991, Hoyt 1995b). Each of the above-mentioned clinicians selects a specific focus with the help of the patient and organizes the treatment around selected goals. The practice of brief treatment requires skillful clinicians who are able to quickly assess the major theme(s). They then proceed to use a variety of therapeutic techniques such as support, insight, interpretation, and sometimes cognitive behavioral methods such as homework, journal writing, and psychoeducation to help the patient resolve his or her problem and understand how to deal with these issues in the future.

Based on the apparent effectiveness of short-term treatment as evidenced by research outcome study results, managed care companies have endorsed a brief treatment approach to mental health care. Essentially, these brief treatment models focus on symptom reduction rather than the alteration of personality structure, goals that are associated with either psychoanalysis or psychoanalytically oriented psychotherapy. Bloom's (1997) review of the research literature suggests that short-term treatment is as effective and long lasting as long-term therapy, regardless of client characteristics or treatment duration. Almost identical findings have been reported for short-term inpatient psychiatric care. Research on treatment outcome has consistently demonstrated that short-term is as effective as long-term therapy in spite of predictions to the contrary. In fact, according to Berg and Miller (1992), the results of a twelve-year study published by the Menninger Clinic, a psychoanalytically oriented treatment and training facility, showed that clients who received brief supportive treatment profited as much from that experience as did those who had undergone extensive, long-term psychoanalytically oriented treatment.

Bloom (1997) also cites Koss and Shiang's (1994) conclusions that brief therapy methods, once thought to be appropriate only for less severe problems, have actually been shown to be effective in treating a wide range of psychological and health-related problems, including severe and chronic problems. Contemporary comparative studies of brief therapy offer little empirical evidence of differences in overall effectiveness between time-limited and time-unlimited therapy, or between alternate approaches to brief therapy. Consequently, brief therapy results in a great saving of available clinical time and can reach more people in need of treatment.

In a recent book entitled *Managed Care and Psychotherapy*, Chambliss (2000) reports on research studies that reflect the efficacy of short-term treatment. Howard and colleagues (1986, as cited in Chambliss 2000) examined data based on thirty years of research with over 2,400 patients. They found that by the eighth session approximately 50 percent of patients were measurably improved and approximately 75 percent were improved by twenty-six sessions. Given the findings and despite the methodological limitations that were noted, the authors speculated that most therapy occurs relatively quickly within a period considered to be brief treatment.

As further confirmation of the validity of short-term treatment, Koss and Butcher (1986, as cited in Bloom 1997) reported that whether by plan or by premature termination, most psychotherapeutic contacts are brief (lasting less than eight sessions). In recent years, partly because of design, brief psychotherapy has become the treatment of choice. Comparative studies of brief and unlimited therapies show essentially no differences in results. Consequently brief therapy results in a great saving of available clinical time and can reach more people in need of treatment.

It has been my experience that many patients are interested in solving their problems quickly and moving on with their lives. They feel that they have been helped if their symptoms disappear and/or if they learn some coping skills that will help them in the future. In addition, some patients, fearing the dependency associated with longer term therapy, are reassured by the fixed number of sessions available to them. This indicates that they will not be caught up in an unnecessarily lengthy course of treatment. Additionally, patients often believe that their problems are not hopeless if they can be helped in a limited period of time. Thus, they approach their problems from a more positive and optimistic stance and seek to acquire problem-solving and coping skills that will enhance their individual and interpersonal functioning.

Finally, planned short-term therapy is applicable to a wide variety of psychiatric disorders as well as acute and chronically stressful life circumstances. Clinical studies have discussed the role of planned short-term therapy in helping patients cope with acute and chronic life circumstances such as aging, bereavement, gay and lesbian issues, hostility, imprisonment, and stress (Bloom 1997).

THERAPEUTIC ISSUES ASSOCIATED WITH
THE PRESENCE OF MANAGED MENTAL HEALTH CARE

There are a variety of issues associated with the beginning, middle, and termination phases of the treatment relationship when the patient's outpatient mental health care is monitored by a case manager who represents a particular behavioral health organization. These issues arise whenever clinicians, whether in private practice, psychiatric hospitals, substance-abuse facilities, social agencies, or outpatient mental health clinics, interact with case managers who represent insurance companies.

Beginning Phase of Treatment

If patients obtain the clinician's name from the insurance company, they may have either positive or negative reactions. For example, people who have had good experiences with physicians that they have been assigned to in the past approach the mental health provider confidently, assured that his or her credentials meet the standards of their company. Initially patients may be concerned with their "fit" with the clinician; however, they also know that if the initial consultation is not satisfactory, they are free to contact someone else. This is similar to patients who pay out-of-pocket in that they are able to move on to another clinician if they don't feel comfortable about the therapist or the therapist's formulation of the problem. In my clinical work, I routinely make a point of reassuring prospective patients that they are not committed to stay and that they will not be penalized by their insurance company if they do not remain. Often the anxiety that patients present masks their fear of what is happening to them and the unknown hands that they find themselves in. Many people have not been in treatment before and are unaware of what to expect in the process; others who have had prior therapy are often fearful about how they will be perceived by the clinician. They feel vulnerable and exposed.

During the initial session, the patient's benefits are reviewed to determine the parameters of treatment, that is, the number of sessions allowed and the frequency of the reports to be made to the behavioral health organization. It is useful for the patient to take part in the discussion of what will be written in the outpatient treatment report. This serves to clarify how the clinician sees the patient, and at the same time solidifies the patient's feelings of trust toward the therapist because they both see what will be reviewed by the case manager. This discussion provides an opportunity to establish goals and clarify symptoms. Most patients have positive feelings toward clinicians who are open and honest about their perception of the problem. The initial discussion also presents patients with an opportunity to alter or change the clinician's impression or to voice objections to the manner in which something may be stated. How the therapist handles this initial evaluation period has implications for the progress of treatment and the patient's confidence in the therapist and in his or her ability to understand and to help.

Unfortunately, some patients have had to terminate with a clinician because their employer suddenly changed insurance companies and the therapist was not part of the new panel. These patients present a special challenge. They are usually angry about having to make a change, and apprehensive about how things will go with a new clinician. They need an opportunity to verbalize their thoughts and feelings of loss, anger, and skepticism about beginning something new with a virtual stranger. At this point, it would behoove the patient and clinician to review the patient's current mental health benefits and to develop a future plan should the same thing occur or should the number of sessions provided prove to be insufficient to meet the patient's needs.

The importance of developing a therapeutic alliance cannot be minimized in this kind of situation. As noted previously, a rapidly established and generally positive working alliance between therapist and patient is a crucial component of brief treatment (Hoyt 1995b, Luborsky and Mark 1991). When a patient begins treatment under circumstances that are less than optimal, it is imperative that a climate of trust be established as rapidly as possible and that clear, realistic options be provided. Patients may feel angry and frustrated that they are not free agents and must use someone on the provider panel because of financial limitations.

Some patients may have accessed a short-term benefit during the last several years and were satisfied with the result. But when another problem arises, they may now discover that their employer has changed insurance carriers and that their original therapist is not on the list. They are then faced with having to choose someone new, generally with no knowledge of the particular therapist, and therefore they may arrive for their new appointment with some apprehension. But since they were pleased with the prior experience, they often anticipate they will have another productive relationship.

> Ms. B. sought help several years ago for feelings of depression associated with her mother's death. At termination, she felt she made good use of her twenty sessions and thought that she did not have to continue with long-term therapy. She contacted her original therapist a year later because her recent divorce had awakened old losses and she wanted to return for help in order to resolve what she feared was another period of serious depression. Upon learning that her therapist was not associated with the new insurance company, she telephoned the company to request a consultation. She was referred to me, strictly on the basis of office location. Although she was initially apprehensive about beginning with a clinician who knew nothing of her past, we were quickly able to establish an excellent working relationship and to focus on the mutually agreed-upon goals. Before the treatment could begin, it was crucial to explore her feelings related to not being able to resume work with her previous therapist and to clarify how that might affect her willingness to begin a new relationship, especially if another insurance contract resulted in my being unlisted, necessitating another change. Ms. B. would not have the financial resources to seek therapeutic help from a provider outside of the insurance network.

In my clinical opinion, patients are rarely concerned about the level of provider qualifications, as they believe that credentials must be in order for the therapist to be on the roster. In fact, Grossberg and Brandell

(1997) note that since the provider has been chosen by the managed care company and given a "preferred" status, transference to the therapist may be more intensive as the therapist is often regarded as having more authority than if the patient had independently arranged for treatment with the therapist. Patients remain concerned about whether or not the individual clinician will be warm, empathic, and understanding of their situation.

Middle Phase of Treatment

Middle-phase transference issues in brief treatment are based on a multiplicity of factors. The presence of the third party (the case manager) or the number of sessions remaining certainly influences the patient's state of mind (Alperin and Phillips 1997, Bloom 1997, Crits-Christoph et al. 1991, Edwards 1997, Mann 1973). Usually there is pressure to see clear progress during the middle phase, especially since termination issues begin to emerge, and there need to be tangible gains made in the work before the termination phase proper begins. Negative transference may be directed at the therapist, who may be regarded as not skilled enough to help the patient within a fixed number of sessions. More commonly, however, the patient directs negative feelings toward the managed care company for not providing more sessions and for being inflexible and unrealistic about the length of time necessary to complete the treatment. Splitting between the therapist and the managed care company must be identified and addressed in the treatment (Alperin and Phillips 1997, Grossberg and Brandell 1997, Saakvitne and Abrahamson 1994). Allowing the patient to remain angry at the case manager and not dealing with the anger generated by treatment issues is therapeutically unwise and perpetuates the patient–therapist collusion to avoid dealing with middle-phase issues and upcoming termination.

Other manifestations of negative transference arise when the therapist is unable to obtain additional benefits. Reactions can switch from seeing the clinician as the hero who has won the case to a helpless victim who has no power (Saakvitne and Abrahamson 1994). The following case exemplifies this phenomenon.

> Mr. M. was referred to treatment because he was depressed and broken-hearted over a breakup with his girlfriend. He revealed a pattern of relationships that all seemed to end in the same way. He would fall in love, idealize his girlfriend, and then begin to become needy, dependent, and demanding of all her attention. Thus, his relationships were characterized by his generosity and tenderness soon being replaced by anger and abusive, demeaning behavior. Goals for the twenty-session course of treatment were to understand what precipitated his needy and angry feeling, and to learn how to stop this destructive behavior so that he could obtain what he ultimately wanted—a warm and loving relationship.
>
> The initial stages of treatment were characterized by the development of a positive and strong therapeutic alliance with the clinician. We worked on identifying the origins of Mr. M.'s neediness and anger. He kept a journal in which he identified relationship situations in which his affection began to change to neediness and then to anger. By the midpoint of our work together, Mr. M. verbalized anger and resentment toward his insurance company for restricting the number of therapy sessions, as he felt that he was reaching an understanding of his problem and wanted to continue treatment. His anger and abusiveness escalated and became unproductive, interfering with the work he could potentially accomplish. It was at this point that I helped Mr. M. to understand that rather than direct his anger at me, he was displacing his hopelessness and frustration for not getting what he wanted onto the managed care company. We were able to understand that his relationship with his mother, whom he saw as both giving and rejecting, and his resultant abuse and criticism of her were being played out in all of his relationships with women. With such insight, his anger abated and he was able to utilize his insights in a positive manner. He recognized that he would take some important tools with him upon

termination and that he had the option to return at a reduced fee should he need more time to work on this issue before the new benefit year began. Although I had offered Mr. M. such an option, he felt that it was important to integrate the insight that he had achieved by being more independent.

It was clear that Mr. M.'s pattern with women was enacted in the therapeutic relationship. He saw the clinician as holding the promise of nurturance; he became increasingly needy and demanding and then angry and abusive. This pattern persisted because he couldn't get what he had always wanted from his mother. He was also able to recognize that his identification with his abusive father was a contributory factor in his "turning" on women at the point that they became sweet and loving to him.

Although there were some realistic elements in Mr. M.'s anger about the limited number of sessions, his anger needed to be redirected to the clinician. The negative transference was then reflected in his disdain toward the therapist, whom he saw as no longer having power or authority. Although the inability to obtain additional benefits was the conscious source of the patient's anger, further work revealed that this was a disguise. His contempt and disdain was a displacement for his feelings toward his mother, whom he saw as having abandoned him just when he was seduced into believing that she would take care of him. If the function of this splitting had not been uncovered, this important insight would not have become conscious and Mr. M. would have continued to enact the frustrating, self-defeating pattern of his behavior that characterized his relationships with women. The contempt that he expressed also had its etiology in his identification with his father, who had alternately abused and loved his mother in the same way.

Termination Phase

This is the most crucial point in treatment, as the gains made must be solidified in spite of the regression often engendered at the thought of leaving the therapist. Many writers have addressed the impact of termination in short-term therapy (Bloom 1997, Budman 1981, Crits-Christoph et al. 1991, Hoyt 1995a, Mann 1973). All have noted the importance of dealing with loss, helping the patient recognize gains made, and interpreting to the patient, if needed. If a patient is not ready for termination on the basis of the severity of the problems, a psychiatric consultation can be requested in order to substantiate the need for additional sessions. Also, many behavioral health organizations endorse the idea of episodic treatment, and the therapist is able to offer the patient the possibility of returning in the future (Chambliss 2000, Grossberg and Brandell 1997, Sauber 1997). The therapist should be prepared to continue seeing the patient at a reduced fee if termination is not appropriate and there are no further options available through the insurance company. This is an important ethical responsibility and must be thought out by the clinician before he or she assumes managed care cases. There are other ethical and legal issues involved in ending with a patient without providing for ongoing care if that seems indicated (Chambliss 2000, Grossberg and Brandell 1997, Higuchi and Newman 1994, Hoyt 1995a, Sauber 1997).

As noted in the example of Mr. M., it is important to interpret the negative transference so that the regression often seen during the termination phase of psychotherapy is not utilized in a self-destructive way by blotting out the gains that have been made in treatment. As Mann (1973) notes, "Time Limited Psychotherapy brings to the forefront of the treatment process the major psychological plague all human beings suffer, namely the wish to be close, to be as one with another, to be intimate, the fulfillment of which demands learning how to tolerate separation and loss without undue damage to our feelings about the self" (p. 43).

COUNTERTRANSFERENCE

There are a number of countertransference issues that are associated with doing brief treatment under the aegis of managed care. Often providers find themselves reacting with anger and apprehensiveness to having a third party involved in their patient's treatment. They may feel that it is intrusive or that their work is being scrutinized by unseen practitioners whose professional training is not known (Saakvitne and Abrahamson 1994). For psychoanalytically trained clinicians, managed care input is especially difficult because they are regularly threatened with the loss of approval on the basis of treatment reports, which seriously threatens the therapeutic alliance and the goals inherently associated with a successful psychotherapeutic outcome. Saakvitne and Abrahamson (1994) report that one's theoretical and clinical orientation can play a part in how managed care is described and experienced in the transference–countertransference matrix. Managed care can become the unwelcome oedipal intruder, the anal sadistic withholding caregiver, the unempathic mother, or the bad object who exiles and then ultimately rejects the patient. In addition, when therapists feel that the pressure of managed care is further complicating their work with difficult patients, additional anxiety may arise, thereby hampering treatment. Two common defenses, splitting and projection, are noted in the context of managed care. Therapists' feelings toward the patient are split, with all negative feelings projected onto the reviewer. This is potentially destructive to the treatment, since one needs the full range of countertransference feelings to understand and treat patients adequately (Alperin and Phillips 1997, Dyckman 1997).

Dyckman (1997) suggests that an important emotion for therapists to consider when working in a managed care environment is their impatience. He believes that pressures to work quickly intrude on the therapy session and reduces the clinician's ability to listen fully, understand the extent of the patient's problems, and fully experience the nuances of the therapeutic relationship. Dyckman suggests that a managed care environment creates impatience among therapists due to a number of factors: (1) a departure from the timetable for the treatment, (2) the perceived need to satisfy third parties, (3) concern about the progress of treatment, (4) doubts about the ability to achieve results in the timetable imposed by managed care, and (5) confusion of process with product and difficulty in departing from a favorite treatment. He also noted that the pressure to work quickly impacts on the therapy session and may reduce the practitioner's ability to listen and to understand the extent of the patient's problems as well as the subtleties of the therapeutic relationship. Self-reflection can minimize these dangers.

A major countertransferential problem for practitioners is in the area of remuneration. What was once the sole province for the practitioner—setting of fees, determining the frequency of appointments, and confidentiality—is subject to the authority of the case manager (Tosone 1998). Clinicians often feel guilty and responsible if they are unable to either help a patient within the time allotted or obtain an extension of benefits. It is not uncommon for the therapist to feel frustrated and hopeless in the face of what may appear to be insurmountable obstacles. Hoyt (1995a) notes that just as the fee-for-service practitioner must guard against the temptation to rationalize unnecessary prolongation of treatment, the HMO therapist must guard against the tendency to undertreat. Institutionalized forces that encourage utilization review and promote rapid turnover of patients need to be balanced against professional standards and values.

Grossberg and Brandell (1997) also speak to the latter point, noting that countertransference reactions and the potential for disjunctive countertransferential responses increase significantly, given that subsequent referrals will come from the managed care company. Loyalty may therefore be more closely tied to the company than to the appropriate treatment of the client. The clinician's judgment about the nature and length of the treatment may be compromised owing to concerns about the managed care company's evaluation. To justify the referral from the managed care company, the therapist may become especially invested in the client's ability to demonstrate functional improvement (as requested by the managed care organization).

Another related area involves countertransference feelings engendered by the sometimes slow payment of bills submitted and/or bills being rejected if the behavioral health organization does not communicate with the financial section of the company in a timely manner about the number of sessions that have been certified. This can create a situation where, after seeing a patient for several weeks or months, the therapist's bill is declined on the basis that the sessions were not reported as certified. Needless to say, it is important that therapists be aware of their feelings about this to the extent that frustration and anger may interfere with the patient's care even though it is not the patient's responsibility to certify sessions or to follow up on mistakes. Unfortunately, providers may find themselves in a difficult financial position because of these errors and become reticent about continuing to treat their patients. An ethical bind is created for therapists. If they continue to see the patient without payment, the loss must be absorbed, but if treatment is interrupted in order to wait for confirmation of certification and/or their money, they are interfering with the emotional well-being of the patient.

CONFIDENTIALITY

Maintaining confidentiality becomes difficult in the era of managed care. All behavioral health organizations require some kind of utilization review, either by telephone or in the form of a regular outpatient treatment report. The concept of revealing information that has been considered sacrosanct is often problematic and creates anxiety in the therapist and patient. If not handled sensitively, the requirements of managed care to provide detailed reports on the treatment progress and diagnosis can pose a serious threat to the newly forming therapeutic dyad. If dealt with appropriately and openly, discussion of the content of the report can be a useful tool and can strengthen the relationship by building trust. It is our responsibility as clinicians to be honest with patients at the onset of treatment and to educate them as to how to best proceed. As mentioned previously, I discuss the content of these forms with patients and obtain their approval as to the appropriateness of what is being reported. Sauber (1997) urges clinicians to review the treatment planning reports with their patients and have patients sign forms indicating that they have read and understood the reports. He believes that it is important for therapists to outline with patients the advantages and disadvantages of the treatment approach.

The presence of a third party also raises questions in terms of how to protect confidentiality and how to ensure that patients' needs will be appropriately met (Roback et al. 1999). The following recommendations are made by Allen (1996), a managed care reviewer himself, to providers who deal with managed care reviewers. He suggests establishing a rapport with the initial reviewer, and asking to speak to the same reviewer every time. He also suggests getting the reviewers' questions in advance and discussing these questions with the patient so that there is joint agreement as to what information will be disclosed. He also stresses the importance of making a strong, clear case to the reviewer and discussing the material in a collegial, nondefensive manner.

CONCLUSION

The therapeutic relationship has been dramatically affected by the advent of managed care and specifically by the addition of a third party assigned to oversee the case. However, once the clinician becomes more accustomed to this new way of showing accountability, the process becomes less cumbersome and the utilization review is less threatening and intrusive. In fact, working with a patient on required reports can often be therapeutic, in that areas to be worked on are specified and goals for treatment are clearly established. This process also provides the patient an opportunity to experience the therapist's understanding of the particular issues being worked on, enabling the development of the working alliance so crucial to a positive therapeutic outcome (Luborsky 1984, Mann 1973).

Managed care has had impact on mental health treatment in multiple ways. It has been beneficial to many people by providing access to mental health benefits they did not have previously because of inadequate insurance coverage or lack of financial resources. Likewise, the continued development and refinement of brief treatment methods and the evidence of their effectiveness have provided help for diverse problems and a wide range of populations. The presence of a case manager has had an impact on the therapeutic dyad in the areas of transference and countertransference. Additional work must take place in order for issues related to these dynamics to be incorporated into the treatment in a constructive manner.

On a positive note, it is striking to see that the stigma that had been associated with accessing mental health benefits is reduced in the managed care model. In fact, individual patients, families, and couples seem to regard their now easy and more affordable access to a mental health counselor in the same way that they think of their primary care physician. They feel free to call for help with a range of problems that they would not have felt comfortable doing in the past.

REFERENCES

Alexander, F., and French, T. (1946). *Psychoanalytic Therapy*. New York: Ronald Press.

Allen, M. G. (1996). Understanding and coping with managed care. In *Impact of Managed Care on Psychodynamic Treatment*, ed. J. W. Barron and H. Sands, pp. 15–25. Madison, CT: International Universities Press.

Alperin, R., and Phillips, D. (1997). *The Impact of Managed Care on the Practice of Psychotherapy*. New York: Brunner/Mazel.

Berg, I. K., and Miller, S. D. (1992). *Working with the Problem Drinker: A Solution-Focused Approach*. New York: Norton.

Bloom, B. (1997). *Planned Short-Term Psychotherapy: A Clinical Handbook*. Boston: Allyn & Bacon.

Breuer, J., and Freud, S. (1895). Studies on hysteria. *Standard Edition* 2:125–134.

Budman, S. (1981). *Forms of Brief Therapy*. New York: Guilford.

Chambliss, C. (2000). *Psychotherapy and Managed Care*. Boston: Allyn & Bacon.

Crits-Christoph, P., and Barber, J. P. (1991). *Handbook of Short-Term Dynamic Psychotherapy*. New York: Basic Books.

Crits-Christoph, P., Barber, J. P., and Kuricas, J. S., eds. (1991). Introduction and historical background. In *Handbook of Short-Term Dynamic Psychotherapy*, pp. 1–16. New York: Basic Books.

Davanloo, H. (1992). *Short-Term Dynamic Psychotherapy*. Northvale, NJ: Jason Aronson.

Dyckman, J. (1997). The impatient therapist: managed care and countertransference. *American Journal of Psychotherapy* 51(3):329–343.

Edward, J. (1997). The impact of managed care on the psychoanalytic process. In *The Impact of Managed Care on the Practice of Psychotherapy*, ed. R. Alperin and D. Phillips, pp. 199–216. New York: Brunner/ Mazel.

Ferenczi, S., and Rank, O. (1925). *The Development of Psychoanalysis*. New York: Nervous and Mental Disease Publication Company.

Grossberg, S., and Brandell, J. R. (1997). Clinical social work in the concept of managed care. In *Theory and Practice in Clinical Social Work*, ed. J. R. Brandell, pp. 404–422. New York: Free Press.

Higuchi, S., and Newman, R. (1994). Legal issues for psychotherapy in a managed care environment. *Psychoanalysis and Psychotherapy* 11(2): 138–153.

Hoyt, M. F. (1995a). Aspects of termination in a time limited brief psychotherapy. In *Brief Therapy and Managed Care: Readings for Contemporary Practice*, ed. M. F. Hoyt, pp. 183–204. San Francisco: Jossey-Bass.

——— (1995b). Brief psychotherapies. In *Brief Therapy and Managed Care: Readings for Contemporary Practice*, ed. M. F. Hoyt, pp. 281–332. San Francisco: Jossey-Bass.

——— (1995c). Characteristics of psychotherapy under managed health care. In *Brief Therapy and Managed Care: Readings for Contemporary Practice*, ed. M. F. Hoyt, pp. 1–21. San Francisco: Jossey-Bass.

Jones, E. (1955). *The Life and Work of Sigmund Freud, Volume II*. New York: Basic Books.

Koss, M. P., and Shiang, F. (1994). Research on brief psychotherapy. In

Handbook of Psychotherapy and Behavior Change, ed. A. E. Bergin and S. L. Garfield, pp. 664–700. New York: Wiley.

Luborsky, L. (1984). *Principles of Psychoanalytic Psychotherapy: A Manual for Supportive-Expressive Treatment.* New York: Basic Books.

Luborsky, L., and Mark, D. (1991). Short-term supportive-expressive psychoanalytic psychotherapy. In *Handbook of Short-Term Dynamic Psychotherapy*, ed. P. Crits-Christoph and J. P. Barber, pp. 110–136. New York: Basic Books.

Malan, D. H. (1976). *The Frontier of Brief Psychotherapy.* New York: Plenum.

Mann, J. (1973). *Time-Limited Psychotherapy.* Cambridge, MA: Harvard University Press.

Mechanic, D. (1999). *Mental Health and Social Policy: The Emergence of Managed Care.* Boston: Allyn & Bacon.

Rank, O. (1947). *Will Therapy.* New York: Knopf.

Roback, H. B., Barton, D., and Castelnuovo-Tedesco, P. (1999). A symposium on psychotherapy in the age of managed care. *American Journal of Psychotherapy* 53:1–16.

Saakvitne, K. W., and Abrahamson, D. J. (1994). The impact of managed care on the psychotherapeutic relationship. In *Psychoanalysis/Psychotherapy, Volume II*, pp. 181–197. Madison, CT: International Universities Press.

Sauber, S. R. (1997). *Managed Mental Health Care.* New York: Brunner/Mazel.

Sifneos, P. (1972). *Short-Term Psychotherapy and Emotional Crisis.* Cambridge, MA: Harvard University Press.

Tosone, C. (1998). *Mandated short-term treatment: impact of managed care on the clinician's countertransference.* Proceedings of the International Social Work Conference, Florence, Italy, March.

Winegar, N. (1997). *The Clinician's Guide to Managed Behavioral Care.* New York: Haworth.

CHAPTER TWO

The Framework:
Theoretical Underpinnings and Characteristics

EDA G. GOLDSTEIN AND MARYELLEN NOONAN

Short-term models that apply the major concepts and treatment principles of current psychodynamic and cognitive-behavioral theories have proliferated in recent years in response to the need to utilize brief interventions with increasing numbers of patients who seek treatment. Most clinicians have not been trained specifically in how to engage in short-term treatment and may find themselves bewildered by the numerous approaches that are available at the present time. Drawing on both psychodynamic and cognitive-behavioral theories, this chapter describes the theoretical underpinnings and major characteristics and components of an integrative and inclusive short-term treatment framework that can serve as guide to practitioners in flexibly implementing interventions.

PSYCHODYNAMIC CONTRIBUTIONS

Psychodynamic short-term approaches are based on the view that early childhood experiences contribute to adult psychopathology. Early brief interventive models that embodied classical psychoanalytic concepts and treatment principles aimed at symptom removal and selective personality change. They advocated insight-oriented techniques including confrontation and interpretation of defenses, maladaptive personality traits and behavioral patterns, and core conflicts. Consequently, they adopted narrow selection criteria, which tended to favor highly motivated and well-functioning patients with a history of adequate adjustment, problems of acute or recent onset, and an ability to relate easily, and excluded those who presented with more severe or chronic deficits (Goldstein and Noonan 1999, Koss & Shiang 1994).

Followers of alternative psychodynamic formulations, such as ego psychology, object relations theory, self psychology, and trauma theory, have recommended different goals, foci, and treatment techniques than those embodied in older short-term treatment models such as Malan's (1963, 1976) intensive brief psychotherapy, Sifneos's (1972, 1979, 1987) short-term anxiety-provoking psychotherapy, Mann's (1973, 1991) time-limited psychotherapy, and Davanloo's (1978, 1980, 1991) intensive short-term dynamic psychotherapy. One consequence of these developments is that brief treatment can be utilized with a broader range of patients than were originally thought to be suitable for short-term treatment.

Classical Psychoanalytic Theory

Classical psychoanalytic theory originated to explain neurotic symptoms and maladaptive personality traits, which Freud saw as resulting from past unconscious childhood conflicts centering on the expression of sexual and aggressive impulses. The id, ego, and superego are crucial structural constructs of Freudian theory and the psychosexual stages (oral, anal, phallic, oedipal) are pivotal in personality development. They generate conflict, defenses, and symptoms, and shape enduring character traits and behavioral patterns. Unresolved oedipal conflicts, in particular, set the stage for later psychopathology.

The goals of psychoanalysis and long-term psychoanalytic psychotherapy were to relieve neurotic symptoms, to modify pathological character traits and defenses, and to produce structural changes in the overall personality. Insight-oriented techniques that aimed at making the unconscious childhood conflicts conscious were utilized. The patient was asked to share fantasies, dreams, and early memories, and to practice free association. The analyst assumed a neutral, abstinent, and anonymous stance, thereby encouraging a therapeutic regression in which patients re-created their early conflicts in the therapeutic relationship or transference. Interpretation of the transference and of the patient's defenses or resistance that arose in the course of the work were the primary foci of the treatment. Because the analyst was nondirective insofar as he or she allowed the process to unfold and intervened only to give appropriate interpretations, the treatment process itself was lengthy and required an extended termination phase in order to work through and resolve the transference relationship. The treatment also tended to minimize the patient's current reality situation outside of the treatment. Likewise, the therapist's reactions (countertransference) to the patient were de-emphasized because it was expected that analysts, through their own treatment, would have worked through any personality conflicts that might impinge on the patient and that they could be objective in their work (Freud 1905, Greenson 1967).

In the short-term version of this approach, therapists are encouraged to be more active and focused in exploring and diagnosing patients' core underlying conflicts that are thought to be responsible for their symptoms and dysfunctional behavior. Short-term goals are similar to but somewhat more limited than those in long-term treatment, aiming at selective rather than total personality change. Therapists are advised to vigorously clarify, confront, and interpret the patient's conflicts, defenses, and resistance as they arise in the transference. It is expected that termination can be accomplished very quickly. This approach necessitates that patients be able to relate easily, possess motivation and psychological mindedness, and display reasonably good functioning and ego strength. Patients who have presenting problems of recent onset are thought more suitable than those who show more chronic and entrenched difficulties.

In expanding Freudian theory, ego psychology emphasized the conflict-free sphere of development, the more rational and conscious areas of functioning, and the ego's role in coping and adaptation. It elaborated on the ego's many innate functions, the importance of developmental tasks associated with life cycle stages and identity formation, the significance of biopsychosocial factors in shaping development, and the significance of ego strength and weakness. Ego psychology focused attention on the developmental arrests and deficits and helped to explain more serious psychopathology than the neuroses. Concurrently, it recognized the significant role of life stressors, such as role transitions, life stages, and traumatic events, in taxing people's coping capacities (Goldstein 1995).

Ego psychology provided the rationale for treatment that aims to restore, maintain, or enhance the adaptive capacity of the ego. Ego-oriented treatment recognized the need for the establishment and maintenance of the therapeutic or working alliance between patient and therapist and expanded the conception of how change occurs, acknowledging that ego support, ego mastery, new learning, problem solving, and corrective relationship experiences can result in improvement. It emphasized here-and-now issues and more conscious thoughts and feelings as well as past childhood events. Rather than being neutral or functioning as a blank screen, therapists were encouraged to be more genuine, to maintain rather than interpret the positive transference, to use the so-called real relationship between therapist and patient as a potentially corrective and reparative force in treatment, and to employ a range of supportive techniques such as exploration, ventilation, acceptance, reassurance, advice, problem solving, and reflection rather than relying mainly on insight-oriented techniques. The use of ego psychology led to an expansion of the range of patients who can be treated in psychotherapy to include those who suffer from preoedipal developmental arrests or who are experiencing more acute reality stressors or life crises (Goldstein 1995).

Ego-oriented interventive principles lent themselves naturally to short-term treatment because of their emphasis on the therapeutic alliance, the goal of improving selective ego functioning, the focus on the present and the patient's conscious thoughts and feelings, and the active repertoire of supportive techniques, including the use of the therapeutic relationship. In contrast to short-term models based on classical psychoanalytic theory, ego-oriented short-term work employs less restrictive selection criteria and thus is suitable to a greater range of patients than traditional short-term approaches (Luborsky 1984).

Object Relations Theory

Rather than focusing on unconscious instinctual conflict or on ego development and ego functioning, object relations theories viewed interpersonal relationships as providing the context in which all personality development occurred (Fairbairn 1954). Although having different emphases, the American and British object relations theorists expanded our understanding of early infant—caregiver attachment and its role in enabling children to internalize what is originally outside and to thereby acquire basic attitudes toward the self and others (self and object representations). They also drew attention to the separation-individuation process, the crucial role of the maternal holding environment in early development, the child's internalization of good and bad objects, and the fragmentation of the personality or severe withdrawal that occurs when the caregiving environment frustrates or is nonresponsive to the child's needs (Fairbairn 1952, 1954, Kernberg 1975, Klein 1948, Mahler et al. 1975, Winnicott 1965).

Object relations theories offered new formulations regarding the origins and nature of primitive or early defense mechanisms. The two most important of these are splitting, in which two contradictory states such as love and hate are compartmentalized and kept apart so that the person experiences himself or herself and others as all-good or all-bad, and projective identification, in which a person puts into another (projects) often anxiety-ridden or disavowed aspects of the self, to the point of inducing the other to experience what is being projected (Kernberg 1975). These concepts have been used to explain certain aspects of severe psychopathology. Although object relations theories have been used to explain the nature of all psychiatric disorders, they made special contributions to our understanding of disturbances in attachment, severe depressive reactions, and borderline and schizoid disorders.

Like the previous frameworks discussed so far, treatment based on object relations theory was generally long-term. Its emphases differed, however, depending on whether the goal was the modification of pathological defenses and internalized self and object representations or the nurturing of the more real aspects of the patient's self experiences and the establishment of new, more positive internalizations. In the former instance, the therapist attempted to help the patient to recognize and to gain insight into the pathological nature of his or her relationship patterns and their origins. The therapist focused on the relationship patterns that were present in the transference, including any manifestations of splitting and projective identification and employed confrontation and interpretation (Kernberg 1975). Alternatively, when the goal was to help the patient connect to his or her true self or to develop more positive internalizations, more experiential rather than interpretative components of the treatment were utilized. The therapist attempted to provide a holding and containing environment in which patients felt safe and secure enough to express their deeper needs and feelings (Guntrip 1973, Winnicott 1965). It is important to note, however, that there is not a clear demarcation between these two approaches. Additionally, in a recent effort to integrate diverse object relations formulations, Mitchell (1993) has pointed out that treatment based on a relational perspective must include an understanding of the contributions of both patient and therapist to the treatment process rather than focusing exclusively on what the patient brings to the therapeutic situation.

Short-term intervention based on object relations concepts and principles recognizes the need for the therapist to be especially active in establishing a holding environment, which will need to be individualized according to a particular patient's needs. Because patients bring deficits in their internalization of good objects, object constancy, and other important psychic structures as well as their primitive defenses, pathological relational patterns, and destructive behavior to the treatment, the short-term therapist must be particularly alert to and able to manage their manifestations in the treatment relationship. For example, accurate assessment of splitting and projective identification can enable the therapist to refrain from reacting to patients in countertherapeutic ways, to confront and interpret patients' distortions or acting-out behavior, and to help patients tolerate their contradictory feelings. Likewise, therapeutic attunement to patients' difficulties in holding on to positive experiences or in being able to soothe themselves can lead the therapist to try various strategies for addressing this problem. The therapist may provide patients with a new type of relationship, help them to use transitional objects in order to maintain a sense of connection with the therapist, or identify ways in which patients can manage their urgent needs and impulses (Stadter 1996).

Self Psychology

In contrast to object relations theory, self psychology placed the self at the center of development. The rudimentary self is innate and has its own developmental track but requires the responsiveness of the caregiving environment for its optimal development. To develop a strong, cohesive self and to have guiding values and ambitions, the child needs to be able to have idealizable caregivers, validation, and affirmation, and to feel a sense of being like others. Selfobjects are those who perform various functions that children cannot do for themselves and who help them maintain a sense of cohesiveness. When the environment responds in an attuned way to the child, the self flourishes. When the self structure is weak and vulnerable as a result of unattuned, neglectful, or traumatic caregiving, both the self-concept and self-esteem regulation become impaired. The person may be at risk for developing severe emotional difficulties or subject to periods of acute disruption (Kohut 1971, 1977).

Although self psychology arose to explain and treat narcissistic disorders, which were not thought to be treatable through classical psychoanalysis, it expanded to encompass a wide range of emotional disturbances, which were viewed as fundamentally related to vulnerability in the self and as requiring self psychological treatment techniques. It also helped to explain many acute reactions in adults that are triggered by disappointment in or loss of needed selfobjects and that are characterized by a diminished self-esteem, depression, withdrawal, and fragmentation (Brandchaft and Stolorow 1984b).

Self psychological treatment rested on the view that patients bring their early unmet or thwarted selfobject needs to treatment, which provides them with a second chance to complete their development. Through the provision of empathic attunement to patients' subjective experience, the therapist enabled them to develop a selfobject transference and attempted to maintain this transference, to repair any disruptions that arose. The restoration of the transference was achieved by exploring and acknowledging how the therapist had disappointed or failed the patient and by examining and explaining how these events are triggering past parental empathic failures. The therapist engaged in empathic interpretations and functioned as a selfobject to some extent. It was thought that repeated experiences of optimal frustration and optimal responsiveness and disruption and repair of the selfobject transference resulted in the strengthening of self structures, improved self-esteem regulation, greater self-cohesion, and the transformation of archaic selfobject needs into those that are less intense (Brandchaft and Stolorow 1984a,b).

Many self psychologists have adopted the views of those writers who describe themselves as intersubjectivists (Stolorow and Atwood 1992, Stolorow et al. 1994). They have argued that the therapist and patient mutually affect one another so that it is necessary to adopt a two-person view of what transpires in treatment.

In self psychological short-term intervention, it is crucial for the therapist to quickly establish an empathic connection to the patient through attunement to the patient's subjective experience, to recognize how the patient's selfobject needs and problems in self-esteem regulation are part of the presenting problem, and to function as a selfobject selectively. This may include validating the patient's feelings, perceptions, and experiences, affirming the patient's strengths and abilities, being a real person, or demonstrating confidence and optimism. An issue in the use of this approach is how to balance staying where the patient is with the need to help the patient more quickly recognize his or her selfobject needs, how they are being thwarted, and how they originated. It is particularly important for the therapist's explanations and interpretations to be made in a sensitive and empathic rather than confrontative manner (Baker 1991, Gardner 1999, Seruya 1997).

Cognitive-Behavioral Theory

Distinctive from but complementary to the psychodynamic formulations discussed so far, cognitive-behavioral theory has become influential in mental health practice. Although cognitive-behavioral theory did not arise as a brief intervention, many of its major concepts and treatment principles are applicable to short-term treatment (Koss and Shiang 1994).

Cognitive treatment had its roots in the work of Adler (Adler and Ansbacher 1956) and gathered renewed interest through the development of Ellis's (1962, 1973) rational-emotive therapy and the later cognitive therapy of Beck (1976) and Beck and colleagues (1979), who attempted to treat depression with cognitive methods. In the 1970s, behaviorally oriented clinicians and researchers began to incorporate aspects of cognitive theory into their work (Craighead et al. 1994).

The cognitive-behavioral model focused on modifying clearly defined ways of thinking and behaving and the current factors that sustain them, rather than on uncovering or exploring the past origins of the behaviors. It attempted to (1) correct misconceptions, unrealistic expectations, and faulty ideas; (2) modify irrational thoughts that relate to the self; (3) enhance problem solving; and (4) improve self-control and

Doing More with Less

self-management (Fischer 1978). The therapist helped the patient bring into focus the thoughts, beliefs, and ideas that are creating and maintaining his or her problems. The approach was reality oriented and educational. It utilized educative and cognitive restructuring techniques, task assignment, modeling, exercises, and problem solving.

Although there is some indication that cognitive-behavioral techniques can be used to modify certain ways of thinking and behaving in those who show more deep-seated personality problems (Beck et al. 1990, Heller and Northcut 1996, Linehan 1993), they have generally been used to change specific and circumscribed target symptoms, traits, and behaviors that the individual is highly motivated to change (Goisman 1997, Koss and Shiang 1994).

Additional Considerations

Recent developments in the study of trauma and cultural and other types of diversity also have significance for short-term treatment.

Trauma

There has been growing recognition that many patients who seek treatment have experienced traumatic events, such as severe physical and sexual abuse, repeated abandonments, parental death and loss, natural disasters, war and combat, dislocation, and domestic and other forms of violence in the recent or distant past. Although recent traumatic events precipitate the need for treatment in some patients, in other instances patients may present with symptoms and problems that are related to earlier traumatic experiences in childhood or at other times in their lives. Because they may not, however, necessarily make the link between their current difficulties and past trauma history or even reveal the presence of traumatic events, it is easy to misdiagnose such individuals, who may be suffering from posttraumatic stress disorder (Gunderson and Chu 1993, Heller and Northcut 1996, Herman 1992, Herman et al. 1989, Kroll 1993).

Practitioners employing short-term approaches need to be alert to the possibility that some patients may be trauma survivors and that their devastating experiences are contributing to their current difficulties. Often patients who have a trauma history present as highly distrustful of relationships, and they use defenses and engage in behaviors that protect their traumatic memories and that have helped them to survive. Many cannot tolerate confrontative techniques and tend to become involved in situations in which they experience repeated revictimization. Frequently, trauma survivors are not initially able to do the work of the treatment because of their lack of a sense of safety and their variable ego functioning. Likewise, it may be difficult for them to tolerate the working through of their traumatic experiences. These features necessitate that the therapist pay considerable attention to the creation of a holding environment for these patients, validate their survival skills, and help them avoid situations in which they may be revictimized. Interventions need to be sensitively timed in order to engage patients in the trauma recovery work (Goldstein 1999).

Gender, Sexual Orientation, Cultural, and Other Types of Diversity

Most personality theories have neglected to fully consider the unique development, experiences, characteristics, and strengths of women, gays and lesbians, people of color, and members of ethnic and religious groups. For example, feminists have criticized psychodynamic theories for using male development as the prototype for understanding women. Likewise, people of color, members of ethnic minorities, and gays and lesbians have been among those who have pointed out the bias that they feel is inherent in traditional formulations of human development and views of maladaptation. They have argued persuasively that practitioners' expectations of what is normal and appropriate behavior and labeling of certain types of attitudes and behavior as pathological are the results of stereotypical, inaccurate, and insufficient understanding of different types of diversity.

Knowledge about different populations is accumulating rapidly and must be integrated into the assessment and treatment process. Clinicians must be aware of their own attitudes and biases, become knowledgeable about different backgrounds and lifestyles, and utilize interventions that are sensitive and responsive to their patients' diverse life experiences.

MAJOR CHARACTERISTICS OF
INTEGRATIVE SHORT-TERM TREATMENT

The integrative short-term treatment (ISTT) framework that is presented and illustrated throughout this book is broad enough to be utilized by clinicians of diverse theoretical orientations. Clinicians using the framework must be able to recognize the overt symptomatology and more subtle manifestations of the full range of psychiatric disorders. With an accurate assessment, the therapist is in a better position to offer the best course of treatment, drawing on the most current thinking and research regarding the efficacy of certain techniques and interventive strategies with patients manifesting certain *DSM-IV* diagnoses.

Because the use of a short-term approach may require clinicians to modify their usual way of working with patients, they must be open to the idea that patients can make improvements in their lives within a limited time-frame. Clinical experience shows that patients seek help for a variety of problems that are responsive to short-term intervention. All too often, however, for understandable reasons, given the extensiveness of many patients' difficulties, clinicians may communicate their doubts about the efficacy of short-term treatment directly or indirectly to their patients. Instead of utilizing a planned short-term approach, they conduct treatment in their customary way, maintaining the hope that patients will find a way to prolong treatment. Opportunities are lost to provide patients with the hope, structure, and focus that they need to make progress in the time available for treatment and to motivate them to extend the treatment should this be possible. Even if short-term intervention is not optimal in a given case, there is good reason to believe that a period of brief treatment that provides patients with some sense of connection and accomplishment, however small, will be helpful in enhancing patients' motivation to return for additional treatment at a later time.

ISTT has the following ten major distinguishing characteristics:

1. The conscious use of time
2. High level of therapist activity
3. Quick engagement
4. Rapid assessment
5. Partialization and focusing
6. Flexibility in approach and technical interventions
7. Differential use of the therapist–patient relationship
8. Emphasis on patients' strengths and capacities
9. Use of collaboration, linkage, and advocacy
10. Acceptance of the limitations of treatment

The Conscious Use of Time

The clinician's and patient's recognition and understanding that treatment must occur within a particular time frame has numerous consequences. A clear structure and focus must be established; active efforts at engagement must be made; partialized, realistic, and attainable goals must be set; a more conscious awareness of the beginning, middle, and ending phases of intervention must be present; and termination must be anticipated from the outset of the process.

High Level of Therapist Activity

It is important for the practitioner to be active from the beginning of the interventive process in structuring the treatment, assessing the problem, establishing a holding environment, engaging the patient, setting goals, selecting and maintaining a focus, enhancing the patient's motivation for treatment, addressing aspects of the patient's behavior that might interfere with the treatment, enabling the patient to manage life outside of the treatment, and monitoring progress. This requirement for a high level of activity may clash with the therapist's usual style or preferences about how to conduct treatment and may result in forced interventions, but it is necessary that the therapist strike a balance between being attuned to and responsive to the patient and assuming responsibility for directing the process.

Quick Engagement

Engagement is an affective and cognitive process. On the affective level, the therapist attempts to create an environment in which the patient feels accepted, understood, listened to, and respected. On the cognitive side, the therapist tries to enlist the patient's view of the problem, his or her attempts to alleviate it, and his or her expectations about what is needed or what would help. In relating to the patient on these two levels, the therapist facilitates the patient's motivation and collaboration in working on the problem. In most psychodynamic approaches, it is customary to underscore the significance of the development of a helping alliance in which the patient's reality ego perceives that the therapist is there to be helpful and enables the patient to agree to the requirements of therapy. But this feature of the treatment is only one component of the task of creating a therapeutic holding environment that helps to stabilize patients, helps them feel safe, enables them to contain and verbalize their feelings, and facilitates their cooperation and trust. This may be particularly important in work with those patients who show severe developmental arrests or present with histories of childhood sexual abuse and other types of early trauma.

Rapid Assessment

Diagnostic assessment involves an understanding not only of the presenting symptoms and problems but also of the patient's personality and his or her life situation. It is important for the therapist to determine the degree to which underlying problems, conflicts, developmental difficulties, long-standing character traits and patterns of relating to others, and vulnerability in self structures are contributing to the presenting problem. The therapist should consider what aspect of the problem is most amenable to change and what internal and external resources are available to help in resolving the problem.

Partialization and Focusing

Partialization, a key principle of the interventive process, makes the work more manageable and less overwhelming to both therapist and patient. Because patients may present with multiple or long-standing problems, the process of setting goals and establishing a focus necessitates prioritizing with respect to what is most immediate or most amenable to change or resolution. Sometimes the selection of a circumscribed aspect of the total problem constellation may be indicated. Likewise, breaking the problem down into smaller elements engenders hope and a sense of greater control. Further, the achievement of modest goals engenders feelings of mastery and enhances motivation.

Together the therapist and patient establish clear goals, which they must keep in the forefront. The therapist helps to maintain the focus, but this is not always an easy task because new concerns may arise or become more pressing throughout the course of treatment. The therapist needs to show flexibility in addressing other issues that arise even if they initially seem unrelated to the identified problem or stated goals. The therapist's task is to determine whether a particular line of discussion is connected to the treatment focus, whether goals need to be redefined, or whether it is necessary to bring the patient back to the main problem.

Flexibility in Approach and Technical Interventions

There is a large repertoire of techniques that can be used effectively with patients in short-term work and it may be beneficial for practitioners to draw on a variety of interventions (Goldstein and Noonan 1999, Koss and Shiang 1994). Techniques such as sustainment, ventilation, and exploration are always employed to some degree in most situations, while other techniques, such as advice-giving, reassurance, mirroring, confrontation, interpretation, homework assignments and tasks, role playing, correcting cognitive distortions, identifying triggers, and rehearsal may be used selectively.

Differential Use of the Therapist—Patient Relationship

The therapist—patient relationship is the vehicle through which the practitioner provides help, and thus it is important for the therapist to actively engage the patient in a positive working relationship from the outset (Perlman 1957). The therapist tends to behave as a benign authority who has the expertise to help the patient or as a collaborator who works jointly with the patient in the treatment process. The relationship often is essential to instilling a sense of hope and fostering motivation. Short-term treatment emphasizes the more realistic as well as the transferential aspects of the interactions between therapist and patient. Empathy, warmth, genuineness, acceptance, active listening, and the provision of a safe "holding" environment are the main ingredients used to establish and maintain the therapist—patient relationship. Respect for diversity in all its forms and a genuine interest in learning about the patient's particular background and life experience is vital to helping the patient feel understood and valued.

The therapist may function as an auxiliary ego for those patients who are overwhelmed or unable to act in their own best interests, provide support and encouragement, educate patients, act as a role model, help patients to access and utilize other resources, or advocate for them. Because so many patients have not experienced validation of their strengths and talents, it may be important for the therapist to function as a new kind of object in their lives.

When the therapist attempts to modify the patient's maladaptive personality patterns and ways of relating to others or to build the patient's internal structure, understanding and working with transference—countertransference dynamics become a more important part of the treatment. Although our understanding of these dynamics has been expanded to include concepts such as projective identification and the selfobject transferences, it is important for clinicians to recognize that their attitudes, behavior, life experiences, biases, and theoretical orientation affect their perceptions of the patient and the patient's behavior in the treatment process (Noonan 1998). Consequently, therapists must always be vigilant regarding how they are affecting patients and tentative in interpreting patients' behaviors as solely related to their internal processes, defenses. or difficulties in relating to others.

Emphasis on Patients' Strengths and Capacities

It is especially important for the therapist to search out, identify, and work with patients' strengths and capacities, although this is not always an easy task. When patients are beleaguered by severe personality or environmental problems, it is useful to recognize that the act of seeking help is a strength upon which to build. For example, even patients who display long-standing and entrenched pathology may possess the motivation to relieve some aspect of their discomfort. Additionally, those who show pervasive ego deficits or other types of developmental arrests may exhibit some areas of intact functioning. Moreover, what may appear to be maladaptive attitudes and behavior may have nevertheless helped some patients to survive.

Use of Collaboration, Linkage, and Advocacy

Collaboration, linkage, and advocacy have a significant role even in psychotherapeutic treatment. The therapist not only draws on the patient's strengths and capacities but may feel called upon to marshal outside resources that can be used to help the patient, such as involving family, friends, and employers or locating entitlement programs, self-help groups, and community agencies and services. Intra- and interprofessional collaboration and work with others in the patient's social network often are needed in linking patients to vital resources and support systems. In some instances, the patient will need an advocate to help obtain what is needed.

Acceptance of the Limitations of Treatment

There are many benefits to short-term treatment, particularly those that result from being able to help the patient make a circumscribed change or attain some resolution of a pressing problem within a brief period of time. There also are some potential limitations, however, for both therapist and patient. It may be difficult for therapist and patient to accept the concept of limited goals and a focus on what is most amenable to change, particularly when the patient's pathology is long-standing and pervasive or arises from profound trauma.

A second possible limitation surrounds separation and loss because the treatment process is designed to come to an end at a specified time. It is understandable that both therapist and patient may wish to prolong the contact either because of the meaning the relationship has to each and the feelings that are aroused in the process of separation, or because of the wish to experience the satisfaction and gratification of the beneficial outcomes of working together over a longer period of time.

MAJOR COMPONENTS OF ISTT

There are fourteen components in the short-term treatment framework presented here, some of which may occur simultaneously:

1. Problem identification
2. Biopsychosocial assessment
3. Engagement
4. Planning the intervention
5. Contracting
6. Implementing the treatment plan

7. Maintaining or altering the focus
8. Monitoring progress
9. Dealing with resistance
10. Managing transference and countertransference
11. Addressing termination issues
12. Reviewing progress and identifying unresolved issues
13. Resolving the therapist–patient relationship
14. Referral and follow-up

Problem Identification

Problem identification is pivotal in brief intervention because it influences every other aspect of the treatment. Although assessment is a continuous activity as new information becomes available, the therapist should develop a beginning understanding of the patient's main symptoms and current difficulties early in the contact. The need for a rapid evaluation necessitates that the therapist actively explores five interrelated areas: (1) the presenting problem, (2) underlying issues that are contributing to or perpetuating the presenting problem, (3) personal or environmental factors that are contributing to the presenting problem, (4) the patient's motivation and expectations, and (5) the patient's internal capacities and strengths and available external resources.

Biopsychosocial Assessment

Although it is not essential to carry out a complete and formal history of the patient, it is necessary for the therapist to make a more extensive assessment of the patient's overall level of personality structure and functioning; the impact of gender, age, sexual orientation, cultural background, and other types of diversity; relationship patterns; hereditary, constitutional, and health factors; family and social network; and the effect of societal attitudes. The therapist does not adhere to a set pattern of questioning, but instead responds flexibly to what the patient presents.

Engagement

The therapist actively, consciously, and purposefully attempts to engage the patient and to create a facilitating environment rather than wait for the therapeutic relationship to develop automatically. It is important to demonstrate interest in what the patient has to say; to convey respect and a desire to be of help; to show acceptance, genuineness, empathy, and warmth, which encourage the patient to share thoughts and feelings; and to structure the treatment in ways that promote the patient's participation, sense of safety, and trust. In some instances in which patients are uncertain about or reluctant to engage in treatment, it is necessary to help them to identify how treatment may be of benefit to them.

Planning the Intervention

In planning the intervention the therapist and patient must partialize and prioritize, identifying those aspects of the patient's presenting and underlying problems that are amenable to change or require immediate attention, or that the patient is motivated to address. Finding some aspect of the problem that can be alleviated quickly allows the patient to experience some sense of accomplishment, engenders confidence, and increases motivation.

Contracting

One way of ensuring that the therapist and patient are proceeding together is for them to make an explicit agreement about the problem to be addressed and the goals, focus, and structure of intervention. This action, called contracting, optimally solidifies the engagement process. It should not be used, however, in a legalistic or mechanical fashion. In situations where a patient may show ambivalence, hesitance, wariness, or resentment about obtaining help, the contract may center on the patient's agreeing to further explore the potential benefits of and concerns about being in treatment.

Implementing the Treatment Plan

The therapist needs to decide what approach and interventions are most appropriate to achieving the individualized goals and foci that have been established. There is considerable variability from patient to patient and therapist to therapist regarding the specific choice of interventive strategy.

Maintaining or Altering the Focus

In short-term treatment, it is particularly important for the therapist to maintain the focus of intervention rather than allowing the process to drift aimlessly into extraneous areas. Sometimes this may require tactfully redirecting patients if they stray too far from the established problem areas that are central to the treatment. The therapist must be flexible, however, because there may be times when the initial focus must be altered or expanded to accommodate changes in patients' lives, to understand their pathology or difficulties, or to address a crisis or pressing need that arises.

Monitoring Progress

The therapist takes responsibility for monitoring the progress or lack of progress in the treatment. The therapist needs to balance the task of ascertaining whether or not the process is leading in some positive direction with the need for letting patients proceed at their own pace. Evaluating progress requires that the therapist start out with some definite ideas about what constitutes positive movement for a particular patient on the way to achieving the interventive goals. Thus, there are early benchmarks that tell the therapist that treatment is moving in the right direction.

Dealing with Resistance

During the interventive process, the therapist must be attuned to and address obstacles that arise in the course of treatment. Sometimes these occur because change itself is difficult and patients are fearful of what is new and unfamiliar, have difficulties altering established and sometimes ingrained traits and patterns, experience negative consequences of change, become discouraged at what seems to be little or slow movement, experience others as nonsupportive, or are stymied in accessing needed resources. At other times, obstacles that arise stem from a patient's inner resistance that reflects early childhood conflicts, ego-syntonic character traits and behavioral patterns, impaired internalized object relations, and self deficits. Additionally, there are obstacles to the interventive process because of issues in the therapist—patient relationship that arise from transference and countertransference reactions.

Managing Transference and Countertransference

There are three significant features of the therapist—patient relationship that are pivotal in the treatment process: (1) the therapeutic alliance, (2) the transference, and (3) the countertransference.

The therapeutic alliance involves the patient's willingness and ability to work jointly with the therapist on the problems for which the patient seeks help. The maintenance and restoration of the therapeutic alliance can be aided by the therapist's monitoring how the patient feels treatment is going, which affords the patient the opportunity to share both positive and negative reactions to the treatment process and permits adjustments to be made. Sometimes it is useful for the therapist to reinforce the concept that the therapist and patient are collaborating, to point out small gains that have been made, and to show confidence that treatment will result in positive changes.

Because short-term treatment is highly structured, time-limited, here-and-now focused, and reality-oriented, and because it emphasizes a high level of worker activity, it often does not stimulate intense transferences. A mild positive transference can be useful in forwarding the treatment, and negative reactions that may develop should be addressed so that they do not interfere with the process. Some approaches, however, in which the goal of treatment is personality modification, stipulate that it is through working with the transference that change occurs. Thus, these approaches deliberately encourage the development of the transference through the use of certain techniques.

Not all of the patient's intense reactions to the therapist are the result of transference. Sometimes the therapist's attitudes, behavior, comments, biases, and insensitivity may evoke appropriate negative responses. It is important for therapists to be self-scrutinizing and open to the possibility that they may be responsible in some way for a patient's strong reactions. Therapists must be alert to the potential impact on the patient of their own life experiences, patterns of relating, unmet needs and wishes, and internal conflicts, and must exercise self-scrutiny and self-discipline in the treatment process. In some instances, patients may induce the therapist to experience the patients' own conflictual feelings or to perform certain roles that repeat earlier dysfunctional relationships patterns. Although it is not always possible to immediately recognize when such a process is occurring, therapists should be alert to their own strong, urgent, indifferent, and other unusual feeling states. As with other types of countertransference, therapists should strive to identify and understand the reasons for their reactions and to refrain from acting upon their feelings in the treatment situation.

Addressing Termination Issues

How the therapist handles termination often enables patients to consolidate the gains that have been made, continue to work on their own, or arrive at a plan for further intervention or referral to other resources. Because of managed care policies, the approximate number of sessions often is predetermined, so the therapist and patient usually can establish the ending date. The reality of termination should be kept in sight from the outset, but the ending phase is initiated when the therapist helps the patient focus on the amount of time and contacts remaining in order to bring intervention to a close. The therapist should introduce the subject of ending at a point that leaves sufficient time to address the relevant issues. The exact amount of time necessary for the termination phase will vary based on the overall number of sessions or time allocated for the treatment.

Because of increasingly rigid policies regarding the time-limited nature of treatment and the severity and chronicity of patient problems, the ending phase does not coincide necessarily with successful achievement of the treatment goals or with resolution of all of the patient's difficulties. The wish to continue the treatment may interfere with the ways in which the therapist and patient address the ending of treatment. Ignoring or minimizing discussion of termination issues may result in a lack of closure or in inadequate planning for the posttreatment period.

Reviewing Progress and Identifying Unresolved Issues

A necessary part of the termination process and an important means of helping patients cope with their possible anxieties and fears about ending treatment is the discussion of their progress, identification of unresolved issues, determination of additional work to be done in the time remaining, and identification of the steps that patients can take or activities or resources that they can pursue that may be beneficial after treatment ends. Along with exploring patients' perceptions of their progress, the therapist also should share his or her observations regarding their accomplishments and why or how these have occurred. It also may be beneficial to help patients anticipate that some temporary setbacks may occur.

Resolving the Therapist–Patient Relationship

Because patients tend to exhibit their usual ways of coping with endings or stressful situations when they are faced with termination, it is useful for therapists to be prepared for this eventuality. Endings may engender an acute sense of loss, particularly in patients who have rarely, if ever, experienced a caring, accepting, and respectful relationship or in those who have come for help at a time of significant loss and need. Endings also frequently engender feelings about previous losses that patients have experienced that intensify clients' reactions to termination. Some patients may experience the end of treatment as a form of rejection and abandonment.

Therapists, too, have a variety of reactions to the process of ending that stem from both the current relationship with the patient and past experiences with others. It is important for therapists to be in touch with their own feelings about termination.

There are positive aspects to the termination process for patients that stem from attainment of their goals, from positive experiences with the therapist, and from the benefits that result from their enhanced sense of mastery or from dealing with earlier unresolved issues. "Because experiences of success and mastery accrue to the ego's overall sense of competence, the ability to move forward in the present can lead to an enhanced sense of self-esteem and competence" (Goldstein 1995, p. 225).

Referral and Follow-Up

Although adjunctive services may be integrated into the treatment process from the outset, sometimes additional resources are necessary at termination. Such activity may be essential to helping the patient achieve goals, sustain the gains that have been made, or address new or additional problem areas.

It may be important in many instances for the therapist to leave the door open and to convey that it is not a failure or weakness if the patient needs to return in the future. Likewise, in some cases, it is useful to establish a time for and means of follow-up, usually within a month of ending. Such contact helps patients to feel that the therapist still is available and has an ongoing interest in the patient.

CONCLUSION

Although short-term treatment is not appropriate for every patient, it can make an important difference in the functioning of a broad range of patients. Ideally, the assessment of the nature of the patient's problem and a decision about possible solutions should determine the nature of intervention. In actual practice, however, it is often the goals, structure, policies, and resources of the practice setting or insurance carrier that influence the nature and duration of treatment. In today's practice arena, long-term or differential forms of treatment may not be available or reimbursable. Practitioners may be faced with certain dilemmas and constraints in their efforts to help patients. It may be necessary to be active in providing a sound rationale for patients to access their insurance benefits, in establishing good working relationships with case managers and medical reviewers employed by managed care organizations, in helping patients to obtain needed resources and services, and in altering or expanding agency policies and service arrangements.

REFERENCES

Adler, A., and Ansbacher, R. (1956). *The Individual Psychology of Alfred Adler*. New York: Basic Books.

Baker, H. S. (1991). Shorter-term psychotherapy: a self-psychological approach. In *Handbook of Short-Term Dynamic Psychotherapy*, ed. J. P. Barber and P. Crits-Christoph, pp. 287–318. New York: Basic Books.

Beck, A. (1976). *Cognitive Therapy and the Emotional Disorders*. New York: International Universities Press.

Beck, A. T., Freeman, A., and Associates. (1990). *Cognitive Therapy of Personality Disorders*. New York: Guilford.

Beck, A. T., Rush, J. A., Shaw, B. F. and Emery, G. (1979). *Cognitive Theory of Depression*. New York: Guilford.

Brandchaft, B., and Stolorow, R. D. (1984a). The borderline concept: pathological character or iatrogenic myth? In *Empathy II*, ed. J. Lichtenberg, M. Bornstein, and D. Silver, pp. 333–358. Hillsdale, NJ: Analytic Press.

——— (1984b). A current perspective on difficult patients. In *Kohut's*

Legacy: Contributions to Self Psychology, ed. P. E. Stepansky and A. Goldberg, pp. 117–134. Hillsdale, NJ: Analytic Press.

Craighead, L. W., Craighead, W. E., Kazdin, A. E., and Mahoney, M. J., eds. (1994). *Cognitive and Behavioral Intervention: An Empirical Approach to Mental Health Problems*. Boston, MA: Allyn & Bacon.

Davanloo, H. (1978). *Basic Principles and Techniques in Short-Term Dynamic Psychotherapy*. New York: Spectrum.

———— (1980). *Short-Term Dynamic Psychotherapy*. Northvale, NJ: Jason Aronson.

———— (1991). *Unlocking the Unconscious*. New York: Wiley.

Ellis, A. (1962). *Reason and Emotion in Psychotherapy*. New York: Lyle Stuart.

———— (1973). *Humanistic Psychotherapy: The Rational-Emotive Approach*. New York: McGraw-Hill.

Fairbairn, W. R. D. (1952). *Psychoanalytic Studies of Personality*. London: Tavistock.

———— (1954). *An Object Relations Theory of the Personality*. New York: Basic Books.

Fischer, J. (1978). *Effective Casework Practice: An Eclectic Approach*. New York: McGraw-Hill.

Freud, S. (1905). On psychotherapy. *Standard Edition* 7:257–282.

Gardner, J. R. (1999). Using self psychology in brief psychotherapy. *Psychoanalytic Social Work* 6:43–86.

Goisman, R. M. (1997). Cognitive-behavioral therapy today. *The Harvard Mental Health Letter* 13:4–7.

Goldstein, E. G. (1995). *Ego Psychology and Social Work Practice*. New York: Free Press.

———— (1999). Integrative short-term treatment of the borderline patient. *Psychoanalytic Social Work* 6:87–112.

Goldstein, E. G., and Noonan, M. (1999). *Short-Term Treatment and Social Work Practice*. New York: Free Press.

Greenson, R. (1967). *The Technique and Practice of Psychoanalysis, Vol. I*. New York: International Universities Press.

Gunderson, J. G., and Chu, J. A. (1993). Treatment implications of past trauma in borderline personality disorder. *Harvard Review of Psychiatry* 1:75–81.

Guntrip, H. (1973). *Psychoanalytic Theory, Therapy, and the Self*. New York: Basic Books.

Heller, N. R., and Northcut, T. B. (1996). Utilizing cognitive-behavioral techniques in psychodynamic practice with clients diagnosed as borderline. *Clinical Social Work Journal* 24:203–215.

Herman, J. (1992). *Trauma and Recovery*. New York: Basic Books.

Herman, J. L., Perry, J. C., and van der Kolk, B. (1989). Childhood trauma in borderline personality disorder. *American Journal of Psychiatry* 146:490–495.

Kernberg, O. F. (1975). *Borderline Conditions and Pathological Narcissism*. New York: Jason Aronson.

Klein, M. (1948). *Contributions to Psychoanalysis: 1921–1945*. London: Hogarth.

Kohut, H. (1971). *The Analysis of the Self*. New York: International Universities Press.

———— (1977). *The Restoration of the Self*. New York: International Universities Press.

Koss, M. P., and Shiang, F. (1994). Research on brief psychotherapy. In *Handbook of Psychotherapy and Behavior Change*, ed. S. L. Garfield and A. E. Bergin, pp. 664–700. New York: Wiley.

Kroll, J. (1993). *PTSD/Borderlines in Therapy*. New York: Norton.

Linehan, M. M. (1993). *Cognitive-Behavioral Treatment of Borderline Personality Disorder*. New York: Guilford.

Luborsky, L. (1984). *Principles of Psychoanalytic Psychotherapy: A Manual for Supportive-Expressive Treatment*. New York: Basic Books.

Mahler, M. S., Pine, F., and Bergman, A. (1975). *The Psychological Birth of the Human Infant*. New York: Basic Books.

Malan, D. (1963). *A Study of Brief Psychotherapy*. New York: Plenum.

———— (1976). *The Frontier of Brief Psychotherapy*. Cambridge, MA: Harvard University Press.

Mann, J. (1973). *Time-Limited Psychotherapy*. Cambridge, MA: Harvard University Press.

———— (1991). Time-limited psychotherapy. In *Handbook of Short-Term Dynamic Psychotherapy*, ed. P. Crits-Christoph and J. P. Barber, pp. 17–43. New York: Basic Books.

Mitchell, S. (1993). *Hope and Dread in Psychoanalysis*. New York: Basic Books.

Noonan, M. (1998). Reconceptualizing the difficult patient: an interactive approach. *Clinical Social Work Journal* 26(2):129–141.

Perlman, H. H. (1957). *Social Casework: A Problem-Solving Process*. Chicago: University of Chicago Press.

Seruya, B. B. (1997). *Empathic Brief Psychotherapy*. Northvale, NJ: Jason Aronson.

Sifneos, P. (1972). *Short-Term Psychotherapy and Emotional Crisis*. Cambridge, MA: Harvard University Press.

———— (1979). *Short-Term Psychotherapy: Evaluation and Technique*. New York: Plenum.

———— (1987). *Short-Term Dynamic Psychotherapy*. New York: Plenum.

Stadter, M. (1996). *Object Relations Brief Therapy*. Northvale, NJ: Jason Aronson.

Stolorow, R. D., and Atwood, G. (1992). *Contexts of Being: The Intersubjective Foundations of Psychological Life*. Hillsdale NJ: Analytic Press.

Stolorow, R. D., Atwood, G., and Brandchaft, B. (1994). *The Intersubjective Perspective*. Northvale, NJ: Jason Aronson.

Winnicott, D. W. (1965). *The Maturational Processes and the Facilitating Environment*. New York: International Universities Press.

CHAPTER THREE

Short-Term Psychodynamic Treatment of Children and Adolescents

JUDITH MISHNE

THEORETICAL OVERVIEW AND TREATMENT PERSPECTIVES

There are numerous perspectives and formulations used to define and characterize a variety of short-term models of treatment. For example, Goldstein and Noonan (1999) differentiate between models in mental health practice and those in social work practice. In mental health practice, they cite (1) the psychodynamic model, (2) the crisis interventive model, and (3) the cognitive-behavioral model. The myriad social work practice models are presented historically and chronologically: (1) the early diagnostic model, (2) the functional model, (3) the ego psychology and the evolving diagnostic (psychosocial) model, (4) the problem-solving model, (5) the crisis interventive model, (6) the task-centered model, (7) the cognitive-behavioral model, and (8) the ecological perspective and life model. Practitioners are developing and using a variety of newer techniques based on hypnosis, biofeedback, gestalt techniques, spirituality, narrative, and social constructionist approaches. Some advocates insist on a correct model for a given population.

While I respect new efforts to reach specific client groups, I do not endorse the exclusive use of one model for treating children and adolescents. I have chosen not to experiment with some of the existing models, have reservations about some, and am partial to others, particularly the crisis and psychodynamic integrative psychoanalytic models.

The short-term psychodynamic treatment model includes basic theories, techniques, and assumptions of traditional and contemporary psychoanalytic theory. Messer and Warren (1995) classify the basic models of brief psychodynamic therapy into the drive/structural model of Malan, Davanloo, and Sifneos; and the relational model of Luborsky, Horowitz, Weiss and Sampson, and Strupp and Binder. Mann's model is called the integrative psychoanalytic model, embracing the four psychologies: drive, ego, object, and self psychology. An eclectic model of brief dynamic therapy is represented by Garfield, Gellak, and Gustafson.

"The practice principles of crisis intervention include (1) time-limited interventions, (2) worker flexibility, (3) high level of worker activity, (4) circumscribed specific goals, (5) the identification of tasks to be mastered. The interventive process emphasizes ventilation, clarification, reassurance, direct influence, supporting strengths and the mobilization of inner and outer resources" (Goldstein and Noonan 1999, p. 28).

All psychodynamic models posit that problems have developed out of early childhood experiences, traumas, developmental deficits, and/or long-standing personality patterns. Relying on a life-span developmental approach requires that attention be given to child development; developmental changes in family relationships; sexuality; issues of separation, individuation, and predictable or expectable challenges; crisis; and transitions. "In a developmental lifespan approach to psychotherapy, the patient's problem is defined in terms of an adaptive failure, usually in the face of new demands from the patient's total life situation. These demands may be accidental, or they may result from the developmental processes itself such as graduating from high school" (Messer and Warren 1995, p. 283).

In the case of Ellen, which is presented later in this chapter, the emphasis is on a developmental perspective, with a crisis intervention focus on the situational factors in psychopathology and on the emotional crisis, rather than on the intrapsychic structure of personality. The use of an integrative psychoanalytic theoretical model is based on the practitioner's belief that these theoretical outlooks are complementary, rather than mutually exclusive (Mann 1973, Mann and Goldman 1982, Mishne 1993, Pine, 1988, 1989, 1990). It follows that the psychodynamic psychoanalytic idea of life-span development requires consideration of particular stage-specific issues and conflicts, which are handled with a here-and-now emphasis and possibly with a crisis intervention orientation, "suggesting therapeutic foci that do not require sustained exploration of early life, as in the case with more traditional open-ended psychodynamic approaches" (Messer and Warren 1995, p. 282).

The crisis intervention approach, alone or in tandem with other short-term models, ideally improves the patient's capacity to attain new and more stable adaptive structures, and to manage stress with improved self-regulation, drive modulation, enhanced self-esteem, and more satisfying age-appropriate object relations. Advocates of crisis intervention de-emphasize the importance of stable and enduring personality characteristics and instead focus on the qualities of the situation and the interaction between the patient and the environment (Budman and Gurman 1988).

Studies find that children are commonly seen in outpatient psychotherapy for six sessions or less, in a variety of private and clinic settings. Yet the literature on time-limited psychotherapy is remarkably sparse. It would seem that much psychotherapy of children is time-limited more by default than by plan, due to a variety of factors: parental resistance, poorly executed referral of the child and parents, lack of flexibility of clinics and agencies, and the skill of the therapist. "Given these realities, there is a pressing need for the development and application of planned, time-limited psychotherapy to maximize the usefulness of psychotherapeutic intervention" (Messer and Warren 1995, p. 284).

The psychodynamic developmental perspective appears uniquely suited to provide guidelines for an individualized assessment and treatment planning for ongoing work with children and adolescents and their parents. This perspective demonstrates the patient's failure to attain developmental milestones in an expected sequence, as well as breakdowns, arrests, or regressions in the areas of cognitive development, social and emotional development, and development of self-structure, which form the basis of identity. This developmental look at the child can be matched with understanding the corresponding parallel development of parents (Benedek 1970) and the required developmental changes in parenting (Mishne 1996, Taffel 1991). The crisis intervention approach seems equally suited to work with young patients who are in the process of change, traversing developmental milestones, resolving developmental crisis, on the way to object and self-constancy, or are experiencing separation-individuation, with the ultimate goal of achieving the consolidation of personality at the conclusion of adolescence.

INCLUSIVE AND EXCLUSIVE CRITERIA

Many clinicians and authors state that selective criteria for time-limited psychodynamic child psychotherapy are similar to those for adults. Suggested criteria include a problem of recent nature; an ability to engage, to relate, and to sustain object ties; a high degree of motivation; and an overall history of adequate adjustment.

The *DSM-IV* category of adjustment disorder is particularly amenable to a short-term treatment approach because of the following characteristics:

A. The development of emotional or behavioral symptoms in response to an identifiable stressor(s) occurring within three months of the onset of the stressor(s).

B. These symptoms or behaviors are clinically significant as evidenced by either of the following:
1. marked distress that is in excess of what would be expected from exposure to the stressor.
2. significant impairment in social or occupational academic functioning.
C. The stress-related disturbance does not meet the criteria for another specific Axis I disorder and is not merely an exacerbation of a pre-existing Axis I or Axis II disorder.
D. The symptoms do not represent bereavement.
E. Once the stressor (or its consequences) has terminated, the symptoms do not persist for more than an additional six months (APA 1994, pp. 273–274)

Adjustment disorders can present in acute form (less than six months of disturbance) or chronic form (lasting more than six months) and with specific accompanying characteristics such as depressed mood, anxiety, or disturbance of conduct. Additional to the clinical and personality disorders to be noted under Axis I and II, and medical conditions under Axis III, Axis IV is particularly important in regard to delineating the inordinate range of psychosocial and environmental problems. Clients commonly selected as optimal candidates for short-term treatment should not suffer overwhelming environmental or psychosocial stressors, and should score at the higher end of the Global Assessment of Functioning (GAF) scale, that is, the final item of the *DSM-IV* multiaxial assessment.

Lester (1968) notes that most important is the task of evaluating the child's movement through successive developmental phases without serious impasse or breakdown. Anna Freud emphasized that the key to a child's or adolescent's future mental health did not lie in the discernible symptoms, regressions, or arrests at the time of the diagnostic evaluation; rather, it was dependent on the child's progressive line of development, despite symptoms and inhibitions.

Thus, the types of problems considered amenable to brief psychotherapy would be various circumscribed problems, transient regressions, reactive disorders, and mild exaggerations of otherwise age-appropriate behaviors. Short-term therapy would also be appropriate for children and adolescents who could develop a working relationship fairly easily, maintain a focus, and demonstrate basic trust, flexibility, and responsiveness to interpretations, suggestions, and reflections. Parental motivation and an appropriate emotional climate in the home must exist such that a treatment plan can be formulated and sustained with continuity and predictability.

Exclusion of children and adolescents with long-standing characterological difficulties and ego weakness is appropriate, as such patients need long-term care and often a range of interventions, such as protective services and referral to residential facilities and inpatient services. As with the adult patient population, youths with less severe psychopathology will be more responsive to brief and/or crisis intervention psychodynamic therapy than will those with chronic developmental difficulty. Object loss, distorted parenting, maternal or paternal deprivation, family psychopathology, psychotic symptoms exhibited by child and/or parents, and traumatic abuse all suggest the need for long-term treatment. The selected criteria of adolescents for time-limited short-term or crisis treatment is similar to the selective criteria of children and adults. Davanloo (1992), Malan (1976), Mann (1973), and Strupp and Binder (1984) emphasize the patient's motivation, the presence of clear precipitants to the current crisis, a capacity for basic trust reflected in the existence of prior relationships of reasonable depth and duration, sufficient ego strengths to facilitate rapid engagement and disengagement, affect tolerance, and some degree of psychological mindedness such that the current difficulties and/or crisis is recognized as located, at least in part, in the self (Messer and Warren 1995).

Distinctions are made between more circumscribed milder problems and those that are more chronic, pervasive, severe, and characterological. Adolescents who are psychotic, drug or alcohol addicted, sociopathic, prone to excessive acting out and impulsivity, or resistive or difficult to engage in therapy are not appropriate candidates for short-term interventions. This would include many with preoedipal arrests or borderline personalities, and those with other severe personality or character disorders.

Evaluation of prior developmental accomplishments is important, as is a thorough assessment of the role of the family, particularly with younger adolescents, to determine suitability for short-term treatment. Parents who are motivated and easily engaged can and do make essential contributions to the treatment efforts. In contrast, severe family pathology and parental resistance generally undermine treatment, and thus the tasks of engagement and relationship building require lengthy treatment approaches.

Adolescents can often be especially difficult to engage because of their oppositional struggles to develop autonomy and independence. They fear facing their inadequacies or establishing any relationship with an adult authority figure.

TREATMENT GOALS

Because of the brevity of the treatment process and contact in crisis or short-term treatment, there is no attempt to restructure the child's personality. Rather, the interventions are aimed at "modifying the existing balance of forces, both internal and external to the child" (Messer and Warren 1995, p. 285). Goals include symptom reduction and restoration of equilibrium. Sometimes underlying issues can be resolved. The clinical focus commonly centers on some discernible, easily identified current stressor or life situation, with therapeutic efforts focused on lessening or modifying the home environment, parental handling, or the child's style of coping, thereby bringing some relief and lessening the child's anxiety or depression, so that the child (and parents) resume more adaptive and satisfying ways of interacting. The major goal is to assist the child in resuming a progressive line of development.

This work often requires assisting the parents as well. Parents often know what they should do, and they want to, but they may be paralyzed by internal or external inhibitions. "Internal inhibitions arise from excessive anxiety, trying too hard, or identifying too strongly with the child or one's own parents. Anxiety about a child's negative reaction, including accusations that the parent does not love the child, often inhibits too many parents. Often parents need permission to express their feelings, and to exercise their own judgment" (Mishne 1996, p. xviii). External inhibitions may be due to anxiety and confusion about conflicting advice, or pressures due to marital or work-related demands.

Providing guidance, interpretations, advice, active modeling, and environmental manipulations all can constitute valuable short-term work with parents, whereby the goal is not one of personality change or promoting insight, but rather of helping parents restructure the child's environment in such a way that there is optimal use made of all dimensions of child development, for example, attachment and separation-individuation (a universal arena of conflict in childhood) (Bowlby 1969, Erikson 1950, Mahler 1968, Sarnoff 1976).

Psychodynamic crisis theory and short-term therapy with parents would also commonly require attention to self-regulation and mutual regulation, to thereby help the parents provide the child with a relatively constant attuned other. Beebe (1994) notes the dynamic process of mutual, dyadic regulation in the infant—mother relationship as well as the self-regulating capacities. When the infant does not receive sufficient help to regulate its internal states, the child resorts to forms of self-regulation, often pathological. The structure of self and sense of identity evolves in a relational context and so it is crucial to focus on the parent—child relationship and the nature of the object ties, in any and all short-term therapy with children and adolescents, throughout the life cycle, from infancy to the older adolescent years.

As noted in work with children, a developmental perspective is particularly useful in the formulation of clinic focus and treatment goals in brief psychotherapeutic interventions with adolescents. Because of the brevity of the treatment, the aims or goals are not to seek any restructuring of personality, "but rather the alleviation of a developmental impasse or crisis. Thus, the therapeutic focus will be framed in terms of the life situation of the adolescent, invariably centered within concentric relationships with family, peers, and the larger community" (Messer and Warren 1995, p. 300). Two central and common developmental themes serve as organizing structures for the creation of a treatment focus—identity formation and separation-individuation. A third task, that of negotiating issues of sexuality and competitiveness, is understood as a framework for interventions with older teenagers (Messer and Warren 1995).

Erikson (1968) had defined the central task of adolescence in terms of "identity formation" versus "role confusion." This follows the distinctive character of early adolescence, that is, disengagement from the parents, which causes the young person to search, at times frantically, for new attachments and new love objects (Blos 1962). Middle adolescence (ages 14 to 17) or adolescence proper is characterized by a more intense emotional life and a turning toward heterosexual love concurrently with increased withdrawal of cathexis from the parents, causing impoverishment of the ego, pain, and mourning at the surrender of parent–child ties.

> The phase of adolescence proper has two dominant themes: the revival of the oedipal complex and the disengagement from primary love objects. This process constitutes a sequence of object relinquishment and object finding, both of which promote the establishment of the adult drive organization. One may describe this phase of adolescence in terms of two broad affective stages: "mourning" and being "in love." The adolescent incurs a real loss in the renunciation of his oedipal parents and he experiences the inner emptiness, grief, and sadness which is part of all mourning. [Blos 1962, p. 100]

During middle adolescence, there are two sources of internal danger. One is the weakness of the ego when defenses are inadequate to successfully bind in aggression and depression, and the other is the anxiety aroused by emotional attachment to a sexually desired object. "Cognition has become more realistic, objective and analytical. Interests, skills, and talents have emerged and self-esteem is more stable. Vocational choices are being considered and sorted out realistically, yet unreconciled internal strife still resists transformations. Conflicts are in sharp focus, to be resolved, it is hoped, in the next phase of adolescence/maturation" (Mishne 1986, p. 18).

Late adolescence is viewed as a stage of consolidation and stabilization, and we anticipate and expect greater clarity, purposeful actions, predictability, constancy of emotions, stable self-esteem, and more mature functioning. In an attempt to avoid identity diffusion the older adolescent may engage in some experiments with negative identity, an identity based on hostility toward and distance from roles approved by family and society. While there is no overall resolution of earlier infantile conflicts, we see a more predictable and stable arrangement of derivation, defenses, and personality style.

Supporting mastery of the above developmental tasks, on the way to self-constancy, consolidation, and stability, commonly can constitute the foci and goals for treating the adolescent patient. Adolescents are far from homogeneous as a clinical population, merging at one end of the range with children and at the other end with adults. Mann (1973) and Sifneos (1979) note that some of the most important models for brief psychodynamic treatment of adults were developed in work with older adolescent populations, such as college students. The literature on the modification of brief psychodynamic psychotherapy for younger adolescents is exceedingly sparse, but overall we can make the following generalizations on brief psychotherapy of adolescents.

Because of the common difficulty in engaging adolescents in treatment, work often requires efforts to develop a working relationship that does not compromise the teen's autonomy or impose intolerable conditions (Blos 1983). This may require a greater level of activity and responsiveness than is usually the case with psychodynamic treatment (Meeks 1971). There may need to be greater flexibility around the structuring of the therapy situation and more willingness to exploit positive aspects of the transference and the real relationship. Additional commonly employed techniques include use of clarification, confrontation, and interpretation, provision of empathy, support, acceptance, reassurance, and education; the clinician's demonstrating active listening;

and where appropriate, referral(s) for additional supports (Goldstein and Noonan 1999). Collaboration, linkage, and advocacy are common techniques in short-term work, and all are offered with an emphasis on the client's strengths.

CASE ILLUSTRATION—ADOLESCENT

Assessment

Ellen, a 17-year-old high school senior, was referred by her parents during a crisis. The senior year is often viewed as a universal crisis, as students complete college applications and await admissions decisions. Ellen is a most attractive, very slim, and petite blonde, who is bright, very articulate, and very dramatic in self-presentation—much like her mother, who struggles with self-regulation. Both are often excessively strident, anxious, and quick to express temper, tears, and feeling overwhelmed. Ellen and her mother describe family frenzy and recent intense discord over the uncertainties of Ellen's college admission, as well as her articulated strong fears about graduating and leaving home. She has deliberately forced herself to apply to colleges away from home, although not too far away to preclude visits home on weekends. With shame and anger, Ellen gave tearful accounts of her disinclination to leave her beloved, familiar high school and peer group. She recognizes the irrationality of her desire not to grow up and go away to school, as well as of her fanatic preference for one of the eight colleges she applied to.

Ellen has become a very strong, high-achieving, and hard-working student, but she had a setback at the end of her junior year. Her grades dropped because of her unavoidable excessive absence due to Lyme disease. Additionally, she does not do well, certainly below her potential, on standardized tests such as the SAT exams. She is panicky that these realities will mar her chances for acceptance at her first choice. While she's managed to improve her grade point average in the first semester of her senior year, she remains extremely anxious, uneven in academic performance, and at constant odds with her parents about use of the phone, care of her room and clothes, and driving privileges. She had recently ended a taxing and unsatisfying relationship with a long-term boyfriend, who was having inordinate difficulty in letting go. In the social context of her private school, other male friends keep their distance to avoid this rejected suitor's wrath. Girlfriends are loyal and supportive, and Ellen is included in all parties and school and peer group social events.

Ellen is an only child, born to older parents who had all but given up hope of ever having a child. Her parents have had chronic marital difficulty that has continued, despite their engagement in marital and individual therapy, and they are on antidepressives. The father, an under-employed lawyer, is a traffic judge. He has had long-standing work problems, with resultant financial pressures, and the mother, a former teacher, now works part-time for her brother at a job with flexible hours to accommodate her enormous burdens in caring for her mother, who is suffering from dementia and Alzheimer's disease.

Ellen, the light of her parents' lives, is currently at odds with both her parents; despair and anger dominate the emotional tone at home. All three normally evidence considerable ego strengths, but currently regression is paramount, particularly in the realm of regulation of affects, whereby rage and explosive anger are expressed routinely. Ellen's autonomous functions, such as memory, show some temporary impairment on tests in school. There's been a decline in mastery and competence and in the synthetic and integrative ego functioning of Ellen and both parents. Father struggles with his unsatisfactory, low-paying job, which entails long hours, and he attempts to gain self-control by attending services at his cherished Catholic church twice a day, where he previously had positions of prestige. Mother feels overwhelmed by her mother's problems, her limited financial resources, her unsatisfying job, and, most important, the new stressors in her relationship with her daughter. In contrast to her husband, mother finds no solace and seeks no contacts at church. She turns to work, earning and saving money as best she can, therapy, and her extended family for support and comfort. The parents both have health problems. Father had a heart attack and suffers from emphysema, and continues to chain smoke, which causes a running battle with his wife and daughter. Mother struggles with her weight and with some torn ligaments in one leg that have proved resistant to healing.

Developmentally, Ellen demonstrates behavior suggestive of considerable reactive regression, which is causing ego exhaustion and depletion. We can hypothesize that the parental conflict created additional interference in her final separation-individuation and oedipal resolution, which was semicompromised originally, given her intense attachment to her parents, which interferes with greater decathexis from them. Separation anxieties and fears about genuine individuation appear to be masked by the overriding affect of anger and angst. Because of the genuine psychological mindedness possessed by Ellen and her parents, mother particularly, fears about growing up and leaving home are also articulated. As Ellen has not been able to complete separation and individuation, so too is she struggling with an incomplete oedipal resolution.

Multiaxial Assessment of Ellen:

Axis I: Adjustment disorder with separation anxiety and depressed mood.

Axis II: Reactive reaction of adolescence.

Axis III: None.

Axis IV: Problems with primary support group, the parents, regarding anxieties about graduation and separation.

GAF score: 50–60.

Beginning Phase of Treatment

Because of the crisis nature of Ellen's presenting problems and stress, therapy was offered immediately, and it was stated that help and relief could possibly occur quickly. The therapeutic efforts centered on mobilizing and enhancing this adolescent's motivation, as well as her mother's motivation, to relieve discomfort and strife. Weekly appointments were scheduled with both. Father's long hours precluded his being seen regularly. (He was seen twice, and had several phone appointments.) In the course of the assessment, Ellen and her mother acknowledged that some of Ellen's fears about graduation and separation from the family might be due to her parents' overinvolvement, especially in her schoolwork. They rationalized that other parents behaved in similar ways, due to the academic demands at her school and the general level of competitiveness regarding academic achievement, grade point averages, and college acceptances. At ages 10 and 11, Ellen procrastinated and commonly did sloppy last-minute work. This caused her parents to push, prod, and oversupervise her, as well as to engage themselves in her projects and assignments. They provided excessive help with compositions by going to the library and doing research for her. The father recounted the same efforts from his own parents, and noted his subsequent very fine high school grade point average. Questioning revealed, however, that he had almost flunked out of college his freshman year. It took several weeks to pry the parents loose from Ellen's schoolwork, at this time of senior-year regression, and they were helped to see that their daughter might suffer a fate similar to her father's unless she was allowed to do her work herself, albeit at times with all-night study stints that they'd have no control over once she departed home and lived in a college dorm. Ellen had developed computer skills and thus had no need for her mother's typing papers for her, and, in fact, she could effectively handle her work, though not often in accord with the parents' notions about time management.

Ellen's strengths were emphasized with her parents to improve their reality assessment and to remind them that Ellen had achieved very good grades and handled all the details of college applications, including getting references and writing essays. Ellen's intellectual curiosity, academic ability, and solid circle of friends were also highlighted. Ellen never was tempted to experiment with drugs, sexual intimacy, or any form of acting out and her parents, her mother especially, needed to be reminded of these important realities. Her mother would explode over comparative trivia, such as a disheveled bed and bathroom during the week, even though Ellen did a thorough cleaning of her room and bathroom on the weekend, and did her personal laundry. Money was often an area of conflict, as mother gave double messages about saving and economy concurrent with overly generous expenditures for Ellen in regard to clothes, special summer programs, and vacation trips. The contract specified mutually determined problem areas, and of particular focus was self-regulation and striving for less discordant modes of communication between Ellen and her parents.

Middle Phase

Ellen and her mother, in separate and joint sessions, ventilated and expressed their rage and frustration at the current breakdown of rapport and communication. They explored the basis of this recent strife, and recognized the depth of their positive attachment and fears about the impending separation. In separate sessions, the mother bemoaned what her life would become when Ellen went away. She dreaded day-to-day life with her unavailable and ungratifying husband and her demanding, disoriented mother. Ellen is her major source of pleasure and pride, and parenting her daughter is her major source of achievement and positive self-esteem. She recognized her dilemma about letting go, concurrent with Ellen's recognition of her fears for her mother once Ellen is no longer at home. Both could engage in rational discourse and reflection in sessions. The mother, born in Europe, at times recognized her old-fashioned concepts about filial responsibility, as well as her jealousy that her daughter had greater freedom than she enjoyed in her youth. She had been forced to accept the traditional female role of the family's worker, cleaner, and helper, in contrast to her two brothers, who had fewer familial duties. She was aware of her Italian, Old World notions and excessive expectations of having a dutiful daughter.

The mother, at times reluctantly, accepted direct advice, guidance, and education about appropriate expectations of adolescents, and what was and was not in the range of adolescents' normal self-assertion. Following numerous theatrical and hysterical outbursts, the mother could demonstrate some humor, along with genuine rapport with the clinician, and thereby would not resist efforts at mediation by the therapist, who she recognized was not taking sides but was allied with both mother and daughter, respectfully and empathically, to facilitate better communication, to restore their better coping capacities, and to help them regain their prior positive equilibrium.

In the context of lending ego, mirroring, and structuring, the therapist could set limits about tone of voice and language used. In the context of the treatment sessions, mother and daughter were helped to see and experience the basic underlying feelings of loyalty and love, and their fear of being apart. In response to the clinician's mediation and advocacy, some tasks and assignments were agreed upon, such as Ellen's not leaving damp towels strewn about. Her mother was helped to tolerate Ellen's need for privacy and to stop inspecting her daughter's room. Mother and daughter were helped to maintain proper boundaries, regarding who should call the colleges to make inquiries and appointments for interviews, as well as who should put the final editing touches on personal essays on the college applications.

During the course of therapy, the therapist—patient relationship— the therapeutic alliance, transference, and countertransference—and the real relationship were reflected upon by Ellen, her mother, and the clinician. Davanloo (1992) believes that the establishment of a working relationship is a prime objective of treatment, and it should be done very early. In fact, Ellen's parents already had an alliance with this clinician from a prior therapy contact, and the good rapport stimulated their return. Their daughter, in tandem with the clinician, quickly developed a mutually respectful and trusting rapport with the therapist (Bauer and Kobos 1987).

With adolescents, the therapeutic alliance is seen as emanating out of the adolescent's "conscious or unconscious wish to cooperate and readiness to accept the therapist's aid in overcoming intense difficulties and resistance" (Sandler et al. 1980, p. 45). In addition to the positive feelings for the therapist, the alliance is based on the ego's accurate appraisal of a need for self-understanding and its gratification at being understood. Adolescents will look to therapy for relief only if they have the capacity for self-observation and some awareness that there is a problem. Ellen demonstrated this capacity to self-observe and to acknowledge her own inappropriate tantrums and outbursts.

The treatment relationship with Ellen and her parents is best described as a positive real relationship without transference, as there was no displacement onto the clinician of feelings and affects from past parental objects. The clinician's responses were counter-reactions, that is, reality-oriented factors, rather than responses that emanated out of the clinician's unconscious (Giovacchini 1985). The clinician was able to continually experience positive regard, respect, and compassion for Ellen and her parents. There was an uninterrupted positive and effective patient–therapist fit. In the context of a positive real relationship, empathic warmth, attention, listening, and active participation were consistently discernible. The parents and Ellen knew that they could count on an unbroken bond of commitment, compassion, and interest from the therapist.

Termination

The specified period of treatment time is particularly germane in considering clinical work with adolescents who are bound to their present concerns and anxieties and generally uninterested in their pasts. Novick (1977) describes what he calls the adolescent's "unilateral treatment plan," in which termination is planned at the onset, for example, to occur at the end of the school year. The treatment contract is often set in conjunction with the academic year.

Ellen did not get into the college of her choice on the early admission option, but was later admitted from the waiting list. She was accepted at several other colleges that she applied to as safe schools. She was distraught about not being admitted early at her first choice, but she arranged for some on-campus interviews, handled herself well, and, given her ever-improving academic record, was later accepted. Her delight and relief were palpable!

Following this good news, the treatment focus moved back to Ellen's feelings of loss about graduation and her struggles to complete final semester assignments. Ellen was also consumed with concerns about the senior prom and various school parties. Several male friends proved attentive despite the social pressures from her former, possessive boyfriend. Thus, mother and daughter experienced the pleasures of shopping for a prom dress and clothes for college—rites of separation/individuation.

There were some struggles about summer employment. Ellen wanted to remain connected to her school, via a low-paying job as counselor at the school's summer camp program. Her mother wanted her to seek more lucrative employment. A relative offered her an impressive summer job at a brokerage firm, and Ellen eagerly accepted the position, given her interest in math and business. She felt quite grown up taking the subway into midtown to her office. Additional treatment foci entailed discussions of her changing social life and separating from old friends, all standard fare for college-bound youth, a reality that Ellen joyfully embraced, along with fears about making new friends.

In the course of the ending phase, Ellen and her mother reviewed the treatment process and recognized that unresolved issues may resurface or reverberate once she's at college, such as homesickness, exam anxiety, and procrastination about completing assignments. Ellen decided that she would not seek counseling at her college. If need be, she would resume contact with me, via phone or in person, since the commute was an easy one.

The concluding phase of treatment constitutes a rehearsal for the future (Ekstein 1983) whereby energy is available for investment in new relationships and new experiences. Like parents, therapists hope their adolescent patients will not falter, but rather will be fortified to master the tasks of life, love, and attachment (Mishne 1986). And so, with considerable hope and confidence, Ellen's treatment was concluded after thirty-two sessions, with patient and clinician gratified that substantial gains had been made.

CASE ILLUSTRATION—CHILD

Assessment

Betsy, 3 years old, is beautiful, outgoing, verbal, and animated. She is small for her age. She is a dusky brunette, with dancing brown eyes and a quick and ready smile. Her parents are upper-middle class, well educated, psychologically minded, and knowledgeable about child development. They had great difficulty conceiving a child. The mother suffered three miscarriages and an ectopic pregnancy. The parents then sought in vitro fertilization to maintain a pregnancy. Despite the low success rate of this procedure, Betsy was conceived and the pregnancy went smoothly. Amid the joy and relief at finally having a healthy child, the parents have experienced continued anxiety about her progress and development. Subsequent in vitro attempts for a second child failed, and Betsy would be their only child. The parents recognize their overinvolvement and anxiety about their special, cherished only child, and contemplate the possibility that they flood her with their high level of anxiety.

Betsy is described as often anxious and intimidated by boisterous youngsters at her play groups and gym programs, and she seems afraid to try new activities such as swimming. She appears to recoil from parental pressures to participate and to excel. The more her parents pressure her to behave more actively and assertively, the more she holds back. She seems afraid to try for fear of failing and disappointing her parents yet again. The parents expressed grave reservations about how Betsy would perform in school admission interviews and on psychological tests administered as part of the admissions procedure. Their anxieties in fact created a self-fulfilling prophecy; their very intelligent and creative child performed badly, froze, resisted some school interviews, would not separate from her parents, and on the testing was scattered and erratic in performance.

The parents previously had been in treatment with the clinician, with whom they'd maintained a warm connection, and so they returned for help in this crisis period of applying for school placement following

Betsy's nursery school experience, seeking short-term treatment—parent guidance for themselves and play therapy for Betsy.

The parents were relieved to be seeking help, comfortable with the clinician, and aware that insight about their anxiety provided little relief or improved self-modulation. They had tried to self-soothe, and discussed the situation easily and frequently at home, to no avail. The parents demonstrated considerable ego strengths, as evidenced by self-awareness, good reality testing, positive object relations, and mastery and competence in most spheres of their life. The current crisis of testing and evaluation of Betsy had produced some real regression in regulation and control of affects and impulses, and defenses failed to bind because of anxiety. Betsy mirrored their anxiety in testing and stressor situations when she was confronted with new and unfamiliar peers, tasks, or challenging new sports activities. When not stressed, Betsy performed and interacted well with peers, teachers, and parents. Betsy clearly evidenced movement out of the primary dyad, and achievement of separation-individuation and self and object constancy. She appeared appropriately engaged in an oedipal attachment to her father, and an appropriately loving, albeit at times ambivalent connection to her well-attuned and understanding mother.

Multiaxis Assessment

Axis I: Adjustment disorder with anxiety.
Axis II: Reactive reaction of early childhood.
Axis III: None.
Axis IV: Problems with primary support group, that is, her excessively
           anxious parents.
GAF: 70.

Beginning

Because of the crisis nature of the presenting situation, treatment was offered immediately, and it was recognized that with assistance, improvement could possibly quickly occur, given the parents' and child's strengths as well as the positive connection between the family and the clinician, who, in fact, was not a total stranger to Betsy. She had been brought to the office on numerous occasions since her birth for visits. Betsy was seen weekly in play therapy, and the parents were seen weekly in individual and joint sessions. It was recognized by parents and clinician that although the crisis was of recent origin, there were earlier antecedents. Parental anxiety was very much related to the struggles to have a child. Additionally, the father was also contending with old feelings that resurfaced in regard to a deceased child from his prior marriage. This daughter had died in a tragic accident more than a dozen years prior, and the father contemplated that possibly his style and manner of pressuring Betsy was because she must compensate him for this prior loss by being a superchild. The mother recognized that she unconsciously often supported the father, out of her devotion to him and the wish that his current family make up to him for all the prior hurt and pain he endured.

We agreed on an immediate focus, namely, family shared anxiety and the dilemma of Betsy's school placement, since she was not admitted to any of the schools the parents had applied to. We did not attempt to work on the father's eternal mourning process, but rather partialized and recognized that different parental approaches were required to give both Betsy and the parents some relief and a better sense of competence.

Because of the parents' prior experience in therapy, scant attention was paid to discussion of cancellation, to the therapist's availability, or to confidentiality, attendance, and fee payment (Goldstein and Noonan 1999). Betsy needed some preparation for the concepts of weekly appointments and confidentiality, as is realistic for a child so young.

Middle Phase

Betsy engaged in creative play therapy and demonstrated, via her enactments, dollhouse play, and drawings, her anxiety as well as her aspirations for better functioning with peers. Her hopes, fears, and reflections were played and acted out, and her parents talked out their worries and fears.

With parental permission, contact was made with Betsy's teacher and school principal, and it was possible to establish some collaborative contact that proved to be supportive to Betsy. Her teachers were sensitized to some of the specifics about what had created the recurrent cycles of parental pressure and anxiety.

The clinician was able to actively provide explanations, clarifications, advice, and reassurance about Betsy's solid endowment and potential. The parents came to share the therapist's view that Betsy's intelligence qualified her for the most rigorous of schools, but her temperament, anxiety, and reluctance to aggressively compete suggested that she would do her best in a less demanding, less competitive setting than the schools the parents had initially selected. The parents' modified views of the wide range of options enabled them to alter their expectations and to improve the child–school fit. With support, advice, and guidance from the clinician and nursery school staff, the parents opted to keep Betsy in nursery school an extra year, to lessen the pressures, and to conform to the realities of their child's character style, temperament, and small physical size. They were also responsive to parent education and guidance about specific parenting techniques that enabled them to contain impulses to push and pressure Betsy and demand performance from her.

Termination

The planned short-term work concluded after four months and twenty child sessions and twenty parent sessions. During this concluding phase, the family relaxed in the newly established home environment of greater attunement, confidence, and ease. Betsy's doll play showed over and over how "the baby" was happily able to become a bigger, more active, and smiling girl. The parents' improved sense of themselves and their daughter enabled them to feel calmer and more secure about her potential and their abilities as parents. Termination was undertaken with comfort and confidence. There was no intense transference or countertransference, that is, the kind of displacement commonly seen in more intensive, longer-term treatment. Rather, building on the therapeutic alliance that had long existed, the parents continued to enjoy what had always been a connection of excellent fit and rapport, one characterized by respect, regard, compassion, and genuine affection. Because of the prior therapy connections, the therapist was keenly aware of the parents' prior life experiences, traumas, strengths, and vulnerabilities. Betsy and her parents knew that they could rely on future contact with the clinician if the need arose in the future. Trust, attunement, and commitment best characterized the treatment relationship.

There has been follow-up by the parents and Betsy. The family has kept in informal but meaningful contact, calling once or twice a year to schedule time to drop by for a chat. All three have come on occasion, but more commonly the visit is made by the mother and Betsy. The focus of such follow-up sessions is to engage in a warm exchange and report life events and how things are going. Betsy's school progress is impressive, both academically and socially, and child and parents radiate pleasure, confidence, and a real sense of competence. Parental, professional and personal issues are also discussed, and there was one interval of a series of regular appointments with mother and father, when they were alarmed by the father's unexpected but short-term health problems.

The ending phase helped the family members review and consolidate their progress, and consider further work that might be necessary. The parents both have great humor and verve, and often joked about the distinct possibility of choosing to seek future short-term treatment when Betsy enters adolescence, or starts to date, or when she faces SAT exams. "Since we pressured her during the SATs for nursery, we don't want to make that mistake again."

DISCUSSION OF TECHNIQUES

The aforementioned techniques are universal practice procedures, utilized in an active and here-and-now format in short-term treatment cases. Ventilation and discussion of life events and feelings is crucial to impart the facts and issues that constitute the presenting problems, and to inform the clinician, and often clarify for the client, what are the overt and covert pressing concerns. To learn more, professionals commonly must explore, clarify, and engage in discussion to arrive at a course of action or selection of options for the work ahead. Partialization and the selection of a realistic focus makes the work manageable. Given greater clinician activity in short-term work, the goal is to quickly educate, guide, and advise clients about a myriad of issues, such as roles, age-appropriate expectations, tasks, and self-regulation of affects.

Ideally, all is done in the context of a positive relationship. There is no time to work through character resistances, and/or powerful irrational negative transference—countertransference displacements. Clients need to feel respected and safe, and when provided empathy, attunement, and encouragement, can share more readily in a warm and safe holding environment. Feeling secure, they can trust, listen, and respond, confident that self-determination is basic in the unfolding professional relationship. It is particularly important that strengths and accomplishments are identified to provide hopefulness and a belief that change and improvement is possible. These techniques were utilized in the short-term work with Betsy and Ellen.

Because of the motivation and strengths exhibited by both Betsy and Ellen and their parents, there was no need to set limits about client behavior in sessions. Both sets of parents were very competent and knowledgeable adults who did not need information about adjunctive resources or other services. Similarly, confrontation was not necessary, as the parents and the adolescent, Ellen, could self-observe and note their maladaptive defenses and dysfunctional patterns of interacting, as well as speculate as to why. They all were able to offer interpretations and clarifications of patterns of thinking and feeling about possible reasons for their perceptions, actions, and behaviors, and could amplify hidden and irrational ideas that had been determining behaviors.

The less well endowed client commonly does need greater therapist outreach, confrontation, role modeling, mirroring, and lending of ego even in the realm of performing concrete services for clients. In such cases providing a real object experience of shared experiences (with job applications, resume writing, accompanying a client to an agency, etc.), often is necessary. In such situations, the therapist may have to facilitate verbalization, that is, help put thoughts into words (Goldstein and Noonan 1999).

The myriad of techniques and interventions are selected, based on a careful individualized biopsychosocial assessment of each case, with attention to ego and superego strengths, deficits, the success or failure at handling developmental tasks, and the positive or negative features of the social environment, family, and extended family structure, health, and comfort or discomfort with sexual orientation, and ethnic and cultural background. The more vulnerable the client or client system, the more active the therapist must be to compensate, by providing clients structure, modeling, mirroring, and new ways of thinking, feeling, and perceiving themselves, their significant others, as well as the critical and impinging life events that often constitute the crisis that prompted them to seek help.

CONCLUSION

Research suggests the efficacy of a structured or time-limited psychotherapy with children. Parad and Parad (1968) found that explicit time limits reduced the likelihood of premature terminations, pointing to parental motivation as the determining factor. Smyrnois and Kirby (1993) found that children in time-limited psychotherapy show as much improvement as those treated in long-term psychotherapy, which indeed may be because long-term treatment commonly is for more disturbed and chronically troubled youth. Overall, the literature on time-limited psychotherapy with children is remarkably sparse (Messner and Warren 1995).

The issue of suitability would require identification of which children would likely benefit from brief treatment, and this requires assessment of the child's social and familial milieu to a greater extent than in the treatment of adults. Because of the influence of family and community, these variables have a disproportionate impact on the likelihood of treatment success. With adult patients, parents are internalized objects, but with younger patients parents impact profoundly and affect the child's functioning and ability to participate in psychotherapy.

With younger children, the focus is not explicitly stated, as it is with adults treated with short-term models of intervention. Likewise, many clinicians do not make explicit use of time limits since young children do not have a sufficiently developed sense of time. All contracting is done exclusively with the parents.

The older adolescent can utilize the agreed-upon short time interval, as well as some specificity regarding focus and partialization, and so can be more actively involved in the process of contracting. Because separation and loss are central issues for adolescents, brief short-term treatment often is particularly well suited for the teenager engaged in separation and individuation.

Concurrent with recognizing the substantial gains that can be achieved in short-term treatment of children, adolescents, and their parents, it must be stressed that criteria and suitability, based on assessment, are key in selection of this intervention. Concerns must also be articulated, as clinicians face "the current trend towards corporatization of psychotherapeutic practice and the large scale deployment of time-limited psychotherapy models as the only available therapeutic option" (Messer and Warren 1995, p. 329).

Indeed this modality has been misused, in planning for young clients, adults, and the elderly, due to the current sociopolitical process in determining clinical practice by third-party payers and managed care personnel. This poses many difficult ethical, clinical, and political questions and dilemmas, as we witness the "industrialization of psychotherapy taking place outside the traditional arenas of scholarship, research, and reasoned clinical discourse" (Messer and Warren 1995, p. 331). Two unpublished doctoral dissertations note this dilemma, as well as the concerns experienced by seasoned child therapists faced with universal designs for allotted sessions for child-focused work (see Burton 1999 and Miller 1999). Too often of late, prescriptions for short-term treatment are mandated across the board by managed care programs, which remain deaf and oblivious when confronted with therapists' clinical assessments and recommendations for long-term care.

Messer and Warren (1995) caution about overly optimistic advocacy for brief therapies, even for extremely disturbed patients. These authors cite the countertransference phenomenon of grandiosity, as clinicians long for a sense of competence, effectiveness, efficiency, and control. A second source of therapeutic overoptimism is out of some clinician's need to "deny the more painful and unpleasant aspects of the human experience by minimizing emotional suffering. It is all too easy to accept our patient's superficial solutions to life's experience because it makes our jobs easier" (p. 332). Seemingly many overly zealous advocates of brief therapies may never hear the full extent and nature of their client's pain and suffering. Because children and adolescents are "captive clients" rarely independently seeking help, they cannot be considered advocates for their own therapy. Additionally, many parents are resistive to any therapy recommendation or referral, due to guilt, fear, denial, or a wish to maintain family secrets. These resistive parents' children generally cannot be considered as appropriate for short-term therapy.

All findings demonstrate that appropriate recommendations for short-term work should be made in situations where there is evidence of problems and/or symptoms of a recent nature, a high degree of motivation, and fairly adequate progression through the successive developmental phases of childhood and adolescence. Additionally, the child and parent must demonstrate capacity for basic trust, and the ability to respond to interpretations, suggestions, and reflections. Relative ego strengths, affect tolerance, and some degree of psychological mindedness are additional characteristics that appropriate child, adolescent, and parent clients demonstrate, as appropriate candidates for short-term treatment. Interestingly, these characteristics are identical to those needed for optimal use of insight oriented, intensive, uncovering long-term treatment. The clinical distinction regarding recommending short-term or long-term treatment rests on evidence of emotional or behavioral symptoms of a reactive sort, in response to clearly identifiable stressor(s).

REFERENCES

American Psychiatric Association (1994). Quick Reference to the Diagnostic Criteria from *DSM-IV*, pp. 273–274. Washington, DC: APA.

Bauer, G. P., and Kobos, J. C. (1987). *Brief Therapy: Short-Term Psychodynamic Intervention.* Northvale, NJ: Jason Aronson.

Beebe, B. (1994). Representation and internalization: three principles of salience. *Psychoanalytic Psychology* 11:127–165.

Benedek, T. (1970). Parenthood during the life cycle. In *Parenthood: Its Psychology and Psychopathology*, ed. E. J. Anthony and T. Benedek. Boston: Little, Brown.

Blos, P. (1962). *On Adolescence: A Psychoanalytic Interpretation.* New York: Free Press.

———— (1983). The contribution of psychoanalysis to the psychotherapy of adolescents. *Psychoanalytic Study of the Child* 38:577–600. New Haven, CT: Yale University Press.

Bowlby, J. (1969). *Attachment and Loss, Vol. 1—Attachment.* New York: Basic Books.

Budman, S. H., and Gurman, A. S. (1988). *Theory and Practice of Brief Therapy.* New York: Guilford.

Burton, F. (1999). *An exploratory analysis of psychoanalytically oriented social workers treating children and adolescents: their counter-reactions to the managed care environment and the effect on the therapeutic relationship.* Ph.D. dissertation (unpublished). New York: New York University.

Davanloo, H., ed. (1992). *Short-Term Dynamic Psychotherapy.* New York: Jason Aronson.

Ekstein, R. (1983). The adolescent self during the process of termination of treatment: termination, interruption or intermission. In *Adolescent Psychiatry Vol. 9: Developmental and Clinical Studies*, ed. M. Sugar, S. Feinstein, J. Looney, et al., pp. 125–146. Chicago: University of Chicago Press.

Erikson, E. H. (1950). *Childhood and Society.* New York: Norton.

———— (1968). *Identity: Youth and Crisis.* New York: Norton.

Freud, A. (1962). Assessment of childhood disturbances. *Psychoanalytic Study of the Child* 17:149–158. New York: International Universities Press.

——— (1965). *The Writings of Anna Freud Vol. 1: Normalcy and Pathology in Childhood: Assessment of Development.* New Haven, CT: Yale University Press.

——— (1977). The symptomatology of childhood: a preliminary attempt at classification. In *An Anthology of the Psychoanalytic Study of the Child: Psychoanalytic Assessment: A Diagnostic Profile,* ed. R. Eissler, et al. New Haven, CT: Yale University Press.

Giovacchini, P. (1985). Introduction: countertransference responses to adolescents. In *Adolescent Psychiatry Vol. 12: Developmental and Clinical Studies,* ed. S. Feinstein, M. Sugar, A. Esman, et al., pp. 447–448. Chicago: University of Chicago Press.

Goldstein, E. G., and Noonan, M. (1999). *Short-Term Treatment and Social Work Practice: An Integrative Perspective.* New York: Free Press.

Lester, E. (1968). Brief psychotherapy in child psychiatry. *Canadian Psychiatric Association Journal* 13:301–309.

Mahler, M. S. (1968). *On Human Symbiosis and the Vicissitudes of Individuation.* New York: International Universities Press.

Malan, D. H. (1976). *The Frontier of Brief Psychotherapy.* New York: Plenum.

Mann, J. (1973). *Time-Limited Psychotherapy.* Cambridge, MA: Harvard University Press.

Mann, J., and Goldman, R. (1982). *A Casebook in Time-Limited Psychotherapy.* New York: McGraw-Hill.

Meeks, J. E. (1971). *The Fragile Alliance.* Baltimore: Williams & Wilkins.

Messer, S. B., and Warren, C. S. (1995). *Models of Brief Psychodynamic Therapy: A Comparative Approach.* New York: Guilford.

Miller, J. (1999). *An investigation in the perceptions of children's mental health treatment center leadership in a managed medicaid environment: organizational readiness for the New York State Medicaid special needs plans.* Ph.D. dissertation (Unpublished). New York: New York University.

Mishne, J. (1986). *Clinical Work with Adolescents.* New York: Free Press.

———— (1993). *The Evolution and Application of Clinical Theory: Perspectives from Four Psychologies.* New York: Free Press.

———— (1996). *The Learning Curve: Elevating Children's Academic and Social Competence.* Northvale, NJ: Jason Aronson.

Novick, J. (1977). Termination of treatment in adolescence. In *Adolescent Psychiatry Vol. 5: Developmental and Clinical Studies,* ed. S. Feinstein and P. Giovacchini, pp. 390–412. New York: Jason Aronson.

Parad, J., and Parad, H. (1968). A study of crisis oriented planned short-term treatment: Part 1. *Social Casework* 49:346–355.

Pine, F. (1988). The four psychologies of psychoanalysis and their place in clinical work. *Journal of the American Psychoanalytic Association* 36:57–59.

———— (1989). Motivation, personality organization and the four psychologies of psychoanalysis. *Journal of the American Psychoanalytic Association* 37:51–64.

———— (1990). *Drive, Ego, Object and Self.* New York: Basic Books.

Sandler, J., Kennedy, H., and Tyson, P. L. (1980). *The Technique of Child Psychoanalysis: Discussions with Anna Freud.* Cambridge, MA: Harvard University Press.

Sarnoff, C. (1976). *Latency.* New York: Jason Aronson.

Sifneos, P. (1979). *Short-Term Dynamic Psychotherapy: Evaluation and Techniques.* New York: Plenum.

Smyrnois, K. X., and Kirby, R. J. (1993). Long-term comparison of brief unlimited psychodynamic treatment with children and their families. *Journal of Consulting and Clinical Psychology* 61:1020–1027.

Strupp, H. H., and Binder, J. L. (1984). *Psychotherapy in a New Key: A Guide to Time-Limited Psychotherapy.* New York: Basic Books.

Taffel, R. (1991). *Parenting by Heart.* Reading, MA: Addison-Wesley.

CHAPTER FOUR

Brief Treatment Approaches in Work with Dementia Sufferers and Their Families: Pre- and Postdiagnosis

HARRIET RZETELNY

Dementia is a profoundly distressing condition to sufferers and to their families. Although the *Diagnostic and Statistical Manual of Mental Disorders* (*DSM-IV*) (APA 1994) defines dementia strictly by the psychological and behavioral manifestations of the disorder, the majority of dementias, especially those occurring in the elderly, are the result of chronic, long-term disease processes. These processes eventually destroy, little by little, that which makes people most uniquely human—their ability to think and to know, to use language richly and fully, to plan for the future, to recognize loved ones and themselves. The emotional impact of this loss on families is well documented (Stone et al. 1986), and for many years the primary focus of treatment has been on helping families manage the symptoms and cope emotionally and concretely with the ravages of the condition (Cohen and Eisdorfer 1986, Lampert 1986, Mace and Rabins 1999). In recent years, personal narratives have been published that highlight the effect of the condition on the sufferers (Davis and Davis 1989, McGowin 1993). James Thomas, a sufferer of Alzheimer's disease, which is the major cause of dementia in older people, writes in a diary he kept during the early phase of his disease: "No theory of medicine can explain what is happening to me. Every few months I sense another piece of me is missing. My life . . . my self . . . are falling apart. I can only think half-thoughts now. Someday I may wake up and not think at all . . . not know who I am. Most people expect to die someday, but who ever expected to lose their self first" (quoted in Cohen and Eisdorfer 1986, p. 22). Clinical treatment efforts have now been broadened to include people in the early stages of the disease (Brechling and Schneider 1993, Drickamer and Lachs 1992).

This chapter applies Goldstein and Noonan's (1999) integrated short-term treatment (ISST) approach to work with sufferers of chronic dementia and their families at two critical points in the course of the condition: pre- and postdiagnosis. It begins with a discussion of the *DSM-IV* (APA 1994) criteria for the diagnosis of dementia, including criteria for differential diagnosis of other conditions dementia may resemble, and addresses key assessment and emotional issues for sufferers and their families that are amenable to focused, brief treatment approaches. Two case examples from the author's practice, one where she functions primarily as a therapist and another where she functions primarily as a case manager, illustrate how these issues emerge and how clinicians in different settings can work with these families. Concrete issues will be touched on briefly, as there are many excellent sources of information on helping sufferers and their families plan for their concrete needs. Two particularly noteworthy examples are *The 36-Hour Day* by Mace and Rabins (1999) and *The Loss of Self* by Cohen and Eisdorfer (1986), which offer comprehensive suggestions to family members on all aspects of dementia care, such as finding home-based services, choosing a nursing home, and dealing with caregiver stress.

INCLUSION AND EXCLUSION CRITERIA

Dementia is a clinical condition characterized by multiple cognitive deficits, including memory impairment. According to the *DSM-IV*, memory impairment is the essential feature and is required to make the diagnosis of dementia. At first, sufferers may forget the names of people, where they parked the car, or the name and location of their bank. As the disease progresses, they may not be able to repeat simple instructions or remember what day it is or what they ate for their last meal. In the later stages, they may no longer remember where they live, when they were born, or even who they are.

The *DSM-IV* specifies that a diagnosis of dementia must include, in addition to memory loss, one or more of the following: (1) aphasia—a disturbance of language function exemplified by the failure to remember the names of people or the details of events; (2) apraxia—the inability to carry out simple motor activities, such as putting one's left hand to the right side of one's face, despite intact motor skills; (3) agnosia—the failure to recognize or identify common objects; and (4) a disturbance in executive skills, such as those involved in planning, organizing, and sequencing. Additionally, the disturbances must be severe enough to cause significant impairment in social or occupational functioning and represent a decline from previous levels of functioning. For example, a mentally retarded person who had lifelong impairments in one or more of the above areas would not be diagnosed with dementia unless he or she developed a condition such as Alzheimer's disease in addition to the preexisting mental retardation.

In the *DSM-IV* the diagnosis of dementia does not imply an etiology. Dementia may be caused by one or more of a variety of physiological conditions such as Alzheimer's disease, AIDS, vascular disease, head trauma, or long-term substance abuse. Butler and colleagues (1991) point out that dementia, especially in the elderly, is often confused with other conditions such as delirium and depression, as all three can cause memory loss and confusion in this population. The *DSM-IV* defines delirium as a condition that usually develops over a short period of time and is characterized by a disturbance of consciousness that is recognized by a reduced clarity of awareness and loss of ability to focus, sustain, or shift attention. A common example of delirium in the general population is alcohol intoxication—the feeling of being drunk. Although delirium can be caused by many conditions ranging from simple dehydration to life-threatening infections (Butler et al. 1991), there is ample documentation for the fact that delirium in the elderly is frequently brought about by overmedication, especially of antianxiety agents, pain killers, and sleeping pills (Raffoul 1986). A complicating factor is that individuals with dementia may also have a delirium and/or be depressed (Verwoerdt 1981). If a quick diagnosis of dementia is made simply on the basis of the memory loss reported or observed during a routine visit to a physician, these other conditions may go untreated. Clinicians working with patients who evidence memory loss must advocate for a comprehensive evaluation to determine what conditions are causing the memory loss. This ensures that appropriate treatment can be instituted, including a complete medical and social history, basic medical tests and lab work, neuropsychological tests (a mental status exam, brain scans), and other diagnostic tests as necessary (Butler et al. 1991).

Table 4–1, compiled by the author, outlines for the clinician the main points of difference between dementia, delirium, and depression in the elderly.

DSM-IV *Coding Procedures*

Dementia is coded on Axis I according to its etiology (for example, 294.9—dementia due to HIV disease), and the disease process is also coded on Axis III. Only dementia of the Alzheimer's type and vascular dementia have codable subtypes. Dementia of the Alzheimer's type is coded according to predomininant features: 290.11—with delirium; 290.13—with depressed mood; and 290.10—uncomplicated. Alzheimer's disease, code 331.0, should also be coded on Axis III. Vascular dementia is coded 290.41 with delirium, 290.43 with depressed mood, and 290.40 for uncomplicated. In addition, the cerebrovascular condition, if it is known, should be coded on Axis III.

THEORETICAL PERSPECTIVES

Goldstein and Noonan's ISTT approach draws from three basic short-term treatment models: (1) crisis intervention, (2) psychodynamic, and (3) cognitive-behavioral. In addition, they make special reference to family-oriented ISTT, in which the approach is broadened to include work with the entire family (Goldstein and Noonan 1999). In short-term work with dementia patients and their families, elements of all of these models come into play.

Because chronic dementia generally comes on over time, there is usually a period prior to seeking a diagnosis where patients and their families go through a crisis state. According to crisis theorists such as Parad and Parad (1990), this involves a disequilibrium in the functioning and coping ability of the sufferer and family along with the accompanying emotional states of denial, anxiety, anger, depression, and, sometimes, paranoia. Family systems theorists are concerned with the impact of a change in one family member on the entire family system (Hartman and Laird 1983). The mental functioning deficits brought about by chronic dementia and the subsequent changes impact profoundly on the individual with dementia and everyone in the family. Relationships can become severely stressed as patients begin exhibiting behaviors that are typical of the disease process but not yet understood by the individual or family. They can no longer complete their daily activities or fulfill their roles in the family system.

Ellis (1962) and others working in the cognitive field point to the cognitive distortions, irrational thinking, and self-defeating behaviors that, in their view, are at the root cause of the emotional problems people experience. It is common to see cognitive distortions and maladaptive behaviors as family members blame themselves or one another for disease-related changes in the patient. When people live alone and they are unable

Table 4–1.

The Characteristics of Dementia, Delirium, and Depression

Characteristic	Dementia	Delirium	Depression
Onset	Generally slow onset over months or years.	Generally quick onset over days or weeks. Associated with underlying medical conditions such as metabolic disorders, bowel impaction, infection, inadequate nutrition, dehydration, or overmedication.	Usually associated with major change or loss such as death of spouse, change of residence, onset of major health problem. Can be a side effect of certain medications. May be associated with lifelong history of depression.
Progress	Usually slow but persistent decline from previous level of functioning. Although not all dementias are chronic, a dementia of the Alzheimer's type is chronic and irreversible, but symptoms can be treated.	Acute but temporary decline in functional level. Can regain previous level of functioning if underlying condition is treated and if it is not superimposed on a preexisting dementia.	Symptoms can be reversed or halted with treatment. Without treatment, may become chronic.
Distinguishing features	Multiple cognitive deficits including memory impairment plus problems with language, abstract thinking, learning, motor skills, and/or information processing.	Disturbance of consciousness with reduced clarity of awareness. Short-term. Functional level can often be regained with treatment.	Disturbance of mood. Memory impairment often *selective* (i.e., unimportant or painful information). Cognitive impairments related to mood.

to recognize, or are in denial about, the symptoms of the disease process, they may also endanger themselves through self-neglect and their inability to complete activities of daily living (Verwoerdt 1981).

Psychodynmic models view early developmental issues or deficits as key to understanding present problems (Goldstein and Noonan 1999). Children and spouses may have many unresolved dependency issues that can emerge as they struggle with the increasing demands the sufferer places on them (Lustbader and Hooyman 1994). Adult children who are still engaged in the separation-individuation process may be thrust into what Blenker (1965) calls the filial crisis. She characterizes this as a stage in adult development in which adult children struggle to assume increasing responsibility for parent care; this often takes place in the context of many unresolved parent–child conflicts. Underlying dysfunctional coping mechanisms and sibling rivalries can rise to the surface as family members argue among themselves as to what is really happening and what should be done (Silverstone and Hyman 1976).

Although Bumagin and Hirn (1990) and Drickamer and Lacks (1992) are generally in favor of involving the patient in the diagnosis, most family-centered treatment approaches are aimed at helping caregivers manage the patient and deal with their own stress rather than focusing on intervening with the family system. As far as the author knows, there are no specific short-term models for treating the dementia patient *and* the family as a unit. The family-oriented ISTT model, when adapted to the special needs of dementia patients and their families, can serve as a useful conceptual tool for providing short-term treatment to this patient population, particularly in the early stages of the disease.

ISTT recognizes that "each individual's personality organization and interaction with others and the world forms a distinct constellation . . . composed not only of externally observable behaviors but also of the particular subjective meaning that the person gives to his or her experience" (Goldstein and Noonan 1999, p. 35). Therapists working with dementia patients and their families must recognize that each individual in the family system will experience the disease in unique and different ways. In addition, the family as a whole must be assessed according to its particular "structure and development; patterns and styles of communication; cultural background and degree of acculturation; . . . environmental conditions; . . . strengths and problem-solving capacities" (Goldstein and Noonan 1999, p. 257).

The following two case examples illustrate these issues.

Case Example 1: The Brixton Family

Althea Brixton has been the primary caregiver to her husband, Robert, who suffered a stroke several years ago that left him partially paralyzed. She is in her early sixties and he is in his seventies. Robert continues to be the dominant force in the marriage and in the family. For the past eight months or so, Althea has been exhibiting certain behaviors that are very upsetting to Robert. For example, within the last month, she failed to pick up prescriptions that he had called into the pharmacy, left packages at the store, and has had difficulty following instructions. Additionally, she hasn't wanted to go to the theater and other activities they would normally attend. He reacts by yelling at her, which only makes her cry.

Their daughter, Linda, who lives nearby, is angry with both her parents. Her father calls her in a rage about Althea, and Linda feels caught in the middle. Linda has had to run over to her parents' house to complete chores her mother has been unable to do. She has urged her mother to get household help, but Robert won't have any strangers in the house and Althea won't go against Robert's wishes. Linda wants her brother, Samuel, to talk to Robert. Samuel, however, thinks his mother is chronically depressed and wants Linda to tell their physician to put her on antidepressants. Once the depression has lifted, he believes, his parents' lives will go on as usual. "It's too late for Mom and Dad to change," he tells Linda. "I'm not going to get involved in this." Linda is very resentful about Samuel's laissez-faire attitude and has accused him of not being able to "stand up to" his father.

Case Example 2: The Lopez Family

Rita Lopez, age 76 and widowed for many years, lives alone in an apartment in the city. One of her neighbors has noted that at times Mrs. Lopez appears confused, disheveled, and agitated, behaviors that are not characteristic of her. At other times she doesn't seem to recognize her friends. The neighbor called a local case management agency and explained the situation. She said that she telephoned Rita's daughter, Jean, but Jean told her she and her mother weren't getting along.

The case manager tried to visit Mrs. Lopez but Mrs. Lopez wouldn't let her in. She then called Mrs. Lopez's daughter, Jean, to discuss the situation. Jean is very angry with her mother. She stated that she has had an argumentative relationship with her mother for her entire life, and recently it has gotten worse. She related an incident in which her mother called up in tears, insisting that she come over because she didn't receive her social security check. Upon arrival, Jean found the social security check lying uncashed in a drawer. When she confronted her mother, Rita yelled at her for prying and accused her of only wanting her money. Jean suspects her mother has started drinking. At times she has found her mother "totally out of it," as if she were drunk. Rita has also stopped taking care of her apartment and has started wearing dirty clothes, something she had not done previously. "My father was an alcoholic," Jean tells the case manager. "Now she's starting, too? I've had it up to here with her."

Discussion

In both examples, uncharacteristic behaviors have thrown the individual and the family into a state of disequilibrium approaching crisis. Althea Brixton is no longer able to function as caregiver to her ailing husband. Neither she nor her family members understand what is really happening to her. Her husband responds by being angry and attempting to bully her into compliance. Both children recognize that something is wrong, but are unable to talk to their father about it, squabbling as to what should be done. Rita Lopez, who lives alone, has been acting in ways that are alarming to people who know her and exacerbating an already anger-filled relationship with her daughter. Jean, caught up in her angry misinterpretation of her mother's behavior as being directed against her, is ready to throw up her hands. Obscured is the fact that Rita is misplacing her social security checks, has periods of being "out of it," and may be functionally impaired and endangering herself.

THE BEGINNING PHASE OF TREATMENT

Treatment Goals

Cohen and Eisdorfer (1986), Butler and colleagues (1991), and others have stressed the need for either obtaining or helping the family to obtain an accurate diagnosis and workup as soon as possible. Goldstein and Noonan (1999) discuss the major tasks in the early stages of family-oriented ISTT as fostering communication and facilitating "family members' agreement on the difficulties on which they want to focus jointly" (p. 256). Dementia sufferers and their families lack knowledge about the symptoms of the disease and may be in denial or disagreement about the cause of the behavioral changes they are experiencing or observing (Lampert 1986). It is the author's experience that the clinician must state up front the possibility that these behavioral changes may be due to an organic or medical condition. This stance enables the family to consider the need to obtain an accurate diagnosis. The author, therefore, suggests the following three treatment goals for the prediagnosis phase of work:

Obtain a Comprehensive Medical Evaluation and a Sociofunctional Assessment

In short-term work with suspected dementia sufferers, the first treatment goal is to obtain a comprehensive medical evaluation and diagnosis, and a socio-functional assessment. Since several other conditions can present as dementia, a comprehensive workup will help the clinician, the patient, and the family know what they are dealing with and how to intervene. A thorough medical evaluation is much easier to undertake if the patient has good health care coverage and a good relationship with the health care system. Families differ, however, in their ability and willingness to obtain and utilize medical services. Cultural or ethnic beliefs that foster mistrust of the medical establishment and/or favor alternative or folk medicine, and the lack of accessibility by some ethnic groups, especially low-income minorities, to health care resources have been well documented (Baker 1990, Lustbader and Hooyman 1994). In the beginning, the therapist may have to work carefully with a family from a different culture in order to build trust. Lustbader and Hooyman (1994) suggest an open, conversant approach that acknowledges the clinician's unfamiliarity with the family's culture as a way to show genuineness and build rapport. The clinician may also have to advocate directly with the health care system to ensure better access for clients without insurance coverage.

In the meantime, the clinician should complete a thorough sociofunctional assessment of the patient and family. This can add substantially to the overall medical diagnosis, especially as it documents the previous level of function. It also aids in appropriate planning and referrals if there are major problems in accessing or utilizing the health care system. Clinicians skilled in biopsychosocial assessments need to add functional, cognitive, and risk factor components to their assessments (Kane 1990, Verwoerdt 1981). Patients in the beginning to moderate stages of cognitive impairment may have problems completing their activities of daily living, especially the instrumental activities of daily living (IADLs). Kane (1990) defines these as "complex activities that support independence" (p. 75), which include banking, shopping, cooking, self-medicating abilities, driving, and using transportation. Individuals who are living alone or with volatile caregivers, may be in danger of abuse or self-neglect (Verwoerdt 1981). If they cannot manage their finances, they may be in danger of financial exploitation, having their utilities turned off, or possibly eviction. Clinicians should find out how patients are managing each daily task. If they are unable to complete the task independently, the therapist needs to inquire who is doing it for them and how willing and reliable is this person?

Although current models of assessing the mental functioning deficits associated with dementia usually don't refer to concepts such as ego functioning, defenses, and primary and secondary process, the author has found them a useful enrichment to a multidimensional assessment. Excellent summaries of the ego functions and the defenses can be found in Goldstein and Noonan (1999).

As the ability to use secondary process thinking breaks down, patients are no longer able to delay or inhibit the expression of impulses. They are easily overwhelmed and subject to overreactions (called catastrophic reactions) at the most minor stimuli. Judgment becomes impaired, as do autonomous functions such as memory, learning, perception, and attention. Defensive functioning, however, remains intact during the early to moderate stages of the disease process and may intensify as patients experience increasing amounts of anxiety about what is happening to them and are unable to use secondary process to moderate their responses. For example, individuals who use projection (attributing unacceptable thoughts and feeling to others) as a primary defense may accuse others of stealing from them when they can no longer remember where they put something.

Table 4–2, adapted and expanded by the author from one developed by Kane (1990), highlights the components of a multidimensional assessment.

If it can be obtained, a complete medical and psychological evaluation will either rule out other possible diagnoses such as delirium or depression or confirm the existence of a medical or affective condition that can then be treated. There have been some recent advances in the use of pharmacological therapies such as Aricept (donepezil) to improve memory function for patients in early to mild stages of the disease (Blazer 1998). The timely introduction of these drugs depends on an early diagnosis. The multidimensional assessment should document the progress of cognitive and functional decline to aid the physician in making an accurate diagnosis. It is also important to ensure that the medical diag-

Table 4–2.

Components of a Multidimensional Assessment

Physical	Other medical conditions, drugs taken, history of physical symptoms; utilization of hospitals and physicians; cultural/religious beliefs about sickness and its causes
Emotional	Psychiatric diagnosis, affective states (depression, anxiety, etc.), alcohol/substance abuse; adaptability
Self-care	IADL: cooking, cleaning, laundry, driving, taking medications, paying bills, and managing money; ADL: bathing, grooming, dressing, feeding, toileting, walking, continence
Ego functions	Judgment; reality testing; impulse control; defensive functioning; stimulus barrier; autonomous functioning
Cognitive	Memory (short- and long-term); following instructions; planning and problem solving; orientation to time, place, and person; state and level of awareness
Social	Relationships: household composition, other family and their willingness/ability to help; burden on family/caregivers; other confidants; social network; activities: prior and current
Environment	Home: safety, conveniences; neighborhood: access to shops and services, safety; community: availability and accessibility of health, social, and other services
Risk factors	In immediate or life-threatening danger?; self-neglect or endangering behaviors; volatility or abusiveness of caregiver; unable to manage finances; potential for financial exploitation or physical abuse

nosis is conducted by physicians and other providers who are trained in this area. Physicians in general practice, especially old-time family doctors, lack the knowledge and skill to undertake a comprehensive evaluation. The Alzheimer's Disease Education and Referral Service, of the National Institute on Aging, can provide information and referrals about the disease. Local chapters of the Alzheimer's Association can also provide information and referral.

Educate the Individual and Family About the Possibility of a Disease, the Behaviors that May Be Arising Because of It, and Why an Accurate Diagnosis is Necessary

Before an evaluation can be undertaken, the family members need to be aware that the patient's behaviors they are witnessing and/or reacting to may be caused by a physical or emotional problem. In case 1, above, Althea's forgetfulness and inability to follow instructions, so upsetting to Robert, may be due to a progressive dementia, a medical or pharmacological condition, depression, or some combination of these factors. It is important to note that a diagnosis cannot be made on the basis of behavior alone, but behavior can provide clues to the underlying disorders. Before a diagnosis is made, it is best to focus on all of the treatable conditions (e.g., overmedication) that might be causing the behaviors. The clinician should keep any information provided to the family on dementia very general and within the realm of possibility, not certainty. Dementia is very frightening to people, and patients and their families need to absorb this information gradually (Cohen and Eisdorfer 1986). Family members will have their unique way of handling the information. Be sensitive to, and supportive of, these variations as long as they do not interfere with the goal of obtaining an evaluation. Don't overwhelm the individual and family with too much information before the diagnosis is confirmed, but give enough so that they will be prepared for whatever the diagnosis might be.

If there is religious and/or cultural resistance to, or distrust of, Western medicine, the clinician may need to become very active and creative in finding ways to help the family overcome its resistance. He or she should certainly provide information about the many acute physical conditions that could be causing the behaviors and point out the consequences of not obtaining a medical evaluation. The clinician might ask for permission to contact a religious or community leader known to the family members who can speak to them about the need for medical intervention. If all the indications are pointing to dementia, the clinician can, at least, start working with the family around managing the condition until a more complete evaluation can be undertaken. The clinician may need to help the family secure entitlements such as Medicaid, or advocate with a managed care company to ensure that necessary medical tests and procedures are authorized and paid for.

Enable Family Members to Act Effectively Together

To obtain a comprehensive evaluation and to plan patient management, the family members must be able to act effectively together. This means different things for different families. For some it means sharing the tasks; for others it means supporting the efforts of the primary caregiver. The clinician needs to quickly assess the family's level of cohesiveness and style of functioning and be flexible in approach. The clinician might be able to work with the entire family, possibly focusing on the one family member who either is the primary caregiver or holds the power in the family and without whose say-so no plan can be carried out (Smith Barusch 1987). The objective, in brief treatment, is not necessarily on changing the family dynamics per se. Rather, to paraphrase Goldstein and Noonan (1999), the clinician works to modify and restructure selected aspects of the family's pattern of relating to each other so that they can function more effectively together around achieving a limited goal, which in this case is obtaining an evaluation and diagnosis.

Process

People who are experiencing cognitive impairments usually don't refer themselves for treatment. More often, the referral is made by a member of the family or another person worried about the patient's ability to continue caring for him- or herself. Family members often don't agree about the necessity for calling in outside help, and one or more key players may be particularly afraid or resistant. The ISTT and other short-term models stress the importance of quick engagement in the beginning phase of work (Parad and Parad 1990). In engaging the reluctant or resistant client and/or family member, Shulman (1992) stresses the importance of the clinician's facing his or her own feelings about the engagement, especially if the patient or family member is angry or hostile. He states, "Beginning discussion with a resistant client [entails] clarifying [the] purpose, clarifying [our] role, and reaching for feedback. A negotiation process takes place, but this time the potential obstacles to a working relationship must be part of the discussion. In affect the [clinician] asks the [patient] if they can work together in spite of the barriers that may block their efforts" (p. 93). In the ISTT model, the clinician is highly active in the beginning phase of treatment, "identifying the problem to be assessed, setting goals, focusing interventions, and monitoring progress" (Goldstein and Noonan 1999, p. 58).

In case 1, presented above, the clinician was contacted by Linda, the Brixtons' daughter. During the initial phone interview, Linda presented the problem as one in which her mother was getting increasingly worn out from caring for her father, who was getting very angry. Linda needed help in convincing her parents to locate and accept some homecare assistance. The excerpt that follows illustrates how the clinician began the assessment and education process with Linda. She began by obtaining specific examples that documented how Althea had changed from a prior level of functioning, and expressed her concern that these behavior changes might either reflect cognitive loss or depression.

Clinician: What specific things are causing you to seek help now?
Linda: Well, my father was never an easy man. And since the stroke, life hasn't been easy for my mother, God knows. But she's been getting so much more tired and worn out.
Clinician: Give me some examples of what you mean.

Linda: She just hasn't been up to doing things that she used to do.

Clinician: Like what? (She maintains her focus on obtaining concrete examples, causing Linda to think about them.)

Linda: She went shopping and left the grocery bags at the store. She forgot all about picking up a prescription he had called in—she must have really been tired to do that. He's always yelling at her. And then he calls me up and I have to come over and do it. And then he yells at me, too. And I'm losing my patience with both of them. And Samuel is no help. Ever since he went on antidepressants, he thinks that's the solution to everything.

Clinician: Sounds like the situation has been getting worse over time. (Linda agrees.) Linda, I'm concerned about these changes in your mother. Forgetting to pick up a prescription and leaving a package at the store might be signs of some kind of early memory loss. Or it might be depression. I want to get a better sense of what's going on with her.

Home visits are a useful tool in work with dementia patients because they enable the clinician to assess the environment and the individual's functioning within it. The clinician discusses the advisability of making a home visit for this purpose. Linda wants Samuel to be present, but after some questioning Linda admits that her brother doesn't really want to be involved. The clinician suggests that Linda ask Samuel to be present, but that he doesn't have to come unless he wants to. She helps Linda strategize ways of approaching the situation with her father. The objective is not to help Linda resolve her problems with her father. It is to enable the family members to act more effectively together so that a comprehensive evaluation can be undertaken.

Linda: I don't think my father would let you in. He doesn't want any help. He just wants my mother to be the way she used to be.

Clinician: But she's not, is she?

Linda: No. And that's the problem.

Clinician: Let's strategize a little about how to approach your father. You may have to be a little assertive.

Linda: I've never been able to be assertive with my father.

Clinician: I know this is going to be hard for you, but I think it's necessary. How about if you begin by expressing your concern about your mother's health, and what will happen to both of them if she gets sick? Yelling at her doesn't seem to get her back the way she was. If she gets sick, who's going to take care of her *and him?*

Linda: I don't know if that would make a dent with him. He's so stubborn.

Clinician: Try it. If it doesn't work, give me a call back, and we'll come up with something else.

In brief, focused treatment, the clinician needs to be more directive and use suggestions, advice, persuasion, and reinforcement much more liberally than she might in a long-term treatment situation (Goldstein and Noonan 1999, Parad and Parad 1990). Using some of the strategies that the clinician suggested, Linda is able to get her father to agree to a home visit. During the home visit, the clinician quickly assesses Robert as narcissistic, very self-involved, and the dominant force in the family. Since each family member may have a subjective definition of the problem, the clinician needs to listen carefully to each person's view of the problem and its causes (Goldstein and Noonan 1999, Hartman and Laird 1983). Additionally, the clinician needs to be aware of the power dynamics in the family and may need to work within the existing power structure (Haley 1980, Smith Barasch 1987). She therefore focuses her initial attention on engaging Robert and turning him into a therapeutically. She also doesn't challenge his position as family power broker. If she does, he could well become an obstacle to any further treatment.

Robert: Well, my daughter tells me you've gotten her real upset about her mother. I think she's just a little tired. I'm a big job for her. I used to do everything myself. Ran a whole department down at the old company. Twenty-five men depended on me to make all the decisions. Now I can't even get to the drug store to pick up my own prescriptions.

Clinician: It must be very hard for you not to be able to do all the things you used to do.

Robert: It sure is. Ever since the stroke . . . (He tells her all about the stroke, its complications and treatment, while Althea and Linda sit and listen.)

Clinician: It sounds like it made a big change in your life.

Robert: It sure did. But we were doing okay. As long as I could tell the wife here what needed to be done and she could do it.

Clinician: And now?

Robert: Well, if she would just be a little more organized, I think she could get a lot more done.

Clinician: I realize how important it is for you to get these things done. And maybe I can help you in that area. (The clinician is beginning the contracting process with Robert around *his* concerns.) But Linda feels things may be getting a little more difficult for her mother. I'd like to ask Mrs. Brixton how she thinks she's doing. (The clinician directs this comment to Robert, joining with the family's pattern of communication in which all exchanges go through Robert. Robert shrugs one shoulder, giving tacit permission.)

Clinician: Mrs. Brixton, your husband and daughter asked me to make this visit because they've both been a little concerned about you. Can you tell me how you think you are doing?

Althea starts to talk a little about some of her problems, which include some health concerns of her own—a urinary tract infection, fatigue, and other things. She doesn't mention her memory problems. As the clinician listens, she gently asks some questions—"When did this start?" "How has your appetite been? What did you eat for breakfast?"— that allow her to begin evaluating Althea's memory function and ability to recall dates and details. The clinician also uses her own observations to comment on Althea's memory problems and to begin the discussion about the need to get a medical evaluation for Althea. She starts with the least threatening of the possible diagnoses.

Clinician: Mrs. Brixton seems to be having a little trouble remembering things. Sometimes stress can interfere with memory function.

Robert: That's right. She's probably just a little stressed.

Clinician: Maybe that's true. And perhaps an antidepressant could help her. But there are a couple of other conditions that could be producing the memory problems. We won't know, though, until we get a good medical evaluation for Mrs. Brixton.

Althea cannot remember what she ate for breakfast or when her urinary tract infection began. Depressed people usually do not suffer this type of memory loss. Although she is tired, her state of consciousness is not impaired. She is not "out of it" as she would be if she were suffering from a delirium. Based on her initial assessment, the clinician is leaning toward a diagnosis of dementia, which would then have to be confirmed by a complete evaluation. Because the Brixton family has good health care coverage, they are able to obtain a comprehensive evaluation within a short period of time.

In case 2, presented above, the goal is to get Mrs. Lopez evaluated to determine what is causing her behavioral changes. Since Mrs. Lopez won't let the clinician in, the clinician approaches the daughter, Jean, and engages her on the mother's behalf. At the very least, she will get some more background information that will help her determine the level of risk for Mrs. Lopez and decide whether or not this case should be referred to protective services. She schedules a visit with Jean.

Jean: Like I told you on the phone, she's totally impossible. As if I was interested in her money! Do you know how much money I've put out for that woman? She needed a dress for Maria's wedding. Who bought it for her? Me. Anything she ever needed, who was there to do it? Me. I've had it. I don't want anything more to do with her.

Clinician: It sounds like you've always been there for her, but that you're pretty angry at her right now. (The clinician quickly engages with Jean around *her* feelings.)

Jean: I am, let me tell you. The priest tells me I have to honor my mother. But I don't have to take abuse from anyone who doesn't appreciate what I do for them. My mother took it from my father. I'm not going to take it from her.

Clinician: I can understand why you don't want to take any more abuse from her, but sometimes mental or physical conditions can cause older people to act like that.

Jean: She's mental all right.

Clinician: You've described several things to me—she's not taking care of herself and her apartment the way she used to. She's misplaced her social security checks. (The clinician stays focused on pinpointing the problem behaviors.)

Jean: And then gets angry at me.

Clinician: Yes. How long has she been like this?

Jean: (thinks for a minute) It's been a few months, now. Not that she's ever been easy, you understand. But it's really gotten worse the last few months.

Clinician: What you're describing sounds like memory loss or confusion. The fact that it's fairly recent and that she seems "out of it" at times might mean that there's some condition that's causing it. You think it's alcohol, but other conditions cause the same kind of thing. Do you know what medication she takes?

Jean: She's always taking something or another—sleeping pills, pain killers. Who knows with that woman?

Clinician: And if she's drinking on top of it, it could be getting her very confused and forgetful. And since this is very scary to people, when they begin to lose their memory and they don't know what's happening or why, she blames you instead. Then she doesn't have to think about what may be happening to her. (Jean is silent.) I'm really concerned about her. If she's misplacing her checks, then she may not be paying her bills or her rent.

Jean: I better check with her landlord.

Clinician: That's a good idea. I'd also like to visit her, with you, and see if I can get a sense of what's going on with her.

Jean: She wouldn't let you in the last time.
Clinician: If she really is suffering from memory loss, she probably won't even remember who I am.

To evaluate Mrs. Lopez, the clinician needs to engage Jean as an ally and enable her to act more effectively with, or on behalf of, her mother. The clinician quickly assesses Jean as a basically involved daughter who is very angry with her mother for behaviors she doesn't understand. The clinician begins the process by expressing her concern and explaining some of the reasons why her mother might be behaving the way she is. Once Jean understands the possible reasons for and consequences of her mother's behavior, she is willing to work together with the clinician as they plan a visit together.

When they arrive, Mrs. Lopez is in bed. She is slurring her speech and is so confused that she doesn't even recognize her daughter. Jean immediately assumes her mother has been drinking and is ready to walk out. The clinician doesn't smell any alcohol and responds to the situation by calling 911. Mrs. Lopez is admitted to the hospital where she is diagnosed as having had a transient ischemic attack (TIA)—a temporary deficiency in the brain's blood supply. She improves somewhat, but after a month Mrs. Lopez continues to experience memory loss and other cognitive symptoms. The doctor adds a diagnosis of dementia related to vascular disease.

SHORT-TERM TREATMENT
IN THE POSTDIAGNOSIS PHASE

After a diagnosis of dementia is made, patients and their families typically go through an initial grief reaction followed by an extended mourning period that can go on for months and years as patients lose more and more of themselves. Their families experience the slow loss of all that they love in that person, one piece at a time. One patient in the author's practice called it "death without end," and Rabins (1984) labels this period "chronic grief."

At the same time, since most dementia patients elect to remain at home, at least during the early to moderate stages of the condition, they and their families need to learn how to manage the condition and to begin planning for increasing incapacity. Cohen and Eisdorfer (1986) and others discuss the issues about which families need information, such as home care, day treatment programs, financial planning and management, and the assistance available to help families cope with the condition. Caregivers need help with stress reduction and obtaining respite. Eventually, they will need information about selecting a nursing home. While there is still enough cognition left, patients need to make out living wills, appoint their health care proxy, decide on the distribution of their assets, and put their affairs in order. The American Association of Retired People (AARP) has an extensive publication list that provides practical information on planning for incapacity. The Alzheimer's Association can supply reading lists about the disease for patients and their families and information about resources. Local chapters run support groups for family members. Some chapters also run support groups for sufferers in the early stages of the disease.

Treatment Goals

The treatment goals for the postdiagnosis phase of work with dementia patients and their families are (1) to help the patient and family members understand and work through their grief reactions; (2) to enable the family to begin long-term planning; and (3) to connect the patient and family to local resources, support groups, and other sources of information and support. The therapist may be continuing with a family that he or she has already been working with and may need to renegotiate the treatment goals. The clinician may also be beginning work with a family that seeks help after the diagnosis. As in the prediagnosis phase, the family must often work through their emotional issues before they can plan effectively together (Cohen and Eisdorfer 1986). The following discussion focuses on the first of the three goals.

Upon hearing the diagnosis of a chronic, long-term dementia such as Alzheimer's disease, patients and their families typically experience many feelings as they struggle to come to terms with the issues of loss of self, dependency, and autonomy; vulnerability and incapacity; and loss of prior roles and relationships. Patients and their spouses must assume different roles in the relationship as men become caregivers to their wives and caregiving women take over more and more of the roles previously assigned to their husbands, such as getting the car serviced and mowing the lawn. Adult children must mourn the loss of the parent they knew and accept increasing responsibility for decision making (Lustbader and Hooyman 1994).

The first response to hearing the diagnosis is almost always denial (Cohen and Eisdorfer 1986). In brief, focused treatment, the clinician has to act quickly to help the patient and family work through this denial so they can begin long-term planning. Worden (1982) calls this work *accepting the reality of the loss*. "Denial can be practiced on several different levels and take various forms, but it most often involves either the facts of the loss, the meaning of the loss, or the irreversibility of the loss" (p. 11).

In beginning postdiagnosis grief work with the Brixton family, the clinician began by starting where each person was in the grieving process. After Althea was diagnosed with primary degenerative dementia of the Alzheimer's type, Robert developed a vague gastric problem that needed constant attention. He wouldn't talk about his wife's condition, nor would he allow anyone else to do so. All discussion was focused on the battery of tests he needed to undergo and the failure of the medical establishment to help him. Samuel, after an initial period of shock and guilt about not being more sensitive to his mother's problems, was determined that his parents would maintain the same quality of life they always had. He planned outings for them and wanted the clinician to urge them to attend. He bought his mother every vitamin and homeopathic preparation on the market that promised memory improvement. "We can beat this thing," he kept saying. Through a self-focused somatization on

Robert's part and an inability to recognize his mother's deterioration on Samuel's, both father and son continued to deny the reality of the loss they were experiencing. Althea went on worrying about her husband and his condition as if she hadn't heard her own diagnosis. Linda's period of denial was briefly characterized by shock: "This couldn't be happening to my mother." She then went into a period of anger at her family for their refusal to deal with the situation, alternating with feelings of helplessness and hopelessness as she feared that her father would never accept any home-care assistance and the burden of care would fall on her. The clinician decided to begin the grief work with Althea. This was, in fact, her disease. She arranged to see Althea alone because she knew she was more likely to talk about herself without Robert present.

Clinician: Althea, how are you doing?

Althea: Okay, I guess.

Clinician: I know you must have been feeling a lot of things since you heard the diagnosis.

Althea: Well, I guess I couldn't take it in at first. I still don't know.

Clinician: Do you think the diagnosis is an accurate one?

Althea: Accurate?

Clinician (very gently): I mean, do you think the doctors are right? That you do have Alzheimer's disease?

Althea: I'm afraid to think about it. I'm losing my mind. (She starts to cry.) What's going to happen to Robert? I can't take care of him anymore. I don't know what to do.

Clinician: That's what I'm here for. To help you and Robert decide what to do. (Althea continues to cry. Clinician takes her hand.) I know how upsetting this is to you . . . something you didn't expect. (She hands Althea a tissue and lets her cry it out.)

Althea: It's still hard to believe. (She wipes her eyes.) Robert hates it when I cry.

Clinician: You have a right to cry, Althea. Robert isn't suffering from this. You are. (Althea nods.)

Clinician (after a short period of silence): How are you managing?

Grief work with Althea involved helping her to accept the reality of the loss. In the author's experience, touch can be a potent form of communication with dementia patients as long as it is nonthreatening. Althea goes on to talk about the hard time she is having with Robert's refusal to show any awareness of her condition or accept any help in the house other than a twice-a-week homemaker and shopper. Althea is beginning to express some anger at Robert as she struggles to cope with what is happening to her and his failure to provide her with support. Linda has been supportive but still can't confront her father, nor does she know what to say in response to her brother's continued denial. The therapist suggests that Linda join a caregivers support group run by the local chapter of the Alzheimer's Association, which she agrees to do.

The therapist next tried to talk to Robert and Althea together, or Robert alone, but he wouldn't see her when she came to the house. He claimed it was because of the pain and discomfort of his condition, but the therapist understood this as a form of his denial. She arranged a family session at the house with Althea, Samuel, and Linda, to which she invited Robert. At first he wouldn't leave his room, but when he realized the family was going to talk with or without him, he joined them. A brief excerpt from the beginning of the session follows. It illustrates how the therapist stays focused on providing continued information about the condition and its impact on his mother's functioning to help Samuel work through his denial and accept the reality of the losses his mother is facing. She is less successful with Robert.

Clinician: I've called this meeting because Althea is having a lot of problems managing in the house and we have to come up with a plan to help her.

Robert: I got her a cleaning lady. What else does she want?

Linda: That's only two days a week. What about the rest of the days?

Robert: What is there for her to do? She just has to get me my meals and call the car service when I need to go to the doctor. What's so difficult about that? Why can't she do it?

Linda: Daddy, Mom has Alzheimer's disease!

Robert: I don't believe it!

Clinician: What's your view, Samuel?

Samuel: The doctor didn't say it was Alzheimer's disease. He said it was primary degenerative dementia. That's not the same thing. I've done some reading about dementia. There've been some very good results from vitamin therapy, especially lecithin and vitamin E. Also, there are some drugs on the market now that stop memory loss.

Clinician: Samuel, doctors don't always give a diagnosis of Alzheimer's disease because there aren't any diagnostic tests that can pinpoint it with certainty. But primary degenerative dementia means just about the same thing. (Samuel shakes his head in disagreement.) Degenerative means that it's going to get worse over time. As far as I know, the drugs may halt memory loss for a while, but nobody knows for how long. And vitamin therapy might help your mother feel a little peppier or better overall, but nothing will reverse the memory loss she already has. She's going to need increasing amounts of help in taking care of herself and your father.

Samuel: She can go on for a long time. (Samuel continues expressing his belief in the power of vitamins and drugs to forestall the worsening of symptoms.)

Clinician: Linda, I can see by the expression on your face that you may have some different thoughts about this.

Linda (very upset): Sammy, all the vitamins in the world aren't going to stop this from happening. (Turning to her mother) Forgive me, Mom, but Sammy has to know the score . . . how bad this can be.

Clinician: Linda is right, Samuel. Your mother has told me that it's becoming harder and harder for her to do things like prepare meals. Your parents have been eating mostly out of cans because she can't remember how to cook. Last Friday afternoon when I visited, your father was still in bed because your mother couldn't help him get up and get dressed.

Samuel (shock and disbelief evident on his face): Is this so?

Althea (crying): I can't . . . I can't . . . I just don't know.

Once Samuel began to work through his denial, he allied with his sister in advocating for some additional help in the house. Robert was still unable to talk about Althea's Alzheimer's disease or acknowledge her increasing incapacity. By staying engaged with Robert around his own needs, the clinician was able to convince him to hire a home-care worker for four hours a day. As Robert said, "It's the only way I'm going to get any help around here."

Turning to case 2, while Mrs. Lopez was in the hospital, Jean took over financial management for her mother to ensure that her bills would be paid. Mrs. Lopez was discharged from the hospital with four hours of home care daily to help her manage. However, she has become very depressed and is unwilling to attempt the tasks she still can do. Every time Jean visits, she berates the home-care worker for not making her mother do more things for herself. Jean finally calls the clinician in tears. "This is not my mother. I don't know what that home-care worker is doing to her, she's making her way too dependent. My mother has become a different person." The clinician arranged to accompany her on a visit to her mother's apartment.

Clinician (after reintroductions): Mrs. Lopez, your daughter Jean asked me to stop by with her and see how you're doing.
Mrs. Lopez: Who did you say you were? (The clinician repeats her name.) Oh. It's hard for me to remember sometimes.
Clinician: That must be very upsetting to you.
Mrs. Lopez: It is . . . you don't know.
Clinician (with much empathy): You look sad. (Mrs. Lopez doesn't say anything; she continues to look sad.) Your daughter Jean is worried about you. (She stops and lets Mrs. Lopez take this in.) She says you don't want to dress yourself anymore. Or feed yourself. (She stops again. When Mrs. Lopez doesn't respond, she adds:) That's not the mother she knew.
Mrs. Lopez (looks at Jean and then away): I'm not that mother anymore.
Jean: Mama, if you would only try. You could still do so much.

Mrs. Lopez (to clinician): She doesn't know.

Clinician: She wants you to be the old mother she knew.

Mrs. Lopez: I'm not. No more.

Clinician (indicating some photos on the buffet): This one looks like you as a young woman. (Mrs. Lopez nods.) You were a beautiful woman.

Mrs. Lopez: Not anymore.

Clinician: You don't feel like the same woman you were anymore. (Mrs. Lopez bows her head in silence.)

Clinician (indicating another photo): And this one looks like Jean. Was this at her confirmation?

Mrs. Lopez (looking up): I made her that dress. She was so beautiful in it. So beautiful. (She looks at Jean.) She's the beautiful one now.

Jean (tears gathering in her eyes): You never told me I was beautiful. You never liked my hair. You never liked my clothes. You never liked anything about me.

Mrs. Lopez: I just wanted you to be more beautiful. (She starts to cry.)

Clinician: You wanted the best for her. (Mrs. Lopez nods.) It sounds like you loved her very much. (Mrs. Lopez nods again and says a few words to Jean in Spanish, calling her "Juanita.")

Jean (crying now): I love you too, Mamacita.

Dementia sufferers and their families must grieve the loss of the person they knew. Jean is angry with her mother for not being the same woman she always was. As much as she and her mother quarreled, the "old" mother was familiar to her. She displaces her anger onto the homemaker, blaming her for "doing too much" and causing her mother's increasing incapacity. Mrs. Lopez, meanwhile, is mourning the loss of the woman she used to be. Mrs. Lopez wants Jean to understand that she can't do what she used to do. The clinician had planned to discuss helping Mrs. Lopez do more things for herself, but she quickly recognizes that Mrs. Lopez and Jean both need to mourn and possibly reconnect in some more meaningful way. She switches gears and decides to stay with the feelings Mrs. Lopez is expressing. Since Mrs. Lopez is losing complex language skills and her ability to verbalize her feelings in any detail, the clinician uses the visual stimulus of the photographs to help Mrs. Lopez connect to herself as a younger woman. She empathizes and reflects back her understanding of Mrs. Lopez's feelings of loss (thereby clarifying them for Jean) without attempting to make her feel better. Butler and colleagues (1991) discuss the need for people who are facing dissolution and death to try to put things in order and resolve problematic relationships. Mrs. Lopez wants to let Jean know, while she still can, that she has always loved Jean very much. In the middle stages of dementia, old memory is more intact than recent memory. Patients will often revert to their first language at times of deep emotion, as Mrs. Lopez does. The clinician helps Mrs. Lopez reach out to her daughter by saying the words that Mrs. Lopez feels but can't quite manage to say.

CONCLUSION

Short-term treatment is an invaluable approach to help dementia patients and their families through critical points in a chronic disease process. The two case examples illustrated the use of short-term treatment techniques such as rapid assessment, a high level of worker activity, partialization and focusing, flexibility of approach, and an emphasis on clients' strengths and capacities (Goldstein and Noonan 1999) at the pre- and postdiagnosis points of the disease. There are many other points where short-term treatment techniques can be effective, such as managing difficult behaviors at home, planning for residential care, selecting and supervising home-care providers, and helping the primary caregiver deal with the stresses of caregiving.

Living with dementia is a long and painful process for patients and their families. Short-term treatment focusing on helping families deal with their emotional reactions to the disease can free them to build more supportive relationships with each other and to act more effectively together to plan for and obtain necessary services and assistance.

REFERENCES

American Psychiatric Association (1994). *Diagnostic and Statistical Manual of Mental Disorders*. Washington, DC: American Psychiatric Association.

Baker, F. M. (1990). Ethnic minority issues: differential diagnosis, medication, treatment and outcomes. In *Minority Aging*, ed. M. S. Harper. DHHS Publication #HRS (P-DV-90-4). Washington, DC: U.S. Government Printing Office.

Blazer, D. (1998). *Emotional Problems in Later Life*. New York: Springer.

Blenker, M. (1965). Social work and family relationships in later life with some thoughts on filial maturity. In *Social Structure and the Family: Generational Relationships*, ed. E. Shanas and G. Streib, pp. 218–230. Englewood Cliffs, NJ: Prentice Hall.

Brechling, B., and Schneider, C. (1993). Preserving autonomy in early stage dementia. *Journal of Gerontological Social Work* 20:17–33.

Bumagin, V., and Hirn, K. (1990). *Helping the Aging Family*. Glenview, IL: Scott, Foresman.

Butler, R., Lewis, M., and Sunderland, T. (1991). *Aging and Mental Health: Positive Psychosocial and Biomedical Approaches*. New York: Macmillan.

Cohen, D., and Eisdorfer, C. (1986). *The Loss of Self: A Family Resource for the Care of Alzheimer's Disease and Related Disorders*. New York: Norton.

Davis, R., and Davis, B. (1989). *My Journey into Alzheimer's Disease*. Wheaton, IL: Tyndale House.

Drickamer, M., and Lachs, M. (1992). Should patients with Alzheimer's disease be told their diagnosis? *New England Journal of Medicine* 326(14):123–134.

Ellis, A. (1962). *Reason and Emotion in Psychotherapy*. New York: Lyle Stuart.

Goldstein, E., and Noonan, M. (1999). *Short-Term Treatment and Social Work Practice*. New York: Free Press.

Haley, J. (1980). *Leaving Home*. New York: McGraw-Hill.

Hartman, A., and Laird, J. (1983). *Family-Centered Social Work Practice*. New York: Free Press.

Kane, R. (1990). Assessing the elderly client. In *Handbook of Gerontological*

Services, ed. A. Monk, pp. 55–89. New York: Columbia University Press.

Lampert, A. (1986). Helping families deal with Alzheimer's disease. *American Journal of Alzheimer's Care and Related Disorders.* Winter:32–36.

Lustbader, W., and Hooyman, N. (1994). *Taking Care of Family Members: A Practical Guide.* New York: Free Press.

Mace, N., and Rabins, P. (1999). *The 36-Hour Day: A Family Guide for Persons with Alzheimer's Disease.* Baltimore: Johns Hopkins University Press.

McGowin, D. (1993). *Living in the Labyrinth: A Personal Journey through the Maze of Alzheimer's.* San Francisco: Elder Books.

Parad, H., and Parad, L. (1990). *Crisis Intervention, Book 2: The Practitioner's Sourcebook for Brief Therapy.* Milwaukee, WI: Family Service of America.

Rabins, P. (1984). Management of dementia in the family context. *Psychosomatics* 25(5):369–375.

Raffoul, P. (1986). Drug use among older people: focus for interdisciplinary efforts. *Health and Social Work* 11(3):197–202.

Shulman, L. (1992). *The Skills of Helping.* Itasca, IL: F.E. Peacock.

Silverstone, B., and Hyman, H. (1976). *You and Your Aging Parent.* New York: Pantheon.

Smith Barusch, A. (1987). Power dynamics in the aging family: a preliminary statement. *Journal of Gerontological Social Work* 11(3/4): 43–54.

Stone, R., Cafferata, G., and Sangl, J. (1986). *Caregivers of the frail elderly: a national profile.* National Center for Health Services Research, Public Health Service, U.S. Department of Health and Human Services. Rockville, MD: National Center for Health Services Research.

Verwoerdt, A. (1981). *Clinical Geropsychiatry.* Baltimore: Williams & Wilkins.

Worden, W. (1982). *Grief Counseling and Grief Therapy: A Handbook for the Mental Health Practitioner.* New York: Springer.

CHAPTER FIVE

Short-Term Treatment of Substance-Abusing Clients

SHULAMITH LALA ASHENBERG STRAUSSNER
AND PATRICIA ROSE ATTIA

The abuse of alcohol and other drugs (AOD) takes an incalculable toll on our society, and there are few, if any, settings where clinicians are not confronted with the direct or indirect impact of AOD on their clients and family members. Brief treatment has proven to be effective in helping numerous substance abusers minimize the impact of their alcohol and drug abuse (Bein et al. 1993, USDHHS 1998).

This chapter discusses substance-related disorders (SRDs) and the use of brief interventions to motivate and treat individuals impacted by alcohol and other drugs. A case vignette illustrates some of the issues and dynamics in short-term treatment of a substance-abusing client.

THE SCOPE AND IMPACT OF SUBSTANCE ABUSE

The full scope of alcohol- and other drug-related problems is often underestimated and minimized since problems related to AOD are frequently mistakenly attributed to other causes. Moreover, as pointed out by Liese and Najavits (1997), "until the mid-1980s, the field of psychotherapy largely ignored substance abuse, viewing it as a superficial symptom of more important underlying problems" (p. 468). Today, professionals are increasingly more aware that substance abuse has to be treated in its own right, and that in order to accomplish this clinicians need to have specialized knowledge and skills.

While preference for a given substance may differ among different individuals and communities, substance abuse disorders are found in both men and women (Straussner and Zelvin 1997), in every ethnic and cultural group in the United States (Straussner, in press), and among individuals of every age—from the preadolescent to the elderly.

According to government estimates, about 14 million Americans, almost 10 percent of all adults in the United States, suffer from alcohol abuse and dependence (USDHHS 1997a), and approximately 5.5 million Americans are dependent or abuse other drugs (Gerstein and Harwood 1990). The abuse of alcohol and other drugs is a major factor in motor vehicle injuries and deaths; in homicides, suicides, and accidental overdoses; in domestic violence; in sexual and physical abuse of children; and in rape. It contributes to numerous criminal activities, as well as to various physical disorders including liver, pancreas, and heart diseases; some cancers; and the spread of sexually transmitted diseases (USDHHS 1997a). An estimated half of all new cases of AIDS are related to injection of drugs, and a growing number of infections are also found among the sexual partners of intravenous drug users (NIDA 1996). These dynamics affect a disproportionate number of African Americans and Hispanics (Day 1999).

While substance abuse has a significant impact on individuals, it also severely affects their family members (Straussner 1994). That impact is particularly profound when the substance abuser is a pregnant woman. According to Gerstein and Harwood (1990), over 100,000 pregnant women annually are in need of drug treatment. Children born of alcohol-abusing mothers may suffer from a variety of fetal alcohol syndromes, while children born of cocaine- and amphetamine-using mothers frequently suffer from attention deficit and hyperactive disorders and learning problems (Nadel and Straussner 1997). A majority of "HIV-infected newborns have mothers who were infected through their own drug use or through sexual activity with a drug user" (NIDA 1996, p. 10).

Alcohol and other drugs are also important components in numerous other Axis I and II disorders, particularly mood and anxiety disorders, schizophrenia, eating disorders, and borderline and antisocial personality disorders. Such co-occurring disorders have to be carefully assessed, and all disorders identified have to be treated in their own right.

ASSESSING AND DIAGNOSING SUBSTANCE-RELATED PROBLEMS—INCLUSIONARY CRITERIA

Although millions of Americans use alcohol and other psychoactive substances, not everyone experiences a problem due to such use. It is therefore helpful to conceptualize the use of alcohol and other drugs as existing on a continuum ranging from nonproblematic substance use, to abuse, and finally to dependence or addiction (Straussner 1993).

According to the fourth edition of the American Psychiatric Association's (APA 1994) *Diagnostic and Statistical Manual of Mental Disorders* (*DSM-IV*), substance abuse is defined as the maladaptive pattern of use of substances resulting in one or more of the following: failure to meet one's role obligations, placing oneself in dangerous and/or illegal situations, and/or experiencing persistent social or interpersonal problems. These symptoms have to be experienced within a 12-month period of time (APA 1994).

The *DSM-IV* defines substance dependence as the existence of at least three of the following seven symptoms within a 12-month period:

1. Tolerance, as defined by either a need for increased amounts of a substance to achieve a desired effect or diminished effect with use of the same quantity of substances.
2. Withdrawal, as characterized by specific withdrawal syndromes

defined for each substance or ingesting a substance to relieve or avoid withdrawal symptoms.

3. Taking the substance in larger amounts or over a longer period than was intended.
4. A persistent desire or unsuccessful efforts to reduce or control use.
5. A great deal of time spent obtaining, using, and recovering from substance abuse.
6. Important social, occupational, or recreational activities are given up or reduced because of substance use.
7. The substance is continued despite knowledge of serious physical or psychological problems related to the substance use.

In essence, substance dependence refers to compulsive and continued use of a substance despite adverse consequences. The terms *alcoholism* and *drug addiction* are synonymous with substance dependence (Straussner 1993). Once individuals have been diagnosed with substance dependence, they can never be diagnosed with the less severe diagnosis of substance abuse.

In addition to the *DSM-IV* criteria, there are numerous assessment tools that are frequently used to diagnose substance-abusing clients. These include the Addiction Severity Index (ASI), the CAGE test (an acronym for the four symptoms that it assesses: CUTTING down on one's drinking; being ANNOYED when criticized for one's drinking; feeling GUILTY about drinking; and taking a drink as an EYE OPENER when waking up), and the Drug Use Screening Inventory–Revised (DUSI-R), among others. Most important, since the abuse of substances, as well as withdrawal from certain substances, can be fatal, clinicians working with substance-abusing clients need to be aware of the kind of substances the individual is using and the impact of a particular substance on the person's brain and daily functioning.

Classification of Substances

The potential for addiction of different substances varies greatly; for example, narcotics or crack cocaine have a much higher potential for addiction than alcohol or marijuana. Nonetheless, every individual taking a mind-altering substance in sufficient quantity will experience a physiological impact or a state of intoxication. Moreover, many substances, if taken in large doses over a long period of time, will lead to addiction or physiological dependence regardless of the individual's predisposing characteristics or intent. Thus it is important to understand the physiological impact of drugs on the human brain and body.

Substances of abuse can be classified into various categories depending on their effect on the central nervous system (Straussner 1993). The most frequent categorization is as follows:

Central Nervous System Depressants

These are substances that slow down or sedate the excitable brain tissues. Such sedation affects the brain centers that control speech, vision, coordination, and judgment. The individual also experiences increased agitation and excitability when coming off these drugs—a withdrawal effect commonly known as a hangover. Once an individual becomes addicted to central nervous system (CNS) depressants, unmonitored withdrawal from these substances can be life threatening. Moreover, combining two or more CNS depressants can result in a potential effect in which the consequences are more devastating than if these substances were taken sequentially. Alcohol, barbiturates, tranquilizers, anesthetics, and solvents are some of the most commonly abused CNS.

Narcotics or Opiates

These drugs decrease pain by binding to specific receptors in certain brain areas. This category includes opium and its derivatives, such as morphine, heroin, and codeine, as well as methadone, and other synthetic painkillers such as Demerol, Darvon, Percocet, and Talwin. These substances are more addictive than the CNS depressants and result in severe physical agitation during withdrawal. However, while very unpleasant, withdrawal from these substances is not dangerous.

Central Nervous System Stimulants

Stimulants produce a feeling of elation, increased heart rate and blood pressure, and decreased appetite. This category includes substances such as amphetamines ("speed," "crank"), cocaine (including crack), drugs such as Dexedrine and Ritalin, and caffeine and nicotine. Large doses of such stimulants as amphetamines and cocaine can produce acute delirium, irrational and violent behavior, and psychotic symptoms such as hallucinations, paranoia, and hypersexuality. At times these symptoms can be difficult to distinguish from schizophrenia. Withdrawal from these substances can lead to severe feelings of depression, including suicidality.

Psychedelics or Hallucinogens

These drugs produce gross distortions of thoughts and sensory processes, altering perception and inducing a psychosis-like state, often with visual hallucinations. The most familiar hallucinogens are LSD (lysergic acid diethylamide), PCP (phencyclidine), and mescaline. Two of the newer hallucinogens are Ecstasy and Special K. Ecstasy, or MDMA (methylenedioxymethamphetamine), also acts as a CNS stimulant. Psychedelics are less physiologically addictive than other substances; however, they may precipitate psychosis in vulnerable individuals. Some scientists also include large or highly potent doses of marijuana (and hashish) under the category of hallucinogens. However, at lower doses, marijuana can act as a mild stimulant, sedative, and even as an analgesic. It is important to note that the marijuana used today is much more potent than that used during the 1960s and 1970s. Frequent use of marijuana by adolescents and young adults has been correlated with the development of the so-called amotivational syndrome, characterized by passivity and lack of ambition leading to poor school and work performance and personality deterioration (Straussner 1993).

As can be seen from the above discussion, different substances have a differential impact on a person's mood and behavior regardless of the individual's personality. Thus, familiarity with the impact of the various substances on a person's behavior and thinking process is a crucial aspect of clinical assessment and treatment.

THEORIES OF ADDICTION-EXCLUSIONARY CRITERIA

There does not appear to be a single explanation for why some individuals who use substances start to abuse them or become addicted while others do not. The factors most frequently cited are genetic predisposition, physiological changes brought on by the substance, sociocultural factors, and familial and psychological dynamics. Among the numerous psychological explanations, psychodynamic, learning, and behavioral theories have been utilized in understanding and treating substance abusers (for a fuller discussion, see Straussner 1993). It is the last two—learning and behavioral theories—that offer the best conceptual understanding to the brief treatment of AOD-abusing clients, and these will be elaborated upon later in this chapter. Nonetheless, it is important to keep in mind that when we treat substance-abusing individuals we are dealing with a "multivariate syndrome in which multiple patterns of dysfunctional substance abuse occur in various types of people with multiple prognoses requiring a variety of interventions" (Straussner 1993, p. 11).

TREATMENT PERSPECTIVES AND APPROACHES

As pointed out by Abadinsky (1997), "There are probably as many approaches to treating and preventing drug [and alcohol] abuse as there are theories to explain the phenomenon itself" (p. 162). A 1997 publication by the National Center for Substance Abuse Treatment (US-DHHS 1997b) lists fifty research-based substance abuse treatment strategies. It is no wonder that during the past twenty-five years an entire industry has developed to prevent and treat addiction. The various programs address the physiological and psychosocial needs of the substance-abusing clients and range from medically monitored detoxification facilities, to in-patient rehabilitation and residential programs, to intensive or weekly outpatient treatment programs. Specialized programs for dually diagnosed clients (Morell 1997, Orlin and Davis 1993), for homeless individuals (Scheffler 1993), for adolescents (Feigelman and Feigelman 1993), for those suffering from AIDS (Strum 1993), for those under the supervision of the criminal justice system (National Center on Addiction and Substance Abuse 1998), and for many other special needs can be found in many communities. Finally, self-help (mostly, although not exclusively, twelve-step–based programs) offered invaluable, easily accessible, and free help to millions of substance abusers and their families (Spiegel 1993, Straussner and Spiegel 1996). The existing treatment programs are based on varying treatment philosophies and utilize a variety of interventive approaches, many of which are well suited for brief treatment.

SHORT-TERM TREATMENT APPROACHES FOR SUBSTANCE-ABUSING CLIENTS

Goldstein and Noonan (1999) describe the ten major distinguishing characteristics composing what they term the integrative short-term treatment approach:

1. The conscious use of time
2. A high level of worker activity
3. Quick engagement
4. Rapid assessment
5. Partialization and focusing
6. Flexibility of approach and technical interventions
7. Differential use of the therapist–client relationship
8. Emphasis on client strengths and capacities
9. Collaboration, linkage, and advocacy
10. Acceptance of the limitations of treatment

To varying degrees, all these characteristics are appropriate to the treatment of individuals abusing alcohol and other drugs.

Short-term treatment is not a new concept in the field of addictions. With the exception of lifelong methadone maintenance provided to those individuals who have been dependent on heroin (Friedman 1993), or the long-term (up to two years) residential therapeutic communities where the goal is to "demolish and rebuild" the personality structure of narcotic- or stimulant-abusing young clients, much of the traditional substance abuse treatment has been based on brief but highly intensive interventions. Aimed mostly at treating those abusing alcohol and other CNS depressants, these traditional approaches were based on the so-called Minnesota model (O'Dwyer 1993), which consisted of an inpatient twenty-eight–day drug-free, rehabilitation program, usually followed by referral to twelve-step programs such as Alcoholics Anonymous. Only the most difficult patients with little community support, those who have had a number of relapses, or those with other overt psychopathology were referred for longer-term inpatient treatment or for ongoing outpatient supportive therapy and psychiatric monitoring.

The traditional, time-limited, approach to the treatment of alcohol and other drugs has required rapid assessment and a high level of therapist activity focused on a limited goal (usually abstinence from all mood-altering chemicals). Collaboration, linkages, and advocacy, and acceptance of the limitation of treatment to address the multiple problems that were frequently the correlates of substance abuse were built into this treatment model. What this traditional approach did not offer was flexibility of interventive approaches that would permit a differential emphasis on individual strengths and capacities.

With the coming of managed care, the uniform twenty-eight–day inpatient treatment approach disappeared, to be replaced by a more individually tailored, mostly outpatient-based treatment. Moreover, there has been a growing focus on a harm-reduction approach that aims at limiting or reducing the consequences of substance abuse for the individual and society. Understanding the disease concept is not a goal of harm reduction, nor is total abstinence (MacCoun 1998).

Currently, even detoxification, which traditionally has been provided by a brief stay at a medically monitored, inpatient setting, and has often served as the source of referral for treatment, has become shorter. Increasingly, there is pressure to detoxify patients in ambulatory settings, with the use of inpatient detoxification units limited to those with life-threatening withdrawal symptoms. Unfortunately, such brief detoxification does not allow time for establishing a therapeutic relationship that can be utilized to motivate clients to enter further treatment. Consequently, a different approach to motivating clients has developed during the past decade, much of it based on Miller and Rollnick's (1991) motivational interviewing and on Prochaska and DiClemente's (1982, 1992, Prochaska et al. 1992) stages of change model. It is these approaches, combined with cognitive-behavioral and problem-solving models, that offer more effective approaches to the treatment of the typically resistant alcohol- and drug-abusing patients. The nonmechanistic and flexible use of these approaches emphasizes the individual's strengths and capacities, and helps develop the ego strength and flexible use of defenses that are essential for healthy functioning in today's stressful environment (Goldstein 1995).

The following section describes the motivational, cognitive behavioral, and solution-focused treatment models and applies them to a case example.

ASSESSING AND INCREASING MOTIVATION TO CHANGE: THE STAGES OF CHANGE MODEL

Prochaska and Diclemente (1982, 1992, Prochaska et al. 1992) identified five stages of motivation to change, with each stage requiring different treatment strategies. This stages of change model stresses the importance of developing an individualized protocol for each person that matches the intervention to the stage of change. Unlike the twelve-step—based programs, the goal of treatment based on the change model is not to get the client to agree that he or she is an alcoholic or drug abuser, but rather to move the person to the next level of change. According to the authors, while regression or relapse can occur at any stage, people generally do not skip any of the stages of change. In their study of cigarette smokers, the authors found that it took going through all the stages an average of four times before individuals were able to quit smoking (Prochaska et al. 1992). Thus, for some clients the goal of short-term substance abuse treatment may consist of moving them through only one or two stages—not necessarily achieving full recovery or lifelong abstinence. The five stages are precontemplation, contemplation, determination, action, and maintenance.

"Resistance to recognizing or modifying a problem is the hallmark of precontemplation" (Prochaska et al. 1992, p. 1103). A patient who is at this stage is not ready to address a problem or consider the possibility of change since he or she is not even consciously aware that a problem exists. The clinician's task is to get, or maintain, the person in treatment by gently increasing the client's awareness of the problem through such techniques as psychoeducation about problems related to substance abuse, and by raising doubts and increasing the level of anxiety about the individual's current state of functioning. Psychoeducation can consists of didactic lectures, provision of literature or films, and/or discussion of such topics as the signs and symptoms of substance abuse and addiction, the impact of substance abuse on the brain and body, and the impact on family members (Straussner 1993). Such education provides cognitive, non–ego-threatening understanding of the dynamics of substance abuse and is usually more effective than direct confrontation in helping individuals begin to contemplate their use of substances.

In the contemplation stage, the patient may be thinking about the problem, but is not necessarily ready to do anything about it. The task of the clinician is to increase awareness of the benefits of change through the use of reflection and open-ended questions, and by offering options that make the individual feel empowered to move ahead to the next stage of determination, or pre-action. According to research studies, the ideal number of options is three: fewer options feel too limiting, while more than three are experienced as too overwhelming (Prochaska, personal communication, 1998).

During the determination stage the client feels "I have to do something about this problem" or "Something has to change," yet he or she is not fully ready to take action to effect change. At this point, the clinician can help the client explore the pros and cons of change by generating possible options and solutions to the problem without pushing the individual to premature action.

In the fourth stage, the action stage, the client, with the support of the clinician, implements the change plan. The task of the clinician is to provide affirmation and support the patient in the change effort. Once such change takes place, it needs to be maintained—otherwise regression or relapse occurs. During the maintenance stage, the clinician needs to help the client continue with the change process by identifying and using effective relapse prevention strategies. Should relapse occur, the treatment goal changes to prevention of possible demoralization through support, encouragement, and provision of accurate, reality-based information that will move the client back to the preparation or action stage.

Miller and Rollnick's (1991) five principles of motivational interviewing provide a useful framework that helps motivate clients to move from one stage of change to another. The five general principles are expressing empathy, developing discrepancy, avoiding argumentation, rolling with resistance, and supporting self-efficacy. The goal of motivational interviewing is to create an internal motivation for change despite the fact that a client may enter treatment due to external pressures. These principles are in line with traditional ego-supportive approaches (Goldstein 1995), but with a more specific, goal-oriented focus. For example, if a heroin- and crack-abusing unemployed man states that his treatment goal is to find a well-paying job, the clinician's insistence on his attending Narcotics Anonymous meetings will naturally be met with resistance since this recommendation is more appropriate for a client in the preparation or action stage, not one who is in precontemplation or even contemplation stage. It is the job of the clinician to provide feedback to the client that illustrates the discrepancy between his ability to achieve the desired goals and his continuing use of substances. To be effective, such feedback has to be provided within an empathic environment that avoids argumentation or direct confrontation of resistance, and one that supports the individual's self-efficacy.

This approach has been conceptualized in the FRAMES model (Bein et al. 1993, Miller and Sanchez 1993): feedback, responsibility, advice, menu, empathy, and self-efficacy. By providing feedback, the clinician helps clients recognize contradictions. Responsibility for change rests with the client, and this awareness avoids power struggles during treatment. Advice is doled out sparingly and emphasizes strategies that the client has effectively utilized in the past. A menu of options is offered to the client. Empathy, rather than confrontation, characterizes the tenor of each clinical intervention. Self-efficacy entails the client's belief in his or her own ability to change.

Cognitive-Behavioral Treatment Approaches

In addition to the change model, current effective short-term treatment approaches for substance abusers tend to utilize elements from cognitive-behavioral treatment approaches, such as rational-emotive therapy (Ellis et al. 1988) and Beck's cognitive therapy (Beck et al. 1993).

Rational Emotive Therapy

In the book *Rational Emotive Therapy with Alcoholics and Substance Abusers* (1988), Albert Ellis and his colleagues describe a process that leads to drug/alcohol abuse and prescribe a method for intervening in this destructive cycle. According to the authors, the individual experiences an activating event, followed by irrational beliefs and emotional distress. The patient then seeks to reduce the emotional distress by using a substance, which leads to a temporary reduction in the emotional distress, only to repeat this cycle at a future time. The clinician's task is to teach clients how to reduce the distress by disputing their irrational belief and learning new coping mechanisms to deal with the original event. For example, a young woman may irrationally believe that she cannot cope with an event, such as a breakup with a boyfriend, without using alcohol. The clinician helps her recognize the activating events or triggers (such as seeing her boyfriend on the street), identify the irrational beliefs ("I cannot live without him," "I am unlovable," etc.) that are evoked, and then "dispute" each of those beliefs through exaggeration ("Seeing him on the street will give you a heart attack?"), or through other approaches that point out the irrationality of these beliefs and bring in reality. The patient then is helped to reinterpret the situation and her own active role in it, and to consider various options of responding to this problem in a less destructive manner.

Similarly, cognitive therapy (Beck et al. 1993) seeks to reduce "excessive emotional reactions and self-defeating behaviors by modifying the faulty or erroneous thinking and maladaptive beliefs that underlie these reactions" (p. 27). Clients learn to recognize urges or cravings that can lead to substance use and relapse. The cognitive model blends easily with a twelve-step program such as Alcoholics Anonymous (AA) that encourages participants to stay away from people, places, and things that can lead to relapse. Attendance at AA or Narcotics Anonymous (NA) meetings and calling a sponsor instead of picking up a substance are new coping skills that replace the old, dangerous ones. The National Institute on Drug Abuse has found that focusing on a person's behavior, in addition to addressing the cognitive aspects (i.e., a cognitive-behavioral focus), has been particularly successful in treating cocaine addicts (US-DHHS 1998).

Solution-Focused Treatment Approaches

Solution-focused brief therapy (SFBT) (Berg 1995, Berg and Reuss 1998) also emphasizes the importance of the collaborative relationship between the client and the clinician. While traditional substance-abuse treatment programs are based on the disease model, the paradigm shift in SFBT is to focus on solutions rather than problems. During assessment and treatment, the clinician helps the patient understand what allows for periods of sobriety and abstinence, rather than focusing on causes of relapse. The focus, consequently, is on what the person is capable of doing, not on the problem.

The utilization of SFBT is highly effective in motivating clients to effect change without needing to understand the causes of their problems. It is a particularly effective approach in working with adolescent or other highly resistant, often involuntary clients, who are more interested in getting rid of the negative consequences of their problems rather than changing themselves.

CASE ILLUSTRATION

The following case illustrates the use of various techniques from the theoretical models discussed above within a framework of short-term treatment mandated by the patient's insurance.

History

Lisa is a 36-year-old single, Caucasian female who was referred to a clinician in an outpatient mental health clinic following a brief hospitalization due to an overdose of a combination of pills and alcohol. The overdose followed a fight with her boyfriend. Lisa was seen in individual therapy for a total of twelve weekly sessions.

Lisa had a seven-year history of treatment at several mental health agencies. Her treatment records indicated a long history of polysubstance abuse and her diagnoses also included mood and personality disorders. When asked about her goals for treatment, Lisa stated, "I'm here because I'm sick and tired of living the life I have."

Lisa described herself as a "garbage head"—a slang term for someone using many substances, and the first of her many self-deprecating comments. She was the youngest of three children of a middle-class alcoholic couple, and her mother was also addicted to pills. Lisa stated that her mother told her that she was an "an accident," and that her parents did not want any more children. Although very bright, Lisa had learning difficulties in school and dropped out of college in her sophomore year after becoming involved with a man who supplied her with pills and marijuana. She had her first suicide attempt after he left her, and was hospitalized and treated for depression, but not for her use of substances.

Lisa's substance abuse history indicated alcohol use that began when she was a young child and "sucked the liquor off the napkins" at her parents' cocktail parties. Lisa's use of chemicals increased during her adolescence. She stole her mother's pills from the medicine cabinet, and started using marijuana, in addition to drinking an increasing amount of alcohol. She felt that the use of these substances took away the pain of being unwanted and helped mitigate the tribulations of being a teenager. As a young adult, Lisa described continuing substance use, promiscuity, anhedonia, depression, and feelings of loneliness.

At the time Lisa came to treatment, she was living in a room that she rented from a couple. In exchange for minimal rent, she babysat for their children. Lisa also worked a few hours a day in a cafeteria of a large company. She disliked her job but felt unable to look for something else. She had minimal health insurance that she paid for herself and that provided very limited coverage for outpatient treatment.

Assessment

Lisa presented as an articulate, intelligent woman with compassion for others, insight, and a willingness to assess her situation objectively. Both depression and polysubstance dependence were long-standing disorders. Although she had received years of treatment, she was skeptical of the benefits of therapy. Her mother's constant reminders that Lisa was unwanted and both parents' substance abuse were clear contributors to Lisa's poor ego functioning and developmental fixations. The early onset of drug and alcohol abuse interfered with her psychosocial development and probably contributed to her learning problems, although she may have had an undiagnosed learning disability. She used drugs and alcohol to deal with her loneliness and depression; however, these substances further contributed to her depression and sense of helplessness.

She was diagnosed with as follows:

Axis I: Polysubstance dependence (304.80)
            Major depressive disorder (296.33)
Axis II: Borderline personality disorder (301.83)
Axis III: None
Axis IV: Few social supports
            Meager income
            Unsatisfying employment
Axis V: GAF (Global Assessment of Functioning) = 45 (current)
            GAF = 60 (highest during the past year)

Engagement

The first few treatment sessions were devoted to establishing a working alliance, and assessing the magnitude of Lisa's substance abuse, depression, and suicidality and her motivation to change. It also focused on developing a treatment contract that included specific goals and objectives.

Initially, Lisa had great difficulty looking ahead, which contributed to her inability to set goals. She could not imagine life any differently. The clinician asked her to pretend that while asleep one night a magical transformation appeared and all Lisa's wishes had come true the next morning. Utilizing the "magic question" (Berg 1995) helped Lisa envision a new life for herself, and this then helped her to identify treatment goals, which included refraining from suicide attempts, reducing her depression, and having better relationships with people. Lisa did not want to discuss her drug and alcohol use and refused to consider the recommendation to attend any twelve-step meetings.

The clinician remained empathetic and nonjudgmental, and during the next couple of sessions kept gently pointing out the ways in which drug and alcohol abuse might have contributed to Lisa's feelings of

depression, suicide attempts, and difficulties establishing healthy relationships. Lisa acknowledged the discrepancy between her stated goals
and her difficulties in working toward them, and agreed to monitor the
effects of substance use on her mood and functioning by keeping a diary
(see Orlin and Davis 1993 for specific format).

Middle Phase

The five or six sessions that composed the middle phase of treatment
concentrated on developing concrete objectives to achieve the goals
identified on the treatment plan. The clinician utilized various treatment
approaches, including the use of homework worksheets to monitor Lisa's
mood, and the provision of information on community resources to meet
new people and psychoeducational literature on dual diagnosis. Since Lisa
was taking antidepressant medication, she found the literature about the
potentiating effects of combining her prescription medications and the
use of alcohol of great interest, and was eager to talk about her concern.
She continued to use a worksheet to monitor the effect of drug and
alcohol intake on her mood and suicidal thoughts. She charted feelings of
euphoria for two to three hours after alcohol or marijuana use followed by
hours, and even days, of depression.

The clinician helped Lisa identify the activities that enhanced her
sense of well-being, and monitored whether engaging in these activities
led to improved mood and reduced her use of substances. Lisa obtained a
library card, joined an environmental group, and remained on medication.
In addressing her relationship issues, the clinician helped Lisa make lists
of the pros and cons of resuming her relationship with her boyfriend. Lisa
identified his consistent dedication and love as essential to her feeling
good about herself. She was also proud of her ability to stay in a
committed relationship. However, his daily marijuana use was identified
as a potential trigger to her own use of marijuana. Lisa described herself as
"a magnet for shit-heads" and believed she could only attract abusive
relationships. The clinician gently challenged this distortion by remind-
ing Lisa that many of her current relationships were not abusive. Utilizing

a problem-solving approach, the clinician helped Lisa looked at her ability to maintain relationships with people who were not abusing her or abusing drugs or alcohol. The clinician also helped Lisa challenge and dispute her distortions about her inability to change and her negative self-view. When Lisa gradually realized that her perceptions of others were distorted, she began to challenge her thinking outside of the therapist's office. This reduced conflict in all of her relationships.

During the ninth session the clinician reminded Lisa that they only had three sessions left. Lisa said she was very sad because she felt that she was finally getting somewhere in therapy. Sessions ten and eleven were spent reviewing her progress, identifying situations that could be triggers for dangerous behavior, and figuring out how she could avoid them. Although Lisa did not want to make a commitment to total abstinence from alcohol, she had stopped smoking marijuana and using all nonprescription drugs. She continued to feel disappointed by the way her boyfriend and co-workers were treating her, but she was able to refrain from disturbing verbal altercations—something she was unable to do previously, both at home and at work. By session eleven, Lisa decided to resign from her job and followed through on a referral for vocational assessment and training and for an application for Medicaid.

Lisa was tearful throughout the final session. She said that she had done well in therapy because she sensed that the clinician liked her. The clinician said that she liked and respected Lisa as someone who had survived a traumatic childhood, demonstrated great resiliency, and had a fine sense of humor, compassion for others, and personal integrity. Each statement was supported by examples from previous sessions. When Lisa said that this made leaving all the more difficult, the clinician pointed out that these qualities would enhance all of her future relationships.

Although Lisa continued to refuse to attend any twelve-step groups and did not want to consider a referral for additional individual treatment elsewhere, she did agree to consider attending a woman's group once her Medicaid insurance came through. She began reading self-help books about why women make poor choices and seemed less obsessed about maintaining her relationship with her boyfriend. She greatly enjoyed her volunteer work and was making new friends there.

Treatment was successful at enhancing Lisa's ego functioning, reducing dangerous behavior, developing new skills, and connecting her to community resources. Observable changes included reduction in drinking and total abstinence from other drugs, increased use of consequential thinking, reduction in suicidal ideation and elimination of suicide attempts, recognition of the need to remain vigilant around self-deprecating thoughts, recognition of her strengths, commitments to a volunteer job and an environmental campaign that give her a sense of accomplishment, and the maintenance of prescription medication.

DISCUSSION OF TECHNIQUES
AND TREATMENT APPROACHES

Throughout treatment, "one can support and enhance areas of strength and marshal them to help the client cope more effectively" (Goldstein 1995, p. 68). Lisa learned to handle stress without drugs, developed a realistic view of herself and the world, increased the use of consequential thinking and judgment, and improved her interpersonal relationships.

Utilizing Prochaska and DiClemente's (1992, Prochaska et al. 1992) stages of change model, the clinician determined that Lisa was in the contemplation stage when she came into treatment. "Serious consideration of problem resolution is the central element of contemplation" (Prochaska et al. 1992, p. 1104). Lisa knew that there were serious problems in her life, yet she was not ready to take action at that point. She readily engaged in the process of self-reevaluation and this inspired her to continue the change process. Specific interventions, such as value clarification and the miracle question (Berg 1995), helped her focus on her treatment goals.

Throughout treatment the clinician used Miller and Rollnick's (1991) principles of motivational interviewing, which helped Lisa move through the stage of contemplation to action. One of the major goals of motivational interviewing is to create discrepancy between clients' goals and their behavior. When Lisa's alcohol binges and drug use increased her negative feelings about the world and her sense of hopelessness, the clinician was able to demonstrate the discrepancy between her use of chemicals and her stated goals.

The clinician's tone and manner were consistently empathetic throughout the treatment process. Lisa's ambivalence about stopping her abuse of substances and her frustrating relationship with her boyfriend were explored, and the clinician helped her assess their pros and cons. Lisa was offered a menu of outside resources and a menu of techniques. She was comfortable with the goal-focused treatment, the cognitive-behavioral approaches, and the focus on her daily functioning. Her refusal to attend Alcoholics Anonymous meetings was respected. The ability to make her own decisions within the menu of services enhanced her self-efficacy, while the clinician studiously avoided confrontation of the resistance.

To work continuously toward the enhancement of ego functioning, the clinician challenged Lisa's distortions regarding her inability to change and her self-deprecating beliefs. When Lisa made self-degrading comments or self-defeating statements about her ability to change, the clinician used examples from Lisa's history to help her reframe her sense of self. The combination of reframing and gentle confrontation of cognitive distortions helped Lisa internalize the capacity to address her own self-defeating thinking. Practicing new skills outside of the session and doing her homework assignments helped her to take advantage of the time between sessions (Kadushin 1998). While the twelve sessions did not resolve all of Lisa's problems, they did help to diminish her substance abuse and improve her social skills, and they helped her to feel better about herself.

CONCLUSION

Drug and alcohol problems continue to plague our society, and research findings do not support the theory that longer treatment necessarily leads to better outcome. Given the current reductions in public and private sector health care funding, short-term treatment is often the only option available to many substance-abusing clients. Continued research is needed to assess the outcome of short-term treatment and to home in on which clients can achieve maximum benefit from which technique.

It is typical for many substance-abusing clients to be externally motivated for treatment, and to have few social supports and poor ego functioning. The short-term theories and techniques described in this chapter can help many substance abusers make better use of treatment, and can prevent clinicians from getting entangled in power struggles that are detrimental for both the patient and the therapist.

REFERENCES

Abadinsky, H. (1997). *Drug Abuse: An Introduction.* Chicago: Nelson-Hall.

American Psychiatric Association. (1994). *Diagnostic and Statistical Manual of Mental Disorders, 4th ed.* Washington, DC: Author.

Beck, A., Wright, F., Newman, C., and Liese, B. (1993). *Cognitive Therapy of Substance Abuse.* New York: Guilford.

Bein, T. H., Miller, W. R., and Tonigan, J. S. (1993). Brief interventions for alcohol problems: a review. *Addiction* 88:315–336.

Berg, I. K. (1995). Solution-focused brief therapy with substance abusers. In *Psychotherapy and Substance Abuse: A Practitioner's Handbook*, ed. A. Washton, pp. 223–242. New York: Guilford.

Berg, I. K., and Reuss, N. H. (1998). *Solutions Step by Step: A Substance Abuse Treatment Manual.* New York: Norton.

Day, D. (1999). *Health Emergency 1999: The Spread of Drug-Related AIDS and Other Deadly Diseases among African Americans and Latinos.* Princeton, NJ: Dogwood Center.

Ellis, A., McInerney, J., DiGiuseppe, R., and Yeager, R. (1988). *Rational Emotive Therapy with Alcoholics and Substance Abusers.* Boston: Allyn & Bacon.

Feigelman, B., and Feigelman, W. (1993). Treating the adolescent substance abuser. In *Clinical Work with Substance Abusing Clients*, ed. L. Straussner, pp. 233–250. New York: Guilford.

Friedman, E. G. (1993). Methadone maintenance in the treatment of addiction. In *Clinical Work with Substance Abusing Clients*, ed. L. Straussner, pp. 135–152. New York: Guilford.

Gerstein, D. R., and Harwood, H. J. (1990). *Treating Drug Problems, Vol. 1.* Washington, DC: National Academy Press.

Goldstein, E. (1995). *Ego Psychology and Social Work Practice*, 2nd ed. New York: Free Press.

Goldstein, E., and Noonan, M. (1999). *Short-Term Treatment and Social Work Practice: An Integrative Perspective.* New York: Free Press.

Kadushin, G. (1998). Adaptations of the traditional interview to the brief-treatment context. *Families in Society: The Journal of Contemporary Human Services* 79(1):346–357.

Liese, B. S., and Najavits, L. M. (1997). Cognitive and behavioral therapies. In *Substance Abuse: A Comprehensive Textbook*, ed. J. H. Lowinson, P. Ruiz, R. B. Millman, and J. G. Langrod, pp. 467–478. Baltimore: Williams & Wilkins.

MacCoun, R. J. (1998). Toward a psychology of harm reduction. *American Psychologist* 53(11):1199–1208.

Miller, W., and Rollnick, S. (1991). *Motivational Interviewing: Preparing People to Change Addictive Behavior.* New York: Guilford.

Miller, W., and Sanchez, V. (1993). Motivating young adults for treatment and lifestyle change. In *Issues in Alcohol Use and Misuse by Young Adults*, ed. G. Howard, pp. 57–75. Notre Dame, IN: University of Notre Dame.

Morell, C. (1997). Women with depression and substance abuse problems. In *Gender and Addictions: Men and Women in Treatment*, ed. S. L. A. Straussner and E. Zelvin, pp. 223–242. Northvale, NJ: Jason Aronson.

Nadel, M., and Straussner, S. L. A. (1997). Children in substance abusing families. In *Children in the Urban Environment: Linking Social Policy and Clinical Practice*, ed. N. K. Phillips and S. L. A. Straussner, pp. 154–174. Springfield, IL: Charles C Thomas.

National Center on Addiction and Substance Abuse (CASA). (1998). *Behind substance abuse and America's prison population*. New York: Author.

National Institute on Drug Abuse (NIDA). (1996). *Drug abuse and drug abuse research: the fifth triennial report to Congress from the Secretary, DHHS*. Washington, DC: National Institute of Health.

O'Dwyer, P. (1993). Alcoholism treatment facilities. In *Clinical Work with Substance Abusing Clients*, ed. S. L. A. Straussner, pp. 119–134. New York: Guilford.

Orlin, L., and Davis, J. (1993). Assessment and intervention with drug and alcohol abusers in psychiatric settings. In *Clinical Work with Substance Abusing Clients*, ed. S. L. A. Straussner, pp. 50–68. New York: Guilford.

Prochaska, J. O., and DiClemente, C. C. (1982). Transtheoretical therapy: toward a more integrative model of change. *Psychotherapy* 19:276–288.

——— (1992). Stages of change in the modification of problem behaviors. In *Progress in Behavior Modification*, ed. M. Hudson, R. Eisler, and P. Miller, pp. 184–214. New York: Academic Press.

Prochaska, J., DiClemente, C., and Norcross, J. (1992). In search of how people change: applications to addictive behaviors. *American Psychologist* 47:1102–1114.

Scheffler, S. (1993). Substance abuse among the homeless. In *Clinical Work with Substance Abusing Clients*, ed. S. L. A. Straussner, pp. 291–329. New York: Guilford.

Spiegel, B. R. (1993). Twelve-Step programs as a treatment modality. In *Clinical Work with Substance Abusing Clients*, ed. S. L. A. Straussner, pp. 153–170. New York: Guilford.

Straussner, S. L. A. (1993). An introduction to clinical practice with substance abusing clients. In *Clinical Work with Substance Abusing Clients*, ed. S. L. A. Straussner, pp. 3–32. New York: Guilford.

——— (1994). The impact of alcohol and drug abuse on the American family. *Drug and Alcohol Review* 13:393–399.

———, ed. (in press). *Ethnocultural Factors in Addictions Treatment*. New York: Guilford.

Straussner, S. L. A., and Spiegel, B. R. (1996). An analysis of 12-step programs from a developmental perspective. *Clinical Social Work Journal* 24(3):299–305.

Straussner, S. L. A., and Zelvin, E., eds. (1997). *Gender and Addictions: Men and Women in Treatment.* Northvale, NJ: Jason Aronson.

Strum, D. P. (1993). AIDS and intravenous drug users: issues and treatment implications. In *Clinical Work with Substance Abusing Clients,* ed. S. L. A. Straussner, pp. 330–350. New York: Guilford.

U. S. Department of Health and Human Services (1997a). *Ninth special report to the U. S. Congress on alcohol and health.* Washington, DC: U.S. Government Printing Office.

———— (1997b). *50 strategies for substance abuse treatment.* Center for Substance Abuse Treatment, SAMHSA. Washington, DC: U. S. Government Printing Office.

———— (1998). *A cognitive-behavioral approach: treating cocaine addiction.* National Institute on Drug Abuse, NIH. Washington, DC: U. S. Government Printing Office.

CHAPTER SIX

Brief Treatment with Schizophrenic Patients*

HELLE THORNING AND ELLEN P. LUKENS

Schizophrenia is a long-term chronic illness with severe psychosocial implications for the patient and family members. It is characterized by pervasive impairment in social, cognitive, affective, and daily functioning. Recent advances in neuroscience have revolutionized the treatment options for patients who suffer from schizophrenia, and this has had a rippling effect in all of the biopsychosocial domains of the illness. With advances in biological treatments, particularly more effective antipsychotic medications, and in the psychosocial realm with more advanced psychoeducational and rehabilitative approaches, there are grounds for optimism and hope. Consequently, there are raised expectations that patients who suffer from schizophrenia can do better. Long gone are the days when patients were expected to sit endlessly and aimlessly in

*The authors gratefully acknowledge permission to reprint excerpts from "Since My First Break: An Update," by Daniel Frey.

hospitals and in outpatient day programs. The current emphasis is on rehabilitation and movement toward recovery. Patients are expected to move between different levels and systems of care: from inpatient to outpatient, from rehabilitation to recovery, and from illness to wellness. Munich (1997) describes this change as an evolution from the therapeutic community to a continuum of care, thereby replacing the traditional hospital setting with a range of ambulatory-based alternatives.

In witnessing and talking to individuals struggling with schizophrenia one is struck by the courage and strength needed to combat and deal with what can be terrifying symptoms (Thorning and Lukens 1996). Transitioning between settings, professionals, and raised expectations, coupled with the unpredictable nature of schizophrenia, makes for perplexing and stressful times. It is during these times that short-term interventions become so important.

In 1992, the Agency for Health Care Policy and Research and the National Institute of Mental Health funded the Schizophrenia Patient Outcomes Research Team (PORT) to develop and disseminate recommendations for the treatment of schizophrenia based on existing scientific research (Lehman and Steinwachs 1998a). The recommendations were based on extensive reviews of the treatment outcome literature, and the twenty-nine recommendations address medications, adjunctive pharmacotherapies, electroconvulsive therapy, psychological interventions, family interventions, vocational rehabilitation, and assertive community treatment/intensive case management. In addition, the PORT study also examined the current patterns of usual care.

These findings indicated that the current treatment practices fell considerably short of recommendations based on the best evidence found for treatment efficacy. The researchers found astonishing rates of inappropriate dosages of antipsychotic medications, untreated depression and side effects, inadequate family support, and minimal vocational rehabilitation and community-based treatment programs (Lehman and Steinwach 1998b). The difficulties in the translation of research findings into practice were quite evident. This all-encompassing study was embraced by both the American Psychiatric Association (APA) and the National Alliance for Mental Illness (NAMI), the powerful family and consumer-advocacy organization. Subsequently the PORT study's recommendations were adopted as "best practices" for the treatment of schizophrenia (American Psychiatric Association 1997, Flynn 1998). The recommendations clearly specify that schizophrenia is a complex illness requiring a host of different treatment modalities: medication, psychological treatment, family interventions, education, vocational rehabilitation, and a service system that integrates all of the above. In addition, the authors strongly urged the psychiatric community to find ways of implementing these recommendations.

Although there is a call for vast improvement of treatment for patients who suffer from schizophrenia, the other pull in today's political climate is the endorsement of managed care. The paradigm of managed care calls for more efficient, outcome-based treatments, with managed care companies primarily interested in reducing costs. In reality, "managed care" often simply means a reduction in visits that are authorized for reimbursement with specific guidelines for specific diagnosis (Dzieglewski 1996). As the United States nears the third decade of managed health care or "managed behavioral health," state mental health, policy, and managed care officials are looking at the problem of how to construct services for patients who suffer from long-term chronic and persistent mental illnesses (Hughes 1999). Because the managed care paradigm is applied primarily to a healthier population (Michels 1998), it can be problematic when dealing with a chronic illness with an uneven and episodic course, one that clearly calls for flexible and comprehensive pharmacologic, psychotherapeutic, psychosocial, and rehabilitative interventions that are, over time, integrated with different level of care systems.

In this current health care climate, it is difficult to foresee if and when psychological treatment for patients with schizophrenia will find its place in managed care. On the one hand it is reasonable to anticipate a trend toward less available individual psychotherapy for patients who suffer from schizophrenia, since these patients are covered by Medicaid

(Dinakar and Sobel 1999). On the other hand, Hogarty and colleagues (1997) posit that "in the late-twentieth-century America, the maintenance of patients with schizophrenia might increasingly become the responsibility of a single primary clinician as necessary mental health services become less available, inaccessible, or 'downsized' by policies of cost containment and managed care" (p. 1505).

Presently, many states are moving toward mandatory assignment for patients with schizophrenia to behavioral managed care companies (Dinakar and Sobel 1999). The Office of Mental Health in New York State is working on implementing a Special Needs Plan (SNP) in which there will be a shift of patients from fee for service Medicaid to capitated managed care plans. The goal is to create a system of individualized care for persons whose severity and duration of mental illness result in substantial functional disability. These individuals require mental health services on a more than incidental basis and need intensive mental health services that offer the expertise and array of services to better meet their complex needs (New York State Office of Mental Health, Section 1, Section 44401 of the Public Health Law[1]).

With the advent of managed care and practice guidelines, a short-term intervention model for patients who suffer from long-term chronic illnesses is necessary. Presently, the treatment system is in a state of flux. Clinicians, trained to treat patients on a long-term basis, are struggling to define what they do and how they can have a positive impact on patients' lives in a shorter period of time. Often clinicians report feeling inadequate in their attempt to help patients on a short basis, experiencing their work as not providing "real treatment." In actuality, clinicians often see patients and their families for relatively short periods of time. This chapter discusses how to focus one's treatment efforts, given the complicated variables associated with schizophrenia and the time limitations.

---

1. This document can be viewed on the State of New York's website: http://www.omh.state.ny.us.

CHALLENGES IN THE TREATMENT OF SCHIZOPHRENIA

Although there has been vast enhancement of the understanding of the illness, in many ways schizophrenia remains a mystery. Those struggling with it and those providing support or treatments are well aware of the suffering and the challenges it presents. The course of schizophrenia remains unpredictable, and the precise etiology and pathophysiology of schizophrenia continue to elude us (Amador and Ratakonda 1996). Schizophrenia is most likely a heterogeneous illness with multiple etiologies, and evidence of neurobiological abnormalities support a biological disease model for schizophrenia. The most current research consensus suggests that schizophrenia is likely a product of brain vulnerability based on factors that originate in neurobiological, genetic, prenatal, or perinatal abnormality. Psychosocial stressors combined with this vulnerability lead to dysfunctional changes that may emerge in late adolescence or early adult life and increase over time, interfering with the individual's neurochemistry, and psychological and interpersonal experiences (Munich 1997). The most viable models for understanding the disorder are multivariate and biopsychosocial in nature, and involve the interaction of diathesis and stress factors to explain the incident and course of the disorder (Freeman 1989, Nicholson and Neufeld 1992, Yank et al. 1993).

Schizophrenia carries a great deal of stigma for patients and their families. In many respects, it seems that stigma guides how priorities are set in the national health care debate and shapes resource allocation in schizophrenia research and treatment options.

DIAGNOSING SCHIZOPHRENIA

There are still many unresolved dilemmas regarding the diagnosis of schizophrenia. However, there have been some major leaps in establishing the reliability and validity of our diagnostic system (Brekke and Slade 1998). Establishing a valid diagnostic category requires a scientific and clinical consensus in five areas: (1) phenomenology (signs, symptoms, and traits), (2) etiology, (3) course, (4) prognosis, and (5) treatment responsiveness (Millon 1991).

Phenomenology (Signs, Symptoms, and Traits)

Schizophrenia is characterized by psychosis as the defining feature (APA 1994). Other disorders such as dementia of the Alzheimer's type or substance-induced delirium may present with psychotic symptoms, but not as defining features. The term *psychosis* has historically been defined in a number of different ways, but not one definition has achieved universal acceptance. Defined broadly, psychosis can be characterized by a dramatic disruption and impairment of reality testing. In schizophrenia this refers to one or more of the following psychotic symptoms: delusions, hallucinations, thought disorders, disorganized speech, disorganized or bizarre behavior, and catatonic behavior. It is important to note that *reality* is defined in modern diagnostic terms, and it is recognized that in some cultures certain experiences, such as hearing the voice of a dead relative, are considered not psychotic but rather normative (Brekke and Slade 1998).

Delusions are false beliefs that are well established and inaccessible to reality testing. Delusions can range from the bizarre ("An alien has taken over control of my internal organs") to the externally based ("I am under surveillance by the CIA"). Delusions that express loss of control over mind and body are generally considered to be bizarre. Ninety percent of people suffering from schizophrenia are, at some point in the course of the illness, delusional (Cutting 1990, 1995). Typically, delusions are fixed in the person's belief system and are not amenable to reasoned argument.

Hallucinations are sensory perceptions of something that is not there and can occur in all five sensory domains: auditory, visual, tactile, olfactory, gustatory. By far, auditory hallucinations are the most common and characteristic of schizophrenia. They are usually experienced as voices, either familiar or unfamiliar, but distinct from one's own thoughts, and can be experienced as either inside or outside of one's head. Hallucinations may also be a normal part of a religious experience, and thus have to be considered with the social context. Approximately 50 percent of people suffering from schizophrenia experience hallucinations (Cutting 1990, 1995).

Disorganized thinking (also called *formal thought disorder* or *loosening of associations*) has been argued by some to be the single most important feature of schizophrenia, but also the most problematic to identify due to the inherent difficulties in coming up with objective definitions. Disorganized thinking takes many forms in schizophrenia. One of the most common examples of disorganized speech is *derailment,* in which unrelated or weakly linked related topics are interwoven in sentences or phrases. Another form is referred to as *ideas of reference.* A young man hospitalized in a long-term facility came for his session. As he caught a glimpse of walking shoes in the corner of the office, he looked perplexed and asked, "You want to have sex with me?" The clinician's shoes took on special meaning and confused him as they gave him a message regarding her sexual intentions. *Bizarre behavior* is apparent in a number of ways such as odd dressing, sexually inappropriate behavior, or unpredictable swearing or yelling.

The symptoms described above are categorized as the positive symptoms. They represent behavior that is exaggerated or an overrepresentation of normal function. The positive and disorganized symptoms can have explosive and dangerous elements, in contrast to the negative symptoms, which include lack of motivation, social withdrawal, poor hygiene, and difficulty comprehending the contextual meanings of words. Patients often are confused by nonverbal cues and often fail to communicate intended meanings to others (Munich 1997). Included in the diagnosis are symptoms of flat affect, alogia (impoverished thinking), and avolition (inability to initiate and persist in goal-directed activity) (Brekke and Slade 1998). More than half the people who suffer from schizophrenia show evidence of one or more negative symptoms during the course of the illness (Cutting 1990, 1995).

The symptoms of schizophrenia are manifestations of impaired basic and social cognition coupled with poorly regulated affect, which produces certain challenges for the clinician. In addition, patients are often unaware of the full impact of their illness and symptoms, which makes it difficult to formulate mutual treatment goals.

Unawareness of Illness

Although the prominent clinical feature of *poor insight* is not a diagnostic criterion for schizophrenia per se, it is one of the most important clinical phenomena directly influencing treatment. In the last several years, investigators have increasingly turned their attention to poor insight as an important feature of the illness (Amador and Kronengold 1998).

Clinicians have noted the seeming indifference to or unawareness of illness displayed by many of these patients, who do not know that they are ill and thus behave in a way that is grossly inconsistent with their own best interest (Lysaker and Bell 1998). Likewise, persons suffering from schizophrenia have often expressed frustration and anger toward clinicians, family members, and friends, who, they believe, force them to take medication and comply with treatment for an illness they feel they don't have. As Amador and Kronengold (1998) point out, poor insight, defensive denial, inappropriate attitudes about illness, indifference reactions, evasion, and external attributions reflect important underlying conceptual differences and semantic preferences among patients. Poor insight can be understood as a defense mechanism protecting the person from self-assessment that might be overwhelmingly demoralizing, or defending against ambivalence and unconscious conflicts that are threatening (McFarlane and Lukens 1998). Conversely, it suggests a cognitive deficit model in which there is impairment in the psychological processes of inductive reasoning, linking thought to affect, and/or generating and monitoring plans and action. Recent studies of poor insight have included an examination of the relationship among neuropsychological deficits, particularly in the frontal lobe, which may account for at least some cases of poor insight (Amador and Kronengold 1998).

Neuropsychological models of impaired insight typically attribute the disturbance to any of a variety of core deficits in the processing of information. In neurological disorders resulting from injuries to the brain, such as agnosognosia, patients' inability to grasp the magnitude of their difficulties is quite similar to the unawareness of illness we see in schizophrenia. *Agnosognosia*, a term introduced in 1914 by Babinsky, as cited in Sackeim (1998), refers to a phenomenon commonly seen in patients following right-hemisphere lesion, where they deny paralysis on the left side of the body. In neurological disorders, as in schizophrenia, patients generally cannot be confronted with the discrepancies in their understanding. John Strauss (1998) details his interaction with a patient delusional about being pregnant. She was convinced of her pregnancy, as she had been pregnant before, and felt certain of what she was feeling. Concomitantly, she also reported being celibate for two years, and sleeping in her jeans to prevent anything from happening. "Ms. P. seems to be struggling with her feeling that she is pregnant (delusion) but also somewhat anchored in the other realities of her life that would indicate that she is not" (p. 355).

In summary, while the etiology remains unclear, insight is a complex and multidimensional phenomenon which includes the following:

1. Failure to recognize signs, symptoms, or disease (lack of awareness)
2. Misattribution of the source or cause of signs, symptoms, or disease
3. Failure to appreciate the implausibility of perceptual experiences or beliefs
4. Failure to derive appropriate cognitive representation despite recognition of pathological signs, symptoms, and disease
5. Inappropriate affective reactions despite recognition of pathological signs, symptoms, and disease
6. Inappropriate behavioral response (actions) despite recognition of pathological signs, symptoms, or disease (Sackeim 1998).

Schizophrenia and Medication

The treatment of a serious mental illness such as schizophrenia most commonly consists of an integrated approach of medication and psychosocial therapy. Although nonmedical clinicians cannot prescribe medication for schizophrenia, it is crucial to have a sufficient knowledge base to work effectively with the patient, family, and treating physician. This treatment arrangement is often referred to as a "split treatment," the objective of which is an open and productive interdisciplinary collaboration.

Advances in psychotropic medication for schizophrenia have been made at a steady pace since these drugs were first introduced following World War II. It is widely accepted, but still hypothetical, that persons with schizophrenia have a relatively high concentration of the neurotransmitter dopamine, or a high sensitivity at its receptor sites, in pathways extending into the cerebral cortex and limbic system (Bentley and Walsh 1998).

Psychotropic medication primarily works by modifying natural events that occur in the synapses of nerve cell pathways in specific areas of the brain, and subsequently affect brain functions by

1. altering presynaptic activity to prompt neurotransmitter release,
2. altering postsynaptic activity to affect receptor binding,
3. interfering with normal reuptake processes, and
4. altering the manufacture of receptors (Bentley and Walsh 1998).

For a useful review of advances in psychopharmacology see Opler (1996) and Bentley and Walsh (1998).

Medication adherence is an ongoing issue for most patients suffering from chronic illnesses. Besides the considerable and uncomfortable side effects that may act as a deterrent to taking medication, the meaning of taking medication also plays an enormous role in compliance. Understanding the patient's subjective experience with psychiatric medication, coupled with the meaning that taking medication has for that individual, is crucial to both the relationship development and the design of interventions strategies geared toward medication management (Sarti and Cournos 1990). Weight gain of up to sixty or seventy pounds is a prominent side effect of the medications, which are referred to as "atypical neuroleptics," and can create self-esteem and body-image problems for the patient. In addition, patients take on the look of a "mental patient" (slowed down mentally and motorically), which negatively impacts both the family and patient. A mother said, "Now she really looks as sick as she is." Since clinicians work most closely with the patient, family, and significant others, they can play a major role in medication management. The psychological treatment of schizophrenia necessarily must be closely linked with somatic treatments; hence, the clinician must work closely with the patient, family, and prescribing physician in the role of collaborator, consultant, educator, monitor, and advocate (Lukens and Thorning 1998).

PSYCHOTHERAPY RESEARCH FOR PATIENTS WHO SUFFER FROM SCHIZOPHRENIA

In the 1960s and 1970s a series of studies examined the role of psychotherapy in the outcome of schizophrenia (Brookhammer et al. 1966, Karon and VandenBos 1972, May and Tuma 1965). These studies were primarily based on now-outdated paradigms, such as psychotherapy versus medication, and supportive therapy versus investigative (exploratory) treatment (Fenton 1997). These studies were generally of limited quality and provided little confidence in the validity and reliability of the results (Penn and Mueser 1996, Thorning and Lukens 1996). Therapy research provided little or no evidence of the efficacy of individual therapy as the sole treatment for schizophrenia (Munich 1997). Coinciding with the outcome of these studies, patients began to be discharged to the community, and many patients were found to be noncompliant with medication when direct supervision was withdrawn. The responsibility for caring for and supervising the treatment of patients with schizophrenia shifted from an institutional setting to the family.

In 1995 Hogarty and his colleagues published the first psychotherapy study that took into consideration the biopsychosocial nature of schizophrenia. Hogarty and colleagues (1997) conceptualized a model for an individual therapy they called "personal therapy," which is a carefully described and tested model of individual intervention. Personal therapy is a disorder-relevant and disorder-specific intervention. The treatment (1) is theoretically grounded in the stress-vulnerability model, (2) considers stress-related affect dysregulation as contiguous to the exacerbation of symptoms, (3) is a sequential use of interventions based on the patient's stage of recovery, and (4) is flexible in the use and range of therapeutic techniques to accommodate both individual needs and deficits (Fenton 1997, Hogarty et al. 1995, 1997). The goal is to increase the patient's ability to recognize the stages and processes of recovery, and to develop and internalize coping strategies necessary to manage external stimuli.

DEFINING CORE TREATMENT CONCEPT
IN SHORT-TERM TREATMENT

At present, there is no cure for schizophrenia, but treatment is seen as a way to decrease morbidity as well as mortality (APA 1997). With the overall goal of affecting improvements in patients' quality of life, the objective of short-term treatment is to reduce the vulnerability to psychiatric decompensation by alleviating symptoms, reducing the risk for relapse, and improving psychosocial adjustment. This corresponds to the American Psychiatric Association's practice guidelines, which suggest that "the general goals of treatment are to decrease the frequency, severity, and psychosocial consequences of episodes and to maximize psychosocial functioning between episodes" (APA 1997, p. 7). Thus, integrated psychosocial interventions are needed to help prepare individuals to cope with their illness, strive for greater self-sufficiency, and achieve a better quality of life.

Although schizophrenia is a long-term illness, the clinician is rarely involved for the duration of the patient's illness or for the duration of the patient's lifetime. Rather, a clinician enters into a patient's life at a particular point in the course of the illness. The assessment and intervention strategies must therefore take a multidimensional view of the patient, including the type of illness, its duration, the phase of the illness (acute, subacute, or rehabilitative), the individual's developmental stage, and the family or community support system. For example, a 17-year-old boy, newly diagnosed and suffering with acute symptoms, faces the developmental task of separation-individuation. A 25-year-old woman, in a somewhat stable period of her illness, is faced with the developmental task of forming intimate relationships, having children, developing a career, and finding a place for herself in society (Erikson 1985). The interrelationship between the illness and the individual's developmental stage, warrants different interventions of varying intensities over the person's lifetime (Adler et al. 1995). In this context, designing interventions that specifically address the needs of patients at a particular time in their life, with attention given to specific symptomatology, facilitates identification of both short- and long-term goals.

At this time, there is no existing model for a brief intervention for schizophrenia; the proposed model of short-term treatment emphasizes the nodal points of the individual's life in the context of the person, family, and illness. The focus is not on dealing with the etiology of the illness but on a rehabilitative psychotherapy that stresses psychological management, which requires an integration of multiple, conjoint treatments (biological, social, and psychotherapeutic). Guze (1998) suggests that this approach to psychotherapy is similar to rehabilitative medicine, which is not focused on etiology but on helping the patient cope with a disability, thereby increasing self-confidence and skills leading to mastery and achievement. Both originate from the idea that people in pain and distress, and fearful of dealing with persistent disability, can benefit from exploring their subjective experiences with a clinician.

The emphasis of the short-term model is on understanding the moment in time, the critical time, when the clinician encounters the patient. For patients with schizophrenia, this often occurs during the times of transition in the phase of their illness, from psychotic to nonpsychotic, or vice versa. This, is turn, leads to transitions in situational settings, from inpatient to outpatient care facilities or the reverse. The role of the clinician is to connect patients with social supports in all areas of their life. Consequently, a significant portion of the treatment strategy is geared toward an integration of various interventions, such as psychopharmacology, as well as occupational, vocational, recreational, and family therapy. For this to be successful, fruitful collaboration with clinicians from other disciplines is essential.

Short-term treatment of patients with schizophrenia follows many of the same elements as described in the brief treatment of other populations (Budman 1981, Goldstein and Noonan 1999). Historically, brief treatment for schizophrenics was considered inappropriate, due to their fragility and their inability to tolerate the abrupt termination of the treatment relationship. Yet, as treatments of patients became more fragmented and time-limited, it became necessary to develop a short-term model that addresses the multifaceted needs of the schizophrenia patient.

Patient selection, brevity, therapy focus, and therapist activity are the parameters that distinguish short-term treatment (Dzieglewski 1996, Groves 1996). In the model presented here, brevity, focus, and therapist activity are central components, but patients are not excluded due to severity of symptoms. As Hogarty and colleagues (1995) suggest, interventions are instead tailored specifically to the disorder at *all phases* of the illness.

Ten core elements of short-term integrated treatment, as outlined by Goldstein and Noonan (1999), can also be applied to short-term work with patients who suffer from schizophrenia:

The Conscious Use of Time

With a chronic illness such as schizophrenia, the clinician's conscious use of time and realistic goal setting are particularly essential, as the patient's underlying problems most likely will not resolve in the time period allotted. Additionally, the limitations of the care setting will further guide the shape and pace of the intervention.

A High Level of Activity on the Part of the Clinician

Patients with schizophrenia are often isolated from others and have trouble forming attachments. The clinician must actively engage patients and their system of support, and then identify the scope of the interventions, set goals, and facilitate collaboration between family members and other clinicians involved. Goldstein and Noonan (1999) stress the importance of educating patients about the treatment process through ongoing explanations of the nature of the interventive process and explorations of their reaction to the treatment. With schizophrenia, therapeutic activity is further guided by the stage of the illness. For example, in the acute phase of the illness, patients are more likely to be hospitalized and the initial emphasis is often on psychiatric stabilization. The non-medical clinician at this point focuses on creating a safe haven for the patient as well as facilitating the adjustment of the family or significant others to the trauma of having a relative hospitalized. Orientation to the hospital setting and staff and to the treatment offered is a crucial element in creating an environment in which both the patient and the family can begin the process of healing. As the patient stabilizes, the clinician moves to address the patient's personality, stressors and vulnerabilities, social and living supports, economic resources, and family availability and level of engagement (Munich 1997).

Quick Engagement

Engagement is dictated by the phase of the illness. For example, engagement during the acute phase of illness is characterized by firmness and directness, but also carried out with tact and sensitivity. An acute episode or decompensation is a devastating experience for the patient. Patients may have been engaged in behavior that has had negative impact on their social relations. Their anxiety is high, and inevitably there is an assault on self-esteem; in the case of a chronic patient who is relapsing, there is a sense of failure (Munich 1997).

In outpatient settings the patient's underlying symptomatology can create certain challenges for the clinician. Patients struggling with paranoia can have difficulty engaging with a new clinician due to fear and lack of trust. Unaware of their illness, patients may feel that treatment is unnecessary, stating "I am not ill." Understanding the patient's subjective experience and attributions of the illness is an important component in establishing a fruitful treatment relationship.

Rapid Assessment—A System-Oriented Biopsychosocial Inquiry

Rapid assessment is the cornerstone of short-term treatment. A comprehensive multiaxis assessment takes into consideration the phase of the illness, the developmental stage of the patient, and the family life-cycle phase. Through the assessment period, the nodal points for interventions are identified. For example, Daniel Frey, 23 years old, the managing editor for *New York City Voices*, writes about the process of recovering from schizophrenia:

> It is really hard to live with this disease even when it is being managed by medications because one of its main symptoms is "delusion." Often I need to question what is real or delusional. I was waiting on the street for a bus in the Bronx one night, not too late at night—about 9:30 P.M. And there was a lot of activity in the area. But the feeling of being the only white kid on the street suddenly came over me, making me feel alone and vulnerable, maybe even a target. I became uncomfortable. On the bus I thought a man was looking at me with angry eyes. I later asked myself: "Is it me or is it the disease?" [Frey 1999, p. 3]

Frey is trying to understand his perceptions of his surroundings, given that his view of the world has been distorted dramatically during the acute phase of his illness. He is trying to put his subjective experience of the world into a meaningful cohesive story that can help him assess his own behavior and feelings. In this transitional phase from psychosis to nonpsychosis, this is not an easy task.

John Rolland (1988, 1994) created a psychosocial typology for the purpose of examining the relationship between the individual dynamics, the family, and the illness. Rolland's typology charts the illness on three dimensions: (1) illness type, with respect to the onset, course, outcome, and degree of incapacitation; (2) time phase of the illness, that is, acute or chronic; and (3) universal and illness-specific components of family functioning, such as the family's illness belief system and transgenerational history of illness and loss. We suggest including the developmental tasks of the patient as well. Often the onset of illness occurs in late adolescence or in early adulthood and may span a lifetime. Adler and colleagues (1995) identify three main stages of the adult life cycle, each accompanied by a critical transition: early adulthood (ages 17 to 39), middle adulthood (ages 40 to 65), and the final stage of adulthood (from age 60 and on, overlapping with the transition that occurs in middle adulthood between ages 60 and 65).

For patients who are in their late adolescence or early adult years when they first become ill, the developmental tasks of separation-individuation are illustrated in Daniel Frey's account of an interaction with his family:

Since I have been diagnosed with this illness my parents want to have more control over my life than I want them to have. They don't really trust that I am taking my medication after I do something that they perceive as irrational. If they panic, I'm not comfortable with the idea that they can put me away in the hospital. Why should I suffer from their insecurities? . . . Recently I had some back pains that kept me up for hours when I needed to sleep. I thought that getting some fresh air might help. The persistent back pain made me irritable, which is why I did not bother telling my father that I was going for a walk at 3 o'clock in the morning. I just left the house with the door slamming behind me. I hate having to tell my father everything I am about to do, but this is the pattern I have gotten into these past months since my first break. When I got home about a half-hour later, my father was upset and grilled me with questions I did not want to answer. I just wanted to be left alone with my back pain. [Frey 1999, p. 3]

Frey describes the dilemma he and his family are facing. Rolland's (1994) topology facilitates an interactional thinking about the relationships between the illness type, the phase of the illness, and family functioning (Lefley 1996).

Partialization and Focusing

As the points for intervention have been identified, the clinician and patient work together on a stepwise plan to accomplish the goals. Partializing and focusing on measurable objectives allow patients to be less overwhelmed by the many difficulties they will likely encounter. Schizophrenia often affects patients' cognitive abilities. Identifying mutual objectives and goals can be challenging, as patients may be unaware of their illness. As patients begin to develop realistic plans, they are faced with the resulting impact of the illness. A process of mourning can ensue as they identify what they have lost as a result of their illness. For example, a young woman who was majoring in psychology and had dreams of becoming a child psychologist must come to terms with the fact that she is no longer able to sit in a classroom, study, or engage in student activities the way she could prior to the onset of her illness. Due to persistent hallucinations and thought disturbances, she must now consider volunteering in a thrift shop, something that requires a dramatic shift in her thinking and her sense of self. The goal of the clinician is to be sensitive to the patient's experience as plans for recovery are being formulated.

Flexibility of Approach and Technical Interventions

Psychological disruption has a profound impact on the patient's sense of self, often leading to eruption of regressive manifestations such as primary-process thinking. Nonetheless, as we consider the neurobiological evidence, it is likely that the manifestation of psychosis has no counterpart in normal development. The symptoms manifested in adult schizophrenia are most likely caused by a biological disease process, and therefore cannot be considered as evidence of defenses or psychological deficits (Willick 1990). Given such evidence, short-term therapy must be rehabilitative and must emphasize psychological management.

In the short-term integrative treatment model (Goldstein and Noonan 1999), the intervention is supportive in nature and derived from an ego-oriented point of view. Focus is on discovering and supporting ego strengths and on recognizing signs of relapse. The clinician strives to be reality based; uses straightforward, conversational language; is interactive and educational; underscores the identification of environmental stressors; and helps to solve problems in living. In this vein, the clinician provides a holding environment for patients as they move through critical periods of transition.

Helping patients adopt a hopeful stance is an important component of short-term integrative treatment. Coming to terms is not a passive acceptance of the status quo, but an active stance of identifying options and opportunities for change, and beginning to reestablish a sense of equilibrium (Lukens and Thorning 1998). The narrative models of treatment facilitate this process.

The process of rediscovering and reconstructing an enduring sense of the self as an active and responsible agent provides the patient with a crucial source of improvement. Four basic aspects of the recovery process that may be seen as involving the rediscovery, reconstruction, and utilization of a functional self have been identified through qualitative interviews with persons struggling to recover from prolonged psychiatric disorders (Davidson and Strauss 1992): (1) discovering the possibility of a functional sense of self; (2) taking stock of the strengths and weaknesses of the self and assessing possibilities for change; (3) putting into action some aspects of the self and integrating the results of these actions as reflecting one's actual capabilities; (4) using an enhanced sense of self to provide a refuge from illness from which to battle symptoms. The narrative model is based on a constructivist theory, which stresses strengths, and on social constructionism, with its emphasis on personal history, cultural perspective, and diversity in the personal experience of the illness (Crowger 1994).

Psychoeducation is another powerful strength-based treatment approach emphasizing the teaching of information and skills patients need to cope and manage the illness, as well as advocating for the best possible treatment options (Lukens et al. 1999). The content includes information on epidemiology, diagnosis, medications and their side effects, and the course and outcome of schizophrenia. Psychoeducation is distinguished from a purely educational approach in that it is conducted in the context of treatment, where the pacing and timing of the educational intervention is guided by the clinician (Lukens and Thorning 1998, Lukens et al. 1999). Models that incorporate the patient as an active treatment collaborator and participant in setting the stage for rehabilitation elicit and foster a more functional sense of self and can contribute positively to improvement.

Differential Use of the Patient–Clinician Relationship

Patients with schizophrenia often exhibit a certain inwardness, intensity, and instability in relating to others. The clinician must interact with the patient in different ways, depending on the patient's situation. For instance, one might use a straightforward approach while educating the patient about the illness.

Emphasis on Patient Strengths and Abilities

The emphasis is on identifying the patient's strengths and abilities, with the goal of instilling a sense of mastery and control over a chaotic and overwhelming illness. The narrative and psychoeducational approaches hence provide a vehicle for education, empowerment, and change (Lukens and Thorning 1998).

Collaboration, Linkage, and Advocacy

The clinician rarely works in isolation with a patient, but rather in the context of an interdisciplinary team. Since the treatment system is fragmented, the need for a collaborative approach with other clinicians and service systems is of paramount importance. Forming a partnership with the patient's family as equal participants in the treatment further enhances the possibilities of successful treatment. Psychoeducation has been particularly successful when conducted in multiple family groups, where families meet together with other families. In addition to increasing the knowledge base of patients and families about mental illness, it also serves the important function of decreasing isolation and stigma (McFarlane et al. 1995). For patients with schizophrenia who are unable to work, connecting them to appropriate entitlements and advocating for the best treatment options are important components of short-term treatment.

Acceptance of Limitations of Treatment

Integral to brief treatment is the notion of a clearly specified end point. For patients with schizophrenia, treatment termination with a specific clinician may be connected to discharge from one care setting to another. As such, termination of the therapeutic relationship indicates either improvement or decline in the patient's level of functioning. Although the treatment has been defined as short-term from the beginning, termination of the relationship can also elicit strong feelings for the clinician, who may feel guilty for "rejecting" or "abandoning" the patient, or simply sad for having lost a gratifying and intense relationship. The clinician may also be mourning the fact that he or she is no longer needed as an object for the patient (Messer and Warren 1995).

The ending of the treatment, "working through termination," has been described in the literature as a very painful event for the patient, one that can engender strong emotions of grief, loss, anger, and abandonment. However, this has not been supported by research, which shows that patients may instead feel a sense of accomplishment and success as they approach the end of treatment. Groves (1996) suggests that patients return for multiple courses of mental health treatment over a life span. The norm for patients with a chronic mental illness is to encounter stressful times in the life cycle, face certain developmental tasks, and be in treatment numerous times with various therapists.

> Under the best of conditions, relationships with professionals other than psychotherapists are not regarded as terminating at all. They are seen as intermittent. For example, the accountant, lawyer, family doctor, or barber may have a permanent relationship with clients and perhaps their families, although the actual face to face contact occurs only for specific tasks or problems. Such a tie may last a lifetime. [Rabkin 1977, p. 211]

In summary, brief interventions should be constructed to attend to the chief complaint presented by the patient, define the nodal point in the biopsychosocial context, and utilize interventions that help the patient through a particular critical time. The following case presentation illustrates the principles of short-term treatment. The intervention consists of three months of treatment, two sessions per week, with a woman recently discharged from an inpatient psychiatric hospital.

TREATMENT ILLUSTRATION

Ann is a 37-year-old, white single unemployed college graduate of an upper-middle-class background and the older of two sisters. Since her late teens, she has struggled with psychiatric problems. In college she performed at a very high academic level and achieved multiple awards and honors. She was considered the intellectual in the family and aspired to become an academician. While in high school, she was extremely driven by her academic pursuits, which gradually extended to controlling her eating and exercising behaviors. In her second year of college, she suffered from anorexia nervosa which led to her first hospitalization. Upon discharge and returning to school, she continued to do well academically, but her eating disorder persisted.

Ann's parents divorced when she was in her mid-teens, and both parents have since remarried. Her father has remained in close contact with her over the years, while her mother, unable to face Ann's illness, withdrew and now sees her only intermittently. For most of her adult life Ann has been estranged from her sister. For the last five years Ann has lived with her boyfriend, Rick, in an apartment paid for by her father. Her boyfriend also has psychiatric difficulties, but the two of them have developed a mutual relationship of reciprocity and support. Ann's psychiatric history has been characterized by multiple hospitalizations, day programs, and therapists. Over the years her illness has been marked by symptoms of hallucinations, thought disorder (particularly ideas of reference), decline in cognitive abilities, and loss of motivation. She presents with a mixed picture of positive and negative symptoms. Her disappointment in herself has left her with constant suicidal ideation (although she always brings herself to the hospital if she fears that she will attempt suicide). She has been unable to define herself in relationship to her illness, and her main modus operandi is casting blame on her parents for causing her illness, on her therapists for not curing her, and on the treatment system for being insensitive to her needs. At times this can take on a paranoid flavor. Furthermore, she experiences intense anger, frustration, and disappointment because she has not been able to live the life she had hoped for.

Ann was referred for outpatient short-term treatment upon discharge from her seventh hospitalization. It was deemed by the inpatient clinical staff that she could benefit from individual psychotherapy in the transitional phase from inpatient hospitalization to community living. The stated objectives for the referral were (1) to solidify the gains achieved during hospitalization with regard to stabilizing medication, (2) to receive support as she emerged from terrifying psychotic symptoms, and (3) to connect with a broader social network in the community. The overall goal was for Ann to become more at ease with herself and her disability, freeing her to identify her strengths.

Although Ann had symptoms consistent with the diagnosis of schizophrenia for some years, this was the first hospitalization where schizophrenia was the final diagnosis. In addition, this was also the first time that Ann was treated with a new atypical neuroleptic medication, clozapine. Since she had been on the new medication, her weight had rapidly increased by fifty pounds. In addition, her attendance to personal hygiene declined. This seemed to be connected with her general inattentiveness, lack of motivation, and a general feeling of malaise. The treatment was designed to consist of two sessions per week for approximately three months. In addition, Ann was returning to a psychiatrist for psychopharmacological treatment. Previously, she had attended many of the day-treatment programs in her community, but at this time refused to participate.

The course of treatment for the short-term model will be discussed in three phases. Each phase emphasizes different aspects of the treatment as Ann moved through the intervention.

The Beginning Phase: Adjusting to Transition

Adjusting to the transition from hospital to community parallels Ann's transition from an acute psychosis to a subpsychosis. Reemerging into reality is complicated, as she has to learn to watch for stimulation that can trigger psychosis. At this time, after having been through similar episodes, she is now more aware of the impact that schizophrenia has had on her life. Developmentally she is out of sync with her peers. She is struggling with issues of separation-individuation and attempting to define issues of independence, given the fact that she still needs her family's support. At the same time she is also facing the developmental tasks of early adulthood. Sadly, her biological clock is ticking without allowance for her illness, and she has to make a decision about having a child.

Ann arrived for her third appointment and immediately began talking about having seen several babies with their mothers on the way to my office.

Ann: It really makes me feel like I want to have children. I see them, and I wonder how it would be, you know, to be a mother. But I was asleep all day, I didn't even get out of bed until my appointment with you. I feel shaky and depressed. How could I ever think about having a baby?

Clinician: Thinking about having children is something a lot of women your age think about.

Ann: Yes, I know. But they can. I mean it wouldn't be good if I did. I'm not able to take care of myself. But I think I would have been a good mother.

Clinician: What would it have been like, do you think?

Ann: I think perhaps I would have stayed home. I would read a lot to them, perhaps go to the park. But I can't. I'm not well.

Clinician: Many factors are weighed when making a decision about having a child or not. It's not an easy thing in life.

Ann: Yes, but it sometimes feels like I'm the only woman who doesn't have children. . . . But I can't have a child. I can't even take care of myself. How can I take care of a baby? Babies need a lot of care.

Clinician: Your face looks sad now. Does it make you feel sad to think about this?

Ann: Yes, it makes me sad. (She is silent for a long time.)

Clinician: What are you thinking about?

Ann: I'm thinking about what I should have for dinner. I can't make up my mind. I'm eating too much and not feeling like exercising. I'm getting so fat.

Clinician: Perhaps thinking about not having children makes you feel sad. Maybe also sad about having gained weight from being on your new medication—all of which reminds you of your illness and how it has affected your life.

Ann: Ever since I was a little girl I wanted to have children. I like children. I used to babysit a lot. Even when I was getting sick again and in the middle of my third breakdown, I was able to babysit. It was about the only thing I could do. I would sit with John and watch him play. I would pretend to be his mother. When he went to sleep, I would have all these horrible thoughts in my mind, I could barely function.

But I did take care of him for a while. Then one day, I called the parents and told them that I had to go to the hospital. I miss John a lot. I relate better to kids.

Ann continued to reminisce about her relationship with John. The clinician listened to the painful mourning process, the changed course of her life, and her struggles to come to terms with her illness. Appropriate to Ann's developmental phase, her maternal feelings have reemerged after a period of being grossly psychotic. Her ability to see more clearly how her illness has changed her life is a sign of progress, yet it is also a precarious stage. As patients with schizophrenia come out of the state of psychosis and reenter reality, the pain of what they have lost due to the illness can be so powerful that it leads to devastating feelings of despair. This transition clearly is a critical time during which the clinician must be able to bear witness to the pain of lost opportunities experienced by the patient and at the same time closely monitor the patient's ability to tolerate this process. Harkavy-Friedman and Nelson (1997) summarized the literature on suicidal risks in patients suffering from schizophrenia and identified two groups: those with poor premorbid functioning, where an increase in suicidal risk was seen as related to impulsiveness and a poor ability to problem-solve; and those who were aware that their previous expectations for the future were less likely to be met, leading to demoralization and hopelessness. Suicidal ideation was one of Ann's most disturbing feelings. Thus, the clinician adopted a stance of frequent monitoring of suicidality and exploration of what thoughts triggered the suicidal ideations. Ann was very clear that she wanted to live, and complied with a working contract that involved her either contacting the clinician or presenting herself to the hospital. Toward the end of the beginning phase, Ann moved from actively mourning toward beginning to think about her future goals.

Ann: I want to feel better soon, so that I can have children. I also need a husband I can really love. Rick is okay for when I'm sick, but he's not the kind of guy I want to marry.

Clinician: I know that you're anxious to get on with your life, and that is precisely what we will be working on together for the next couple of months. This is an important time in your life, and we will be working on a plan for you to get back on your feet after your hospitalization. What do you think would be helpful?

Ann: I want to marry someone and get back to acting.

Clinician: Those are great goals. Recovering from being ill may take some time and some adjustment, so we should think about the smaller steps you can take to get there.

Ann: Yes, I feel shaky. I'm still feeling that I can be overpowered by this thing that you call psychosis. It's like I'm walking next to a tidal wave that can overpower me at any time. It seems like I have no control. I'm on the edge all the time.

Clinician: It's important that we think together about what we can do to make you feel in charge of your life again.

The clinician here acknowledges Ann's feeling of urgency, of wanting to get better and catch up developmentally. The overall goal is defined, and the clinician and the patient are beginning to partialize the tasks at hand. At the same time the patient is trying to manage her symptoms.

Middle Phase: Building the Social Network

During this phase, the main task is to facilitate the expansion of the patient's social network in order to decrease isolation and to help her rejoin the world. As Ann already had been involved with traditional day programs, the clinician attempted to put together an alternative program driven by Ann's particular interest. Taking risks was a scary proposition, as too many stimuli brought on psychotic symptoms. Ann feared that psychosis was the contributing factor to staying at home, often in bed.

At the time of her tenth appointment, Ann called the clinician indicating that she wasn't coming in for her session. Difficulty in making it to the office was indicative of her difficulties in moving on in her recovery process. She was also easily overwhelmed and overstimulated by her environment. With time of the essence and moving from a flexible stance, the clinician proceeded with a phone session. As the objective for this phase was to help Ann become more involved outside of her house, identifying her interests and strengths became the main focus. However, suggestions from others were often met with negativity. It became clear that exposure to new situations and to stimuli made her feel "invaded" and psychotic.

Ann: I can't come in today, I just feel so bad.
Clinician: Bad in what way?
Ann: I can't explain it. I'm so tired I can't leave the house.
Clinician: Are you feeling suicidal?
Ann: I guess. But I'm not feeling that now.
Clinician: It seemed that you were able to manage the feelings and didn't need to have to call me.
Ann: No, I think that after I have slept all day I don't feel suicidal.

After some exploration of the types of stressors she might have encountered, she said that watching TV the evening before had upset her.

Clinician: Tell me more about what happened last night when you were watching TV.
Ann: Rick was sitting in the living room, and we both like this one show about the woman lawyer. I had to watch the TV from the other room last night, I couldn't be in the same room. It was too much. The TV was very loud. Still, after we turned the TV off, I couldn't fall asleep. I was just lying there, thinking about the people in the show wondering about why they did what they did.
Clinician: It sounds like there were a lot of things going on that made it difficult for you while you were watching TV and later when you were trying to sleep. You made a good decision for yourself in putting some distance between the stimulation of the TV and yourself. Could you have talked to Rick about turning down the volume?

Ann: I didn't think of it. I know that he likes the TV to be loud. I also thought that it's strange that I can't have it loud. That is so weird.

Clinician: It's not weird. Sometimes a lot of noise put together with a lot of visual stuff can be overwhelming. Being able to regulate how much you're exposed to is important for you. Do you think that Rick would be receptive to your asking to turn down the volume?

Ann: Oh, yeah. He would be good about that. But still it was hard to let go of the story.

Clinician: Was there something in particular that disturbed you?

Ann: I was watching the show with the woman lawyer and in the middle of the scene she was seeing things, you know the little naked man.

Clinician: Did it seem like she was hallucinating? That must have been kind of frightening.

Ann: Yes, it got me upset, you know, thinking of when I was ill and seeing things.

Clinician: It's not surprising that it was upsetting for you to see the actress on TV have hallucinations like you did. You were reminded of something quite terrible that happened to you.

Ann: Yes, and I am always afraid of that happening again.

Clinician: When you feel afraid like that you start feeling suicidal.

Ann continued to talk at length about what being psychotic is like for her. Retreating to her apartment and to her bed is her way of keeping herself safe. Understanding that she is not just lazy but protecting herself was helpful for her self-esteem. Gaining detailed information about her subjective experience allowed the clinician to gain useful understanding that can guide both clinician and patient to address a particular obstacle and, in Ann's situation, offset suicidal ideation.

Ann was then able to recount some of her experiences during her psychotic episodes. This was the beginning of her being able to put together a sequence of events that had been extremely frightening during her hospitalization. This narrative approach was useful for her and helped put together her story. In addition, discussing her home situation in such detail allowed us to explore her environment and possible areas of overstimulation that were getting in her way.

Clinician: You worked very hard at making sure that you protect yourself. Like putting some distance between you and the TV. Is there anything else you can do to have a bit more of a buffer zone?
Ann: I could turn the volume down, although my boyfriend likes the TV to be loud. I could go into the other room and close the door and read.
Clinician: Those are great suggestions. You've been home from the hospital only a short time, and you may still be quite sensitive to noise and overstimulated from the shows that you watch on TV. It's not so uncommon that when you first leave the hospital you sleep more. Perhaps you need to give yourself some more time to unwind before you can expect to fall asleep. I know that you like the shows late at night. But they probably also stimulate your mind, which can make it difficult to fall asleep.

For patients transitioning from a psychotic state, sleep can serve as a buffer and a protective measure against overstimulation. Identifying sleeping as a way that Ann is dealing with her sensitivity to stimulation helped her identify other ways of taking control of her environment and illness. By self-moderating her exposure to stimulation, she was able to begin to regulate her movements, which enabled her to feel more comfortable in risking new involvements. In a psychoeducational manner the clinician was able to use the stress-diathesis model to help Ann understand that either too much or too little stress can cause difficulties. Although sleeping is a helpful tool for gaining control after too much stimulation, too much sleep can cause unnecessary boredom and isolation from others.

In this middle phase of Ann's treatment, various groups in the community were identified and explored, such as an alternative program and a self-help group for patients recovering from schizophrenia. Her involvement in the self-help group enabled her to find out about a theater group. Although she was not ready to join, she was able to attend several of the group's performances, which provided her with the possibility of joining at a later date.

With permission from the patient, the clinician also reached out to the patient's father. Like the patient, he too had a very difficult time coming to terms with his daughter's illness, and both agreed to join a multiple family group. This proved to be extremely beneficial for the patient and her father, as they together began to develop a common language for how to understand Ann's illness. Although this group was a time-limited one, the connections with other families and the family advocacy group, National Alliance for Mental Illness (NAMI), were beneficial.

Closing Phase: Launching

In this final phase of the treatment, Ann began to explore various options and interests. An avid reader when not ill, Ann began to read again. She allowed herself to read nonfiction books and was able to achieve a sense of accomplishment about her increased ability to concentrate. Helping her to understand the severity of the trauma of her illness made her more forgiving of herself for not having accomplished the dreams of her adolescence. This allowed her to pursue other avenues. For example, in a late session, after a friend gave Ann a computer, she actively began to seek out computer training programs.

Ann: I went to the computer program yesterday. I like the atmosphere there, although it was busy, it was like being in school again. But today, I slept all day—just couldn't get out of bed.
Clinician: I'm glad to hear that you went. We know that you sleep more after you try something new.
Ann: Yes, and I didn't feel sick. I felt okay. But I don't know if I can take the course now. I wish I could.
Clinician: It may take you some time to find what you like. Right now you're trying new things, seeing what and how much you can deal with.

The fact that you slept more today doesn't mean that you will not be able to do something again tomorrow. Plus, you were able to come in to see me.

Ann was able to discuss how she was feeling about reentering the world.

Ann: I feel like I've been away for a long time, and everything has moved away from me. I used to be involved with the latest. I was a feminist and very politically involved. Now everything has to do with computers and I don't know anything. I have so much to catch up with. Everyone is ahead of me.

Clinician: Being ill and spending time in hospitals is like being away. In a sense you're reacclimating yourself and you need to take one day at time.

Ann: Yes, that's what we discussed at the group the other night. And at the family meeting my father also heard from the other parents that you need patience recovering from mental illness. I guess we both needed to hear that.

Although at the onset of her short-term treatment Ann had set long-term goals for herself of marriage and returning to her acting career, she had been able to partialize and focus on some key obstacles to building her social network. This was an important move toward recovery.

Although the three-month time frame for treatment was brought up throughout the treatment, termination was actively worked on for the last four to six sessions. As Ann was better able to regulate stimuli and establish buffer zones, she was also able to move into outside activities. Her attachment to the multiple family and the self-help groups grew. In addition, her interest in attending the computer training program became more solidified and she worked on a plan to register. Counting the sessions left, Ann became more critical of the clinician, stating that therapy had not helped her at all. As Mann (1996) suggests, it is necessary for the clinician to deal directly with the patient's reaction to termination to ensure that the termination facilitates a process of maturation and not regression. Not surprisingly, the patient expressed a great deal of ambivalence regarding termination, fearing that leaving the clinician would trigger regression. However, underscoring the gains the patient had made in the relatively short period of time allowed her to experience a new sense of accomplishment, and as such, a successful ending of the treatment. In addition, the ending of this treatment accentuated the fact that she was moving forward in the process toward recovery.

CONCLUSION

We have described some of the challenges in working with patients who suffer from a long-term illness such as schizophrenia and who are facing critical times in their lives. For patients whose lives have been impacted in so many ways because of the symptoms of the illness, addressing the everyday problems in living from a strengths-based perspective can yield optimism and hope. Clinicians must use the diversity of their skills and flexibility to treat this illness and be sensitive to the needs of this population, given the changing health care environment.

Today there is a need to establish well-described and well-researched brief interventions for patients with schizophrenia, as evidenced-based treatment clearly should be the norm for clinical practice. The model described here is an attempt to develop a short-term treatment relevant to today's practice arena.

REFERENCES

Adler, D. A., Pajer, K., Ellison, J. M., et al. (1995). Schizophrenia and the lifecycle. *Community Mental Health Journal* 31:249–262.

Amador, X. F., and Kronengold, H. (1998). The description and meaning of insight in psychosis. In *Insight and Psychosis*, ed. X. F. Amador and A. S. David, pp. 15–33. New York: Oxford University Press.

Amador, X. F., and Ratakonda, S. (1996). The diagnosis of schizophrenia: past, present and future. In *Schizophrenia: New Directions for Clinical Research and Treatment*, ed. C. A. Kaufman and J. M. Gorman, pp. 5–17. Larchmont, NY: Mary Ann Liebert.

American Psychiatric Association. (1994). *Diagnostic and Statistical Manual of Mental Disorders*, 4th ed. Washington, DC: Author.

——— (1997). Practice guidelines for the treatment of patients with schizophrenia. *American Journal of Psychiatry* 154:1–63.

Bentley, K. J., and Walsh, J. (1998). Advances in psychopharmacology and psychosocial aspects of medication management: a review for social workers. In *Advances in Mental Health Research: Implications for Practice*, ed. J. B. W. Williams and K. Ell, pp. 309–342. Washington, DC: NASW.

Brekke, J. S., and Slade, E. S., eds. (1998). *Schizophrenia*. Washington, DC: NASW.

Brookhammer, R. S., Meyer, R. W., Schober, C. C., and Piotrowski, A. Z. (1966). A five year follow-up study of schizophrenics treated by Rosen's "direct analysis" compared with controls. *American Journal of Psychiatry* 123:602–604.

Budman, S. H. (1981). Looking toward the future. In *Forms of Brief Therapy*, ed. S. H. Budman, pp. 461–466. New York: Guilford.

Crowger, C. (1994). Assessing client's strengths: clinical assessment for client empowerment. *Social Work* 39:262–268.

Cutting, J. (1990). *The Right Cerebral Hemisphere and Psychiatric Disorders*. New York: Oxford University Press.

——— (1995). Descriptive psychopathology. In *Schizophrenia*, ed. S. R. Hirsh and D. R. Weinberger, pp. 15–27. Oxford, England: Blackwell Science.

Davidson, L., and Strauss, J. S. (1992). Sense of self in recovery from severe mental illness. *British Journal of Medical Psychology* 65:131–145.

Dinakar, H. S., and Sobel, R. N. (1999). Managed care and psychotherapy for schizophrenia. *American Journal of Psychiatry* 152(2):336–337.

Dzieglewski, S. F. (1996). Managed care principles: the need for social work in the health care environment. *Crisis Intervention and Time-Limited Treatment* 3:97–110.

Erikson, E. (1985). *Childhood and Society.* New York: Norton.

Fenton, W. (1997). We can talk: individual psychotherapy for schizophrenia. *American Journal of Psychiatry* 154(11):1493–1495.

Flynn, L. M. (1998). Commentary. *Schizophrenia Bulletin* 24(1):30.

Freeman, H. (1989). Relationship of schizophrenia to the environment. *British Journal of Psychiatry* 155(suppl 5):90–99.

Frey, D. (1999). Since my first break: an update. *New York City Voices: A Consumer Journal for Mental Health Advocacy* 5(3):3.

Goldstein E. G., and Noonan, M. (1999). *Short-Term Treatment and Social Work Practice: An Integrative Perspective.* New York: Free Press.

Groves, J. E. (1996). Introduction: four "essences" of short-term therapy: brevity, focus, activity, selectivity. In *Essential Papers on Short-Term Dynamic Therapy,* ed. J. E. Groves, pp. 1–27. New York: New York University Press.

Guze, S. B. (1998). Psychotherapy and managed care. *Archives of General Psychiatry* 55:561–562.

Harkavy-Friedman, J. M., and Nelson, E. A. (1997). Assessment and intervention for the suicidal patient with schizophrenia. *Psychiatric Quarterly* 68(4):361–375.

Hogarty, G. E., Kornblith, S. J., Greenwald, D., et al. (1995). Personal therapy: a disorder-relevant psychotherapy for schizophrenia. *Schizophrenia Bulletin* 21(3):379–393.

——— (1997). Three-year trials of personal therapy among schizophrenia patients living with or independent of family, I: description of study and effects of relapse rates. *American Journal of Psychiatry* 154(11):1504–1513.

Hughes, W. C. (1999). Managed care, meet community support: ten reasons to include direct support services in every behavioral health plan. *Health and Social Work* 24(2):103–111.

Karon, B. P., and VandenBos, G. R. (1972). The consequences of psychotherapy for schizophrenic patients. *Psychotherapy: Theory, Research and Practice* 12:143–148.

Lefley, H. P. (1996). *Family Caregiving in Mental Illness, Vol. 7.* Thousand Oaks, CA: Sage.

Lehman, A. F., and Steinwachs, D. M. (1998a). At issue: translating research into practice: the schizophrenia Patient Outcomes Research Team (PORT) treatment recommendations. *Schizophrenia Bulletin* 24(1):1–10.

——— (1998b). Patterns of usual care for schizophrenia: initial results from the schizophrenia Patient Outcomes Research Team (PORT) client survey. *Schizophrenia Bulletin* 24(1):11–32.

Lukens, E. P., and Thorning, H. (1998). Psychoeducation and severe mental illness: implications for social work practice and research. In *Mental Health Research: Implications for Practice*, ed. J. B. W. Williams and K. Ell, pp. 343–364. Washington, DC: NASW.

Lukens, E. P., Thorning, H., and Herman, D. B. (1999). Family psychoeducation in schizophrenia: emerging themes and challenges. *Journal of Practical Psychiatry and Behavioral Health* 5(6):314–325.

Lysaker, P. H., and Bell, M. D. (1998). Impaired insight in schizophrenia: advances from psychosocial treatment research. In *Psychosis and Insight*, ed. A. F. Amador and D. S. Anthony, pp. 307–317. New York: Oxford University Press.

Mann, J. (1996). Time-limited psychotherapy. In *Essential Papers on Short-term Dynamic Therapy*, ed. J. E. Groves, pp. 66–96. New York: New York University Press.

May, P. R. A., and Tuma, A. H. (1965). Treatment of schizophrenia: an experimental study of five treatment methods. *British Journal of Psychiatry* 111:503–510.

McFarlane, W. R., and Lukens, E. P. (1998). Insight, families and education. In *Insight and Psychosis*, ed. X. F. Amador and A. S. David, pp. 317–331. New York: Oxford University Press.

McFarlane, W., Lukens, E., Link, B., et al. (1995). Multiple family groups and psychoeducation in the treatment of schizophrenia. *Archives of General Psychiatry* 52:679–687.

Messer, S. B., and Warren, C. S. (1995). *Models of Brief Psychodynamic Therapy: A Comparative Approach.* New York: Guilford.

Michels, R. (1998). The role of psychotherapy: psychiatry's resistance to managed care. *Archives of General Psychiatry* 55:564.

Millon, T. (1991). Classification in psychopathology: rationale, alternatives, standards. *Journal of Abnormal Psychology* 100:245–261.

Munich, R. L. (1997). Contemporary treatment of schizophrenia. *Bulletin of the Menninger Clinic* 61(2):189–221.

Nicholson, I. R., and Neufeld, R. W. J. (1992). A dynamic vulnerability perspective on stress and schizophrenia. *American Journal of Orthopsychiatry* 62:117–130.

Opler, L. (1996). Pharmacologic treatment of schizophrenia: Where have we been, where are we now, and where are we going? In *Schizophrenia: New Directions for Clinical Practice and Treatment*, ed. C. A. Kaufman and J. M. Gorman, pp. 165–176. Larchmont, NY: Mary Ann Liebert.

Penn, D. L., and Mueser, K. T. (1996). Research update of the psychosocial treatment of schizophrenia. *American Journal of Psychiatry* 153(3):607–617.

Rabkin, R. (1977). *Strategic Psychotherapy.* New York: Basic Books.

Rolland, J. (1988). A conceptual model of chronic and life-threatening illness and its impact on families. In *Chronic Illness and Disability*, ed. C. S. Chilman, E. W. Nunnally, and F. M. Cox, pp. 17–107. Thousand Oaks, CA: Sage.

——— (1994). *Families, Illness and Disability.* New York: Basic Books.

Sackeim, H. A. (1998). Introduction: the meaning of insight. In *Insight and Psychosis*, ed. X. F. Amador and A. S. David, pp. 3–15. New York: Oxford University Press.

Sarti, P., and Cournos, F. (1990). Medication and psychotherapy in the treatment of chronic schizophrenia. *Psychiatric Clinics of North America* 13(2):215–228.

Strauss, J. (1998). Epilogue. In *Insight and Psychosis,* ed. X. F. Amador and A. S. David, pp. 352–357. New York: Oxford University Press.

Thorning, H., and Lukens, E. (1996). Schizophrenia and the self. In *Schizophrenia: New Directions for Clinical Research and Treatment,* ed. C. A. Kaufman and J. M. Gorman, pp. 177–188. Larchmont, NY: Mary Ann Liebert.

Willick, M. (1990). Psychoanalytic concepts of the etiology of mental illness. *Journal of the American Psychoanalytic Association* 38:1049–1081.

Yank, G. R., Bentley, K. J., and Gordon, C. T. (1993). The vulnerability-stress model of schizophrenia: advances in psychosocial treatment. *American Journal of Orthopsychiatry* 63:55–69.

CHAPTER SEVEN

A Brief Treatment Approach to Depression

JAMES I. MARTIN

THEORETICAL OVERVIEW
AND TREATMENT PERSPECTIVE

There are numerous models of short-term treatment of depression. Some are based on psychodynamic theories, including Bellak's brief and emergency therapy (Bellak and Siegel 1983, Bellak and Small 1978), Mann's time-limited psychotherapy (Mann 1973), Luborsky's supportive-expressive psychotherapy (Luborsky 1984), and Klerman's interpersonal psychotherapy (Klerman and Weissman 1993). In addition, both Baker (1991) and Martin (2000) have described short-term adaptations of self psychology for treatment of depressed patients. Among the models that draw upon cognitive theories are Ellis's rational-emotive therapy (Ellis 1989) and Beck's cognitive restructuring therapy (Beck et al. 1979). Antidepressant medication may be used adjunctively with any of these models when patients are severely depressed.

In describing the short-term treatment of depressive disorders, this chapter focuses on patients' self-structure, coping capacities, and support networks. It conceptualizes depressive disorders in terms of episodes of depression that occur because of interactions between internal vulnerabilities, stressful life events, and inadequate external support. This conceptualization has been used to explain episodes of schizophrenia (Freeman 1989) and episodes of low self-esteem (Martin and Knox 1997). In this chapter, internal vulnerabilities include self-structure that lacks cohesiveness and coping patterns that are ineffective. Genetic and biochemical factors are other potential internal vulnerabilities. Stressful life events include those deriving from internal sources such as normative developmental transitions, and others deriving from external sources such as victimization. People who have a family history of depression and a self-structure that fragments easily, and who tend to cope with stress through avoidance, are highly vulnerable to experiencing episodes of depression. However, they might experience fewer, shorter, or less severe episodes if they have sufficient external support (including supportive therapy), and they are able to use this support effectively. People without significant internal vulnerability for depression might still experience a depressive episode following the loss of support, or the experience of life events sufficiently powerful to overwhelm their coping capacities.

Self Structure

The problems that people in American society experience are increasingly those that derive from deficits in their self structure (Cushman 1995, Kohut 1977, Lasch 1979). These problems involve the inability to regulate self-esteem and internal tension, and to accomplish life goals (Gardner 1991). Kohut and Wolf (1986) called problems deriving from self-structure deficits "primary disturbances of the self" (p. 178). Kohut (1977) theorized that the increase in these types of problems was a result of changes in the size and structure of American families, but Lasch (1979) asserted that it was an effect of consumerist capitalism. Cushman (1995) associated it with the extreme importance of self-contained individuality in American society and the destruction of family and interpersonal relationships by society's institutions. These factors result in a typical self-construction in which people tend to experience chronic internal emptiness (Cushman 1995).

Kohut and Wolf (1986) conceptualized problems associated with temporary setbacks in self-esteem, tension regulation, or movement toward realistic goals as "secondary disturbances of the self" (p. 178). These problems occur in people with cohesive self-structures when circumstances overwhelm their coping capacities. According to Kohut, people never become completely independent of the need to rely on others in order to maintain their self-cohesiveness (Elson 1986). In this conceptualization, optimal functioning always involves interactions between people's internal self structure and external support systems.

Kohut's (1977, 1984) psychology of the self originated as a theory of psychoanalysis, focusing on the treatment of primary disturbances of the self. More recently, several authors described how it could be adapted for use in short-term treatment with individuals (Basch 1995, Gardner 1991, Martin 1993, 2000). These applications are best suited for treatment of secondary disturbances of the self, including those occurring in people who also have a primary disturbance. They tend to focus on restoring adaptive functioning, rather than on healing deficits in the self structure. However, they can also include efforts to enhance patient functioning.

Coping Capacities

Assessing and, when appropriate, enhancing a patient's ability to cope with stress is of primary importance in short-term treatment of depression. People may experience stress that derives from either internal or external sources. For example, experiencing pubertal changes, beginning a relationship, getting sick, emigrating to another country, losing a job, and being assaulted are all potential sources of stress. People tend to develop individual coping patterns that may include a combination of efforts designed to solve the stress-producing problem and reduce the distress they are experiencing as a result of the problem (Martin and Knox 1995). These efforts can focus on changing the individual's thoughts, feelings, or behavior, or else the environmental conditions that give rise to the problem (Goldstein and Noonan 1999).

Short-term treatment tends to focus on helping patients cope with their problems, rather than on "curing" their mental disorder. Underlying this orientation is the assumption that many patients need professional help only for developing and using more effectively their inherent strengths (Bloom 1997). In particular, some patients might need help in either developing new coping skills or changing their typical coping strategies.

Among the various coping responses that people use, avoidance has particular clinical significance. Avoidance can be a useful coping response on a temporary basis when a problem appears unsolvable, but it may have harmful consequences (Terry and Hynes 1998). For example, a woman with advanced ovarian cancer might feel better if she can forget about the disease affecting her body by keeping her mind occupied with other things. However, if this strategy causes her to neglect her health, her condition may worsen significantly. Similarly, if employees who receive a poor job evaluation start to call in sick regularly, they might experience less distress related to their job, but they might also hasten the possibility of getting fired. The use of avoidance as a coping strategy is associated with depression (Billings and Moos 1984, Terry and Hynes 1998) and other poor outcomes (Kelly et al. 1991, Stanton and Snider 1993). Some patients might drink alcohol, use drugs, or engage in sex compulsively as an avoidance strategy (Martin and Knox 1995). Patients such as these may need help in developing new strategies for solving problems in their lives and coping with stress.

Support Networks

To some extent, people's lives are embedded within an interpersonal web that helps to sustain them. For example, children's resilience in the face of adverse life experiences is largely due to the existence of positive relationships within their families and external support systems (Smith and Carlson 1997). Self psychology theorizes that external sources of mirroring, idealizing, and twinning selfobject functions help to maintain self-cohesiveness, even among people with healthy self-structures. During times of increased stress, people may experience heightened needs for selfobjects. If they are unable to get these needs met appropriately, they might experience a state of self-fragmentation. However, competence in finding appropriate selfobjects and using them effectively helps to maintain a cohesive self state (Martin 2000). Accordingly, short-term interventions might focus either on helping patients to improve these competencies (Basch 1995) or on modifying patients' support networks (Young 1994).

People who are depressed might have difficulty obtaining support from others (Sarason et al. 1986). In some cases this difficulty might result from the direct negative effects of depression on people's abilities to engage in interpersonal interactions of all kinds. For example, people who are depressed might participate in fewer social activities or express less interest in conversations with others. Another reason might be that the same vulnerabilities that predispose some people to depression, such as unstable self-esteem, also make them less able to get their needs for interpersonal support met (Martin and Knox 1995). In one study, gay men who had unstable self-esteem reported less intimacy in their relationships, rated the quality of support from friends and family lower, and used avoidance coping more than gay men with stable self-esteem (Martin and Knox 1997).

The communities in which people live and work also help to sustain them, sometimes in indirect ways. Molinari and colleagues (1998) found that people who rated the quality of their communities poorly on issues such as crime, recreational resources, poverty, and pollution also reported more problems with their emotional and physical health. According to Halpern (1993), members of minority groups are less likely to have mental health problems when they live in communities of people like themselves. Therefore, in assessing patients' support networks and their ability to use them effectively, therapists should consider the quality of their communities. For some patients, short-term interventions might focus on helping them obtain resources available in their community, or on finding a community that is more responsive to their needs.

INCLUSION AND EXCLUSION CRITERIA

Depending on the model used, criteria for inclusion and exclusion are likely to be different. For example, Mann (1991) suggested excluding patients with concurrent narcissistic disorders, or chronic general medical conditions such as rheumatoid arthritis, since they are not likely to benefit sufficiently from brief treatment. For similar reasons, Luborsky and Mark (1991) recommended excluding patients with concurrent personality disorders of any type. Conversely, Basch (1995) urged psychotherapists to initially treat all new patients according to a short-term model, and to change to a longer-term approach only when the initial attempt fails. Failure might occur with patients whose vulnerabilities are so severe that they require ongoing support to maintain their level of functioning, or with patients who present strong resistance to engaging with the therapist.

Contradicting this caution, Walter and Peller (1992) asserted that selecting action-oriented goals that directly relate to what patients want, as prescribed by solution-focused brief therapy, often results in rapid improvement. Short-term treatment of problems related to depression should focus on alleviating depressive episodes, as defined by the *DSM-IV* (American Psychiatric Association 1994), rather than "curing" depressive disorders. Patients who present a history of previous depressive episodes that were refractory to psychotherapy, those complaining of depression that has lasted for several years, and those suffering from melancholic depression might be less likely to obtain sufficient benefit from short-term treatment, especially if it is not accompanied by appropriate medication.

TREATMENT GOALS

The selection of appropriate goals is of primary importance in short-term treatment of depression. According to Bloom (1997), therapists accustomed to longer-term or open-ended therapy must reconsider their conception of cure in order to formulate appropriate goals for short-term treatment. Bloom calls application of the medical concept of cure to psychotherapy "utopian" and "unrealistic" (p. 257) because it assumes that people can achieve perfect solutions to their problems. Instead, Bloom promotes episodic psychotherapy, in which patients seek help whenever they are unable to resolve an issue on their own. In short-term treatment of major depression, goals should focus on relieving the symptoms of the major depressive episode, such as hypersomnia, social withdrawal, fatigue, feelings of worthlessness, and poor concentration. Treatment does not have to be purely behavioral, since many times depressive episodes are associated with identifiable psychosocial stressors (American Psychiatric Association 1994) that might be resolved within a short time frame. Goals are unlikely to focus on changing aspects of the underlying personality structure thought to predispose the patient to experiencing depressive episodes. However, if there is sufficient time available, therapists can also help patients to reduce the possibility of future depressive episodes by enhancing their coping skills and ability to use their support system more effectively.

CASE ILLUSTRATION

Mitchell Stanwick, a 31-year-old white gay man, self-referred to an outpatient psychotherapy program designed for gay men and lesbians who could not afford to see a private therapist. The program allowed patients to see a therapist for no more than ten sessions, often for a minimal fee. Mr. Stanwick called intake the day after Christmas, and he was seen for an initial evaluation two weeks later. After the evaluation he was assigned to a clinical social worker, who began seeing him one week later.

Assessment

According to the initial evaluation, Mr. Stanwick sought help because he was very depressed. He had moved to Boston from Miami six months earlier, in June, to train for a flight attendant job. However, he was fired without warning in July, one week before the end of the training period. He obtained a job as a hotel concierge shortly afterward, but he was fired from that job in September. The patient reported that this was the point at which he became depressed, and that it had been getting worse since then. He complained of sadness and loneliness, frequent crying spells, fatigue, hypersomnia, and recurrent suicidal fantasies. He also reported having hardly any social life, and getting little enjoyment from any of his activities.

Mr. Stanwick reported that his "life has been downhill" since he tested HIV-positive three years ago. At that time he was living in Miami, where he worked as a flight attendant (for a different airline) for several years. His description of life during those years was rather idyllic. He enjoyed his job, he dated, and he felt good. After testing positive he experienced an episode of depression that was treated successfully with imipramine. During that episode, he withdrew socially, shutting himself in his apartment for several days at a time. He called in sick to work frequently, and was eventually fired from his job for excessive absenteeism. The patient also reported that he had seen therapists several other times during the past ten years to work on love relationship problems.

After Mr. Stanwick was fired from the concierge job, in September, he obtained a job as a waiter. He reported that the manager of the restaurant was very interested in him sexually. After he told the manager that he did not share this interest, the manager apparently began treating him very badly. In reaction to this treatment, Mr. Stanwick quit and obtained a different waiter job, one that he continued to hold at the time of the initial evaluation. However, the restaurant was not doing well and the job was not providing much income.

Six months after moving to a new city, the patient found himself without sufficient or reliable income. This was a significant blow to his self-esteem, after living independently in Miami for years. Since moving to Boston, he lived with a roommate who was also HIV-positive, and who was both emotionally and financially supportive. In fact, Mr. Stanwick owed his roommate for the last two months' rent. Nevertheless, he felt deflated by his need for a roommate and the inability to pay his own bills. When asked how far he went with his education, he reported finishing one year of college.

Accompanying Mr. Stanwick's recently turbulent employment history was the recurrent theme of being betrayed or let down. He believed that his being gay and HIV-positive were major reasons why he was fired repeatedly. For example, he lost his job with the first airline as a result of his difficulty coping with HIV seroconversion. However, he was in the process of suing the airline for AIDS-related discrimination, and he hoped to get his job back one day. He believed that the second airline and the hotel both fired him when they found out about his HIV status. He quit the first restaurant job due to apparent sexual harassment.

Although the patient reported a supportive relationship with his roommate, he had not made other friends since moving to Boston. The person to whom he felt closest—Adam, an older gay man and a physician—remained in Miami. Mr. Stanwick lived with Adam for a while after he lost his job. Adam obtained free antiviral medication for him, and was even sending it to him in Boston. It was Adam who prescribed imipramine for him three years ago to treat his earlier episode of depression. Recently, Adam wrote Mr. Stanwick a letter stating that he could not continue sending medication much longer. The patient also reported that he never had a long-term relationship, which disturbed him, although he did have several short-lived boyfriend relationships over the years.

Mr. Stanwick reported poor relationships with his parents, who lived in Texas. His father was a retired airline pilot, and his mother a retired social worker. He described his father as an authoritarian and his mother as a "wimp." He said that his parents rejected him when he came out to them nine years ago. As time passed, their relationship improved, but they rejected him again when he told them about being HIV-positive. Although he found it extremely difficult to do, he recently called his parents to ask for money. However, they refused to help, even though he needed the money to buy antiviral medication and pay rent. Mr. Stanwick's relationship with his older sister was reportedly much better. She often expressed concern about his health, and even promised to send him some money when she could afford it. He did not describe his relationship with his younger sister.

The patient reported that he occasionally drank beer, sometimes as many as six in one night. However, he denied having a drinking problem since he never drank "to the point where I can't walk." He added, "I can do without drinking." He reported trying several recreational drugs in the past, and reportedly used cocaine regularly six years ago. He stated that he continued to smoke marijuana occasionally, but denied current use of other drugs.

Although he had been HIV-positive for three years, Mr. Stanwick remained in relatively good health. He reported having frequent colds and sinus problems, and he had a basal cell carcinoma removed from his face in the previous year.

According to the initial evaluation, Mr. Stanwick wore clothes that were clean but old and somewhat shabby. His speech was articulate. He expressed a somewhat restricted range of affect, and his mood was depressed. His thinking appeared logical and coherent. He had been given the following multiaxial diagnosis:

Axis I: Major depressive disorder, recurrent, mild (296.31)
Axis II: Personality disorder not otherwise specified (301.9)
Axis III: Seropositive for HIV
Axis IV: Inadequate social support, change of residence, multiple job
            losses and underemployment, inadequate finances, inadequate

                source of health care services, discord with parents, AIDS- or
                gay-related discrimination
Axis V: GAF = 50

      The Axis I diagnosis was assigned to the patient because of his report of five symptoms that had been present for more than two weeks. The symptoms were depressed mood, hypersomnia, fatigue, recurrent thoughts of suicide without a plan, and decreased enjoyment of most of his activities. These symptoms represented a change in his functioning as compared to the time when he was living in Miami. Because he reported experiencing a previous episode of depression, he was diagnosed with a recurrent major depressive disorder.

      Although this diagnosis was certainly useful, it did not sufficiently describe Mr. Stanwick's self-structure, coping capacities, or support networks. The clinician assessed these areas by examining the initial evaluation report and asking additional questions during the first session. He considered the patient's depressive symptoms, especially the suicidal fantasies and fatigue, to reflect a state of self-fragmentation. He noted evidence that Mr. Stanwick had previously functioned much better, although this was apparently not his first major depressive episode. The extent of his vulnerability to fragmentation was not clear, based on the available information. However, the clinician thought that the report of his seeing therapists several times for problems related to love relationships might suggest that the current episode of self fragmentation was occurring within the context of a primary disturbance of the self. Certainly, what little was known about his family of origin suggested a developmental milieu that might have been less than empathic to his selfobject needs. In addition, his reported pattern of alcohol use, past abuse of cocaine, and experimental use of other drugs might also have been signs of an enfeebled self.

      As indicated by the Axis IV diagnosis, Mr. Stanwick had experienced numerous stressors during the previous few months. However, the clinician also noted evidence of significant active coping capacities. The patient lost four jobs over the course of six months. Yet with each loss he not only motivated himself to look for a new job, he actually obtained one. In addition, he was pursuing legal action to regain his former flight attendant job in Miami. He was able to move to a new city and find a home and a supportive roommate. When he recognized that he was getting increasingly depressed, he found affordable, gay-affirmative services. The clinician noted that Mr. Stanwick was engaging in his initial interactions with him, perhaps indicating an ability to cue others to at least some of his needs. There was no evidence that the patient relied primarily on avoidance strategies to cope with stress.

However, there was evidence that the patient's support network was inadequate even before he moved to Boston. He lacked both emotional and instrumental support from his parents. Although he described one close friend in Miami, he provided little information about any others. He had not established any long-lasting romantic relationships. The stress associated with moving to a new city might have been alleviated if he had better support, but instead he experienced a dwindling network. Not only did he find little support from his employers, he also recently heard that his friend Adam might not send him free medication anymore. He had not yet established a new network that could respond to his health care needs.

Finally, the clinician wondered if it was more than a coincidence that Mr. Stanwick sought help with the coming of the New England winter. It was true that many people experienced stress during the holiday season. However, the short days, frequent snowfall, and cold temperature might have provided the last straw for Mr. Stanwick, whose conception of home was tropical Miami.

Beginning

Prior to his first session with Mr. Stanwick, the clinician reviewed material from the initial evaluation. His goals for the first session were to engage the patient, to reach his own diagnostic judgment and share them with the patient, and to reach an agreement with the patient about the treatment goals. Mr. Stanwick arrived on time for the session. The clinician noted that he was a tall, attractive man who appeared his stated age. He was dressed very casually in jeans and a sweater. He responded with interest to the clinician's introduction, though his affect appeared blunted. The clinician explained that, in the fifty minutes they had available, he wanted to get a better understanding of Mr. Stanwick's situation and his feelings so he could formulate the most appropriate plan to help him. He added that he would give the patient his impressions and make some recommendations before the session ended. The clinician stated that he had read the initial evaluation and knew that Mr. Stanwick requested help because he was depressed. Since a week had passed since the evaluation, he wanted to know how the patient was currently feeling, and whether anything had changed since last week.

The patient reported that he still felt depressed, although he felt a little better at the present time. He said that little had changed. He was still employed by the restaurant where he was making very little money, especially since he was getting scheduled only about two days a week. The clinician asked a number of questions oriented toward helping the patient understand how he experienced the events that had happened to him. He also asked some questions about the patient's family of origin, especially regarding his parents' reactions to his coming out. Mr. Stanwick reported that his father retired from the Air Force prior to becoming a commercial pilot. The Air Force required the family to move many times during his childhood years. When Mr. Stanwick came out to his parents, his father refused to talk with him about it, and became sullen and angry. The clinician thought it sounded as if his father might have experienced the news as evidence of personal failure on his part, and consequently an injury to his self-esteem. His mother simply cried, as she often did when she was upset.

The clinician summarized that Mr. Stanwick had experienced numerous losses and difficult changes during the previous few months, and that many people would have had difficulty adjusting to them. He added that it was certainly understandable how these losses and changes might have led to feeling depressed. He did not share his impression that the patient was highly vulnerable to episodes of depression, since the parameters of short-term treatment would preclude focus on the vulnerability itself. He explained that they would need to work in a very focused way toward clear goals because of their time limit. As an overall goal, the clinician suggested reducing the patient's symptoms of depression. Based on the information provided by the patient, the clinician suggested the following objectives: to obtain a better job that would provide adequate income; to obtain health insurance; to obtain access to health care services, including a source of antiviral medication; and to improve relations with members of the family of origin. In addition, the clinician stated that he wanted to learn more about Mr. Stanwick's sources of support in Boston, since they might also want to focus on strengthening them. He asked the patient how the overall goal and the objectives sounded to him. Did he believe they captured what he wanted to change in his current life? Would he be on the way to feeling less depressed if he were to accomplish these objectives? The patient agreed to the goal and objectives, stating that if he had a better-paying job, access to health care services, and better support he would probably feel better. Since Mr. Stanwick reported a positive response to antidepressant medication in the past, the clinician also referred him to the mental health division of the local department of health for a psychiatric evaluation.

The clinician said that he would like to use a brief questionnaire to track progress toward reducing Mr. Stanwick's depression. Showing him a copy of the questionnaire, the Generalized Contentment Scale (GCS) (Hudson 1992), the clinician said the best way to use it was to fill it out at the beginning of each session. He would score it right away, so both of them would know the results. He explained that the test would be used to supplement the patient's subjective assessment of his mood. In response to a request for feedback, the patient said that using the test was fine with him. The clinician then asked him to fill out the first one so they could compare the result to later ones. It took about five minutes to fill out and score the questionnaire. The patient's score was 51. Since a score between 30 and the maximum of 100 is an indication of clinical depression (Hudson 1992), the patient's score corroborated both the initial evaluation and the clinical assessment. An additional item on the questionnaire asked how the patient's current mood compared to his mood during the previous week. Mr. Stanwick responded that he felt better at the present time, perhaps indicating his reaction to the first therapy session. He said that the questionnaire was interesting, and that the result seemed to represent how he felt.

Middle

Mr. Stanwick filled out the GCS at the beginning of the second session, and his score was 39. He indicated that his mood was about the same as it had been during the week. He said that he had obtained a new waiter job that was providing more income. He also interviewed for a sales job at a store, which would provide both income and health insurance benefits. He talked about having few good friends, and he told the clinician about the frequent arguments his father had over the years with him, his mother, and his sisters. Near the end of the session, he commented that when he saw previous therapists there never seemed to be enough time to talk about things. The clinician wondered about the extent to which this last comment reflected the patient's transference. That is, the patient might have expected to be disappointed by the clinician, repeating his disappointment by previous therapists and other important people in his life. The comment might also have been an expression of disappointment with the short-term parameters of the treatment contract. The clinician believed it was too early to interpret this comment, and instead responded that he hoped Mr. Stanwick would feel differently this time.

The patient called a couple of hours before the appointed time of the third session to cancel, stating that he could not get out of working late. A week later, he called to change his appointment to the next day because of another conflict with his work schedule. He arrived thirty minutes late for the third session, a morning appointment, and his GCS score was 60. He said that his mood was worse than it had been during the week. He complained that it was so hard for him to wake up and get going in the morning. He also complained of problems with his current job. He felt that the manager did not treat him fairly when he developed the work schedule for the week, and that he did not get as many tables assigned to him as one of his co-workers did. Mr. Stanwick then cried when talking about his lack of friends, adding that the friends he did have let him down. He said that his roommate was talking about moving out of town. During the session, Mr. Stanwick also admitted that his friend Adam had made unwanted sexual advances during the time when he was living in his house. The clinician empathized with his feelings of loneliness and betrayal, but he did not draw a connection to the "doorknob issue" raised at the end of the previous session. In other words, he avoided commenting on the transference. Instead, he focused on the patient's experience of disappointment and betrayal in his work and social relationships. He suggested that they work on trying to improve his current support network. One option was a referral to a support group for HIV-positive gay men.

The patient asked if he could have another session in a few days, not wanting to wait a full week. The clinician agreed, considering the time limit and the subsequent need to attain the treatment goals as quickly as possible. However, he was also concerned about the possibility of stimulating patient dependency on him. Therefore, he added that this should be a one-time exception to the general plan of meeting weekly.

Mr. Stanwick appeared depressed and anxious in the fourth session, which was held four days after the third one. He cried and verbalized anger at having to ask his parents for money, especially since they had never been supportive of him in the past. Although he was angry about their lack of support for him, he did not express this anger directly toward them. Instead, he was angry at the situation. The clinician empathized with his feelings of betrayal and anger, and gave him a referral to the AIDS clinic at a public hospital at which he could receive low-cost services. He also gave him information about a support group for HIV-positive gay men. He also asked Mr. Stanwick to make a list of the people at whom he was feeling angry, in order to help direct his anger away from himself and onto people rather than diffuse situations. He did not administer the GCS at this session because it was less than a week since the last session.

The fifth session was held three days later. The patient's GCS score was 62. He said that his mood was about the same all week. He made the list, which led to further discussion of his difficulty expressing angry feelings directly. Instead, he often felt angry at the situation and became depressed. Since the previous session, Mr. Stanwick talked with Adam, who prescribed Prozac for his depression. He said that he had an appointment at the public hospital's HIV clinic for later that week. To help the patient prepare, the clinician predicted that the clinic might be crowded, and that he might have to wait a long time even though he had an appointment. They spent time talking about what the patient could do to cope with waiting. Mr. Stanwick also said that he called about the support group, and he was planning to join when it began in a couple of weeks.

Mr. Stanwick scored 48 on the GCS in the sixth session. He reported that his appointment at the AIDS clinic was frustrating, but their discussion about what to expect helped him to cope with the situation. He had good feelings about the physician who saw him. He had blood drawn for tests and received antiviral medication. Reflecting the lower score on the GCS, Mr. Stanwick said that he felt better. He was less depressed and more relaxed. Since the last session he called his younger sister, with whom he had not talked in over seven years. By comparing past family experiences with her, Mr. Stanwick realized that his parents did not single him out for bad treatment. This realization made him feel better. He also reported having an interview for a new job next week.

The patient did not show up for the next appointment. When the clinician called him, he reported thinking that the appointment was for the following day. He said that things were going well for him, and rescheduled an appointment for the following week. The clinician wondered whether the missed appointment might be another expression of the transference that appeared in the second session, or a different transference that anticipated the impending termination. As the patient began to feel better, it was also possible that he considered coming to sessions less important than doing other things in his life, especially in view of the limited intimacy of the short-term treatment relationship. In the seventh session, Mr. Stanwick's GCS score was 39. He reported feeling much better. He said that he decided to move back to Miami in a few months, when his roommate was planning to move out of town.

Termination and Follow-Up

In the eighth session, Mr. Stanwick's GCS score was 31. Once again, he said his mood was better than it had been during the week. He reported that he was returning to Miami much sooner than expected because a hearing had been scheduled in response to his appeal. He was leaving in a few days. He said that he was feeling good again, and he was hopeful that he was going to get his old job back. Two weeks later, the patient called from Miami. His message said that the hearing was inconclusive, and a continuance was issued for another month. He decided to remain in Miami, and had already found a place to live. He was looking for a new job. He said that he continued to feel good, and gave the clinician his new phone number.

DISCUSSION OF TECHNIQUES

This case illustrates short-term treatment of major depressive disorder in which the major focus is on supporting and strengthening patients' coping capacities, and secondarily on resolving problems in their social and physical environment. As suggested by Pinsof (1995), the clinician kept the treatment goal and objectives close to the patient's presenting problem. Since Mr. Stanwick's major complaint was depression, the goal was to reduce his symptoms of depression. The clinician based the selection of objectives on the theory that the identified stressors led to the patient's depressive episode. This case illustrates the conscious use of time, as described by Goldstein and Noonan (1999), in its limited and clear focus, and its attention to patient autonomy. The clinician made it clear from the beginning that treatment could consist of no more than ten sessions. As recommended by Goldstein and Noonan (1999), the clinician engaged quickly with the patient, assessed him rapidly, and remained very active throughout the course of treatment.

Because the patient was a gay man living with HIV, the clinician's focus on helping him to cope with external stressors, as opposed to resolving intrapsychic conflicts or building structural deficits, was particularly meaningful. According to Markowitz and colleagues (1993), mood disorders are more prevalent among people living with HIV, perhaps due to the extreme stress associated with this condition. The stress might be even more intense among some HIV-positive gay men because of the devastating impact of the AIDS epidemic on their communities (Cadwell 1998, Dane and Miller 1992, Paul et al. 1995), and the experience of antigay discrimination, prejudice, marginalization, and violence in their daily lives (Granvold and Martin 1999). Especially since Mr. Stanwick believed that he had been victimized by repeated discrimination in employment and other negative circumstances, the therapist wisely used the limited number of sessions to empower him.

According to Goldstein and Noonan (1999), therapists engaged in short-term treatment should work actively to build a positive, collaborative relationship with their patients. In the case example the structure of the initial session illustrated this effort. The clinician explained to the patient the length of time they had available and what would happen during the session. Responsibilities were shared—it was the patient's responsibility to talk about himself and his situation, and the therapist's responsibility to make some recommendations based on his understanding of the patient's story. By telling Mr. Stanwick what he learned from the initial evaluation, the therapist showed that he thought enough of the patient to prepare for meeting him. However, by not relying solely on material from the evaluation, the therapist showed that he was primarily interested in listening to the patient. The clinician suggested the treatment goal and objectives because of the brief number of sessions available and the patient's depressed mood. However, he asked the patient whether they adequately addressed his concerns. If Mr. Stanwick had expressed any reluctance to accept these suggestions, the therapist would have had to negotiate changes in the goal or objectives.

The clinician began intervening immediately by providing a referral for psychiatric evaluation. Doing so in the first session showed that he wanted to help the patient as quickly as possible. It also highlighted the collaborative nature of their relationship. Once again, they shared responsibilities—the therapist used his expert knowledge to provide the referral and the patient needed to follow through on it. Although Mr. Stanwick did not use this referral, he did use some others that the clinician provided. If he showed repeated inability or unwillingness to do so, it would have been important for the therapist to explore the reasons for it. Because of the effectiveness and efficiency of many antidepressant medications, therapists engaging in short-term treatment should always consider referring their severely depressed patients for psychiatric evaluation. Such referral must always be done collaboratively, and the wishes of some patients not to take psychoactive medication must be respected. However, therapists can also provide patients with information about medication and correct misconceptions about them, or they can refer patients to other experts who can do so. For Mr. Stanwick, medication appeared to have additional meaning as a concrete expression of Adam's caring. Thus, receiving a new prescription from Adam, rather than a stranger, was probably much more reassuring. It showed that he still had a relationship with Adam, even as he expected to lose the more transient relationships with his roommate and the clinician.

The therapist's use of the Generalized Contentment Scale (GDS) (Hudson 1992) to measure Mr. Stanwick's depression was designed to demystify treatment and empower the patient by showing him tangible evidence (a numerical score) of his improvement. It also provided the clinician with objective information useful for engaging in ongoing evaluation of his intervention. The GDS is one of several short questionnaires designed to measure depression in adults. Patients answer each of its twenty-five questions with a rating from 1 (corresponding to "None of the Time") to 7 (corresponding to "All of the Time"). After the patient fills out the questionnaire, the clinician can score it quickly and easily. The lowest possible score is 0 and the highest is 100. Scores below 30 indicate that the patient is not clinically depressed, while scores of 30 or more indicate the presence of clinical depression. A decrease in scores over time indicates a reduction in the patient's level of depression. If the patient's scores do not decrease over time, or they increase, the intervention strategy should be changed, consistent with Goldstein and Noonan's (1999) recommendation that therapists engaging in short-term treatment remain flexible in their approach.

The use of questionnaires in clinical practice must abide by ethical standards of informed consent. In the initial session, the therapist explained the questionnaire's purpose, administration process, and scoring, so that the patient could make an informed decision about whether to agree to its use. If the patient did not want to use the questionnaire, the therapist would have had to respect his wishes. In addition, the therapist would need to discontinue its use if he found that it was not fulfilling its purpose or the patient expressed dissatisfaction with it.

In the case example, the patient's scores on the GCS indicated clinical depression each time, although the last two were just above the cutoff score of 30. Across the eight sessions, his test scores initially improved, worsened for a few weeks, and then improved again. The initial improvement might have indicated the establishment of an initial positive transference. After the second session the patient might have felt safe enough to reveal the depth of his depression. The worsening test scores occurred as he began verbalizing feelings of loneliness and betrayal. In addition, they followed an interaction that the patient might have experienced as an empathic failure. When the patient commented about never having enough time to talk in previous therapy, the clinician's response avoided the likely affective meaning of this statement. The patient's statement might have been an expression of his concerns about the limited number of sessions available to him in the current contract. Or it might have been an expression of a mirroring transference in which his need to be heard and acknowledged was accompanied by a fear of empathic failure. On the other hand, after changing two appointments, the patient asked for an additional session. Perhaps this pattern expressed his ambivalence toward the clinician. It also might have indicated the lack of control he had over his work schedule and his mounting disappointments with others. The test scores began improving after the patient had positive contacts with the physician at the AIDS clinic, Adam, and his sister. During this time he also began taking Prozac. Finally, he received word that his appeal would be held in Miami.

In therapy that is this brief, little time can be devoted to exploring patients' transference. In this case, the clinician chose to accept the patient's excuse for changing appointments at face value, especially since one of the major treatment objectives was to help him obtain adequate income through improved employment. If the patient continued to express similar transference material in subsequent interactions, the therapist would need to address it as simply and directly as possible. For example, he could have asked whether the patient felt that he was getting enough time to talk with him. However, in the absence of continued expressions of transference it would be more important for the therapist to stay focused on the surface material.

During the middle phase of treatment, the clinician remained flexible in his approach, employing diverse techniques. Primary among them was his sustained empathic attention, designed to dissipate defensiveness and restore the patient's self-cohesiveness (Elson 1986). Goldstein (1995) describes many of the other techniques that the clinician used throughout the treatment process. These included exploration, description, ventilation, and the sustaining techniques of encouragement and reassurance. He also used the structuring techniques of partializing, focusing, and planning, always important in short-term treatment. The clinician used the structuring technique of homework when he asked the patient to make a list of the people at whom he was feeling angry. Homework helps to maintain movement in short-term treatment because it expands the therapeutic work into the patient's life outside the treatment situation. In doing so it also reinforces the collaborative nature of the therapeutic relationship by distributing responsibility for improvement more equally between the patient and the therapist. The clinician used the educative technique of anticipatory planning when helping Mr. Stanwick prepare for his appointment at the AIDS clinic. By helping him to anticipate likely problems there, the clinician reduced his potential for becoming overwhelmed with frustration and anger, or for overpersonalizing poor treatment by clinic staff.

The clinician also showed flexibility by temporarily increasing the frequency of sessions in response to the patient's request when his depression and anxiety reached a peak. Although increasing session frequency carries with it the risk of increasing emotional intensity, transference, and patient dependency, short time limits tend to counteract this risk. The clinician wisely clarified that the increase would be temporary, and that the overall plan for meeting weekly would remain unchanged. In addition to discouraging dependency, meeting on a weekly basis also minimized the danger of running out of sessions before the treatment goals were achieved.

Termination was unplanned in this case. However, the treatment goal of reducing the patient's depressive symptoms had been achieved. In particular, Mr. Stanwick reported that his mood was much improved, corroborated by two weeks of substantially lower test scores. He seemed to have more energy and hope, and there were no more reports of crying spells or suicidal fantasies. He had increased his income, gained access to medical care, and obtained a source of antiviral medication. However, it is important to remember that his internal vulnerability to depressive episodes was not changed. In that respect he was probably better off returning to Miami, which felt more like home to him, and where he had much better support. The clinician's intervention is likely to have helped reduce the patient's symptoms by empowering him to seek better employment, make contact with his sister, and find needed resources in Boston. Although the reestablishment of Mr. Stanwick's linkage with Adam was probably equally important in the restoration of his self-cohesiveness, his phone call from Miami might have indicated that he valued the brief relationship he had with the clinician.

CONCLUSION

When treating patients with depressive disorders within a limited time frame, therapists should focus on interactions among patients' internal vulnerabilities, coping capacities, and support networks. Understanding the nature of patients' vulnerabilities may help in conceptualizing the support needed to restore a previous level of functioning. For example, patients with primary disturbances of the self may reduce the likelihood of experiencing episodes of depression when they have external resources that provide ongoing support. By contrast, patients with cohesive self-structures who become depressed following circumstances that overwhelm their coping capacities might need only temporary support or help in changing their coping patterns.

Short-term treatment of depressive disorders requires clear, limited goals and objectives that focus on the presenting problem. Therapists should engage quickly with patients and establish a collaborative relationship. Although it is often possible in short-term treatment to use some transference material to increase patient insight, when only a few number of sessions are available the relationship must remain reality-based. Therapists should work actively toward helping patients to achieve the treatment goals and objectives, using a variety of techniques in a flexible manner. Patients like Mr. Stanwick might benefit from longer-term treatment in order to reduce their internal vulnerabilities. However, as illustrated here, such resources are often unavailable. In their absence, patients such as these can obtain significant benefit from treatment that is episodic and limited in scope.

REFERENCES

American Psychiatric Association. (1994). *Diagnostic and Statistical Manual of Mental Disorders*, 4th ed. Washington, DC: Author.

Baker, H. S. (1991). Shorter-term psychotherapy: a self psychological approach. In *Handbook of Short-Term Dynamic Psychotherapy*, ed. P.

Crits-Cristoph and J. P. Barber, pp. 287–322. New York: Basic Books.

Basch, M. F. (1995). *Doing Brief Psychotherapy*. New York: Basic Books.

Beck, A. T., Rush, A. J., Shaw, B. F., and Emery, G. (1979). *Cognitive Therapy of Depression*. New York: Guilford.

Bellak, L., and Siegel, H. (1983). *Handbook of Intensive Brief and Emergency Psychotherapy*. Larchmont, New York: CPS.

Bellak, L., and Small, L. (1978). *Emergency Psychotherapy and Brief Psychotherapy*, 2nd ed. New York: Grune & Stratton.

Billings, A. G., and Moos, R. H. (1984). Coping, stress, and social resources among adults with unipolar depression. *Journal of Personality and Social Psychology*, 46:877–891.

Bloom, B. L. (1997). *Planned Short-Term Psychotherapy: A Clinical Handbook*, 2nd ed. Boston: Allyn & Bacon.

Cadwell, S. A. (1998). Providing services to gay men. In *HIV and Social Work*, ed. D. M. Aronstein and B. J. Thompson, pp. 411–429. New York: Harrington Park.

Cushman, P. (1995). *Constructing the Self, Constructing America: A Cultural History of Psychotherapy*. Reading, MA: Addison-Wesley.

Dane, B. O., and Miller, S. O. (1992). *AIDS: Intervening with Hidden Grievers*. Westport, CT: Auburn House.

Ellis, A. (1989). Using rational-emotive therapy (RET) as crisis intervention: a single session with a suicidal client. *Individual Psychology* 45:75–81.

Elson, M. (1986). *Self Psychology in Clinical Social Work*. New York: Norton.

Freeman, H. (1989). Relationship of schizophrenia to the environment. *British Journal of Psychiatry* 155(suppl 5):90–99.

Gardner, J. R. (1991). The application of self psychology to brief psychotherapy. *Psychoanalytic Psychology* 8:477–500.

Goldstein, E. G. (1995). *Ego Psychology and Social Work Practice*, 2nd ed. New York: Free Press.

Goldstein, E. G., and Noonan, M. (1999). *Short-Term Treatment and Social Work Practice: An Integrative Perspective*. New York: Free Press.

Granvold, D. K., and Martin, J. I. (1999). Family therapy with gay and lesbian clients. In *Family Practice: Brief Systems Methods for Social Work*, ed. C. Franklin and C. Jordan, pp. 299–320. Pacific Grove, CA: Brooks/Cole.

Halpern, D. (1993). Minorities and mental health. *Social Science and Medicine* 36:597–607.

Hudson, W. W. (1992). *The WALMYR Assessment Scales Scoring Manual*. Tempe, AZ: WALMYR Publishing.

Kelly, J. A., Kalichman, S. C., Kauth, M. R., et al. (1991). Situational factors associated with AIDS risk behavior lapses and coping strategies used by gay men who successfully avoid lapses. *American Journal of Public Health* 81(10):1335–1338.

Klerman, G. L., and Weissman, M. M. (1993). Interpersonal psychotherapy for depression: background and concepts. In *New Applications of Interpersonal Psychotherapy*, ed. G. L. Klerman and M. W. Weissman, pp. 3–26. Washington, DC: American Psychiatric Press.

Kohut, H. (1977). *The Restoration of the Self*. New York: International Universities Press.

———— (1984). *How Does Analysis Cure?* Chicago: University of Chicago Press.

Kohut, H., and Wolf, E. S. (1986). Disorders of the self and their treatment: an outline. In *Essential Papers on Narcissism*, ed. A. P. Morrison, pp. 175–196. New York: New York University Press.

Lasch, C. (1979). *The Culture of Narcissism*. New York: Norton.

Luborsky, L. (1984). *Principles of Psychoanalytic Psychotherapy: A Manual for Supportive-Expressive Treatment*. New York: Basic Books.

Luborsky, L., and Mark, D. (1991). Short-term supportive-expressive psychoanalytic psychotherapy. In *Handbook of Short-Term Dynamic Psychotherapy*, ed. P. Crits-Cristoph and J. P. Barber, pp. 110–136. New York: Basic Books.

Mann, J. (1973). *Time Limited Psychotherapy*. Cambridge, MA: Harvard University Press.

———— (1991). Time limited psychotherapy. In *Handbook of Short-Term Dynamic Psychotherapy*, ed. P. Crits-Cristoph and J. P. Barber, pp. 17–44. New York: Basic Books.

Markowitz, J. C., Klerman, G. L., Perry, S. W., et al. (1993). Interpersonal psychotherapy for depressed HIV-seropositive patients. In *New Applications of Interpersonal Psychotherapy*, ed. G. L. Klerman and M. W. Weissman, pp. 199–224. Washington, DC: American Psychiatric Press.

Martin, J. I. (1993). Self psychology and cognitive treatment: an integration. *Clinical Social Work Journal* 21:385–394.

——— (2000). Self psychology theory. In *Theoretical Perspectives in Direct Social Work Practice: An Eclectic-Generalist Approach*, ed. N. F. Coady and P. Lehmann, pp. 145–161. New York: Springer.

Martin, J. I., and Knox, J. (1995). HIV risk behavior in gay men with unstable self-esteem. *Journal of Gay and Lesbian Social Services* 2(2):21–41.

——— (1997). Self-esteem instability and its implications for HIV prevention among gay men. *Health and Social Work* 22:264–273.

Molinari, C., Ahern, M., and Hendryx, M. (1998). The relationship of community quality to the health of women and men. *Social Science and Medicine* 47:1113–1120.

Paul, J. P., Hays, R. B., and Coates, T. J. (1995). The impact of the HIV epidemic on U.S. gay male communities. In *Lesbian, Gay, and Bisexual Identities Over the Lifespan: Psychological Perspectives*, ed. A. R. D'Augelli and C. J. Patterson, pp. 347–397. New York: Oxford University Press.

Pinsof, W. M. (1995). *Integrative Problem-Centered Therapy*. New York: Basic Books.

Sarason, I. G., Sarason, B. R., and Shearin, E. N. (1986). Social support as an individual difference variable: its stability, origins, and relational aspects. *Journal of Personality and Social Psychology* 50:845–855.

Smith, C., and Carlson, B. E. (1997). Stress, coping, and resilience in children and youth. *Social Service Review* 71:231–256.

Stanton, A. L., and Snider, P. R. (1993). Coping with a breast cancer diagnosis: a prospective study. *Health Psychology* 12:16–23.

Terry, D. J., and Hynes, G. J. (1998). Adjustment to a low-control situation: reexamining the role of coping responses. *Journal of Personality and Social Psychology* 74:1078–1092.

Walter, J., and Peller, J. (1992). *Becoming Solution-Focused in Brief Therapy.* New York: Brunner/Mazel.

Young, T. M. (1994). Environmental modification in clinical social work: a self-psychological perspective. *Social Service Review* 62(2): 202–218.

CHAPTER EIGHT

Short-Term Psychodynamic Treatment of Anxiety Disorders

CAROL TOSONE

Fear is sharp-sighted, and can see things underground, and much more in the skies.

Cervantes, *Don Quixote*

Anxiety, panic, worry, and the "fear of fear" (Goldstein and Chambless 1978) are unpleasant but ubiquitous phenomena of everyday life. At the same time, these anxiety-based reactions are also among the most prevalent problems prompting the necessity for medical and mental health care. In fact, approximately 15 percent of the population will suffer from an anxiety disorder at some point during their lifetimes, and the majority of them will evidence at least one additional clinically significant anxiety or depressive disorder at the time of their assessment (Brown and Barlow 1992).

The ubiquity of anxiety is apparent in the numerous clinical entities and manifestations mentioned in the *Diagnostic and Statistical Manual of Mental Disorders*, fourth edition (*DSM-IV*) (APA 1994), including panic disorder with or without agoraphobia, social and specific phobias, obsessive-compulsive disorder, posttraumatic stress disorder, acute stress disorder, generalized anxiety disorder, anxiety that is substance induced or due to a medical condition, and anxiety disorder not otherwise specified.

While these diagnostic disorders can occur concurrently and can share overlapping features, such as fear and anxiety sensitivity (Cox et al. 1999), each may have its own unique etiology and clinical course. A review of the literature suggests multiple theories of anxiety, such as biological (Gorman et al. 1992), learning (Barlow 1988, Clark 1986, Wolpe and Rowan 1988), and psychoanalytic (Bowlby 1973, Fairbairn 1952, Freud 1895, 1900, 1926, Horney 1950, Klein 1975a,b, Kohut 1977, 1984, Sullivan 1953). From these three theoretical perspectives, specific treatment strategies are derived: psychopharmacology (Gorman et al. 1992), cognitive-behavioral treatment (Barlow and Craske 1994), and psychodynamic treatment, respectively. The psychoanalytic approaches are both supportive and insight-oriented in nature, and range from psychoanalysis (Greenson 1967, Kohut 1977, 1984, Rangell 1978) to short-term treatment (Crits-Christoph et al. 1995).

This chapter focuses on the psychoanalytic theories of anxiety, which inform a short-term psychodynamic treatment approach designed specifically for the therapy of generalized anxiety disorder. This approach can be applied to the understanding and treatment of panic and other anxiety-related disorders as well. Case material is presented to illustrate the phases of treatment, from assessment to follow-up, as well as general treatment principles, techniques, goals, and countertransferential concerns in conducting short-term psychodynamic psychotherapy of anxiety disorders.

PSYCHOANALYTIC THEORIES OF ANXIETY

Freudian Perspectives

Since the inception of psychoanalysis, anxiety has been a central concept and focus of therapeutic activity. As such, Freud identified the crucial role anxiety played in the causation and resulting symptomatology of neurosis.

Although his conceptualization of anxiety evolved, Freud maintained its pivotal place in normal behavior and psychic life. What Freud (1895) first termed "anxiety neurosis" or "actual neurosis" bears remarkable similarity to the current *DSM-IV* (APA 1994) diagnostic criteria for panic disorder (vertigo, abdominal distress, paresthesias, intense fear) and shares some of the features for generalized anxiety disorder (irritability, sleep disturbance, worry).

His initial theory of anxiety concentrated on explaining these somatic manifestations, which he asserted were the result of repressed or nondischarged libido. That is, experiences associated with excitation, such as sexual activity or trauma, required motor or verbal discharge. If this discharge was inhibited, as in the case of coitus interruptus, the excitation state (repressed libido) was transformed into anxiety. Referring to this as the "toxic theory," Zerbe (1990) notes it has continued clinical application in the urging of patients to gradually disclose terrifying, unacceptable affects during the course of treatment. In the disclosure process, "intrapsychic de-repression occurs, allowing the noxious anxiety . . . to be diverted in a more productive, positive direction" (p. 173), such as in the subliminatory channels of hobbies and vocational pursuits.

Prior to the articulation of the "signal theory" in 1926, Freud (1900) addressed the issue of anxiety in "The Interpretation of Dreams." He reiterated his conviction that neurotic anxiety arose from sexual sources, illustrating the sexual material present in the associations of anxiety dreamers. Summarizing his theory of anxiety to date, Freud contended that anxiety could result from undischarged sexual excitation and repressed libido, as well as from disturbed somatic processes, especially those involved in breathing.

With the advent of the structural theory and the tripartite division of the mind into id, ego, and superego, Freud (1926) shifted from a physiological basis for anxiety to a psychological model. Anxiety was now viewed as an adaptive function of the ego activated in response to the perception of danger. This perceived danger situation could originate from external environmental events or from internal id and superego demands. Basic danger situations include object loss, loss of love, castration anxiety, and guilt feelings generated by the superego. Intrapsychic conflict results when instinctual urges oppose the ego's environmental realities or the superego's moral prohibitions.

Hence the term *signal anxiety* describes the unconscious institution of defense mechanisms to respond to these danger situations. When symptomatic anxiety occurs, signal anxiety has failed in its function to deactivate the urges and prohibitions that are deemed dangerous. If the danger threshold is too low, the defense mechanisms inadequate, or the perceived danger is overwhelming, Gorman and colleagues (1992) maintain that the symptomatic anxiety will result in a panic state. Two principal goals for short-term psychodynamic treatment of anxiety are to help expand the ego's signal function and to develop better anxiety tolerance. When a therapist explores the subjectively perceived danger situation and helps a patient gain insight through interpretation, Zerbe (1990) maintains that the clinician is employing the "signal theory."

Rangell (1995) notes the universal acceptance of the signal theory and the mixed opinion concerning Freud's former theory, which Freud himself hesitated to abandon. Rangell (1968, 1995), along with Fenichel (1945) and Blau (1952), postulated a unitary theory of anxiety in which both mechanisms exist and operate in tandem. (See Compton [1972] for a comprehensive review of Freud's theories on anxiety.)

Following Freud, numerous psychoanalytic theorists have advanced our understanding of anxiety, most notably Horney (1950), Sullivan (1953), and Fromm-Reichmann (1955) from the interpersonal perspectives, Fairbairn (1952), Bowlby (1973), and Klein (1975a,b) from object relations theories, and Kohut (1977, 1984), the founder of self psychology.

Interpersonal Schools of Thought

Karen Horney (1950), an early cultural feminist, proposed that the painful emotion of anxiety was brought about by hostile, unconscious impulses seeking expression. Presuming the world to be potentially harmful, the person engages in obsessions and addictions as ways to master intense anxiety. In these instances, clinicians need to assist patients in bringing these hostile impulses into consciousness, where they can be better accepted and tolerated.

By contrast, Sullivan (1953) proposed that anxiety arose from the anticipated disapproval of the primary caregiver, usually the mother. Because the child experiences anxiety as toxic, a variety of "security operations" (defenses) are employed to minimize the affect. According to Sullivan, clinicians need to approximate the security of the mother–child dyad in the therapeutic encounter by providing a secure milieu so that patients can gradually develop their own sense of security. His ideas are akin to Winnicott's (1965) formulations about the importance of establishing a "holding environment" in treatment.

Along with Sullivan (1953), Fromm-Reichmann (1955) posited that adults may be appraising others in their environment based on childhood misperceptions. These distorted interpersonal patterns are viewed as a function of anxiety, which, in turn, can generate additional anxiety. The therapist's emphasis here, as with proponents of short-term psychodynamic treatment, is on helping patients recognize how these distorted relationship patterns interfere with their ability to correctly perceive others. In this way, the therapist helps to alleviate anxiety and promote personal growth.

Object Relations Theories

As with the representatives of the interpersonal school of thought noted above, object relations theorists, particularly Klein (1975a,b), Fairbairn (1952), and Bowlby (1973, 1980), have made significant contributions to our understanding of anxiety. Melanie Klein (1975a,b), generally regarded as the progenitor of British object relations theory, held that anxiety was the ego's response to the operation of the death instinct. If the mother's presence cannot be evoked on demand, the infant will experience anxiety in the form of fear of annihilation and death by bad, persecutory part objects. Aggression is introjected in the form of internalized bad objects, and the infant fears persecution from within as well as from outside the self. The infant's feelings of paranoia and persecution constitute the basis of anxiety in the paranoid position, as opposed to the anxiety of the depressive position, which involves preserving an object that is experienced as whole and good (Kernberg 1995). In adult life, manifestations of these early, internalized representational states are evident in paranoid anxiety, as well as in feelings of guilt and inadequacy in being able to maintain positive relationships (Zerbe 1990). Klein's articulation of the processes of projection, introjection, and projective identification inform psychodynamic treatment and are especially relevant in short-term practice where, in the emotionally charged here-and-now atmosphere, patients often flood the therapist with their own raw anxiety (as will be evident in the case example).

Related to Klein's theory, is the work of Ronald Fairbairn (1952), who proposed that the earliest form of anxiety is separation anxiety. When frustrated by the temporary separations from mother, the infant internalizes the object, splitting it into the exciting/libidinal and rejecting/frustration qualities of the mother. The child is deeply dependent on but ambivalently attached to the mother and may oscillate between the desire for closeness and separation. In moving closer toward the mother, the child might feel enveloped or fused (engulfment anxiety), and in the inevitable process of separation, the child might feel lonely and isolated (separation anxiety).

Fairbairn's ideas about the "masochistic defense" and the "internal saboteur" are particularly useful in handling negative therapeutic reactions, which may arise in response to potential treatment progress. The patient, as a result of unconscious guilt from the need to preserve the relationship with the internal saboteur or rejecting object, may unwittingly undermine meaningful external relationships, including the therapeutic one. The intensity and tenacity of a patient's connection to the internal saboteur can also be understood if one extrapolates from John Bowlby's (1973, 1980) work on attachment, separation, and loss. Through his studies of ethology and infant research, Bowlby (1980) observed that "the goal of attachment is to maintain an affectional bond, any situation that seems to be endangering the bond elicits action designed to preserve it, and the greater the danger of loss . . . the more intense and varied are the actions elicited to prevent it" (p. 42).

While Fairbairn (1952) was writing about the power of a relationship to an internal object, Bowlby concentrated on the actual mother–infant dyad and need for mother to provide a secure base for the child. Mothers who fail to be consistently available may have children that develop attachments of an anxious-ambivalent nature (Ainsworth et al. 1978). Anxiety and panic reactions may result from a chronic disturbance in one's sense of safety. In this connection it is also important to note that 20 to 50 percent of adults with panic disorder report symptoms of pathological separation anxiety as children (often school phobia), and that their initial panic attacks were often preceded by the real or threatened loss of a key relationship (D. Klein 1981, cited in Gorman et al. 1992).

Self Psychology

From a self psychological perspective, Kohut (1977, 1984) emphasizes the secure, satisfactory early relationship with mother as setting up the structure for the cohesive self. During early development, the mother serves as a mirroring selfobject and the father as an idealized one. However, Kohut also maintained that selfobjects are essential for psychological health and functioning throughout the life span. Kohut departed significantly from Freud's ideas in fundamental ways, including his views on castration anxiety. Whereas Freud (1905) viewed castration anxiety as a normative event of the oedipal period, Kohut (1977) believed that such anxiety was evidence of the parental selfobjects' failure to provide appropriate, phase-specific empathic responsiveness. *Disintegration anxiety* was the term he used to describe this basic, primitive anxiety. Such anxiety could arise at any phase of development and could be mitigated by the provision of appropriate selfobjects. In treatment the clinician's intellectual interest and affective attunement to the patient serves a vital, corrective selfobject function. (See Zerbe 1990, for a comprehensive and clinically oriented review of the psychoanalytic theories of anxiety.)

To summarize, the theoretical and clinical conceptualization of anxiety has developed substantially since the beginning of psychoanalytic practice. The expansion of psychoanalysis to include relational schools of thought has brought about a greater knowledge of the etiology, processes, and types of anxiety. Long- and short-term clinical practice is enriched by the addition of signal, castration, separation, annihilation, and engulfment anxieties to the professional lexicon.

PANIC AND ANXIETY: DYNAMICS AND DISTINGUISHING FEATURES

Anxiety neurosis was first described by Freud in 1895, but it was not until 1952 that the American Psychiatric Association recognized the syndrome as a distinct clinical entity (Gorman et al. 1992). Prior to the publication of the *DSM-II* in 1952, it was viewed primarily as a "reaction" accompanying other conditions. In 1980, the *DSM-III*, recognizing that spontaneous panic attacks differed qualitatively from chronic anxiety, divided the diagnosis of anxiety neurosis into two distinct categories: panic disorder and generalized anxiety disorder. In 1987, the *DSM-III-R* delineated additional anxiety-related disorders, and the *DSM-IV* (APA 1994) reflected even further complexity in the diagnostic schema.

Fear and worry, core features of panic disorder and generalized anxiety disorder, respectively, are found in all anxiety-related disorders. Researchers have found that these two diagnoses were among the anxiety disorders with the lowest diagnostic agreement (DiNardo et al. 1993, Mannuzza et al. 1989). Additionally, generalized anxiety disorder and panic disorder have a comorbidity rate of 25%, the highest for all of the anxiety-related disorders (APA 1994). Therefore, it is important to describe the dynamics of each disorder and, where possible, to clearly delineate its distinguishing characteristics.

Panic Disorder

Terrifying, unanticipated, "out of the blue" panic attacks are the hallmark of panic disorder. The person is generally engaged in some routine, nonstressful, daily activity, such as eating or watching a movie, when suddenly the individual experiences abrupt, overwhelming physical and psychological sensations. The person is paralyzed by fears of impending death or loss of control, which are accompanied by distressing physical symptoms, such as heart palpitations, tachycardia, sweating, trembling, chest pain or discomfort, feeling choked or smothered, dypnea, nausea or abdominal distress, vertigo, light-headedness, numbness or tingling sensations, and chills or hot flashes. Psychologically, the person may also experience feelings of derealization and depersonalization (APA 1994).

According to the *DSM-IV* (APA 1994), if four or more of these distressing somatic or cognitive symptoms develop abruptly and peak within ten minutes, the person has experienced a panic attack. Although panic attacks are not a codable disorder, the persistent concern about or unexpected recurrence of them, as well as the fear of the health or mental health consequences or altered behavior because of them, will result in the diagnosis of panic disorder. In this context, agoraphobia is a common development. Individuals, particularly women, begin to avoid situations where attacks have occurred and where help is not readily available should another one occur. Panic disorder with agoraphobia is diagnosed three times as often in women than in men (APA 1994).

The label of panic disorder is reserved for individuals who experience panic attacks with some regularity and frequency, although the condition is known to wax and wane with periods of spontaneous recovery followed by additional outbreaks. Before diagnosing someone with panic disorder, it is essential for the diagnostician to rule out panic attacks that may result from drugs or general medical conditions such as hyperthyroidism, hyperparathyroidism, seizure disorders, or cardiac disease. It is also important to determine if the panic attacks are better accounted for by other mental disorders, including those that may be mood based or anxiety related (APA 1994, Brown and Barlow 1992).

Anxiety sensitivity is the strongest predictor of panic disorder and is believed to be both a cause and consequence of the condition (Otto and Reilly-Harrington 1999). Defined as the fear of anxiety sensations, which arises from the belief that these symptoms have harmful psychological, social, or somatic consequences (McNally 1999), anxiety sensitivity is a multifaceted clinical entity and research construct that is evident in most anxiety-related disorders. However, depending on the disorder, different components of anxiety sensitivity may be accentuated.

Most relevant in the assessment of panic disorder is the "catastrophic misinterpretation of certain bodily sensations" (Cox et al. 1999, pp. 121–122). During a panic attack, the person interprets cardiorespiratory and other autonomic physical sensations as being more dangerous than they are in actuality. To a lesser extent the individual may fear cognitive dyscontrol and publicly observable anxiety symptoms. These latter manifestations of anxiety sensitivity are more pronounced in other anxiety-related disorders: in posttraumatic stress disorder, fears of psychological sensations are prominent; in social phobia, there is a dominant fear of publicly observable anxiety; and in generalized anxiety disorder and obsessive-compulsive disorder, fear of cognitive dyscontrol predominates (Cox et al. 1999).

In regard to epidemiology, women are diagnosed with panic disorder twice as often as men, as compared to generalized anxiety disorder where the number of women with the disorder is only slightly greater than the number of men (APA 1994). Panic disorder has also been found to have a strong genetic component; that is, panic disorder tends to run in families (Torgersen 1983).

The psychodynamics of panic disorder do not differ significantly from those of generalized anxiety disorder. Loss is a key dynamic for both disorders. As noted earlier, the actual or threatened loss of an important relationship may precipitate the initial panic attack. Similarly, as with the case example to be presented, generalized anxiety disorder study subjects have been found to have higher rates of trauma related to death, illness, or injury than did nongeneralized anxiety disorder subjects (Borkovec 1994). The panic disorder patients, however, are known to have had early childhood experiences characterized by chronic feelings of frustration and entrapment. This was largely due to insecure attachments to one or both parents who were generally described as frightened, controlling, or critical (Shear et al. 1995). These findings are consistent with Bowlby's (1973) formulation that insecure parental attachments in childhood can lead to a chronically impaired sense of safety in later life.

Generalized Anxiety Disorder

In sharp contrast to the acute, terrifying symptoms of panic disorder, generalized anxiety disorder is characterized by chronic, pervasive feelings of anxiety and worry. As the core feature of generalized anxiety disorder, Borkovec and colleagues (1983) define worry as "a chain of thoughts and images, negatively affect-laden and relatively uncontrollable. [It is] an attempt to engage in mental problem solving on an issue whose outcome is uncertain but contains the possibility of one or more negative outcomes" (p. 10). Despite its potential benefits, Borkovec and colleagues (1983) observe that worry is a cognitive activity that the person feels compelled to engage in, has difficulty terminating unless distracted by environmental stimuli, and cannot prevent its reemergence during the course of a day.

Worry is found in other disorders and is closely linked to the fear process. Its focus, however, will vary depending on the specific diagnosis. For instance, the worry in panic disorder pertains to having a panic attack; in social phobia, there is a fear of being embarrassed in public; and in hypochondriasis, one worries about having a serious illness. In obsessive-compulsive disorder, the obsessional thoughts are qualitatively different from worry in that they are ego-alien intrusions that can be experienced as urges, impulses, and images, as well as thoughts (APA 1994).

The *DSM-IV* (APA 1994) restricts the diagnosis of generalized anxiety disorder to anxiety and worry that are not accounted for by the above-mentioned or other Axis I conditions. Rather, these symptoms of "apprehensive expectation" may occur regularly for at least a six-month period and extend to a number of activities, such as school or work performance. The anxiety and worry are accompanied by at least three of the following six symptoms: restlessness, fatigue, concentration difficulties, irritability, muscle tension, or sleep disturbance. (Children are required to have only one of the six symptoms to qualify for the diagnosis.) The *DSM-IV* (APA 1994) also emphasizes the necessity for the anxiety and worry to cause some degree of impairment in social or occupational functioning.

Although the epidemiology and psychodynamics of generalized anxiety disorder were discussed in comparison to panic disorder, it would be clinically pertinent to address the dynamics of worry. Crits-Christoph and colleagues (1995), reviewing the research of Roemer and colleagues (1991) and Borkovec (1994), as well as their own observations in working with generalized anxiety disorder patients, noted that although these patients have higher rates of trauma than do other patients, they tend to avoid thinking about events they consider traumatic. Worrying seems to serve a defensive function in that it distracts the person from the more distressing affect-laden content. Such content may be related to the death of a significant other or illness involving the self or other.

In applying a dynamic understanding of the research literature to formulate a short-term treatment approach, Crits-Christoph and colleagues (1995) underscore the high level of interpersonal concern associated with worry. Akin to panic-prone individuals, generalized anxiety disorder patients were also insecurely attached in childhood. Their insecurities, however, became manifest largely in their greater enmeshment with the caregiver. In the case to be discussed, Kate is representative of such individuals in that she underwent a role reversal, assuming the role of caregiver to her mother whom she felt the need to protect but also toward whom she held strong ambivalent feelings. In essence, she feared losing the caregiver she loathed.

Culture-Bound Syndromes Associated with Panic and Anxiety

Before turning our discussion to the short-term treatment of anxiety disorders as illustrated in the case of Kate, it would be wise to briefly mention the culture-bound syndromes that feature anxiety-based symptoms. It is clinically imperative to consider the cultural context in which a patient's condition occurs. The *DSM-IV* (APA 1994) enumerates several cultural conditions that mimic the symptoms of panic and generalized anxiety disorder: *Ataque de nervios*, a Latin-American syndrome, often occurs following a stressful precipitating event, such as the death of a family member. It is characterized by uncontrollable crying, shouting, and trembling, and the person may also experience fainting or seizure-like episodes. *Nervios*, a related Latin condition, refers to a more general state of emotional and somatic distress. In Asia, anxiety-type reactions are prevalent. For instance, in Korea, *Hwa-bying*, translated as "anger syndrome," is a condition in which the symptoms of both panic and anxiety are evident; it is to be distinguished from *shin-byung*, which refers to the experiencing of anxiety and somatic complaints, followed by dissociation and the possession by ancestral spirits. *Shen-k'uei* (Taiwan) and *shenkiu* (China) also describes anxiety-related symptoms that are attributed to excessive semen loss, symbolizing the life-threatening loss of one's being or essence. Lastly, *rootwork* refers to the panic-like symptoms associated with the fear of voodoo or witchcraft. This syndrome is frequently encountered in Caribbean cultures.

SHORT-TERM TREATMENT OF ANXIETY DISORDERS

Overview

There are a plethora of long- and short-term treatment models available to the nonmedical clinician, but only a handful are designed exclusively for the treatment of anxiety-based disorders. Among them are panic-focused cognitive behavioral treatment (Barlow and Craske 1994), emotion-focused treatment (Shear et al. 1995), anxiety management training (Gorman et al. 1992), and supportive-expressive dynamic therapy for generalized anxiety disorder (Crits-Christoph et al. 1995).

Research studies have supported the efficacy of several of these latter approaches. Specifically, panic-focused cognitive-behavioral treatment involves the elimination of fears of anxiety sensations and panic episodes through exposure interventions, cognitive restructuring, and training in arousal reduction. Dramatic decreases in anxiety sensitivity were noted in eight-week (Telch et al. 1993) and twelve-week (Penava et al. 1997) cognitive-behavioral programs that utilized these techniques (cited in Otto and Reilly-Harrington 1999). With emotion-focused treatment, Shear and colleagues (1995) focus on the patient's fear and avoidance of negative affects and their triggers. Although the treatment is derived from a psychodynamic model, there is a strong psychoeducational component and emphasis on present-day problems, rather than on interpretation of unconscious conflict. Shear and colleagues (1994) found emotion-focused treatment to be as effective as cognitive-behavioral treatment. In regard to supportive-expressive dynamic therapy for generalized anxiety disorder, Crits-Christoph and associates (1995) found promising results in their pilot study that indicated a significant decrease in the anxiety scores of their subjects. This model serves as the basis for the case illustration.

Short-term supportive-expressive dynamic therapy for generalized anxiety disorder is derived from the core conflictual relationship theme (CCRT) method originally developed by Lester Luborsky in 1984. Messer and Warren (1995) categorize the CCRT method as a relational model of brief psychodynamic treatment and place it in the company of Horowitz's (1988, 1991) person schemas theory, Weiss, Sampson, and the Mount Zion group's (1986) control-mastery therapy, and Binder and Strupp's (1991) cyclical maladaptive pattern model. These approaches view psychopathology in terms of recurrent themes of interpersonal maladaptive behavior. According to Messer and Warren, relational models are more closely aligned with object relations than drive theory because conflict is viewed as arising in the context of interpersonal relationships, not necessarily the result of libidinal and aggressive drives. That is, "a wide range of affects, intentions, wishes and subjectively experienced needs [occur] in relation to others" (p. 119). In addition to sexual and aggressive drives, such conflicts may be related to issues of separation, dependency, and self-integration, and may arise at any stage of development.

The CCRT method, also known as supportive-expressive treatment and supportive-expressive psychodynamic therapy, has been applied in both time-limited and open-ended versions. In addition to generalized anxiety disorder, the CCRT or supportive-expressive treatment method has been found effective in other Axis I disorders, namely major depression (Luborsky et al. 1984, cited in Luborsky et al. 1995a), opioid dependence (Woody et al. 1983, Woody et al. 1994, cited in Luborsky et al. 1995b) and cocaine abuse (Mark and Faude 1995), as well as in the treatment of patients with HIV/AIDS (De Roche 1995).

In the study conducted by Woody and colleagues (1983), patients were randomly assigned to drug counseling alone or to drug counseling plus six months of either supportive-expressive treatment or cognitive-behavioral psychotherapy. While all three treatment groups improved significantly, patients receiving the two psychotherapies demonstrated even greater improvement. In the later study conducted by Woody and associates (1994, cited in Luborsky et al. 1995b), only supportive-expressive treatment was compared to drug counseling, and it was found to have advantages over drug counseling, particularly when measured at one year posttreatment. In an overall meta-analytic review of treatment studies, Crits-Christoph (1992) found evidence for the efficacy of dynamic therapy versus other therapies.

Core Conflictual Relationship Theme Method: General Approach

As noted above, the CCRT method has been applied successfully to a variety of conditions, including generalized anxiety disorder. The CCRT method has a rich history and was inspired by Luborsky's observations of the practice of supportive-expressive psychoanalytically oriented psychotherapy conducted at the Menninger Foundation where he trained. Luborsky's (1984) approach represents an assimilation of the "commonly used techniques in the practice of psychoanalytically oriented psychotherapy" (p. xix). In its short-term version, the CCRT method contains the key elements found in all models of brief psychodynamic therapy: brevity (sixteen-session limit), focus (the CCRT), therapist activity (more active than in long-term psychotherapy), patient capacity to engage and disengage readily (due to the abbreviated nature of the therapeutic relationship), goals (symptom relief and some personality change), and patient selectivity (motivated, psychoanalytically minded patients with sufficient ego strength) (Book 1997, Groves 1996, Messer and Warren 1995). In regard to selectivity, the supportive techniques in the CCRT method suggest applicability to a broader range of patients than for most brief psychodynamic treatments. It should also be noted that the CCRT method is compatible with Goldstein and Noonan's (1999) integrative short-term treatment model discussed in Chapter 2.

As outlined by Luborsky (1984) and later elaborated on by Book (1997), the CCRT method combines two main classes of techniques: supportive ones, which derive from the supportive relationship with the therapist and which are designed to maintain or strengthen the patient's defenses and level of functioning; and expressive ones, which derive from an understanding of what a patient expresses and which are designed to foster an increase in self-understanding through the patient's revelations and through the therapist's interpretations of what has been revealed. Figure 8–1 lists the specific techniques and guidelines for their general use.

Expressive techniques allow the patient to express thoughts and feelings, and then, together with the therapist, the patient reflects on them. For the more psychologically healthy patients, the use of expressive or interpretive techniques is the same as it would be in psychoanalysis. According to Luborsky (1984), the requisite for extensive use of expressive techniques is that patients have adequate ego strength and anxiety tolerance, concomitant with a capacity for reflection about their interpersonal relationships.

Supportive techniques, by contrast, are needed for "patients with character disorders and disruptive alloplastic symptoms" (Luborsky 1984, p. 73). Such patients, by definition, have difficulty tolerating

Figure 8–1.

Level of patient functioning in relation to the use of techniques.
(Adapted from Luborsky [1984] and Book [1997].)

Lower Functioning	Higher Functioning
Continuum	

Supportive Techniques	Expressive Techniques
Continuum	

Supportive Techniques

- Defining the therapeutic frame
- Offering empathic comments
- Maintaining vital defenses
- Maintaining appropriate selfobject transferences
- Setting limits appropriately
- Noting gains
- Returning to the here-and-now perspective
- Demonstrating genuine interest and respect

Expressive Techniques

- Empathic comments
- Clarification
- Confrontation
- Interpretation

anxiety and being self-reflective. Supportive techniques involve helping these patients maintain vital activities and defenses that reinforce their current level of functioning. In addition to specific interventions, support is also inherent in the treatment structure itself. That is, maintaining regular appointment times and length of sessions are important components of a supportive milieu.

Further, Luborsky (1984) proposed that the greater the patient's severity of psychiatric illness, the less expressive and more supportive the therapy needs to be. He underscored the clinician's "freedom" to determine appropriate proportions of supportiveness versus expressiveness. When employing interpretations, he cautioned therapists to limit the extensiveness and complexity of each interpretive statement. With regard to transference interpretations, Luborsky upheld Freud's (1912) principle of going along with the positive and interpreting the negative transference. The more higher functioning the patient, the better able he or she is to respond to and utilize the transference interpretations.

Supportive and expressive techniques are applied to the understanding of the patient's CCRT, the circumscribed focus of therapeutic activity. The CCRT consists of three components: a wish (W), a response from other (RO), and a response from self (RS). The wish occurs in the context of a relationship, and likewise, the actual or anticipated response from that other person occurs in relation to the wish. Subsequently, a person acts in accord with the actual or anticipated response from the other person in regard to that wish. All three aspects, the wish, response from other, and the response from self, are potentially operating in each interaction. To provide greater clarity, let us consider a common type of CCRT pattern found in patients suffering from anxiety and panic. The anxiety-ridden patient who has a history of insecure attachments might wish to have a relationship with someone who is dependable and trustworthy (W). However, the real and/or anticipated response from the other person is one of rejection (RO), which leaves the patient feeling anxious (RS). Often the RS is an Axis I disorder, such as anxiety, substance abuse, or depression, or a psychological state such as sadness, anger, or withdrawal. Treatment may involve any or all of the following: (1) altering the wish to make it a more realistic or mature one, (2) altering one's expectations in regard to the RO, or (3) altering one's RS in regard to the wish or RO experience. The clinician, by virtue of his or her empathic position, offers a reparative RO experience and positively contributes to the changing equation.

Book (1997) emphasizes that the CCRT is a recurrent motif in the person's past and present life, and is at the core of the person's significant interpersonal difficulties. The conflict pertains not only to the disparity of what one wishes for in a relationship and what one experiences receiving, but also to the tension between what one consciously wishes for in a relationship and what one unconsciously seeks in those interactions. That is, one may consciously wish to be treated as an adult by others, yet interact with them in a way that suggests the desire to be dependent on them.

Both Luborsky (1984, 1997) and Book (1997) stress the uniqueness and predictability of an individual's CCRT pattern, one that becomes evident as patients recount relationship episodes from their life experience. Relationship episodes are vignettes or accounts that patients tell the therapist about their interactions with another person or persons. During the assessment process, the therapist is advised to listen attentively to relationship episodes that may be apparent as patients provide details of their developmental history. The patient's psychological mindedness, capacity for insight, and use of defenses in regard to these relationship themes should also be noted. Essentially, such themes occur repeatedly in different current contexts, such as with the therapist, family, friends, co-workers, subordinates, and bosses. These themes are also evident in past relationships, such as with siblings, parents, teachers, and schoolmates. Should a clinician not have the opportunity for a formal assessment period, my experience has been that the very nature of the CCRT pattern ensures its occurrence in the treatment relationship. In fact, as documented by Luborsky and Crits-Christoph (1997), the patient's transference reaction itself is a manifestation of the CCRT.

Core Conflictual Relationship Theme Method: Guidelines for the Treatment of Anxiety Disorders

The collaborative work of Luborsky and Crits-Christoph led the latter author to develop a short-term treatment model for generalized anxiety disorder based on the CCRT method. The following guidelines are derived primarily from the research of Crits-Christoph and colleagues (1995) at the University of Pennsylvania Center for Psychotherapy Research, where I had the opportunity to train in the CCRT method. Given that their method was developed in a research context, some modifications have been made to make their approach applicable to a broader range of anxiety disorder patients in a variety of treatment settings.

Assessment

In a research setting, patient suitability for short-term treatment is often determined by an evaluator who assesses the prospective patient's mental status, *DSM-IV* diagnosis, developmental history, and presenting problem. Generally, patients who are insightful, motivated, possess significant ego strength, and have a history of at least one meaningful relationship tend to do better in short-term treatment. In private practice and in treatment settings that are not research based, the intake evaluator is often the treatment provider as well. In these instances, the clinician is advised to listen for relationship episodes evident in the patient's narrative. Book (1997) suggests that the clinician and patient set up a socialization interview following the evaluation process but prior to initiating therapy. The purpose of this session is to outline the treatment parameters, such as the length and dates of the sixteen sessions, and to discuss the treatment process, particularly in regard to the tentative CCRT. This session also provides the clinician with a valuable opportunity to educate the patient about each of their respective roles in the therapeutic endeavor.

Early Phase (Sessions 1 to 5)

Pragmatically, some clinicians may incorporate the assessment process into the early phase of treatment (as occurs in the case illustration). In this phase, the emphasis is on building a working alliance, which has been associated with better treatment outcomes (Luborsky et al. 1988). This is accomplished by utilizing supportive techniques to build trust and by empathizing with the patient's feelings should negative transferential issues emerge. Patients with an additional Axis II diagnosis are more prone to manifest negative transference reactions. In these instances, it is wise to set boundaries with any behavior that is self-destructive. Additionally, the clinician is cautioned to attend to these issues as they interfere in the treatment process, but to remain focused on the problem of anxiety in relation to the CCRT.

In addition to trust building and preliminary formulation of the CCRT, goal setting is another key task in the early phase. The primary goal is to help the patient understand the CCRT issues involved in the presenting problem of anxiety. Comprehensive personality change is not a realistic goal. Rather, goals should be determined together with the patient and should be focal in nature so as to make them capable of being accomplished.

Middle Phase (Sessions 6 to 11)

Having established a solid working relationship in the early phase, patients generally feel safer and are more open to self-reflection during the middle phase. Their defenses have usually lowered, resulting in the recollection of memories and experiences. The therapist's primary task is to refine the CCRT formulation by illustrating its extensiveness in past and present relationships, including the therapeutic one. This is accomplished by reflecting back to the patient the commonalities found in discussion of his or her relationship episodes. This process is analogous to the working-through process of long-term psychoanalytic treatment.

Should the patient disclose past traumas at this juncture, it would behoove the therapist to discuss them as needed and, where pertinent, to understand the incidents in relation to the anxiety-based symptoms. If the patient shows any signs of decompensation or if the clinician determines that long-term treatment is more appropriate, then the clinician should either shift to a more open-ended treatment or refer the patient for additional treatment elsewhere. Of course, such a decision would depend on the therapist–patient preference and on any constraints inherent in the treatment setting or in regard to financial issues or insurance coverage.

Termination Phase (Session 12 to 16)

Patients who have progressed during the middle phase may experience a resurgence of symptoms in anticipation of termination. The handling of the CCRT during the termination phase becomes the critical focus of intervention. The patient faces the impending loss of the therapist and may fear that his or her goals will not be met by the termination date. Countertransferentially, the therapist may be tempted to collude with the patient by avoiding discussion of termination in favor of more pressing unfinished business. Such a stance deprives both patient and therapist of the opportunity to work through CCRT issues in relation to loss and abandonment. It is recommended that discussion of termination issues begin in session 12, but no later than session 14, to ensure that both parties have the opportunity to process feelings related to impending loss. Mann (1986) asserts that clinicians often have difficulty bringing brief treatment to an appropriate close within the agreed-upon time frame. This is often due to feelings of guilt, as well as the therapist's difficulty tolerating separation and loss.

Booster Phase

Initially designed for research purposes, the booster phase involves scheduling monthly sessions for three months posttermination. The primary purpose of these sessions is to foster further internalization of the therapist's function, that is, to encourage patients to do the work of therapy on their own. Booster sessions also permit the clinician to monitor and reinforce therapeutic gains, and when necessary, to interpret any relapse in terms of the CCRT pattern and loss of the therapist.

Crits-Christoph and colleagues (1995) consider booster sessions an important component of treatment, but also acknowledge concerns that such sessions may "water down" the termination process. It should be noted that such sessions can be a useful option for the patient should the need arise, but that scheduling them can undermine the patient's autonomy. As with the case to be presented, patients will sometimes choose to "check in" or "touch base" following termination, but the decision is their own, not one determined by the clinician.

CASE ILLUSTRATION AND DISCUSSION

Early Phase

Kate is a soft-spoken, self-effacing, Irish Catholic woman in her mid-fifties who presented with a twenty-year history of panic attacks and "jitters." She is slim, attractive, and dresses in a professional manner. As would be her custom for most of our work together, she arrived precisely on time for her first appointment. When I inquired about the circumstances that brought her to treatment, she recounted in a matter-of-fact way her numerous treatment failures, most of which involved medication treatment. I noted her lack of affect, then asked her thoughts about our work together. She veered away from the question, returning to the details of her treatment experiences; this time her dissatisfaction was more pronounced. I acknowledged her disappointment and again asked how those experiences affected her expectations for our work together. In this way, I was both exploring potential transference (CCRT) patterns and alerting her to their impact on our relationship. Had I been working with her on an open-ended basis, I would not have pressed her in regard to treatment expectations. Instead, I likely would have taken note of her lack of response, but not said anything.

Her only hope for our work together was to gain some insight into the psychological causes of her anxiety. She doubted the reassuring comments of her physician, who insisted that her anxiety was solely due to her "sensitive spirit." "There must be more," she countered to him. I took the opportunity to educate her about the treatment process and to foster the working alliance by demonstrating my respect for the insight she has already gained on her own. (Earlier she had stated that she learned more about anxiety medication than about herself.)

Her insights were poignant and extensive. Importantly, she began by attempting to convince me of her intelligence and how others relied on her because of her accomplishments and sense of responsibility. A self-proclaimed perfectionist, she found it difficult to delegate and relinquish control. As a result, she felt burdened by others' expectations and their putting her "last in line." When I asked where this occurred, she said in an exasperated tone, "absolutely everywhere." Friends, family, fellow churchgoers, co-workers, and her boss all sang her praises, but at the cost of her anxiety attacks. (She interchanged the words *anxiety* and *panic*, but her descriptions were unmistakably of severe panic attacks.)

It was not until I asked about the circumstances of her initial attack that the depth of her pain became clear. As she began to talk about her family, she struggled to compose herself as she mentioned her 16-year-old daughter who was killed by a drunk driver fifteen years ago. Kate felt that her daughter was crying out to her before she died and she failed to be there for her. The driver of the car wrote Kate's family a twenty-page letter describing the accident and begging for their forgiveness. Kate regretted not communicating with the elderly man, who she assumes has since died. "If he were here with us now, what would you want to say to him?" I asked. She responded, "I'd tell him that it wasn't his fault. I want to release him from the burden of guilt. God chose this man as his instrument."

Her altruism surprised me, especially since she then went on to talk about her only other child, a son, who, as a budding adolescent, was sexually abused by a church elder. Previously, as a young child he had been molested by the patient's older brother. Kate had yet to tell her mother who was now in her early eighties, fearing that her mother would not believe her and, worse yet, if she did believe her, "the knowledge might kill her." It took Kate's son, Peter, ten years to tell Kate, and subsequently, it took her several more years before she confronted her brother shortly before his death from complications of alcoholism. She was concerned about the impact of such knowledge on her brother's family. Peter, now 30, was single, chronically unemployed, and living at home, which was a tremendous source of shame for Kate and her family. She blamed herself for his choice of lifestyle and his inability to establish a relationship with a woman.

Countertransferentially, I was feeling overwhelmed by the amount and extensiveness of her traumas, when she then added that her panic attacks first began a year or so after she witnessed her father die of a massive heart attack. She was alone and unable to help him as he struggled to breathe. Kate was now the same age as her father when he died. She still missed him and wished that he were alive to help care for her elderly mother who was now in a nursing home. She briefly spoke about her long-standing love–hate relationship with her mother and how her mother did not treat Kate or her family well in comparison with how her mother treated her brother and his family. Even after her brother's death, Kate's mother idealized him, yet she rarely spoke about Kate's deceased daughter. These were all sore points for Kate.

Toward the end of the session, I empathized with much of what she spoke about, especially the many losses and disappointments she experienced in relation to others. Our job would be to understand how these losses and disappointments connected with her need to please others and with her pervasive feelings of anxiety.

The next session she reported felling impressed with our initial meeting and complimented me on my careful listening. (Ostensibly this could be seen as representing the beginning of a working alliance, but it also belied her deep need to please others to ensure having her own needs met.) More importantly, she hadn't realized the accumulation of things that bothered her and queried, "How many blows can a body take?" She began to realize that anxiety was her body's way of saying she was doing too much, yet if she slowed down, others would be disappointed. I commented, "As frightening as the anxiety is, it seems easier than disappointing others." She agreed, recounting all of her church responsibilities and the caregiving responsibilities for her mother. Her mother, she felt, never really appreciated all of her efforts, now or in the past. Kate also felt that she needed people's permission to slow down and it would be difficult to change their view of her, to which I added "and difficult for you to change your view of yourself."

In subsequent early-phase sessions, she began to relate more of her family background. She could not recall her parents saying they were proud of her, nor could she recall their calling her "dear," or "honey," endearing terms Kate routinely called her daughter when she was alive. When I asked her to describe the feelings she experienced as she spoke about the past, she described a gripping feeling in her chest. Kate said, "It's like I'm holding back rather than shouting. I can feel myself holding back now." "And if you let it go?" I asked. She began to cry, later commenting that she makes excuses for her mother, who does not seem to care about her. Her mother, she firmly believed, was more interested in Kate's taking care of her needs rather than the other way around. Kate was realizing that her mother's approval was elusive and conditional. I highlighted her anxiety as a way to express feelings she can't control, linking the anxiety to the "gripping feeling" she expressed earlier. We also talked about her ability to show me her vulnerability (crying), something that she felt was new for her to do. With the exception of the deaths of family members, the only way she let others see her vulnerability was when they witnessed her panic attacks, something that she found embarrassing and humiliating.

Middle Phase

During this phase of treatment, Kate found herself struggling with a range of emotions toward the people with whom she felt closest. Feelings of irritation, annoyance, and anger alternated with feelings of guilt, sadness, loss, and disappointment. She was startled to realize that she felt so much animosity toward her husband, the only person who loved her unconditionally. For much of their time together he held relatively low-paying jobs and, as a school nurse, she assumed the position of family breadwinner. Kate felt guilty for feeling so angry; she tried to reassure us both that it was not her husband's fault as he was wonderfully supportive whenever she had anxiety attacks. "I feel loved when he takes care of me," she said, to which I responded, "When you become anxious, you let other people take care of you. You feel assured of their love and concern." Kate was beginning to recognize that her anxiety attacks allowed her to be dependent on other people. She treated them as she hoped they would treat her when in need: "Maybe this is why I exhaust myself for others . . . to let them know I care. . . . I'm a good person." Kate desperately wanted to be loved for herself and not for the things she did for her husband, mother, and others.

Kate began feeling anxiety symptoms instead of full-blown panic attacks. She also began to address emotionally charged issues that lay dormant for years. For the first time she asked her son to tell her about the details of his abuse. As she began to deal with her own anger, she was better able to hear his anger toward her for not recognizing the signs of abuse. Kate spoke tearfully about her trouble accepting his lifestyle and how she now rejected her son as her mother had done to her. She mourned for her son's lost childhood and her own, and felt that her family suffered as a result of her limitations.

Kate also used treatment as an opportunity to mourn her daughter. She spoke not only of missing her, but of the unfairness in losing a child so needlessly. Kate was cognizant of not wanting to burden others with feelings about her daughter. She was brave to others but secretly bitter and perpetually sad about her loss. Kate was ashamed to admit that she still thought about her daughter every day and, more so, that she really hated the man who killed her. "I'm not being a good Christian," she said. "People would think I'm terrible." We spoke at length about her feeling so unlovable and alone, before I asked if she could feel loved if she were honest with others: "When you are anxious and in need, you feel loved by others. Can you be loved when you're angry?"

Kate truly believed that people cared for her only when she was winning favor with them, that is, when she was doing something to take care of their needs. She was able to test out her emotional honesty in the transference. At work she was asked to take on additional responsibilities without increased pay and she felt helpless to set limits with the supervising nurse. Therapy helped with "old stuff" but hadn't helped her to set limits when she felt others were taking advantage of her. She was able to express disappointment in me and the limitations of our work. We spoke about the importance of her honesty and how expressing her true feelings did not turn me away from her. Instead, it helped me to better understand her and to be more attentive to her current concerns.

Termination Phase

Her frustrations about the treatment process also reflected her growing awareness of termination. There were so many issues left to discuss and she "forgot" that our arrangement was to meet for sixteen sessions. Similar to her view of the issues and people in her life, Kate was disappointed that she wasn't further along in our work. "I came here to put these things away for good and that can't happen," she said. Kate expected herself to be a better patient, and if I were grading her she would anticipate receiving a B or B+, grades not acceptable to a woman accustomed to receiving an A+. We used this as an opportunity to discuss her unrealistic expectations for herself and her perceived need to not disappoint me.

With this understanding in mind, Kate continued to address the most pressing issues. In regard to her mother, she faced the painful realization that her mother would probably never really accept her or her husband. Kate was also able to see that some of her anger toward her husband related to the fact that he could not live up to her mother's expectations either. She held the erroneous fantasy that if she married someone different, perhaps then her mother would have embraced her.

Kate continued to work on the relationships with her husband and son, and was better able to set limits in regard to work and church activities. She reported a resurgence of anxiety when saying no to others, but instead of a "gripping" feeling associated with holding back anger and other difficult emotions, she felt terrified that they would reject her. She continued to worry about others' responses, yet she took chances in those relationships.

Perhaps she made the most progress in mourning her daughter. In the session prior to our last meeting, she was uncharacteristically fifteen minutes late. On her way to the session she witnessed a fatal car accident. Although the bodies had already been removed, the experience evoked images of her daughter's death. She was overcome with grief, sobbing as she called her daughter's name. She missed her "baby" and cried as if she had just heard about her death. Kate described in searing detail what she imagined her daughter's final moments to be like. She would have given anything to trade places with her daughter in order to let her daughter live.

In short-term treatment there are often difficult moments and countertransferential feelings for the clinician. With Kate, I frequently felt helpless, inadequate, and anxious, yet this session proved to be the most difficult. Her pain was so palpable, I found myself wanting to reach out to comfort her. Instead I settled for sitting forward and simply listening, hoping she was not paying attention to my watery eyes. My response seemed woefully inadequate compared to the courage she had just shown in mourning her daughter. Subjectively, bearing witness to her pain helped me to realize my own unfinished business in regard to my mother's death, which, coincidentally, also occurred fifteen years ago.

The final session proved to be difficult as well. "You've become a link to security," she told me. "It will be hard to let this go." Kate spoke about the previous session and worried if she could continue the work on her own. She also wondered if she punished herself for her daughter's death by suffering so much (referring to her anxiety). Kate's insight was testimony to her ability to continue working on her own. We spoke about the other insights she made over the course of our work together, especially how her anxiety ensured the love of others and how she feared that they would not be there for her unless she was doing something for them. Last, we spoke about how she felt I was there for her at her worst (referring to her anger and unresolved mourning) and that she might consider giving others the same opportunity.

As we parted, I assured her that she could contact me if the need arose. She thanked me for what she learned about herself and I silently thanked her as well. Therapy, I believe, can be mutually reparative.

Booster Phase/Follow Up

Kate contacted me six weeks later to report in on how she was doing. She appreciated the offer to meet if she needed to, but things seemed to be going pretty well. She found that she still became anxious, but not as often or as intensely. She did have one major panic attack, but was able to weather it on her own. She internalized the analytic function to some extent and reflected on the panic attack by asking herself, "Am I angry or upset about something?" It was still difficult to say no to others, but she did not let that stop her from doing so. She stated, "I have to take care of myself. . . . I don't need anxiety to do that for me."

Discussion

Kate made important gains in understanding how her anxiety connected to the relationship themes in her life. In treatment she presented numerous relationship episodes that reflected her predicament; she began to appreciate how desperately she sought the love and approval of others, and that this need extended to her family, friends, fellow worshipers, and co-workers alike (the W of CCRT). This wish originated in childhood and manifested itself later in present-day relationships and in the therapeutic encounter. Kate anticipated and at key times received negative responses from others beginning with her parents in childhood. She believed that to receive acceptance from others (an accepting, positive RO), she needed to put their needs before her own (RS), leading to anxiety (another RS). Kate's anxiety (RS), in turn, ensured the attention and care from others (positive RO) and made her feel loved.

In treatment and through the therapeutic relationship, Kate sought to change the nature of the relationship pattern to one where she could receive love from others when she expressed her feelings honestly and openly (RS). Rather than reject her, she learned that others (namely the therapist) could accept and understand her (positive RO). Instead of anxiety, Kate began to respond with genuine, deep-seated feelings (RS) and thus began the process of changing her CCRT pattern. Kate needed to be angry and to mourn, comforted in the knowledge that she would be cared for and understood.

While Kate made important gains in understanding the problems that plagued her for years, it is important to remember that short-term treatment is not a panacea. As with most patients, Kate presented with numerous issues, all of which she experienced as urgent and warranting attention. As her narrative unfolded, my interventions were guided by her desire to understand the core relationship themes in her life. If time permitted more work could have been done, but such is the nature of short-term treatment.

CONCLUSION

There are myriad ways of understanding the complex and universal experience of anxiety. This chapter has examined the psychoanalytic theories of anxiety, approaching the topic from the multiple model perspectives of Freud, interpersonal and object relations schools of thought, and self psychology. Such an approach reflects the pluralism of contemporary psychodynamic practice. Additionally, the concept of anxiety is multifaceted and has been examined in relation to panic and the cultural context in which the symptom occurs. The short-term treatment approach to anxiety has been described and applied to the case of Kate, demonstrating the ways to approach anxiety in a short-term treatment context.

REFERENCES

Ainsworth, M., Blehar, M., Waters, E., and Wall, S. (1978). *Patterns of Attachment: A Psychological Study of the Strange Situation.* New York: Wiley.

American Psychiatric Association. (1994). *Diagnostic and Statistical Manual of Mental Disorders,* 4th ed. Washington, DC: Author.

Barlow, D. H. (1988). *Anxiety and Its Disorders.* New York: Guilford.

Barlow, D. H., and Craske, M. G. (1994). *Mastery of Your Anxiety and Panic II.* New York: Psychological Corporation.

Binder, J. L., and Strupp, H. H. (1991). The Vanderbilt approach to time-limited dynamic psychotherapy. In *Handbook of Short-Term Dynamic Psychotherapy,* ed. P. Crits-Christoph and J. P. Barber, pp. 137–165. New York: Basic Books.

Blau, A. (1952). In support of Freud's syndrome of "actual" anxiety neurosis. *International Journal of Psycho-Analysis* 33:363–372.

Book, H. E. (1997). *How to Practice Brief Psychodynamic Psychotherapy: The Core Conflictual Relationship Method.* Washington, DC: American Psychological Association.

Borkovec, T. D. (1994). The nature, function and origins of worry. In *Worrying: Perspectives on Theory Assessment and Treatment,* ed. G. C. Davey and F. Tallis, pp. 5–34. Sussex, UK: Wiley.

Borkovec, T. D., Robinson, E., Pruzinsky, T., and DePree, J. (1983). Preliminary exploration of worry: some characteristics and processes. *Behavior Research and Therapy* 21:9–16.

Bowlby, J. (1973). *Separation.* New York: Basic Books.

——— (1980). *Loss.* New York: Basic Books.

Brown, T. A., and Barlow, D. H. (1992). Comorbidity among anxiety disorders: implications for treatment and *DSM-IV. Journal of Consulting and Clinical Psychology* 60:835–844.

Clark, D. M. (1986). A cognitive approach to panic. *Behavior Research and Therapy* 28:461–470.

Compton, A. (1972). A study of the psychoanalytic theory of anxiety: I. The development of Freud's theory of anxiety. *Journal of the American Psychoanalytic Association* 20:3–44.

Cox, B. J., Borges, S. C., and Enns, M. W. (1999). Anxiety sensitivity and emotional disorders: psychometric studies and their theoretical implications. In *Anxiety Sensitivity: Theory, Research, and Treatment of the Fear of Anxiety,* ed. S. Taylor, pp. 115–148. London: Lawrence Erlbaum.

Crits-Christoph, P. (1992). The efficacy of brief dynamic psychotherapy: a meta-analysis. *American Journal of Psychiatry* 149:151–158.

Crits-Christoph, P., Crits-Christoph, K., Wolf-Palacio, D., et al. (1995). Brief supportive expressive psychodynamic psychotherapy for generalized anxiety disorder. In *Dynamic Therapies for Psychiatric Disorders,* ed. J. P. Barber and P. Crits-Christoph, pp. 43–83. New York: Basic Books.

DeRoche, P. (1995). Psychodynamic psychotherapy with the HIV-infected client. In *Dynamic Therapies for Psychiatric Disorders,* ed. J. P. Barber and P. Crits-Christoph, pp. 420–443. New York: Basic Books.

DiNardo, P. A., Moras, K., Barlow, D. H., et al. (1993). Reliability of *DSM-III-R* anxiety disorder categories using the Anxiety Disorders Interview Schedule–Revised (ADIS-R). *Archives of General Psychiatry* 50:251–256.

Fairbairn, W. R. D. (1952). *An Object Relations Theory of the Personality.* New York: Basic Books.

Fenichel, O. (1945). *The Psychoanalytic Theory of Neurosis.* New York: Norton.

Freud, S. (1895). On the grounds for detaching a particular syndrome from neurasthenia under the description "anxiety neurosis." *Standard Edition* 3:86–117.

———— (1900). The interpretation of dreams. *Standard Edition* 4/5.

———— (1905). Three essays on the theory of sexuality. *Standard Edition* 7:125–243.

———— (1912). Recommendation to physicians practising psycho-analysis. *Standard Edition* 12:145–156.

———— (1926). Inhibitions, symptoms, and anxiety. *Standard Edition* 20:75–175.

Fromm-Reichmann, F. (1955). Psychiatric aspects of anxiety. In *An Outline of Psychoanalysis*, ed. C. M. Thompson, M. Mazer, and E. Witenberg, pp. 113–133. New York: Modern Library.

Goldstein, A. J., and Chambless, D. L. (1978). A reanalysis of agoraphobia. *Behavior Therapy* 9:47–59.

Goldstein, E. G., and Noonan, M. (1999). *Short-Term Treatment and Social Work Practice: An Integrative Perspective*. New York: Free Press.

Gorman, J. M., Liebowitz, M. R., and Shear, M. K. (1992). Panic and anxiety disorders. In *Psychiatry*, ed. R. Michels, J. Cavens, H. Brodie, et al., pp. 1–14. New York: Lippincott-Raven.

Greenson, R. (1967). *The Technique and Practice of Psychoanalysis*. New York: International Universities Press.

Groves, J. E. (1996). Introduction: four "essences" of short-term therapy: brevity, focus, activity, selectivity. In *Essential Papers on Short-Term Dynamic Therapy*, ed. J. E. Groves, pp. 1–25. New York: New York University Press.

Horney, K. (1950). *Neurosis and Human Growth: The Struggle Toward Self-Realization*. New York: Norton.

Horowitz, M. (1988). *Introduction to Psychodynamics: A New Synthesis*. New York: Basic Books.

——— (1991). Short-term dynamic therapy of stress response syndromes. In *Handbook of Short-Term Dynamic Psychotherapy*, ed. P. Crits-Christoph and J. P. Barber, pp. 166–198. New York: Basic Books.

Kernberg, O. (1995). Psychoanalytic object relations theories. In *Psychoanalysis: The Major Concepts*, ed. B. E. Moore and B. D. Fine, pp. 450–462. New Haven: Yale University Press.

Klein, D. F. (1981). Concepts: anxiety reconceptualized. In *Anxiety: New Research*, ed. D. F. Klein and J. G. Rabkin, pp. 235–263. New York: Raven.

Klein, M. (1975a). *Love, Guilt and Reparation and Other Works: 1921–1945*. New York: Delacorte.

——— (1975b). *Envy and Gratitude and Other Works: 1946–1963*. New York: Delacorte.

Kohut, H. (1977). *The Restoration of the Self.* New York: International Universities Press.

———— (1984). *How Does Analysis Cure?* Chicago, IL: University of Chicago Press.

Luborsky, L. (1984). *Principles of Psychoanalytic Psychotherapy: A Manual for Supportive-Expressive Treatment.* New York: Basic Books.

———— (1997). The convergence of Freud's observations about transference and the CCRT evidence. In *Understanding Transference: The Core Conflictual Relationship Theme Method,* ed. L. Luborsky and P. Crits-Christoph, pp. 307–325. Washington, DC: American Psychological Association.

Luborsky, L., and Crits-Christoph, P. (1997). *Understanding Transference: The Core Conflictual Relationship Theme Method.* Washington, DC: American Psychological Association.

Luborsky, L., Crits-Christoph, P., Mintz, J., and Auerbach, A. (1988). *Who Will Benefit From Psychotherapy? Predicting Therapeutic Outcomes.* New York: Basic Books.

Luborsky, L., Diguier, L., De Rubeis, R., et al. (1994). *The efficacy of dynamic psychotherapy for major depression versus chronic depression.* Paper presented at the NIMH methodology conference on research on treatment of chronic and recurrent anxiety and mood disorders, Bethesda, MD, February.

Luborsky, L., Mark, D., Hole, A.V., et al. (1995a). Supportive-expressive dynamic psychotherapy of depression: a time-limited version. In *Dynamic Therapies for Psychiatric Disorders,* ed. J. P. Barber and P. Crits-Christoph, pp. 13–42. New York: Basic Books.

Luborsky, L., Woody, G. E., Hole, A. V., and Velleco, A. (1995b). Supportive-expressive dynamic psychotherapy for treatment of opiate drug dependence. In *Dynamic Therapies for Psychiatric Disorders,* ed. J. P. Barber and P. Crits-Christoph, pp. 131–160. New York: Basic Books.

Mann, J. (1986). Transference and countertransference in brief psychotherapy. In *Between Analyst and Patient: New Dimensions in Countertrans-*

ference and Transference, ed. H. C. Meyers, pp. 119–127. New York: Analytic Press.

Mannuzza, S., Fyer, A. J., Martin, L. Y., et al. (1989). Reliability of anxiety assessment: I. Diagnostic agreement. *Archives of General Psychiatry* 46:1093–1101.

Mark, D., and Faude, J. (1995). Supportive-expressive therapy of cocaine abuse. In *Dynamic Therapies for Psychiatric Disorders*, ed. J. P. Barber and P. Crits-Christoph, pp. 294–331. New York: Basic Books.

McNally, R. (1999). Theoretical approaches to the fear of anxiety. In *Anxiety Sensitivity: Theory, Research, and Treatment of the Fear of Anxiety*, ed. S. Taylor, pp. 3–16. London: Lawrence Erlbaum.

Messer, S. B., and Warren, C. S. (1995). *Models of Brief Psychodynamic Therapy: A Comparative Approach*. New York: Guilford.

Otto, M. W., and Reilly-Harrington, N. A. (1999). The impact of treatment on anxiety sensitivity. In *Anxiety Sensitivity: Theory, Research, and Treatment of the Fear of Anxiety*, ed. S. Taylor, pp. 321–336. London: Lawrence Erlbaum.

Penava, S. J., Otto, M. W., Maki, K. M., and Pollack, M. H. (1997). Rate of improvement during cognitive-behavioral group treatment for panic disorder. *Behaviour Research and Therapy* 36:665–673.

Rangell, L. (1955). On the psychoanalytic theory of anxiety. *Journal of the American Psychoanalytic Association* 3:389–414.

———— (1968). A further attempt to resolve the "problem of anxiety." *Journal of the American Psychoanalytic Association* 16:371–404.

———— (1978). On understanding and treating anxiety and its derivatives. *International Journal of Psycho-Analysis* 59:229–236.

———— (1995). Affects. In *Psychoanalysis: The Major Concepts*, ed. B. E. Moore and B. D. Fine, pp. 381–391. New Haven: Yale University Press.

Roemer, L., Borkovec, M., Posa, S., and Lyonfields, J. (1991). *Generalized anxiety disorder in an analogue population: the role of past trauma*. Paper presented at the meeting of the Association for the Advancement of Behavior Therapy, New York: November.

Shear, M. K., Cloitre, M., and Heckelman, L. (1995). Emotion-focused treatment for panic disorder: a brief, dynamically informed therapy. In *Dynamic Therapies for Psychiatric Disorders*, ed. J. P. Barber and P. Crits-Christoph, pp. 267–293. New York: Basic Books.

Shear, M. K., Pilkonis, P. A., Cloitre, M., and Leon, A. C. (1994). Cognitive behavioral treatment compared with nonprescriptive treatment of panic disorder. *Archives of General Psychiatry* 51:395–401.

Sullivan, H. S. (1953). *The Interpersonal Theory of Psychiatry*. New York: Norton.

Telch, M. J., Lucas, J. A., Schmidt, N. B., et al. (1993). Group cognitive-behavioral treatment of panic disorder. *Behavior Research and Therapy* 31:279–287.

Torgersen, S. (1983). Genetic factors in anxiety disorders. *Archives of General Psychiatry* 40:1085–1089.

Weiss, J., Sampson, J., and Mount Zion Psychotherapy Research Group (1986). *The Psychoanalytic Process: Theory, Clinical Observations and Empirical Research*. New York: Guilford.

Winnicott, D. W. (1965). *The Maturational Processes and the Facilitating Environment*. New York: International Universities Press.

Wolpe, J., and Rowan, V. C. (1988). Panic disorder: a product of classical conditioning. *Behavior Research and Therapy* 26:441–450.

Woody, G., Luborsky, L., McLellan, A. T., et al. (1983). Psychotherapy for opiate addicts: Does it help? *Archives of General Psychiatry* 40:639–645.

Woody, G., McLellan, A. T., Luborsky, L., and O'Brien, C. (1994). *The outcomes of psychosocial treatments for opiate addicts in three community clinics*. Paper presented at the meeting of the North American Society for Psychotherapy Research, Santa Fe, NM, June.

Zerbe, K. (1990). Through the storm: psychoanalytic theory in the psychotherapy of the anxiety disorders. *Bulletin of the Menninger Clinic* 54:171–183.

CHAPTER NINE

Short-Term Therapy with Eating-Disordered Patients

ELLEN AGOOS

The treatment of eating-disordered patients requires an understanding of the complexities of their behavior and their sense of self in addition to a realization that they have an urgent wish to assume control over their lives and to abstain from their symptoms. In a session a patient may be talking about some important psychological issue, but for many patients their thinking focuses on whether or not they can make it through the day without binging, purging, or restricting. Their basic needs are for survival, safety, and security.

These concerns demand an approach that will help the patient begin to address her[1] symptomatology. One particular form of short-term psychotherapy, cognitive-behavioral therapy, has demonstrated positive effects in reducing the frequency and intensity of binge eating (Fairburn 1995, Garner et al. 1985, MacFarland 1995).

---

1. Because of the prevalence of eating disorders in women, the feminine pronoun is used throughout this chapter to refer to the eating-disordered patient.

As third-party payers demand economy and quality in mental health services, therapists are faced with ever-increasing pressures to treat patients as cost-effectively as possible. The clinical complexity of the eating-disorder syndromes poses a particular challenge for therapists. To be effective practitioners in the era of health care reform and increasingly stringent managed care guidelines, therapists need to be open to brief models and to have the skills that accompany these models. This conceptual adjustment requires therapists to consider focusing on the causes of the symptoms and on uncovering solutions in the patient's own experience.

This chapter outlines the dimensions of a short-term model of treatment for eating-disordered patients, including (1) the characteristics of the model, highlighting the theoretical overview and treatment perspective; (2) a description of the *DSM-IV* (APA 1994) criteria for classification of bulimia; and (3) the general treatment goals. A case illustration demonstrates the specific techniques employed. Though the case example describes the treatment of a bulimic woman, the theory and technique apply to anorexics and compulsive binge-eaters as well.

THEORETICAL OVERVIEW
AND TREATMENT PERSPECTIVE

The short-term model (Fairburn 1995, Goldstein and Noonan 1999, MacFarland 1995) takes advantage of the competencies and resilience inherent in the patient. It offers a unique perspective of identifying exceptions to the problem behavior and using those exceptions as a solution (MacFarland 1995). The therapist must be willing to accept a paradigm shift and ask, "What does this patient need?" and "How can things be better in the future?" A solution-focused, short-term treatment can create more rapid change and empower patients to recognize and appreciate their own personal efficacy and resourcefulness. MacFarland (1995) states, "By focusing on the patient's own mastery experiences related to the eating/restricting/purging behaviors, further entrenchment in the maladaptive behaviors is thwarted or reduced, and the individual is likely to experience a positive ripple effect that will influence other aspects of her life" (p. 13). This is accomplished by amplifying, reinforcing, and highlighting solution patterns and by establishing proximal goals that are salient to the patient.

Fairburn's (1995) cognitive-behavioral model for the treatment of binge eaters details a treatment strategy that targets symptoms including restricting behaviors, binge eating, purging behaviors, and the thoughts and feelings that mediate the performance of these behaviors. The cognitions that have been most frequently targeted include a drive for thinness and body dissatisfaction (Garner and Bemis 1984). Therapist and patient collaborate on the target symptom to be self-managed. Additionally, the use of self-monitoring and diary writing increases success. This model can be easily applied to the treatment of anorexia and bulimia.

MacFarland's (1995) short-term treatment is a solution-based, dynamic approach that enlists, when necessary, outside resources such as family, friends, nutritionists, pharmacologists, and support groups. The use of food journals, cognitive approaches, and "contracting" work add to the multidimensionality of this treatment approach. This approach initiates a new clinical trend in the eating disorder field by emphasizing the significance of highlighting and reinforcing patient competencies. The goal is to help the patient identify exceptions (those times when binging, purging, or restricting is not problematic or to identify other viable existing solution patterns) and help the patient repeat them. The therapist works as a collaborator with the patient, who is an active participant and expert in her own care.

Certain theoretical assumptions underlie the short-term model of treatment (Goldstein and Noonan 1999, MacFarland 1995):

- Eating-disordered patients have the necessary internal resources and competencies to surmount their own difficulties or solve their own problems.

- The patient and therapist work together cooperatively, with the patient functioning as the "expert" in her treatment and defining the goal of therapy.
- Change is viewed as inevitable and constant, and the therapeutic process is based on the belief that one small change in the system effects change in other parts of the system.
- The treatment focuses on what is possible and changeable. The therapist strives to be as economical as possible in obtaining desired therapeutic goals.

My clinical experience using a short-term model has demonstrated that those patients who have a more stable ego, good reality testing, good judgment, high motivation, and previous periods of abstinence can benefit from this more interactive, behavior-focused approach. For those patients whose pathology reinforces the maintenance of the symptom, longer-term analytic work may be required to uncover the resistances and reenactments that militate against change.

INCLUSION AND EXCLUSION CRITERIA

Researchers and clinicians postulate multiple variables that interactively serve as potential pathogenic routes and increase the risk of an individual developing an eating disorder. The more commonly accepted risk factors can be summed up under four variables: sociocultural, familial, individual, and biological (MacFarland 1995).

Sociocultural Variables

- The thin body ideal is valued and the thin body is seen as symbolizing self-discipline, control, independence, attractiveness, and success.
- Women's role expectations are in conflict.

Familial Variables

- Family is highly achievement oriented and perfectionistic.
- Family places great value on appearance and is preoccupied with food, dieting, and bodily functions.
- Family tends to exhibit rigidity, enmeshment, inability to resolve conflicts, and overprotectiveness.

Individual Variables

- The person is usually an adolescent girl who feels overweight.
- The person has an impaired self-concept and general feelings of ineffectiveness.
- The person has marked cognitive distortions related to shape and weight and impaired body image.
- The person has difficulty adapting to the maturational tasks of adolescence, such as separation-individuation, dating, burgeoning sexuality.
- The person tends toward an obsessional style.
- The person has dysphoria, affective instability, and impulsivity.

Biological Variables

- The dysregulation of serotonin (a brain neurotransmitter) results in binge eating.
- The mechanism of satiety (secretion of the hormone cholecystokinin) is impaired.
- The effects of starvation alter mood, cognitive ability, and character traits, causing the eating disorder to become more entrenched and resistant to treatment.
- Restrictive dieting adversely affects satiety cues, which are correlated with binge behaviors, and metabolic rate, which can promote weight gain.

- Strict dieting and exercise can trigger the biobehavioral process that results in anorexia.

Theorists such as Bruch (1962) and Wilson and colleagues (1985) stress the importance of unraveling separation-individuation conflicts and repairing deficits in the ego.

The overlap between the anorexia nervosa and bulimia diagnoses and the tendency of patients to alternate between diagnoses in the course of the disorder are borne out and reported in the literature (Russell 1981) and in clinical practice. Patients tend to swing back and forth from restricting to bingeing with or without purging. Over the course of time, patients can experience both types of symptoms either concurrently or alternately. Sours (1980) points out that anorexia nervosa patients may be anything from starving "cadavers" to binge eaters of normal weight who gorge on enormous meals three to four times a day. The common feature is that all the patients have endured a subjective conflict between, on the one hand, anorexic efforts to lose weight, and, on the other, bulimic impulses threatening to thwart these strivings. Theander (1970) notes that "a conflict arises between the more or less conscious desire to eat and the resistance to satisfy this need" (p. 76). The central disturbance in anorexia is the fear of being overcome and losing control of eating (Chediak 1977). Crisp (1970) describes this phenomenon as "weight phobia." In contrast, the bulimic impulses imply a permanent preoccupation with thoughts and actions concerning food and eating and urges to gorge without restraint.

Thus, food and purging are used to numb "emerging feelings" (Bruch 1962) or to desperately compensate for "feeling empty" (Johnson and Connors 1987). Underneath the bulimic structure, emotions rage and confusion reigns. Life in general feels overwhelming. An imprisoning structure of goals, plans, and predetermined behavior is adhered to, while bingeing and purging serve to express the alien aspects of self and otherwise function to organize, however unsuccessfully, the patient's life (Brisman 1989).

TREATMENT GOALS

Central to the short-term model of Fairburn (1995) and MacFarland (1995) is the hypothesis that there are exceptions—periods of time when the problem does not occur. The focus of the initial sessions is on encouraging the patient to imaginatively project herself into a future situation in which her problem no longer exists. The therapy highlights the patient's ability to generate exceptions, picturing a new life for herself, validating the fact that change is happening and that it can happen rapidly. The therapist and patient work together, forming realistic and achievable treatment goals that are highly specific. Goals emerge from the therapist's questions: "What do you want to be different as a result of coming here?" "How will we know when therapy is finished?" Both therapist and patient need to know where they are going and how to recognize that they have gotten there. Once therapists know what works, they can then focus their therapeutic efforts. When the therapist and patient discover a meaningful exception to the problem, then a solution has probably been discovered and the patient needs to do more of the exception. Suggested techniques such as journal writing (Brisman 1989) in lieu of bingeing are offered. The goals of brief therapy are more limited than traditional therapy.

Developing proximal goals (short-term, readily achievable changes), is essential in this treatment approach. The small steps needed to achieve the larger goal reinforce a feeling of efficacy and mastery, and sustain motivation in the presence of the debilitating and disorganizing symptomatology. Learning to tolerate behavioral slips or lapses is a natural course of treatment. Disordered eating is often triggered by unpleasant events or stressors. Developing skills for dealing with day-to-day problems and stressors is critical. Patients will need support in distancing themselves from impulsive bouts of eating, allowing themselves to feel the anxieties and depression that were masked by their symptom. A primary goal of early treatment intervention is allowing the patient the experience of anxiety, an experience usually avoided if eating is an immediate response to internal stress. Techniques employed to address these goals are demonstrated by the following case and then discussed.

CASE ILLUSTRATION

This case demonstrates a way of working with a bulimic patient in which the short-term integrative treatment model (Goldstein and Noonan 1999), the cognitive-behavioral model (Fairburn 1995), active intervention, assignments, and contracts are integrated to produce a solution-focused treatment. This case illustrates how the therapist constructs a cooperative relationship with the patient in which "your reality, your way of being, your perspective is not superior to the client's" (Gilligan 1990, p. 368). A willingness on the therapist's behalf to discuss bingeing, vomiting, calories, and weight obsession carries a particular importance for the bulimic patient and is central to the treatment. The language of food and weight is the main (and often only) language the patient has for talking about herself, her fears, and her needs. This language informs the treatment, facilitating a symptom-based approach.

Beginning Phase I:
Problem Identification, Biopsychosocial Assessment, Engagement

Linda telephoned the eating-disorder center looking for a therapist who accepts her managed care insurance, and I agreed to see Linda the following week. I liked her the minute I met her. She was eager, anxious, and frightened, yet she offered an easy manner that allowed for early engagement. Linda is a 39-year-old single, white, Jewish woman from a solidly middle-class background. She looks slightly older than her stated age. She is of normal weight at 5'6" and 135 pounds. She is obsessed with her body and body weight and has recently gained 20 pounds. She works in retail clothing as a buyer four days a week and was attempting to start a masseuse business so she could ultimately leave her job. She was a rapid-fire talker who got down to business immediately. She told me that she feels "pulled in all directions. I'm running all over. There's nothing left for me." In addition to her day job, Linda sees private massage clients in the evening. She also works part-time as a masseuse in a spa. She feels confused, unhappy, and overwhelmed by her choices.

Linda supplied me with information about her eating disorder and an evolutionary tale and current status of the frequency of bingeing and purging. There was a conspicuous omission of her childhood and family history. Instead, she placed an emphasis on food, weight, and binge/purge behavior. She was bright, curious, and relieved to be talking about her binge eating. She chronicled her previous treatment efforts in a well-organized fashion, informing me that she had never been in therapy but had been in Overeaters Anonymous for fifteen years, reporting great success and many periods of remission. She had been through "The Forum" on a few occasions and had found deep understanding and relief upon completion of the workshops. An inquiry into the binge/purge behavior revealed its onset to be age 14, at which time her menses ceased. As with many bulimics, the frequency and severity was minimal, increasing rapidly over the course of a few years. At age 17 she became anorexic. Since then, she has alternated between bulimia and anorexia, and is currently binge eating with occasional purging. She outlined her rigid rules of "what works." Her best periods are when she is avoiding white flour, wheat, and sugar. (These are common "taboo" foods of bulimics, anorexics, and compulsive overeaters.) She mentioned that intense binge eating began about three months ago following a twelve-day fast. She felt that the fast precipitated the binge eating and she needed to get it under control. She let me know that she not only wanted to stop bingeing but also wanted to gain a deeper understanding of her current stressors.

Born an only child to parents who were bakers, Linda recalled with amusement spending many after-school hours in the bakery overwhelmed by the searing smell of the fresh baked bread. She recalled her childhood with a distant look that seemed a mirror for how she felt growing up. Childhood was a very lonely and distant experience, distant from her parents, friends, relatives. Her mother, though overprotective, was described as nonnurturing, depressed, narcissistic, fearful, and unable to take care of herself. Linda suspected that her mother was anorexic. Intensity of emotion was focused on her father, a highly critical and cruel man who frequently exhibited rages that frightened Linda. Hornyak and Baker (1989) state that the father is the prime masculine figure in most young girls' lives and that a father's reaction influences a girl's responses to her changing body, her femininity, and herself in general. For Linda, her father was inconsistent, vacillating between being an admirer and a critical judge.

Beginning Phase II: *Assessing Self-Capacities, Engaging, and Beginning Contracting*

During this assessment phase, I learned few historical memories and I realized that we would have to construct a narrative of her life from hypotheses that we would begin to generate throughout the early phases of treatment. I realized that Linda had experienced much pain in her youth, and the lack of memory might be due to a trauma that she quickly revealed. When Linda was 14 her mother died of breast cancer after a long illness. Within a few months her father was diagnosed with cancer and was critically ill for five years until his death when Linda was 21. Linda could barely mourn her mother before being thrust into caring for her father. Having had a tumultuous relationship with her father prior to his illness, Linda was resentful not only of having to care for him but of being robbed of her adolescence. Linda told me of feeling alternately hateful and loving of her father who "also had a nice side. I always wanted his approval."

After her father's death, Linda gained a sizable inheritance, which she rapidly depleted in four years. "I felt like I was finally free and able to live my life. I became very independent. I know I was very reckless and eventually I got myself into D.A. (Debtors Anonymous) in my late twenties. Since then I've been more careful with money."

As a child, Linda was of normal weight and had no apparent eating problems. When faced with the illness of her mother, she began binge eating and started to gain weight. She became more depressed, using food to soothe herself while not facing the wretched feelings of impending loss and abandonment. In late adolescence she became anorexic, losing her hair and her menstrual period for six years. In her twenties, she gained and lost thirty pounds, using Weight Watchers for support.

I learned a detailed picture of the development of the symptoms (i.e., the latent content behind the symptoms, how the patient engages, and her coping skills). I made an assessment of her id, ego, and superego and I began to consider treatment strategies and interventions.

I determined that the short-term integrative treatment approach adapted from Goldstein and Noonan (1999) and cognitive-behavioral work (Brisman 1992, Fairburn 1995) would be well received by this patient. She exhibited the eagerness and motivation to work cognitively and behaviorally. Her ego was highly developed and protected by healthy defenses. Reality testing and judgment were good. Defenses such as dissociation, denial, intellectualization, isolation, projection, and splitting would have interfered with the work. Her defenses and coping capacities seemed to be able to protect her from the disorienting anxiety and chaos she might feel when stopping bingeing. At this point bingeing and purging was the sole prominent impulse disorder. She had not exhibited a chaotic lifestyle or severe personality disturbance. For these reasons I recommended individual treatment on a weekly basis. Her managed care company would authorize up to twenty-five sessions and she and I agreed to work within this time frame using an action-oriented approach.

Though I often recommend group treatment for eating-disordered patients, I decided that this would not be appropriate for Linda, given her numerous group experiences and involvement in Overeaters Anonymous. Group is often recommended for eating-disordered patients because they are isolated and maintain distorted images of body and self (Brisman and Siegel 1985). Brisman (1996) states, "Involvement with others who share these concerns can be an invaluable means of support and feedback. Group also provides a place to explore one's effect on others and vice versa" (p. 41).

Though Linda entered treatment with the specific goal of wanting to be rid of bingeing, she expressed a need to "understand myself a little better and explore some of my underlying issues, particularly why I keep men at a distance." It was clear that she felt stressed and psychically confused, which contributed to her relapse. The work of the short-term therapy would become a mixture of direct intervention with the symptom while at the same time exploring the underlying stressors and interpersonal relationships. In addition, correcting distortions in thinking and ways of perceiving others would facilitate change. Brisman (1996) states, "Eating-disordered patients tend to disavow the effect of interpersonal interactions on themselves and others" (p. 45). She feels that any treatment that does not emphasize what happens between the patient and therapist seriously neglects an important aspect of the patient's difficulties in living and sets the stage for the development of disordered eating patterns in the face of future interpersonal stressors.

Over the course of the initial sessions, I took a careful look at the moments when Linda actually binged or obsessed about food. I encouraged her to keep a journal, not only to record what she ate but more importantly to explore bingeing patterns. In particular, I asked her to note situations, people, and emotions that triggered problems with food and eating. For example, I asked her to note what she was thinking or feeling right before she took that extra portion of food. Linda agreed to keep a journal.

Here is an excerpt from the next session:

Therapist: So how did you do?

Patient: Well, I binged at work three times last week.

Therapist: Did you write in your journal this week?

Patient: Yes, on Monday. I felt so angry at my boss. He's very critical of me and never acknowledges the good job I'm doing. He yells at me and I get paralyzed. I can't fight back.

Therapist: So you eat your feelings instead of expressing them.

Patient: Yeah, I guess I binge when I feel unable to express myself.

Therapist: What makes it hard for you to tell your boss how you feel?

Patient: I'm not sure why I should feel so injured by him. I think I'm seeing him as my father, hearing the criticism but wanting the appreciation.

Over the course of the next few sessions, Linda expressed great sadness about her father's attitude toward her, his inability to acknowledge and appreciate her, and her subsequent sensitivity to people who are critical. She realized it obscured a clearer picture of them and that her immediate reaction was to flee or clam up. Linda was able to understand her transference reaction to her boss, who seemed to genuinely like her and her work. This recognition freed her from the grasp of a relationship that had been causing much stress and psychic confusion. She was able to tolerate some of the internal conflict, allowing her to feel more in control and less needy of him. In turn, a healthier distance was created, resulting in a much improved interpersonal relationship.

Linda used her journal to describe her binges and the accompanying feelings. This helped us understand her stressors and keep her attuned to her inner self. Because eating-disordered patients tend to be externally focused on people, appearances, and body image, it is important to help them pay attention to what they feel is so out of control, namely their inner thoughts and feelings.

Several authors, such as Brisman (1992) and MacFarland (1995), suggest homework assignments with the purpose of increasing the patient's perception of self-efficacy and control to promote change. I felt that Linda could make use of an assignment that would serve to delay or stop a potential binge. I suggested the use of contracting work and asked her if she could reduce her thrice weekly bingeing and purging to twice weekly, telling her to carefully monitor her food and her feelings. I told her that if she was unable to succeed, we needed to understand what interfered with her contract with me. This step requires careful consideration of the thoughts and feelings prior to the binge.

Here is an excerpt from the next session:

Patient: Last weekend not once. This is the first weekend I've been binge-free. But ever since, I've been bingeing and purging my brains out.

Therapist: That's an accomplishment. So what was different this past weekend that you were able to do that?

Patient: Well, I don't know. I was busier this past weekend. I called one of the people I know at work and asked her if she wanted to go shopping. So we did and then went to dinner and a movie.

Therapist: Is that different for you, to call up someone and ask her to do something?

Patient: Yeah, really different. I really don't feel comfortable with anyone anymore. I've lost touch with a lot of people.

Therapist: So how did you decide to go ahead and call this person?

Patient: Well, I decided that I'm sick and tired of being alone and feeling sick and tired. My throat hurts, I have a headache. I'm in the house all weekend. I feel terrible after the weekend. So I picked up the phone. My friend was happy to hear from me. We had a nice time.

Therapist: That's great. Tell me how this helped you as far as your bingeing and purging goes.

Patient: Well, I guess being with someone really helps. It just makes me feel less lonely. I mean I really had a good close circle of friends once.

Therapist: So what do you have to do to have more weekends like this past one?

Patient: Well, I guess I have to be busy. But it's more than that. For me, it helps to be in a relationship. My bingeing and purging is worse now because I have no male or female relationships.

This session helped Linda identify the loneliness, its causes, and possible solutions to alleviate it. We next spoke about alternative behaviors she would be willing to engage in before turning to food—self-soothing behaviors, such as resting, taking a bath, letting herself give in to her feelings, calling a friend, reflecting on her needs other than hunger, and putting these needs into words. I asked her if she could allow the use of "safe" food to soothe her. For Linda, this was not an option. She feared becoming out of control (with reckless abandon) if she ate any of her taboo or binge foods to satisfy a craving. "It's all or nothing with me. I can't just have a little."

In the first two months (approximately eight sessions), Linda made use, in fits and starts, of the contracts and the insights of treatment. She had a burgeoning understanding of how she used food, as well as people and boyfriends, to intrude on her experience and to take away her discomfort. Through her writing, she began to give words to these discomforts such as sadness, loneliness, despair at being overlooked, and mistrust of others. Slowly, the bingeing rituals diminished in intensity and frequency. By the end of the second month, Linda could spend a week to ten days at a time without bingeing. She started to realize a small weight loss and felt proud of her accomplishments. As bulimic patients stop bingeing and purging, they normally realize a weight loss, contrary to what many fear will happen without the protection of purging. Linda maintained a fairly rigid schedule of eating and for the time being the structured regimen gave her a margin of safety against her fear of losing control. Authors such as Fairburn (1995) and Garner and colleagues (1985) agree that eating must become mechanical in the sense that it is determined by a definite and predetermined plan. Early in treatment the patient should make every effort to avoid decisions about eating, since making such decisions will lead to a drifting back into dieting or eating more than desired.

Two months into treatment, Linda was determined to explore her mistrust and how she distances herself from people. She was curious about her dreams, which played out themes of engulfment and imprisonment. She noticed that she worried about becoming too dependent on me. I knew that this would be a difficult but nonetheless inevitable experience for Linda. We explored the historical antecedents of her fear of dependence, her submissiveness in the relationship with her mother and the resultant suffocation she felt, and her fear of being exposed to the punitive father who reduced her to insignificance. We saw the development of her eating disorder as an attempt to assert control over her life, as a way to nurture herself, and as a way to avoid interpersonal relationships, which had been rejecting and abandoning. During this phase, Linda proposed coming to therapy every other week. This led to a discussion of how Linda might be subverting herself in the treatment and what a connection to me meant to her, and how I might threaten her. Was the change of focus from food to more analytic issues too overwhelming?

Patient: I'm feeling less of a need to come here. My eating is much better. I feel like I have a way to go but I can continue the work on my own. Still, I'll be coming every other week so you'll still be here for me.

Therapist: You're feeling you don't need me as much, or are you uncomfortable with needing me weekly?

Patient: I've always done things on my own. I guess I feel more comfortable that way.

Therapist: But this is what you also regret. You feel alone, lonely, and unable to maintain a connection with people.

Now that Linda's relationship with me, not the food, was the primary focus and the therapeutic arena had begun to encompass previously unacknowledged aspects of herself, Linda was feeling more threatened. She was acknowledging previously unexpressed feelings of sadness and loneliness and she was becoming more dependent on me as a reliable person in her life. We were able to talk about this and realize that pushing people away was a repetitive pattern that had resulted in self-imposed isolation, stress, and depression. I encouraged Linda to continue with the present focus for now, believing that underscoring our goals would refocus the work on solution-focused problems and give Linda back a sense of control.

To summarize, during the initial phase of treatment, which lasted two months, keeping a journal, contracting, and thinking of alternatives were successful in delaying and avoiding binges, so that within one month Linda was bingeing just two to three times weekly, and for one week had no binge/purge episodes.

The Middle Phase:
Implementing Interventions, Maintaining and/or Altering the Focus, Monitoring Progress, Dealing with Obstacles, Managing the Therapist—Patient Relationship

During the middle phases of treatment, sessions 9 to 22, we explored employment and her relationships with men. The bingeing occurred once monthly, and Linda and I did not spend time addressing it directly. Under stress, she asked for the structure of specific contracts to "get me through." She moved from rigid, controlled eating to experimenting with her taboo foods, particularly breads and cakes, which she successfully kept down. She was able to control the quantity of these foods without fear that it would lead to a binge. I applauded her efforts and encouraged her continued work on normalizing her eating. The safety of the therapeutic relationship allowed her to try things that she would have been afraid to do on her own. Her confidence extended into the dating and job arenas. Her job became more rewarding and she was asked to work full-time. After careful consideration, she accepted her boss's offer, deciding to forgo a career in massage therapy. She was consolidating her life. It felt more organized, focused, and manageable. She reported a dream: "I'm in a submarine with the Queen Mother. We're upside down, pushing downward. Suddenly, the boat turns itself over and we're floating up to the surface. We emerge from the water."

This dream suggested a positive shift in Linda's self-experience, emphasizing control, competence, and a sense of hope about getting on the right track. I shared these thoughts and added that the Queen Mother may have been me, guiding her down the chosen path. She smiled and as if to agree with this interpretation, she said, "She was blonde, like you."

Power or control is a common theme that emerges in the treatment of eating-disordered patients. Brisman (1992) states that these patients are awakening from a world marked by fitful fluctuations of control and lack of control played out daily around food.

Linda and I engaged in an ongoing exploration of power, dependency, and "hunger" with regard to men. She desperately wanted to be in a relationship but feared submission and loss of her independence. However, submission was her only framework for connecting. She connected to each parent in a submissive manner. With many of the men she dated, she either manipulated a tenuous but persistent hold over them until they registered panic and fled, or she felt suffocated and fled.

The following shifts occurred in the middle phase. The eating disorder abated, and Linda had begun a relationship that was in its second month. She still limited her involvement with this man, but was more willing to gradually let him in—the way she gradually let in her forbidden foods.

> *Patient:* I'm really enjoying spending time with him and I'm not feeling the urge to flee. I guess caring can be genuine and not mixed up with criticism or suffocation.
> *Therapist:* You see, you can have a different experience than you had with your parents.

Linda's personal confidence and self-worth increased. My overt approval of her boyfriend was very important to her and I gave it freely. I knew that Linda still distrusted her feelings and would find reasons to leave the relationship, but eventually she was able to negotiate a nice balance between work, this relationship, and other activities. She enjoyed meals out and did not deny herself much of anything by way of food. She was less concerned about the extra weight. The clinical experiences of Kearney-Cooke (1989) with eating-disordered patients show that improving patients begin to question the goal of a perfect body that is superior to other women's bodies. They see how this goal isolates them and prevents them from developing close relationships with other people.

The middle phase focused on using the therapeutic relationship to gain insight into intrapsychic and interpersonal difficulties. Linda deepened her understanding of the effects of her parents' treatment of her. She developed coping skills and control and mastery over her impulses, fears, and symptoms.

The Termination Phase:
Addressing Termination, Reviewing Progress and Identifying Unresolved Issues, Resolving the Therapist—Patient Relationship, Referral, and Follow-Up

With short-term treatment, the termination phase need not be prolonged. The treatment is generally solution-focused, and once the solutions are found and the patient is restored to a stable level of functioning, the treatment can be viewed as an unqualified success. Toward the fifth month, sessions 23 to 25, the sessions became more repetitive. Linda and I recognized that her insurance would terminate after twenty-five sessions. Again she questioned her need to come to therapy as often. I felt this time that with the assumed security that her boyfriend offered, perhaps Linda could think about winding down. We discussed her concerns of "going it alone," her fear of missing me, and her concerns that without my help her relationship would "mess up." But as the sessions continued, Linda grew more intrigued with the possibility of trying it on her own. We set a termination date for the following month.

Linda was symptom-free, she had resolved her confusion about her career, she functioned in a more stable manner, and she was able to maintain a longer-term relationship. Though Linda wished to continue to share herself and her life in the evolving relationship with me (the good mother), she also realized that she needed to find other people to round out her life, people on whom she could comfortably depend and whom she could utilize for comfort and connection. She wanted to know that she could call if she needed to. When the date approached to leave, after twenty-five sessions, she left without incident. To date, I have not heard from Linda and I assume that she continues to make progress.

Linda's primary goal was restoration of previously symptom-free behavior regarding food. In our brief work together, we not only accomplished this goal but understood the use of the symptom and its interference with interpersonal relationships. This time, being symptom-free was accompanied by an expansion of the inner self and outer world.

TECHNIQUES

Short-term therapy concentrates on a combined approach of interpretive and exploratory work, with an emphasis on changing behavior using a cognitive-behavioral approach. To concentrate only on symptom relief, without exploration, the therapist may wind up focusing on what the patient does, not on who she is (Browning 1985). This not only may reinforce the way the patient identifies herself by doing rather than being, but also may unknowingly replicate earlier familial patterns in which the patient's messy uncomfortable parts are deemed unacceptable. In an effort to be cared for, the patient dismisses and avoids many aspects of her self. She has been encouraged to look good and act good at the cost of a deeper understanding of who she is or what needs may have prompted such behavior in the first place. If the therapist merely contracts with the patient to "clean up the eating disorder," the patient's history of looking perfect at the cost of being known is repeated (Brisman 1989).

Therapy involves the development of coping skills and ego-building functions as substitutes for the patterns of the eating disorder. Feelings, thoughts, and events that may precipitate a binge are explored, and alternative means of handling internal and external stressors are considered (Brisman 1992). Contracts that encourage healthier responses and that limit the binge-purge cycle behavior are made between therapist and patient (Fairburn 1985, Johnson et al. 1983, White and Boskind-White 1981). Behaviors that can delay bingeing are considered. Can the patient write her thoughts in a journal or call a friend? What avenues of self-soothing are available to her?

Krystal (1974) has suggested that with patients such as these, the preliminary work of therapy entails explanation, elucidation, and at times direct reassurance regarding the experience of emotions. For the eating-disordered patient, this means recognizing that emotions are signals to the self that should be listened to and utilized, not avoided through eating.

Discussion of the effect that negative thinking has on eating behavior is essential to correct distortions and interrupt behavior. Eating-disordered women feed themselves many negative monologues, which is typical of the overgeneralization of all-or-nothing thinking in which these patients frequently engage. Goldstein and Noonan (1999) feel that change occurs through the mechanism of correcting distortions in thinking and ways of perceiving the self and others. Challenging the notion that binge-eating and purging are successful weight control methods is another crucial educational tool.

The following techniques are adapted from Yager (1985) and can be modified and applied to anorexics and compulsive overeaters; they were used to help Linda control her binge/purge cycles:

Diary and journal keeping: These activities may help the patient develop increased awareness and an observing ego. Writing the details of the binges and purges and their antecedents and consequences also helps to gain control. The discipline of keeping a diary may be therapeutic and may help patients reduce the frequency of the symptoms.

Contracts: The contract (Brisman and Siegel 1985), is a verbal agreement established between patient and therapist in which the patient agrees to abate and delay binge behavior for a period of time between sessions. For example, a patient who binges and vomits two to three times daily may decide she will forgo bingeing for one day prior to the next session. Someone who binge-purges only once weekly may contract to go the entire week binge-free. Ways of coping, interacting, or self-soothing are discussed and encouraged as alternatives to the binge. The goal is not merely to set up contracts the patient is able to keep, but also to understand what gets in the way of her keeping the contracts in the first place, or what allows for successes she was unable to achieve on her own (Brisman 1989). Contracts need to be realistic and to reflect the beginning of change. Contracts that allow for a high probability of feeling some degree of control over the binge–purge behavior increases patients' feelings of competence in other spheres of functioning as well. Overall, contracts are utilized to emphasize the concepts of choice and control; that is, people are making choices and controlling their behavior even when it is experienced as a lack of control. Giving up the binge-purge "cold turkey" is not encouraged. Patients are asked to respect the feelings behind the binge-purge and to question the underlying needs. They are encouraged to label and find more effective ways of meeting their needs, such as self-parenting.

Normal, planned eating: Many bulimic patients suffer from "dietary chaos" (Yager 1985), and rarely eat normal meals, starving themselves when they are not bingeing. Normal meals are stressed early in treatment. To minimize the threat of too many dietary choices, some patients initially require relatively rigid meal programs.

Basic education about bulimia: Patients need to learn about the nature and treatment of bulimia. Books are recommended, such as Fairburn's *Overcoming Binge Eating* (1995), and patients are encouraged to join Overeaters Anonymous.

Cognitive and insight-oriented corrections of distortions: Techniques include interpretation, confrontation, distancing, externalization, and thought stopping.

Change in patient's environment: Altering certain contingencies including space, time, and people who promote bulimic symptoms has been effective in behaviorally oriented weight reduction programs.

Psychological immunization against food preoccupation: Patients should be informed that persistent food preoccupation following cessation of bingeing and purging behaviors is common. Similarly, they should be informed that periodic backsliding is not uncommon and should not be taken as a sign of an avalanche.

Mental imagery techniques: Such techniques can enable patients to bypass ruminative, intellectualized defenses and to generate unanticipated new perspectives about their symptoms and life situations (Kosbab 1974). Using mental imagery to soothe or calm the raging emotions has helped to forestall binge behavior.

Developing alternative activities: These should be active, not passive like watching television. They should be feasible and enjoyable, not a chore.

Suggest waiting: Urges to binge fade with time (Fairburn 1995). Distract oneself.

CONCLUSION

The eating-disordered patient has retreated from the world of people to a world of food, where she has prematurely established a fragile identity, replete with rules, structures, and inflexible laws as to how she should be.

An approach that attempts to minimize the focus on food and allows for a real relationship in which the patient has an effect on and is affected by another person is the goal of treatment. Contracting to abate binge–purge behavior is the vehicle to help the patient not only diminish impulsive acting out, but also to understand who is doing what to whom. Only then is the patient free to experience various aspects of self that have previously gone under cover (Brisman 1989).

Severity and chronicity of an eating disorder as well as alcohol abuse or substance abuse are important diagnostic criteria and are related to outcome. The longer the patient has been ill and the more severe the personality disorder, the more difficult it is for her to recover. For these patients, a longer-term treatment may be more appropriate. The limitations of time may prevent a deeper analysis of the personality disturbance reinforcing the symptomatology. In addition, eating-disordered patients tend to mistrust and resist any intervention that interferes with their food disorder. The relationship building phase, by necessity, may be of longer duration than allowed with a short-term approach. For those patients, building a therapeutic relationship and exploring underlying issues such as family dynamics must occur well before the patient feels safe enough to give up the use and misuse of food. This phase can often take several months or years.

For patients amenable to the short-term approach, treatment may end successfully though fall short of uncovering deeper intrapsychic and interpersonal problems. For Linda, short-term treatment restored her abstinence, provided insights, and helped her feel more comfortable with intimacy. Had she remained in treatment, we might have worked on issues of depression, abandonment, mourning, and healthy dependency. Given her history of relapse, she may need to consult a therapist in the future but for now Linda was functional and intact. Johnson and colleagues (1990) report that one-year follow-up data suggest that the eating symptoms of bulimic patients without personality disorders are likely to remit in fewer than thirty sessions.

In conclusion, the eating disorders are eminently treatable; however, the prognosis is not uniform throughout the whole population. It is necessary to diagnose the eating-disordered bulimic subgroup into which each patient falls and then determine the approach. The techniques described in this chapter can be modified to apply to bulimics, anorexics, and compulsive overeaters. The approach used was eclectic. Cognitive-behavioral combined with insight-directed strategies provided the techniques to address the bulimic symptomatology.

REFERENCES

American Psychiatric Association. (1994). *Diagnostic and Statistical Manual of Mental Disorders*, 4th ed. Washington, DC: Author.

Brisman, J. (1989). Treatment of the bulimic college student: considerations and complications. In *The Bulimic College Student: Evaluation, Treatment and Prevention*, ed. L. C. Whitaker and W. N. Davis, pp. 191–204. New York: Haworth Press.

———— (1992). Bulimia in the older adolescent: an analytic perspective to a behavioral problem. In *Psychotherapies with Children: Adapting the Dynamic Process*, ed. J. O'Brien, D. Pilowsky, and O. Lewis, pp. 171–187. Washington, DC: American Psychiatric Press.

———— (1996). Psychodynamic psychotherapy and action-oriented techniques: an integrated approach in treating eating disorders. In *Treating Eating Disorders*, ed. J. Werwe and I. Yalom, pp. 31–70. San Francisco: Jossey-Bass.

Brisman, J., and Siegel, M. (1985). The bulimia workshop: a unique integration of group treatment approaches. *International Journal of Group Psychotherapy* 35(4):585–601.

Browning, W. N. (1985). Long-term dynamic group therapy with bulimic patients: a clinical discussion. In *Theory and Treatment of Anorexia and Bulimia: Bio-medical, Sociocultural and Psychological Perspectives*, ed. S. W. Emmett, pp. 141–153. New York: Brunner/Mazel.

Bruch, H. (1962). Perceptual and conceptual disturbances in anorexia nervosa. *Psychosomatic Medicine* 24:187–194.

Chediak, C. (1977). The so-called anorexia nervosa: diagnostic and treatment considerations. *Bulletin of the Menninger Clinic* 41:453–474.

Crisp, A. H. (1970). "Feeding disorder," "nervous malnutrition," or "weight phobia"? *World Review of Nutrition and Dietetics* 12:452–504.

Fairburn, C. G. (1985). Cognitive-behavioral treatment for bulimia. In *Handbook of Psychotherapy for Anorexia Nervosa and Bulimia*, ed. D. M. Garner and P. E. Garfinkel, pp. 160–192. New York: Guilford.

———— (1995). *Overcoming Binge Eating*. New York: Guilford.

Garner, D. M., and Bemis, K. (1984). Cognitive therapy for anorexia nervosa. In *Handbook of Psychotherapy for Anorexia Nervosa and Bulimia*, ed. D. M. Garner and P. E. Garfinkel, pp. 102–146. New York: Guilford.

Garner, D. M., Rockert, W., Olmstead, M. P., et al. (1985). Psychoeducation principles in the treatment of bulimia and anorexia nervosa. In *Handbook of Psychotherapy for Anorexia Nervosa and Bulimia*, ed. D. M. Garner and P. E. Garfinkel, pp. 513–571. New York: Guilford.

Gilligan, C. (1990). Teaching Shakespeare's sisters: notes from the underground of female adolescence. In *Making Connections*, ed. C.

Gilligan, N. Lyons, and T. Hamner, pp. 1–29. Cambridge, MA: Harvard University Press.

Goldstein, E. G., and Noonan, M. (1999). *Short-Term Treatment and Social Work Practice: An Integrative Perspective.* New York: Free Press.

Hornyak, L., and Baker, E. (1989). *Experiential Therapies for Eating Disorders.* New York: Guilford.

Johnson, C. (1985). Initial consultation in patients with bulimia and anorexia nervosa. In *Handbook of Psychotherapy for Anorexia Nervosa and Bulimia*, ed. D. M. Garner and P. E. Garfinkel, pp. 19–51. New York: Guilford.

Johnson, C., and Connors, M. (1987). *The Etiology and Treatment of Bulimia Nervosa: A Biopsychosocial Perspective*, pp. 88–126. New York: Basic Books.

Johnson, C., Connors, M., and Stuckey, M. (1983). Short-term group treatment of bulimia. *International Journal of Eating Disorders* 2:199–208.

Johnson, C., Tobin, D. L., and Dennis, A. B. (1990). Differences in treatment outcome between borderline and non-borderline bulimics at one-year follow-up. *International Journal of Eating Disorders* 9:617–627.

Kearney-Cooke, A. (1989). Reclaiming the body: using guided imagery in the treatment of body image disturbances among bulimic women. In *Experiential Therapies for Eating Disorders*, ed. L. M. Hornyak and E. K. Baker, pp. 11–33. New York: Guilford.

Kosbab, F. P. (1974). Imagery techniques in psychiatry. *Archives of General Psychiatry* 31:283–290.

Krystal, H. (1974). Affect tolerance. *The Annual of Psychoanalysis* 2:197–219.

MacFarland, B. (1995). *Brief Therapy and Eating Disorders.* San Francisco: Jossey-Bass.

Russell, G. (1981). The current treatment of anorexia nervosa. *British Journal of Psychiatry* 138:164–166.

Sours, J. A. (1980). *Starving to Death in a Sea of Objects.* New York: Jason Aronson.

Theander, S. (1970). Anorexia nervosa. *Acta Psychiatrica Scandinavica, Suppl.* 214.

White, W. C., and Boskind-White, M. (1981). An experiential-behavioral approach to the treatment of bulimarexia. *Psychotherapy: Theory, Research and Practice* 18:501−507.

Wilson, C. P., Hogan, C. C., and Mintz, I. L. (1985). *Fear of Being Fat: The Treatment of Anorexia Nervosa and Bulimia.* Northvale, NJ: Jason Aronson.

Yager, J. (1985). The outpatient treatment of bulimia. *Bulletin of the Menninger Clinic* 40(3):203−226.

CHAPTER TEN

Short-Term Interventions with the Mentally Retarded

JOAN L. KLEIN

THEORETICAL OVERVIEW
AND TREATMENT PERSPECTIVE

There are persistent diagnostic and treatment myths about persons who are diagnosed with mental retardation. Perhaps the most insidious one is that these individuals are not treatable and are unresponsive to modern therapeutic interventions. With the belief that mentally retarded persons cannot benefit from psychiatric intervention, many professionals in the mental health field have given low priority to the referral and treatment of this population. A common misconception is that behavioral and emotional problems are a function of retardation and not attributable to difficulties with interpersonal relationships. With the added dimension of mental illness, the professional is often particularly unmotivated to work with this population. Most therapists have a preference for working with verbal, bright patients. They see intelligence as essential for effective work, although current thinking suggests that the necessity for high intellectual endowment has been overemphasized as a prerequisite for psychotherapy (Fletcher and Dosen 1993, Menolascino and Stark 1984). Despite their cognitive deficits, persons who have both a psychiatric and developmental disability diagnosis can be constructively engaged in a rehabilitative process.

With the recognition that no one modality will be successful with all patients, many treatment strategies have been utilized in the attempt to modify behavior. Brief treatment, however, has not generally been the treatment of choice due to the belief that dually diagnosed[1] patients need long-term care, which is inconsistent with managed care's short-term focus. In today's managed care practice arena, clinicians have been forced to reexamine the efficacy of long-term work as the only applicable treatment for this population. Traditionally, Axis II diagnoses on which mental retardation is coded have not been viewed as amenable to brief work (Tuckfelt et al. 1997).

Mental retardation encompasses different levels of intellectual impairment and is coded by its degree of severity. The four categories of retardation are determined by IQ levels, which, according to the American Psychiatric Association's (1994) *Diagnostic and Statistical Manual of Mental Disorders*, fourth edition (*DSM-IV*), are mild, moderate, severe, and profound. This population as a whole requires service, but the nature of the care and treatment needed differs depending on the degree of disability. While it is equally important to recognize that moderate, severe, and profoundly retarded people have distinct needs that must be attended to, short-term treatment is not applicable because of their inadequate level of intellectual functioning. Rather, the benefits of this approach are best recognized with the mentally ill-mildly retarded individual.

The *DSM-IV* conceptualizes a mental disorder as a "clinically

---

1. Dual diagnosis usually refers to the mentally ill, chemically involved population. In 1983, the National Association for the Dually Diagnosed was founded to address the needs of individuals who have the coexistence of mental illness and mental retardation. Therefore, in this chapter, when the term *dual diagnosed* is used, the reference is to this population.

significant behavioral or psychological syndrome or pattern that occurs in an individual and is associated with present distress (e.g., a painful symptom) or disability (i.e., impairment in one or more areas of functioning)" (APA 1994, p. xxi). With the mentally retarded individual, mental illness comprises a full range of disorders, which Menolascino (1983) categorized into the areas of psychoses, neuroses, personality disorders, behavioral disorders, and adjustment reactions.

Brief treatment is a potentially successful alternative to long-term work, particularly if we examine the criteria for situations that are responsive to short-term intervention as described in the integrative short-term treatment (ISTT) model (Goldstein and Noonan 1999). The dually diagnosed often become overwhelmed and need help in restoring previous levels of functioning. They are in need of information, resources, and guidance. Their presenting problems may be limited in scope and situational in nature, and they can benefit from supportive approaches to develop and strengthen ego functions, problem-solving capacities, coping mechanisms, object relations, and self-esteem. When presenting problems are chronic, such as difficulties with interpersonal relationships, poor frustration tolerance, and feelings of loss and abandonment, partializing interventions are helpful with this population. Goldstein and Noonan (1999) note that problems requiring help arise from five areas: the social environment, life events and circumstances, interpersonal relationships, hereditary and constitutional health factors, and personality characteristics. People whose cognitive functioning is not impaired may have deficits in one or more of these areas, but clearly all of these areas have posed problems for the mentally retarded individual. Addressing the issues that are most debilitating to the patient supports the relevance of time-limited intervention.

The ISTT model rests on the social work value of appreciation for the uniqueness of the individual. Nowhere is this concept more important than with the mentally ill-mentally retarded individual whose uniqueness is generally negatively regarded. This individual has, for the most part, been isolated from participation in many activities, such as age-appropriate play, socialization and dating with peers, marriage, and raising a family (Fletcher and Dosen 1993). With deinstitutionalization, this population has become more visible to mental health providers and to the community at large. Most if not all members of this group will require some form of care during their lives. While many are able to live independently, a substantial number are unable to function without supports, and live either with families or in community residences. The majority of mentally ill-mentally retarded people who come for help are not self-referred but rather are sent for treatment by others, and therefore have no awareness of why treatment is being sought or offered to them. Frequently it is the caregiver who initiates referrals because of the patient's maladaptive behavior. Limited cognitive functioning hampers the patient's ability to express feelings, resulting in disruptive and assaultive behavior, which is then diagnosed as the problem (Fletcher and Dosen 1993). As an example, patients who feel anxious or depressed following placement in a residential facility may not be able to talk about their loneliness. Violence, not uncommon with this population, becomes the expression of loneliness and anger (Klein 1992).

The magnitude of the needs of this population can be overwhelming. These patients' vulnerabilities, conflicts, pain, feelings of loss, isolation, and alienation resemble those of the mentally ill nonretarded. Mentally retarded persons require acceptance and approval because so much of their life has been steeped in rejection, failure, frustration, and the stigma of being labeled "retarded" (Bates 1984). Many patients are acutely aware of their differences and limitations, and the reality that they are retarded. Brief work can be attentive to these deficits, providing channels through which success may be attained and acknowledged. There is a challenge in "controlling the causes of maladaptive behaviors and in developing new, alternative remedies" (Gold et al. 1989, p. 838) instead of viewing this population as hopeless and treatment-resistant.

There is a commonality of themes that dually diagnosed patients can explore and work to resolve. Many patients have an inadequate self-image and believe they are incapable of being loved (Menolascino 1983, Selan 1976). They grow up as misfits, with no sense of belonging, and with little peer interaction, resulting from social withdrawal or social rejection. Their negative self-perception has been societally reinforced as they have experienced almost no successful family or school validation. The relationship between clinician and client allows for these feelings to be identified and expressed, with the hope that feelings of inadequacy and anxiety will diminish. The themes of separation and abandonment predominate, and are often helped by ventilating and problem solving with a therapist who understands the experience and the sadness.

Mann (1981) states that "the most poignant and most distinctively human reaction occurs in the face of loss" (p. 28), and that loss affects personality development in multiple ways. It has thus been substantiated that past and present losses constitute a major reason for seeking psychotherapy (Budman and Gurman 1988), and that problems in this area can be addressed successfully in short-term therapy. The patient is helped to work through the loss and to master separation. My experience supports that work on issues of abandonment and loss can be accomplished with a time-limited approach.

INCLUSION AND EXCLUSION CRITERIA

The presence of two distinct diagnoses—mental illness and mental retardation—requires unique approaches to treatment. The need to establish special criteria for diagnosing this population has been well documented (Fletcher and Menolascino 1989). Most prevalent with the population is a "diagnostic overshadowing," which refers to the idea that when an emotional disorder is present in a mentally retarded individual, clinicians are more likely to diagnose the mental retardation and overlook the accompanying emotional disorder. Therefore, emotional disturbance in this population is underestimated, underdiagnosed, and undertreated (Fletcher and Menolascino 1989). There is, however, sufficient convincing evidence that mentally retarded persons can develop the full range of psychiatric disorders. In fact, they are particularly at risk for anxiety, depression, and other mood disorders. They are frequently diagnosed with schizophrenia and personality disorders and, in addition, are often beset with multiple medical and physical handicaps (Reiss et al. 1982).

The combined definitions of mental illness and mental retardation often present a diagnostic dilemma for the clinician who is not sure in which category the person belongs. Therapists must be well acquainted with both mental illness and mental retardation to make a differential diagnosis, and to know how to approach treatment and management of dually diagnosed individuals. Without this, the applicability of a short-term treatment approach cannot be determined. Only professionals with experience in both fields are able to distinguish behavior that is attributable to limited intelligence rather than to the symptomatology or manifestation of poor adjustment or mental illness. During a period of emotional stress, deficits and maladaptive behaviors may significantly increase in severity, and sometimes the exacerbation rather than the onset of behavioral problems is diagnostically relevant. Clinicians often attribute abnormal behavior to mental retardation rather than as part of the phenomenon of mental illness (Borthwick-Duffy and Eyman 1990). Behaviors displayed by this group include difficulty with impulse control; inappropriate emotional outbursts; expressions of anger, sullenness, and stubbornness; and poor adaptation to life's demands (Menolascino et al. 1985). Low frustration tolerance, disruptive aggressive verbal and physical behavior, and narcissism all present major management issues.

It has been shown that the major deprivation of nonexistent or dysfunctional family life contributes to a "detachment syndrome" and an often indiscriminately expressed "affect hunger" (Menolascino and Stark 1984). Individuals lacking functional families have had little or no extended experiences with significant or meaningful relationships and are accustomed to living among minimally involved people. As a result of this affect hunger, many individuals seek attention indiscriminately. Their detachment is often interpreted as an inability to feel, and they are often accused of lacking depth of emotion. The question arises as to whether this is a result of the limitations imposed by the retardation, a defensive measure designed to protect the individuals from the experience of constant loss, or the reflection of inadequate nurturance to which they have been subjected all of their lives.

Many studies, particularly those of Spitz (1965) and Bowlby (1969), have documented the effects of early object loss and institutionalization, both of which have a profound impact on children. The implications are that this set of circumstances produces a detached institutionalized adult, too crippled to function in normal relationships. The work of Spitz and Bowlby support the conclusion that the behavioral characteristics of detachment result from lack of object relatedness and from impersonal care experienced by the individual and not by the underlying mental retardation (Menolascino 1983). In recent years, other theorists have also stressed the importance of maternal relationships on infant attachment and relatedness (Beebe 1985, Lichtenberg 1989, Stern 1985).

In working with dually diagnosed patients, their enormous sense of deprivation and loss becomes apparent. These deep-seated voids and feelings of emptiness and loneliness are inarticulately expressed and often maladaptively acted out, becoming their response to the pain felt at the loss or absence of significant parenting and, in particular, mothering.

The *DSM-IV* underscores two components of the diagnosis of mental retardation. A biologically based limitation of cognitive functioning, as demonstrated by an IQ of 70 or below, and the deficits or impairments in social-adaptive behavior, both with an onset before age 18, represent the dual components of mental retardation (Levitas and Gilson 1989). The biological factor limits the ability to function intellectually and contributes to a series of events that change and limit the range of social-adaptive functioning. As a result of cognitive impairments, distorted development, and limitations in lifestyle choice imposed by the care system, mentally retarded people often present signs of psychiatric disorders differently than nonretarded people. For example, the patient may demonstrate bizarre and disturbed behavior rather than verbalize stress or dysfunction (Menolascino and Stark 1984). Another key factor is that the clinical history may be shaped by the caregiver and not by the retarded person. The caregiver's behavioral observations may obscure symptom clusters suggestive of psychiatric disorders. Developmental disability, deficits in ego functioning, limited intrapsychic resources, and inability to cope point the retarded persons on an alternative track of development, which, when combined with social, political, and economic pressures, places them at increased risk for mental illness. They present with a reduced capacity to withstand stress, a poor ability to resolve mental and emotional conflicts, a lack of social competence, and the potential for being led into difficulty by their associates, all of which may lead to loss of self-control (Klein 1992, Pollock 1944). Mildly retarded individuals are under special stress in that they look normal, rarely exhibiting identifiable signs of their handicap, often leading to unrealistic expectations from others and thus to repeated interpersonal failures.

An individual often reaches 6 to 9 years of age before retardation is medically confirmed, and by this time the individual has often been labeled as deviant, disturbed, and "stupid." Low self-esteem is frequent and the societal stigma is well established, furthering feelings of inadequacy and dissimilarity from the mainstream. The ability to negotiate normal developmental crises, such as differentiation of self from others, autonomous functioning, trust, and intimacy, has not developed (Fletcher and Menolascino 1989). This developmental delay, reduced cognitive ability, and poor ego functioning are disadvantages in dealing with issues typical of the chronological age, and may lead to feelings of frustration and acting out.

Despite these limitations, many individuals are good candidates for brief treatment. Working from a strength perspective, inappropriate behaviors can decrease as treatment progresses. When positive qualities are identified in patients' current environments or in past parental and institutional experiences, these patients can begin to experience the same qualities in themselves. Those individuals not suitable for short-term therapy demonstrate little or no ability to change disruptive behavior; function with a rigid, primitive, defensive structure; show poor motivation; and are unable to form a relationship after a trial period. Ego functions, especially judgment, reality testing, thought processes, and autonomous functioning, if severely impaired, present impediments to treatment (Budman 1981).

TREATMENT GOALS

Goals to be accomplished with mentally retarded individuals resemble those for the nonretarded. The outcome of treatment will rest on the clarity and mutuality of goals. While significant improvement may occur in treatment, the mentally ill-mentally retarded often progress slowly and there may be frequent setbacks and repetitions of dysfunctional behavior. Treatment must be viewed as supportive, to be utilized as needed, rather than as a cure for mental illness. People with disabilities often need help through difficult periods; this requires a realistic understanding from the mental health system that future help may be needed again when other difficult life experiences occur (Fletcher and Menolascino 1989). With this approach, ISTT has value in its recognition that help is possible in a limited period of time. The treatment goals with this population need to be carefully designed and are dependent on sound clinical knowledge of the patient. An individualized treatment plan rests on an assessment that reflects an accurate biopsychosocial understanding of how the patient functions in all areas. The multitude of problems that this patient may present must not overwhelm or obscure the need to find and identify a focus that determines realistic and attainable goals. It is important to make clear to the patient that psychotherapy is not endless; it is goal limited and, therefore, time limited.

With an emphasis on individualized goals, the first step is to determine whether the problem is with the identified patients or with the systems with which they interact (Beasley and Kroll 1992, Levitas and Gilson 1989). As patients are viewed in relationship to their surroundings, external change may be necessary. With this population, a change in the patient's living arrangement is often the environmental intervention of choice.

There is recognition about the need for attention to oppressed and stigmatized populations, but often there is a failure to identify this group among them (Klein 1992). It is well established that mentally ill-mentally retarded individuals exhibit poor self-esteem and have little self-confidence, a result of both inadequate internal resources for coping and the external reinforcements of their inadequacy. Goals need to be formulated in these areas, and patients should be involved in setting the goals. The mutuality of identifying and discussing goals enhances self-esteem because it includes the patient in decision making, something of which most people believe retarded people are incapable. This is an empowering experience for patients who often feel powerless over their lives.

It is generally believed that the most significant goals in working with this population are to help patients (1) understand and accept their disabilities; (2) improve impulse control and frustration tolerance; (3) express feelings and emotions in socially acceptable ways; (4) increase independent decision making and self-reliance; (5) improve self-esteem, self-image, and interpersonal relationship skills; (6) cope with stressful situations; and (7) resolve conflicts of dependency and guilt (Szymanski 1980). These goals are possible for a candidate deemed appropriate for brief work; however, not every patient can be expected to master all of them.

Clinicians have been criticized for focusing more on pathology and limitations than they do on strengths. Practitioners need to be attuned to how the patients have previously attempted to negotiate difficult life experiences and circumstances. Validation of positive efforts is essential to the work; it serves as a goal of treatment as patients are helped to assess and recognize their own successes. Patient progress is relative to the level of functioning and deficits at the outset. With this population, improvement and success must be viewed as a matter of degree and always assessed on an individual basis. Another criticism of individual psychotherapy is that it increases dependency in a patient who is already a dependent person. Therapy must help patients take control of their lives and must address dependency issues. Brief therapy has significant value in that it does not foster the dependency that might emerge in long-term work (Flegenheimer 1993).

If clinicians remain cognizant that mentally ill-mentally retarded people tend to be inadequately equipped to understand or adapt to life's complexities, they can recognize that it is this bewilderment, confusion, and emotional turmoil that bring these patients into treatment. Accepting that many ego functions are impaired, the goals and focus of treatment rest on an amelioration of ego deficits.

CASE ILLUSTRATION

Background and History

Jane was born on December 12, 1979, to Mr. and Mrs. Y. She was the younger of two children. Her brother, Jerome, was four years older, and when he was 18 he left home to live and work in Boston. Mr. Y. was a supervisor at the post office and worked nights, leaving Jane and Mrs. Y. alone most of the time. Mrs. Y. was a homemaker. The family lived in an apartment in the Bronx.

According to her parents' reports, Jane was a frightened and dependent little girl. She often somatized and, when she was faced with problems in school, her mother would keep her home. She was involved with remediation until age 12, but her school performance was poor and her shyness and social maladaptiveness were apparent. She was tested by the Board of Education and achieved a full-scale IQ of 64. She was then transferred to a special school for the retarded.

Jane's mother attempted to protect her from the loneliness and ostracism that she was experiencing, but ultimately Mrs. Y. began to feel overwhelmed by the response of her slow, different child. By age 16, Jane began to exhibit acting-out behavior. She often missed the school bus and would wander around her apartment complex for hours. She was also caught smoking in her room, putting cigarettes out in the wastebasket, taking money from her parents, and becoming sexually promiscuous.

The school recommended residential placement, informing her parents that the school feared for Jane's safety. With feelings of relief and guilt, the parents accepted the referral. Jane was admitted to a residential setting where she responded positively to the structure of the cottage and where she exhibited no self-destructive behavior. Despite this, she continued to have difficulty relating to others and needed constant monitoring. She began reacting to changes in her routine with temper tantrums. Jane maintained close contact with her parents throughout her placement. They visited and she went home frequently on weekends, where they provided the structure she required. At 18 years she "aged out" of this residential setting and was referred to another residence for the mentally ill-mentally retarded.

Shortly after this second placement, Jane was referred to me for brief treatment, as she was exhibiting depression and anxiety. She often withdrew to her room, refusing to speak to anyone, and preferring to be isolated from staff and peers. When less depressed, she appeared agitated and demonstrated aggressive behavior, poor impulse control, and low frustration tolerance. Jane angered easily and often was verbally abusive, which was reflective of her mental retardation. The residential staff were frustrated with her, and her parents were concerned about her depression. No one could understand why she was acting out, as her history had indicated a somewhat successful adjustment to her first placement.

The Beginning Phase

At our first meeting the focus was on understanding the reasons for Jane's behavior, assessing her level of functioning, and determining whether a core issue would emerge so that she could be evaluated as a candidate for short-term work. Jane initially appeared somewhat hostile, withdrawn, and noncommunicative. However, I introduced myself as a therapist and clarified my role. Previous experience had provided her with other therapists so she acknowledged that she understood who I was. I asked her if she knew why she was seeing me. She responded, "I don't know anything."

On a manifest level, this indicated that she didn't know the reasons she came to see me. Her statement had deeper implications, because it undoubtedly reflected her lack of understanding and knowledge in many areas. At the outset, however, in accordance with the beginning phase of a time-limited model (Goldstein and Noonan 1999), my intention was to identify the problem, do a biopsychosocial assessment, begin the process of engagement, and form a therapeutic alliance. I wanted, therefore, to help her to feel comfortable and to understand whether we might work together. She immediately added, "No one tells me anything."

Therapist: Are you saying that no one has told you why you're here today?

Jane: The staff didn't tell me nothing—just "You're going to an appointment."

Therapist: Perhaps I can tell you the reasons that this appointment was made for you. Both your parents and the staff at your residence are worried about you. They have said you seem to be unhappy and often your behavior shows that you are angry and unhappy. Do you think this is true?

Jane: I'm a retard. (The patient did not answer the question, but provided possible essential linkage to her unhappiness.)

Therapist: Can you tell me what you mean by "a retard"?

Jane: I'm dumb. Everyone says I'm dumb. I don't know a lot of things. I can't do a lot of things. I don't know how.

We talked about some of these "things." She identified not reading as well as other people, not handling money, not understanding what others talk about.

Therapist: You mean it's been hard for you to understand these things that other people seem to understand.

Jane: Yes.

Therapist: And people have called you dumb or retarded.

Jane: I don't care.

Therapist: Everyone would be upset by that. Sometimes people say they don't care because they feel hurt. Could that be the way it is for you?

Jane: (she nods) I hate it there.
Therapist: You've been living at the residence for four weeks and you've been unhappy. Can you tell me what you hate?

In the next few minutes, the client spoke about the staff and described their lack of empathy. She was quite verbal in her explanation of where she had been prior to this residence. She added that she was not given much information or preparation for the move. It was my impression that her depression and acting out were less related to adjusting to the new facility and more related to deeper issues, such as abandonment, rejection, poor self-esteem, and feelings of failure, which were triggered by the move. Jane began to express her feelings of abandonment and rejection. The predominant theme that emerged was the void, the deprivation that she experienced, and the continual expression of desire for her mother and her family. Placement had been painful for her because it was a final reenactment of a long history of loss and abandonment. She expressed these feelings in her session.

Jane: I'm alone.
Therapist: You feel alone even though you're living with many residents.
Jane: My mother sent me here and I wanted to be with her.
Therapist: So you feel alone because you are without your mother. Many residents feel the way you do.

Because of intellectual disability, this population is unable to adequately express feelings, and some do not understand the implications of their behavior and illness in the family's decision to place them. Powerful anger emerges at the loss of family, coupled with an unrelenting yearning for home. There is always the fantasy that those who sent them away will rescue them and take them home again. With or without cognizance of the reasons for placement, there is hope that placement is temporary and that someday they will be reunited with their mothers. Their resentment at loss of control over their lives and at someone's decision to place them, without their involvement, leaves them feeling hopeless. They also experience intense feelings of deprivation and failure, and have an insatiable need for the attention, warmth, and nurturance.

It is sometimes difficult with the mentally ill-mentally retarded to arrive at a focus in one or two sessions because much of the provided information is hampered by inadequate cognitive and verbal skills. Often it may take several sessions to accurately determine a core problem area. However, Jane was quite verbal and expressive. With my paraphrasing, repetition, and clarification, we were able to identify her behavior as a symptom of her underlying sadness.

With the recognition that the issues appeared to be around a central core issue, suitable for short-term work, I then proposed that we meet for several weeks to talk about her sadness and anger, the hope being that she might feel happier at the residence. Consistent with a brief model, a goal of the beginning phase is to contract with the patient to work within a brief time frame (Budman and Gurman 1988). It is always important to be cognizant of the intellectual limitations of this population. Therefore, proposing time-limited treatment must be carefully explained and re-peated throughout treatment. The use of visual aids, calendars, and holiday markers are useful tools to foster the recognition of the passing of time. Weekly reminders, especially near termination, are essential (Ep-stein 1992). In these initial meetings Jane demonstrated strengths, such as her ability to identify consequences to her behavior and to show motiva-tion to meet with me. She had successfully adjusted to her previous placement, showing some mastery and competence and an ability to form some attachments. A supportive approach, focused around a central issue, could enhance her problem solving, coping mechanisms, object relations, and self-esteem (Goldstein and Noonan 1999). Supportive techniques, such as encouragement, reassurance, ventilation, and guidance, are effec-tive (Fletcher and Dosen 1993).

In working with Jane, it was apparent that little attention had been given to how she experienced the changes in her life. With the move to the residence, she felt unsupported and unable to express her sadness. Positive adjustment had not occurred. Therefore, the therapeutic relationship was to provide her with a place to feel understood and accepted. Her anxiety and depression could then be alleviated, leading to an amelioration in several areas of functioning.

In the beginning phase of treatment, we talked about her sadness, her feelings of rejection, and her belief that she was bad.

Therapist: So there are many things that make you feel sad.
Jane: (after a pause) I'm bad.
Therapist: What makes you say that you're bad?
Jane: If I was good, my mother wouldn't send me away.
Therapist: You think you were sent to the residence because you're bad?
Jane: Didn't my mother love me? If she loved me, she wouldn't have sent me away.
Therapist: You thought that your mother and father didn't love you. You feel unhappy at this new residence; you thought you were sent there because you were bad. (She nods and I wait a moment.) Perhaps one of the ways that you've tried to tell everyone at the residence that you were unhappy was to break some rules and act very angry.

The Middle Phase

In the middle phase of treatment, the focus, if properly defined, is maintained and the therapist intervenes in ways that help the patient to be self-reflective, enabling the identification and working through of key issues. With this population, limited cognitive functioning may pose impediments to this goal. Jane, however, was able to verbalize many thoughts and was responsive to the therapist's interpretations and clarifications.

In the next few sessions, she spoke about how she thought she was dumb, how she was sad that she might never live at home, and how, if she were smart and good, she would be living with her parents like other "normal people."

Therapist: How are you different from these people?
Jane: They go to regular school because they're smart.

Therapist: Yes, you went to special schools because you needed help with your learning. It wasn't because you were bad that you were in special classes.

Jane: Sometimes I was bad.

Therapist: What did you do that was bad?

Jane: If I couldn't do something, I would yell and scream.

Therapist: What kinds of things couldn't you do?

Jane: When the teacher wanted me to learn about money, I couldn't.

Therapist: So if things were hard for you, you would yell and scream— perhaps as you've been doing at the residence.

Jane: Yes. Maybe I do the same things.

Therapist: You mean you yelled and screamed with your teachers and now at the residence. Did this happen at home, too?

Jane: I cursed. I did bad things. I didn't come home sometimes. I took money.

Therapist: Do you know why you did these things?

Jane: I had no friends.

Therapist: You must have been lonely. Do you know what I mean?

Jane: Yes. I only had my mother and she sent me away.

Therapist: So you didn't have any friends. Your mother was very important to you and then you thought she sent you away and didn't love you. And this was very hard for you.

I empathized with her and repeated some of these thoughts. Then I wanted to help her make connections between her behavior and the need for placement, not as a punishment, but as a necessity. Goldstein and Noonan (1999) identify this time frame for implementing interventions and monitoring progress. Jane was responsive to the exploration of issues.

Therapist: You know some of the things you told me about could have been dangerous to you. What do you think?

Jane: You mean like walking around the streets at night?

Therapist: Yes. And smoking in your room.

Jane: My mother and father said that it was dangerous.

Therapist: What did you think? (She nods in agreement.) Your parents were worried about you. They worried that you could have gotten hurt, that you weren't safe.

Jane: So they sent me away?

Therapist: They looked for a place where you could be safe and where you might make friends with other people and not be so lonely. (She is quiet for a few moments.) You know, mothers and fathers can love their children but sometimes aren't able to help them in the ways that they need help.

Jane: Like my mother?

Therapist: Yes, like your mother and father.

Jane began to understand the reasons she was sent to placement. In the next six to eight sessions, we talked about her behavior, her loneliness, her pain at separation from her mother, and her feelings about her father and his lack of involvement with her. We identified the positive experience of placement—friends, shared activities, and learning new skills of daily living. Her behavior in the residence improved. She was calmer, less depressed and anxious, less isolated, and more cooperative. She began to participate in activities, made a few friends, and became sexually active with several of the male residents, not uncommon with this population and with residential placement.

Termination

After approximately twelve sessions, we began to evaluate her progress and we talked about ending our time together. In a brief treatment model, termination is a time to review progress and identify unresolved issues (Epstein 1992, Goldstein and Noonan 1999, Luborsky 1984, Mann 1981). Cognitive limitations often pose a problem for the therapist when termination is discussed. Again, frequent reminders and visual aids are attempts at addressing anticipated responses to termination, but are not always effective.

Therapist: Ms. S. (social worker at the residence) called to tell me that the staff thinks you're doing well. What do you think?

Jane: I went to a show last night with everyone.

Therapist: You've made friends at the residence. Is that your way of telling me that you're happier at the residence?

Jane: I have a boyfriend.

Therapist: So you have a special friend? (She smiles.) When you first came to see me, we talked about some of the problems you were having at the residence. Do you remember that?

Jane: I don't have so many now.

Therapist: Yes, that's true.

Jane: My mother and father come to the residence. They know all the staff and the residents.

Therapist: So some things have really changed for you. You've made friends and you see your parents often and I'm told you hardly ever yell and scream. You've learned to talk to the staff when things bother you.

Jane: I mostly talk to Cynthia (her counselor).

Therapist: That's really helpful to you. Perhaps this is a good time for us to talk about when we will end our sessions.

Jane: Why can't I talk to you, too?

Therapist: You mean you don't want to end our time together.

Jane: I like coming here.

Therapist: Yes, and I've liked talking to you, too. We've seen each other for twelve weeks (I show her on the calendar). Do you remember when we began to work together, you were unhappy? Now you're not sad or angry the way you were when we first met.

Jane: But who will I talk to?

Therapist: Perhaps it seems to you that if we don't meet, then you won't have anyone to talk to.

Jane: I like you. Why can't I keep coming? (She looks away and appears unhappy.)

Genuine empathic relationships are often lacking for patients who are retarded. With Jane, a strong, positive transference developed and the sessions were valuable to her. It was important to remember, however, that her original belief was that she was sent away by her mother because she wasn't loved. Transferentially she may have believed that I, too, was sending her away. I interpreted that she experienced endings and changes as meaning she was no longer loved. I reminded her that we were talking about ending our work together, not because I didn't care about her, but because she accomplished the goals we had set. We reviewed her progress in communicating and problem solving.

We spent eight more sessions together—four weekly, two every other week, one a month after following termination, and one three months later. Budman and Gurman (1988) state that many psychoanalytically oriented brief therapists believe that treatment should not include follow-up sessions as this implies that the treatment is not really complete and, therefore, should not be terminated. When the central issue is to work through previous separation and loss, this belief is particularly relevant. In contrast, Budman and Gurman differ in that they believe that a patient's return to treatment indicates a positive working alliance. Another reason supporting follow-up sessions is that this often helps to maintain the gains made (Gambrill 1983, Rzepnicki 1991). Based on my previous practice experiences, less frequent sessions during the termination phase have proved successful.

The first few sessions of this phase identified her feelings of loss and rejection similar to those she experienced with her mother. While acknowledging her sadness, I continued to help her recognize her self-improvement. As her parents had, out of caring and concern, looked for another place to provide her with what she needed, she and I could make the transfer to other caring people at the residence. In all of the subsequent sessions, I was attentive to her level of understanding and often repeated previously discussed issues. I encouraged her to verbalize her feelings and, when necessary, I interpreted them for her.

Prior to our next to last session, Jane had a temper tantrum at the residence. Staff couldn't understand this acting out and regressive behavior, and, with the client's knowledge, reported it to me. It is not uncommon for patients who are anxious about termination to regress. There may be a resurgence of problems, or new problems may emerge (Levinson 1977, Luborsky 1984). I wanted to show respect for Jane's ability to discuss what had occurred. It was important for her to know that her report was as valuable in understanding what had happened:

> *Therapist:* The staff told me that there was an incident at the residence when you were screaming and yelling. Is that so?
>
> *Jane:* Yes.
>
> *Therapist:* Do you know what made you so angry?
>
> *Jane:* I wanted to talk to you and they didn't let me.
>
> *Therapist:* What was it that you wanted to talk to me about?
>
> *Jane:* I don't know. (Long pause.)
>
> *Therapist:* Perhaps because we only have two sessions left you behaved the way you did in the beginning when you first came to me. Maybe you thought that we could continue our sessions if you had a tantrum.
>
> *Jane:* I was sad.
>
> *Therapist:* I know. It's hard for you to say good-bye.
>
> *Jane:* I feel sad.
>
> *Therapist:* Yes. Saying good-bye can feel sad. (She nods.) You know you've learned to talk to staff when you're sad and you've been able to control your behavior by talking rather than yelling and screaming. You've shown this to everyone in the past few weeks. You should be proud of what you've been able to do. The staff and your parents have been proud of you, too.

Thus, I reinforced both the gains she had made and her increased ability to take control of her behavior, resulting in her increased sense of competence and mastery.

Separation and loss are issues for clinicians as well as patients, and the clinician must help the patient to experience this loss differently from previous ones. This must represent not an abandonment, but rather a planned ending. Though sad, termination evolves out of a mutually successful venture. The therapist must help the patient put the feelings into the larger context of previous separations. Placing the ending into a historical context allows the opportunity for a corrective emotional experience. The patient is permitted to deal with feelings as well as internalize an aspect of the treatment, and progress in a more functional way (Mann 1981).

Jane continued to progress after our sessions and made a successful adjustment to the residence. While she often verbalized missing her parents, she was better able to understand the reason for their decision to place her and to acknowledge this, not as an abandonment, but as a way to help her with her problems. In total, we worked together for twenty sessions.

TECHNIQUES

Psychotherapy with mentally ill-mentally retarded people can pose difficulties for the therapist as the process demands one's knowledge, skill, insight, and unending patience. Treatment requires a modification of therapeutic techniques according to the patient's language and psychosocial development.

One of the first steps in developing treatment interventions with persons having mental illness and mental retardation is to establish a therapeutic relationship between the therapist and the individual requiring care (Fletcher and Menolascino 1989). It is the alliance between patient and therapist that is essential to the therapeutic process, which is the basis for providing the security to explore and master surroundings (Fletcher and Dosen 1993).

A therapeutic relationship rests on an unconditional valuing of the patient (Sinanson 1992). The therapist must believe these individuals are both entitled to and are capable of achieving a richer life. While the relationship is fundamental to the work with other groups, these individuals are often bereft of significant people in their lives. They can be fearful of becoming attached and are often needier because of the lack of other relationships. They require a therapeutic relationship that provides respect, empathic understanding, encouragement, reassurance, guidance, and genuineness in order to develop trust and promote growth. The therapist attempts to stimulate a rapid working alliance and positive transference (Mann 1981).

Brief therapy does not encourage the same bonding that may occur in longer treatment, but, nonetheless, without a positive respectful relationship, the treatment will fail. Mentally ill-mentally retarded people who have faced repeated lifelong rejection and abandonment can take a longer time to establish a therapeutic relationship. The clinician needs to understand the client's wariness about trusting someone new. Since time is a most important factor in brief treatment, this may present problems. The clinician can help the treatment to progress while simultaneously conveying respect for the emotional distance that exists. In our fourth session, Jane was particularly quiet. I questioned her about this and she responded:

Jane: Why should I talk to you? You'll leave, too.
Therapist: You are afraid to talk to me because you think you will lose me, too.

Countertransferential feelings are common in working with this client population. Workers must be attuned to their own feelings and not allow them to intrude on the techniques and process. Therapists often feel guilty about not being able to cure the patient's retardation or rescue the patient from the unhappiness that it brings (Szymanski 1980). Overprotectiveness, lack of limits, and inappropriate expectations are also countertransferential reactions (Jakab 1970). At times, Jane repeatedly verbalized the same thoughts from session to session and I experienced frustration and feelings of inadequacy regarding my success with her. I was aware of her positive transference and needed to ensure that I did not allow her to idealize me in the transference as a way of soothing my fears of not doing enough for her.

Before any therapeutic intervention is started, a person's current functioning must be understood in relation to external and internal conditions that contribute to its development. Initially, a historical perspective helps in the development of a working hypothesis so that a treatment plan may be devised to focus on the problem behaviors. It is essential to combine the developmental (historical) and functional (contemporary) viewpoints. Some practitioners believe that traditional psychotherapy with this group is less effective than social skills training (Matson 1985), which is aimed at specific target behaviors.

Professionals who have practiced long-term treatment with mentally ill-mentally retarded individuals have utilized techniques from different theoretical schools:

1. Psychodynamic psychotherapy uses psychoanalytic, ego psychology, object relations, or interpersonal theories and techniques, with a focus on changing those aspects of the individual's personality that create problems and distress.
2. Supportive therapy is aimed at strengthening existing personality skills for managing life problems.
3. Counseling is directed toward practice in solving daily living problems, accomplishing social tasks, and developing coping skills (Rubin 1983).

Some of these techniques are equally effective in time-limited treatment. Therapy generally has greater relevance to immediate life experiences than to historical review. While insight is not a goal of treatment, helping the patient to understand that current behavior is connected to and influenced by past experiences has been effective (Fletcher and Dosen 1993). A supportive approach using techniques of encouragement, reassurance, ventilation, and guidance raises self-esteem, independence, and appropriate risk-taking. Concrete demonstration, modeling, and role playing are used to label emotions and illustrate more adaptive defenses (Rubin 1983). Interpersonal skills are also practiced through more directive techniques.

At the beginning of treatment, the patient sometimes requires shorter, more frequent sessions of half-hour duration rather than the conventional schedule of psychotherapy sessions. Frequent sessions are often instrumental in decreasing acting out related to low frustration tolerance and poor impulse control. Conversation, interchange, and therapist activity in the therapeutic process is helpful to the client (Szymanski 1980). The therapist must be a real person, not solely a neutral therapeutic mirror. Retarded people ask many personal questions, characteristic of early stages of development and reflective of their experience of always being questioned. It is, therefore, recommended that the therapist answer their questions, although this is contrary to the neutral stance of the traditional psychotherapist. This therapeutic posture furthers feelings of equality and independence, and works to promote greater self-esteem. Therapists need to be direct, initiating and facilitating the process, especially with patients who need to understand the limits of acceptable behavior.

Sadness has, for the most part, been denied expression and, as a result, turns into anger. The usual mode has been to discourage expression of anger and to "work it off" (Levitas and Gilson 1989). An inappropriate response, akin to rage, emerges. The patient is helped to appropriately express anxiety, anger, sadness, and guilt. It is not uncommon for the therapist to be the only person who has listened and responded to these patients in a respectful, caring, and understanding manner. In general, it is necessary to help them verbalize their feelings and for the therapist to reflect their emotional world back to them. However, ventilation needs to be used selectively as a therapeutic intervention. Ventilation does not always provide a catharsis, but may actually help to escalate the very behaviors that need calming. Aggressive disruptive incidents are often prevented by a combination of ventilation and physical activity away from the setting. This provides out-of-control patients with the safety that they cannot feel within the emotionally charged setting.

Nontraditional, innovative approaches have been utilized where patients are unable to meet the commitment of a traditional setting. I have sometimes recommended that with severely deprived, fragile patients, who cannot tolerate the clinical office setting, therapy can begin outside of the office. Individual sessions may take place on a park bench or other unconventional area. If a resistant patient is more amenable in a less threatening environment, then the therapist is encouraged to begin work in this manner (Klein 1992). Some clinicians believe that concepts and practice based on child psychotherapy should be utilized with this patient population (Levitas and Gilson 1989).

Limit setting, consistency, and structure are essential in working with these patients. They are capable of adhering to structure if they are continually, and in a caring manner, reminded of the schedules they helped to devise. Otherwise, they can be highly manipulative and treatment-destructive. In setting limits and boundaries, the contract should allow the patient to talk about any subject during the first ten minutes, with the remainder of the session focusing on issues related to the treatment and goals. This provides both a cathartic effect and allows the therapist to acknowledge the patient's feelings (Fletcher and Dosen 1993). While these techniques are based on a long-term approach and brief therapy must stay focused on a central issue, this population has major difficulties with impulse control. It may, at times, be necessary and advisable to modify the treatment approach to allow some time for catharsis. Efforts in brief therapy are directed toward teaching the patients to recognize their emotions, especially in regard to the precipitating conditions, and toward replacing usual aggressive behavioral responses with more self-managed, socially appropriate behaviors.

CONCLUSION

In assessing the gains of brief work, the therapist must never lose sight of the complex needs of this patient population. While it has been substantiated that brief treatment is effective, too few professionals have shown interest in conducting research and in treating this population. Harmful attitudes, ignorance, and lack of experience interfere with research, diagnosis, and treatment. While attitudes have been more tolerant over the last few years, stereotypes still exist. These patients are often still viewed as untreatable; intensive work to change current attitudes is essential to providing effective treatment. Measures can be taken to help prevent mental illness in the mentally retarded. Families that have a mentally retarded child can be educated so that the child is less stigmatized by intellectual deficits. This can be accomplished with brief treatment.

Arguments about the effectiveness of psychotherapeutic intervention continue. Some believe that brief psychotherapy is ineffective and a luxury we cannot afford. Others believe that behavioral management alone is most beneficial. The future requires diverse treatment methods with an emphasis on multimodal procedures, including a combination of techniques appropriate to the diagnostic and functional profile of the patient. Additional treatment modalities and facilities are needed, and existing concepts must be challenged. Insight is not an appropriate goal of treatment for the dually diagnosed. Work is directed toward cultivating the patient's potential, always with the belief that change and adaptation are possible.

We cannot cure mental illness and mental retardation, but we can reeducate, change, and develop better coping skills. All of this is possible within the framework of brief therapy. Professionals must understand the range of systems—the community social service system, the agency system, the family, the peer/reference group, and the individual's intrapsychic system. They also need to focus on biopsychosocial adaptation, human ecology, and maladaptation or incompatibility, all of which require professional actions that are both preventive and remedial. Every professional has an ethical obligation to be well grounded in these systems.

The professional community must recognize special needs of special populations and make these needs known to helping agencies. There must be a commitment to obtaining services and directing energies to effect social change for disadvantaged people. Change, as difficult as it may be, can and does occur with the mentally ill-mentally retarded. The scales for measurement, progress, and success need to be realistic and accurate. Establishing criteria for success that are clinically and statistically significant is an area of professional concern in assessing treatment effectiveness (Matson 1985). Optimism, motivation, therapeutic intervention, knowledge, and empathy are all determinants in the process of change. This is a challenge. With innovative, improved services, long-term needs of the mentally ill-mentally retarded can be met within a framework of brief therapy.

REFERENCES

American Psychiatric Association. (1994). *Diagnostic and Statistical Manual of Mental Disorders*, 4th ed. Washington, DC: Author.

Bates, W. J. (1984). Multi-modal treatment of mental illness in institutionalized mentally retarded persons. In *Handbook of Mental Illness in the Mentally Retarded*, ed. F. J. Menolascino, pp. 219–230. New York: Plenum.

Beasley, J., and Kroll, J. (1992). Who is in crisis? The consumer or the system? *National Association for the Dually Diagnosed Newsletter* 9(6):1–5.

Beebe, B. (1985). Mother/infant mutual influence and precursors of psychic structure. Paper presented at the New York Meeting, Frontiers of Self Psychology, April.

Borthwick-Duffy, S. A., and Eyman, R. K. (1990). Who are the dually diagnosed? *American Journal of Mental Retardation* 94(6):586–595.

Bowlby, J. (1969). *Attachment and Loss: Vol. 1. Attachment*. New York: Basic Books.

Budman, S. H., ed. (1981). *Forms of Brief Therapy*. New York: Guilford.

Budman, S. H., and Gurman, A. S. (1988). *Theory and Practice of Brief Therapy*. New York: Guilford.

Epstein, L. (1992). *Brief Treatment and a New Look at the Task-Centered Approach*, 3rd ed. New York: Macmillan.

Flegenheimer, W. (1993). *Techniques of Brief Psychotherapy*. Northvale, NJ: Jason Aronson.

Fletcher, R. J., and Dosen, A. (1993). *Mental Health Aspects of Mental Retardation: Progress in Assessment and Treatment*. New York: Lexington.

Fletcher, R., and Menolascino, F. (1989). *Mental Retardation and Mental*

Illness: Assessment, Treatment, and Service for the Dually Diagnosed. Lexington, MA: Lexington.

Gambrill, E. (1983). *Casework: A Competency-Based Approach.* Englewood Cliffs, NJ: Prentice Hall.

Gold, I. M., Wolfson, E. S., Lester, C. M., et al. (1989). Developing a unit for mentally retarded-mentally ill patients on the grounds of a state hospital. *Hospital and Community Psychiatry* 40(8):836–840.

Goldstein, E., and Noonan, M. (1999). *Short-Term Treatment and Social Work Practice: An Integrative Perspective.* New York: Free Press.

Jakab, I. (1970). Psychotherapy of the mentally retarded child. In *Diminished People,* ed. N. H. Bernstein, pp. 145–150. Boston: Little, Brown.

Klein, J. (1992). *The story of Hope House: a residential program for the mentally ill-mentally retarded.* Unpublished doctoral dissertation, The Union Institute.

Levinson, H. R. (1977). Termination of psychotherapy: some salient issues. *Social Casework* 58(8):480–489.

Levitas, A., and Gilson, S. (1989). Psychodynamic psychotherapy with mildly and moderately retarded patients. In *Mental Retardation and Mental Illness,* ed. R. Fletcher and F. Menolascino, pp. 71–110. Lexington, MA: Lexington.

Lichtenberg, J. D. (1989). *Psychoanalysis and Motivation.* Hillsdale, NJ: Analytic Press.

Luborsky, L. (1984). *Principles of Psychoanalytic Psychotherapy.* New York: Basic Books.

Mann, J. (1981). The core of time limited psychotherapy: time and central issue. In *Forms of Brief Therapy,* ed. S. Budman, pp. 25–44. New York: Guilford.

Matson, J. L. (1985). Emotional problems in the mentally retarded: the need for assessment and treatment. *Psychopharmacology Bulletin* 21(2): 258–260.

Menolascino, F. J. (1983). Bridging the gap between mental retardation and mental illness: overview. In *Mental Health and Mental Retardation,* ed.

F. J. Menolascino and B. M. McCann, pp. 3–64. Baltimore, MD: University Park Press.

Menolascino, F. J., Ruedrich, S. L., Golden, C. J., and Wilson, T. E. (1985). Diagnosis and pharmacotherapy of schizophrenia in the retarded. *Psychopharmacology Bulletin* 21(2):316–321.

Menolascino, F. J., and Stark, J. A. (1984). Research and future directions. In *Handbook of Mental Illness in the Mentally Retarded*, ed. F. J. Menolascino and J. A. Stark, pp. 399–402. New York: Plenum.

Pollock, H. M. (1944). Mental disease among mental defectives. *American Journal of Psychiatry* 101:361–363.

Reiss, S., Levitan, G. W., and McNally, R. J. (1982). Emotionally disturbed mentally retarded people. *American Psychologist* 37(4):361–367.

Rubin, R. (1983). Bridging the gap through individual counseling and psychotherapy with mentally retarded people. In *Mental Health and Mental Retardation*, ed. F. J. Menolascino and B. M. McCann, pp. 119–128. Baltimore, MD: University Park Press.

Rzepnicki, T. (1991). Enhancing the durability of intervention gains: a challenge for the 1990s. *Social Service Review* 65(1):92–111.

Selan, B. H. (1976). Psychotherapy with the developmentally disabled. *Health and Social Work* 1:73–83.

Sinanson, V. (1992). *Mental Handicap and the Human Condition*. London: Free Association Books.

Spitz, R. A. (1965). *The First Year of Life*. New York: International Universities Press.

Stern, D. (1985). *The Interpersonal World of the Infant*. New York: Basic Books.

Szymanski, L. S. (1980). Individual psychotherapy with retarded persons. In *Emotional Disorders of Mentally Retarded Persons*, ed. L. Szymanski and P. Tanguay, pp. 77–78, 132–133, 267. Baltimore, MD: University Park Press.

Tuckfelt, S., Fink, J., and Warren, M. P. (1997). *The Psychotherapists' Guide to Managed Care in the 21st Century*. Northvale, NJ: Jason Aronson.

CHAPTER ELEVEN

Brief Treatment of Clients with Chronic Medical Conditions

GRACE HYSLOP CHRIST, MARY SORMANTI,
AND SUSAN OPPENHEIM

At the beginning of the twentieth century, when the state of medical and public health knowledge limited treatments, Americans frequently died at a young age from infectious and parasitic diseases. As sanitation, nutrition, and living conditions improved, antibiotics were discovered and medical technology advanced, deaths from infectious diseases declined steadily and children and young adults survived longer. Newborns and young infants now survive even in the face of serious health problems that previously would have taken their lives. Biomedical advances have also extended the lives of the elderly with disabilities and life-threatening chronic illnesses. Consequently, greater numbers of people in our society have limitations in functioning associated with many common diseases such as heart disease, asthma, diabetes, arthritis, and cancer (Hoffman and Rice 1996). Chronic illnesses are distinguished from acute illnesses by their duration (three months or longer), their effects on quality of life, and their interference with normal life functions (Sidell 1997).

The increase in the prevalence of chronic illness, the broad impact of associated disabilities, and the cost of caring for such patients, often at home rather than in the hospital, have encouraged health professionals to rethink their way of providing care. Increasingly attention is paid to the psychosocial aspects of care, including illness-related distress, quality of life, and impact of the illness of the patient's family and support network. For clinicians this means that regardless of their work setting (e.g., acute care hospital, community agency, private practice), they are likely to confront patients who have a chronic illness or are caring for an individual with a chronic illness.

Brief treatment models such as integrated short-term treatment (ISTT) are ideally suited for individuals with chronic illness because their problems often concern specific psychosocial adjustments to illness-related occurrences, and frequently they have developed considerable ego strengths and had accomplishments prior to the occurrence of the illness or as a consequence of coping with its associated stresses. These strengths can be mobilized to facilitate rapid change. Furthermore, ongoing long-term therapy may be contraindicated as it can undermine an individual's careful balancing of necessary dependency required by the illness experience and assertion of realistic independence that fosters a sense of mastery, control, and self-esteem.

There is also a natural fit of brief treatment with chronic illness. The treatment model is usually brief, but episodic over time. Because of the changing health care scene during the last decades of the twentieth century, the emphasis on limiting unnecessary health service utilization has meant that much of the care provided is administered by managed care organizations. Brief treatment is synergistic with managed care's emphasis on "solution-focused health and mental health interventions, approaches that clearly prioritize episodic treatment over ongoing . . . support" (Volland et al. 1999, p. 12).

TREATMENT PERSPECTIVES

Patients who have chronic illnesses often need help in managing crises related to treatment, developmental changes, or life transitions that are more complicated due to the presence of illness or disability. Such crises may include expected changes in the treatment process, such as the anxiety experienced at the end of a treatment protocol, or unexpected occurrences such as a disease exacerbation or recurrence. Normative developmental tasks such as establishing a career, forming intimate relationships, or child bearing can also become quite complicated and stressful when they occur during the illness experience. In addition, patients with chronic illness may find job loss, job promotion, or necessary geographic moves more stressful as a consequence of their condition. Brief treatment focuses on normalizing the greater challenge patients experience from such developmental changes and life transitions. In these situations patients need help in solving related problems or in acquiring additional skills and resources that will help them to cope effectively.

Brief treatment is also particularly suited for work with individuals with chronic illness because it emphasizes the rapid mobilization of ego strengths. Although some chronically ill patients may present with symptoms of suicidality and depression that are severe enough to qualify them for a *DSM-IV* diagnosis, their symptoms suggest a treatment approach that is different from one that would be indicated for individuals with severe and persistent mental illness. Their symptoms are likely to be reactive to a life situation rather than psychopathology. They often have greater underlying ego strengths and capacities and are able to respond quickly to therapeutic approaches that are focused on their salient issues. Some have a considerable period of symptom-free life experience before their illness, during which they developed ego strengths and accumulated successes in problem solving, developing coping skills, and mastering of developmental tasks. They may have honed special abilities to deal with a range of stresses as a consequence of meeting the challenge of illness and treatment. For example, the Internet has become a primary resource for many patients, providing specific information and social support through facilitating communication with other patients in similar situations. Teaching patients how to use such resources has been shown to be effective in helping them cope (Gustafson et al. 1993, 1998). The presence of the illness may also have encouraged the development of "steeling qualities" in their ability to cope. In other words, their symptoms are likely to reflect adaptive reactions to highly stressful situations rather than the existence of persistent psychopathology. Although their strengths may be temporarily overwhelmed by the illness situation, brief treatment wisely identifies and builds on these strengths.

Finally, the structure of brief treatment may be helpful to individuals with chronic illness because it meets necessary dependency needs, for a limited period of time, but then focuses on mobilizing strengths and capacities the individual needs to cope independently with illness over a lifetime. Individuals with chronic illness struggle with the fact that they need to be dependent on others for treatment, care, and assistance. While accepting this necessity, those who cope successfully also search for areas in which they can assert themselves and gain control and mastery, which builds confidence and self-esteem. Open-ended, nondirective therapies may encourage greater dependence than is necessary or helpful, given the nature of the challenges patients confront.

Three goals are integral to brief treatment with individuals with chronic illness: (1) help the patient maintain a sense of mastery and control over a disease and treatment process that often seems to be beyond their control, (2) use a broad range of inventive approaches to help the patient maintain a sense of self-esteem and meaning that is constantly challenged by illness, and (3) promote the development of an effective support network (Lapham 1986, Strauss and Glaser 1975).

THEORETICAL OVERVIEW

While all theoretical frameworks of human behavior are used in short-term work with chronic illness, the two models most relevant are crisis intervention theory (Parad and Parad 1990) and problem-solving theory (Goldstein and Noonan 1999, Perlman 1957). In addition, the eco-systems perspective of Germain and Gitterman (1982), and Meyer (1983) provides a structure for conceptualizing the fit between the demands of the illness and the resources and abilities of patients, the support network, and the social and medical care system within which their illness is treated.

Crisis Intervention Approaches

Most chronic illnesses are characterized by a series of phases, crises, or nodal points around which individuals experience special problems in coping. The medical, social, and psychological demands of these situations may overwhelm the individual's usual means of coping and problem solving and are therefore critical points for intervention (Christ 1991, Lapham 1986, Loscalzo and Brinzenhofeszoc 1998, Rolland 1994). The therapist needs to understand the particular crisis points in the illness as well as the anticipated illness trajectory for the patient. While patients may inform the clinician about these dimensions of their illness, the clinician often needs to obtain confirmation from a physician. Patients may (unconsciously) deny the severity of illness or they may believe that their prognosis is more hopeless than it really is.

The illness trajectory includes anticipated duration, course, associated disability and limitations, and expected outcome (Corbin and Strauss 1988, Rolland 1994). As an example, in cancer, such phases include diagnosis, treatment, treatment completion and continuing care, illness exacerbations, and terminal illness (Christ 1991). Rolland (1994) suggests that common phases for all chronic illnesses may include crisis, chronic, and terminal phases. Pollin (1994) identifies diagnosis, disease exacerbation, and the end of a treatment protocol as critical points for intervention. At these times patients may experience heightened feelings of distress that include fear, anxiety, confusion, desperation, helplessness, and loss of control. Pollin describes a brief treatment model that targets eight major fears of the individual with a chronic illness, fears that are often exacerbated during particular illness phases: (1) fear of loss of control, (2) fear of loss of positive self-image, (3) fear of dependency, (4) fear of stigma, (5) fear of abandonment, (6) fear of expressing anger, (7) fear of isolation, and (8) fear of death.

Goals of psychosocial treatment during illness and related crises are

(1) to relieve patients' acute distress; (2) to empower them to master the emotional, cognitive, and behavioral tasks demanded by the illness stage; and (3) to assist them to return to their highest premorbid level of coping, and if possible improve baseline coping. To do this, however, it is necessary to understand how illness demands are affecting the patient's personality, strengths, vulnerabilities, and learned ways of coping.

Eco-Systems Perspectives

While external situations identified in Germain and Gitterman's (1980) life model cause stress for many individuals, these situations can become crises for patients with chronic illness. These domains of stress include life transitions and traumatic life events, environmental pressures, and dysfunctional interpersonal relationships. Further, individuals with chronic conditions are vulnerable to a pileup of stresses or multiple stresses that can overwhelm their capacity to cope (McCubbin et al. 1998).

The demands of a new stage of development or embarking on a major life transition (Erikson 1959, Germain and Gitterman 1980), such as establishing independence, developing intimate relationships, or choosing a career, can create stress for which patients seek counseling. A change in job or living situation can also increase stress since with each change patients must reconstitute their views of themselves in the context of the new situation, confronting again their limitations, barriers to full functioning, and the need for accommodation.

> Molly was a competent African-American adolescent when she was diagnosed with a cancer that required treatment at a hospital far away from her home. Her father, an attorney who had previously been somewhat distant due to his work, was able to relocate his activities so that he could work near the hospital and regularly visit with her. As a consequence she got to know him much better. When she finished college she decided to give up her previous love of science and enter law school so that she could follow her father's

career interests. Molly found herself very confused and unhappy during her first year of law school as the actual work was not what she enjoyed. Consequently, she dropped out. Her husband was supportive of her need to take time out, but her parents were angry, disappointed, and frightened by what seemed to be unacceptable quitting or giving up on a commitment. Molly began to experience ambiguous neurological symptoms with no identifiable cause, became depressed, and felt herself to be a failure. After four brief treatment sessions she was able to explain to her parents that she dropped out because law was not what she really wanted to do; she was doing it to please her father. She realized that with all her medical treatment she had become more interested in science and medicine. Eventually she completed medical school.

This example demonstrates how the realistic demands for a more dependent relationship with parents during the illness conflicted with mastery of normative adolescent developmental tasks of increasing individuation and separation from parents (Blos 1962). Molly's gratitude to her parents for supporting her through the illness and her continuing dependence on their approval made it difficult for her to have confidence in her own emerging interests when they conflicted with those of her parents. With the onset of young adulthood she needed to integrate the reality of her illness in a new way. Not only was it important for her to understand her situation, but also she needed to be able to communicate this to her parents, who were also unaware of how the illness had prolonged unnecessary dependency in their relationship with each other.

Problem-Solving Approaches

The problem-solving model, developed in social work by Perlman (1957), emphasizes the need to partialize and prioritize patients' problems, and encourage them to consider alternative coping approaches and to expand rational thinking about their situation. Current research into problem-solving approaches has developed from cognitive-behavioral theoretical frameworks (D'Zurilla and Goldfried 1971, Nezu et al. 1999). These approaches teach specialized problem-solving skills that patients can use to address existing problems, as well as prepare for future challenges in more effective ways. Strategies that promote active problem solving and coping behaviors have been empirically demonstrated to be effective in reducing depression and anxiety in patients with cancer and other chronic illnesses (Nezu et al. 1998, 1999). In addition, people who exhibit flexibility in their problem-solving efforts are better at coping with the stresses of chronic illness (Rolland 1994). Problem-solving skills that can be taught include problem orientation (i.e., an optimistic or pessimistic expectation of successful resolution), problem definition and formulation, generation of alternatives, decision making, and implementation and verification of the solution. This approach is well suited to the complex multiproblem situations faced by individuals with chronic illnesses. While the disease cannot be cured, patients can continue to affirm their competence and maintain self-esteem through the process of mastering various challenges as they arise. The importance of effective problem solving in maintaining self-esteem is demonstrated in the following example:

> A group of women who had recovered from breast cancer spoke frequently about their fears of recurrence and how they cope with that uncertainty. When one woman did experience a recurrence, the leader wondered whether the group would be able to continue in the face of this confrontation with their worst nightmare. The affected woman met with the group to discuss her situation. One group participant said to her, "You think you are our worst nightmare, but you are not. Our worst nightmare is that this would happen to us and we would be unable to function, to find and engage in additional treatment, to talk with our family and friends about it, to continue on with our lives with strength, dignity, and courage. That is our worst nightmare." The woman who had the recurrence decided to continue with an active treatment group rather than this

posttreatment group so that all participants would be dealing with similar illness and treatment issues.

The problem-solving approach builds on data that suggest that those who cope well with stress, whether it be a serious illness, job loss, or a natural disaster, are those who don't deny the adversity or tragedy of the situation, but are able to see it as a challenge, to make positive changes in their life and their relationships, and who can derive some positive meaning out of the situation (D'Zurilla and Nezu 1982, Lazarus and Folkman 1984, Rowland 1989, Taylor 1983, Telch and Telch 1985). Problem-solving approaches aim to empower patients by giving them critical tools that promote a sense of mastery and self-efficacy to improve self-esteem. Adults who adapt well to chronic illness also use active coping strategies such as engaging in a partnership with professionals about their condition and building a network of individuals who have had similar experiences.

COMMON FEATURES OF
TREATING CHRONICALLY ILL INDIVIDUALS

Chronic illness confronts individuals with complex problems that involve the interaction of at least three different domains (Dimond 1984):

1. The medical treatment and physiological reactions
2. The social responses of family, friends, co-workers, and health care workers
3. The individuals' psychological response to their condition shaped by age, gender, and cultural expectations as well as individual appraisals and experiences.

The practitioner assesses not only each individual domain but also the interaction between domains. The goal is to enhance a positive, mutually reinforcing process rather than a negative, mutually destructive interaction, which is often occurring when the patient enters treatment. Neglect of any one of these areas may prevent an optimal understanding of the patient's situation and make it difficult to identify the most salient issues for intervention. The practitioner aims to help the patient maximize opportunities presented in the illness experience as well as cope with its adverse consequences. Clinical practice with the chronically medically ill is characterized by the following unique features:

1. The responses of individuals with chronic illness are shaped by the impact of the disease on their developmental level at the time of the onset of the disease, the way it changed their lives then, and its changing meaning to them during their subsequent life course. The ability to master sequential developmental tasks, and maintain a positive appraisal of the illness and a realistic understanding of its causes and consequences over time affects adaptation (Lazarus and Folkman 1984, Mathieson and Henderikus 1995, Rowland 1989).

2. Critical to providing therapeutic interventions with chronically ill individuals is helping them to balance mourning losses caused by illness and treatment with recognition and affirmation of strengths and remaining capacities (Moynihan et al. 1988). Significant strengths such as courageous endurance, successful navigation of obstacles, and creative coping with numerous physical adversities are often taken for granted by patients. Yet an individual's recognition of strengths and achievements is necessary to maintain self-esteem. Patients may present as defensive, angry, or witholding based on underlying, and often unconscious, fears of dependency, abandonment, and rejection. Similarly, exaggerated assertions of capabilities may cover fears of vulnerability, inadequacy, and failure. It is important to remember that anger can be a source of motivation to overcome the many obstacles created by the illness.

3. In their effort to "keep the illness in its place" and not let it dominate their lives (Gonzales et al. 1989), patients may deny its impact on their reactions or minimize the importance of their

emotions and perceptions. Conversely, patients may become pre-occupied with the demands of illness to the exclusion of more pleasurable activities and growth experiences.

4. Living with chronic illness requires considerable expense. Even with insurance coverage, there are many out-of-pocket costs. Insufficient funds for treatment, rehabilitation, functional or cosmetic surgery, and routine living expenses can be very stressful for these patients and can limit the types of intervention options available to them. Consequently, case management roles such as obtaining resources and teaching advocacy skills may have the greatest impact on patients' well-being (Francoeur et al. 1997).

5. Individuals with chronic illness may initially express anger at the therapist based on previous encounters with health care professionals and others who were overwhelmed with the complexity of the illness situation. Health care professionals are more comfortable with acute, discrete episodes of illness rather than the uncertainties of chronic conditions. Patients may have been victims of social rejection, alienation, and isolation based on others' fears and lack of knowledge of their condition.

6. Patients may engage in high-risk behaviors such as failure to participate in rehabilitation, noncompliance with treatment, and self-medication with drugs and alcohol that require careful assessment. Such behaviors may reflect efforts to deny their vulnerability and to cope with depression. In these situations, confrontation of the potential destructiveness of their behaviors is necessary to provide a safe environment for psychosocial treatment.

7. Individuals with chronic illness may prefer episodic therapy, that is, intensive intervention during an illness or social or psychological crises. Following these episodes, they may want to terminate therapy and normalize their life when the illness crisis has passed. For example, after a course of hospital-based treatment, patients may want to distance themselves from hospital support and engage community services. Such self-assertion can be helpful. Following completion of a medical treatment protocol, therapy is generally

aimed at integrating the impact and meaning of the particular exacerbation, treatment, and illness effects.

> Rachel, a 43-year-old mother with two small children, was diagnosed with breast cancer. She began psychotherapy after her chemotherapy was completed. While she was on chemotherapy she had participated in a therapy group and had consulted with various professionals about how to manage the side effects of her treatment. After treatment was over, she wanted help controlling her anxiety about recurrence since she was no longer actively fighting the disease. She also wanted help in managing her relationship with her husband and children within the context of the possible threat to her life and with her new sense of vulnerability.

8. The therapeutic role with individuals with chronic illness often emphasizes a consultative and collaborative style in therapy that conveys respect, but encourages the patient's initiative and independent action. The clinician educates, promotes positive cognitive appraisals, sets limits on negative thinking and behaving, and encourages the development of a positive sense of meaning and identity (Mathieson and Henderikus 1995, Taylor 1983). In this way, patients are engaged as active participants, their fears of helplessness and dependence are diminished, and self-esteem is enhanced.

SPECIFIC FOCI

The following treatment foci guide the clinician in brief treatment with chronically ill adults. They provide a structure that supports a rapid but comprehensive assessment based on accumulated knowledge, frames the most salient issues that help to prioritize the work, and encourages an openness to unexpected and highly idiosyncratic issues that may emerge.

Listen Carefully to the Presenting Problem

Given the wide range of responses to experiences, the clinician must listen carefully to the specific nature of the presenting problem and elicit patients' descriptions of their concerns. Showing interest and concern for the patients' present problem, as well as understanding the impact of their past experiences, will help to diminish the patient's anger from previous negative encounters with health professionals. Patients may have a long history of frustrating interactions with multiple providers within the health care system who have become overwhelmed with the complexity of their case and have not been responsive to their needs.

Clarify the Illness Trajectory

To assess an individual's coping with an illness, the clinician must first understand where the patient falls on the illness trajectory. For example, when initially diagnosed with a life-threatening illness, most individuals and their families fear death is imminent. In reality, many life-threatening illnesses can be successfully treated for extended periods, if not cured. On the other hand, some illnesses, such as AIDS or some forms of cancer, result in a dramatically shortened life expectancy, placing patients almost immediately into the terminal illness phase. The clinician helps patients align their perceptions and emotional responses with medical realities. This may be accomplished in one session or it may require multiple brief treatment sessions to work through the patient's rage, shock, and fear.

> A 32-year-old man presented as enraged and hopeless following his diagnosis with HIV. Feeling his life was over, he had bouts of excessive drinking and subsequent work absences, which resulted in his dismissal from numerous jobs as a chef. He blamed his previous girlfriend, his family, and society for what he viewed as his hopeless situation. He dismissed the clinician's efforts to empathize and provide solace, and he sometimes ended sessions early or had little to say. Nevertheless, he continued to keep his appointments with his

clinician and complied with his medical treatment. The clinician normalized the patient's feelings within the context of diagnosis, had the patient's depression evaluated by a psychiatrist for medication, and emphasized the importance of keeping medical appointments. The clinician also encouraged the patient to reconnect with people in a support network that had previously been important to him, and highlighted the positive results of medical tests as they were reported to him. In fact, the patient's illness seemed to be under control and, with new treatments, the patient's physician believed he had a life expectancy of at least five years and likely more. The clinician also recognized the patient's efforts to keep finding new jobs, his commitment to work, his strong relationship with some family members and friends, and his courage in following through on difficult diagnostic procedures. After six sessions, the patient began to express feelings of optimism and encouragement about his situation. He stabilized his job situation, and began to describe some pleasurable times with family and friends.

Identify the Psychosocial Tasks of the Illness Phase

Each illness phase confronts patients with adaptive tasks that must be mastered. Helping the patient fulfill these tasks may frame the clinical role. For example, the phase of continuing care following treatment for cancer includes the following adaptive tasks (Christ 1991, Christ et al. 2000):

- Recognize fear of less medical surveillance.
- Confront sense of emptiness/abandonment now that the crisis is over.
- Relinquish medical care team as primary source of support.
- Obtain support from those outside the medical care team.
- Reengage with pre-illness activities, functions, and tasks.
- Cope with residual physical impairments and psychological stresses.
- Reevaluate priorities within the context of illness.

The clinical role in response to these tasks may include:

- Normalize the patient's fears, anxieties, and conflicting feelings.
- Provide information about community resources.
- Facilitate return to normative tasks and functions.
- Encourage patient/family recognition of strengths and coping skills.
- Facilitate grief of perceived losses.
- Prepare patient/family for potential complications and late effects.
- Provide structure for continued medical and social work services.

Assess Patient Safety

Failure to comply with treatment for chronic illnesses can be life threatening. Therefore, the clinician assesses patients' understanding of the illness and the way of managing the treatment, and inquires about high-risk behaviors such as alcohol and substance abuse, as well as suicidal thoughts related to depression and/or to the illness condition. In some situations the patient could commit suicide by simply not taking medication, by overdosing on stockpiled prescription medication, or by other forms of neglect of self. The presence of a medical illness is, in fact, a risk factor for suicide (Depression Guideline Panel 1993), with AIDS patients reported as having one of the highest suicide rates (Mancoske et al. 1995). Clinicians find it helpful to initiate a discussion of suicide with newly diagnosed AIDS patients and then to monitor their thinking about this at various points in the illness process. Individuals with secondary neurological or sensory impairments may be especially vulnerable because their coping capacities have been reduced.

Emphasize the Patient's Strengths, Build Self-Esteem, Support a Positive Body Image, and Enhance a Sense of Mastery and Control

As discussed above, a chronic illness and its consequences can undermine patients' acceptance of personal strengths as they confront their physical vulnerabilities. Without acknowledgment of strengths, self-esteem is compromised. Physical disabilities can also undermine a positive body image, further reducing self-esteem. Many patients feel less attractive as a consequence of having an illness. It is important to identify ways individuals can continue to take care of their bodies and exercise some control over their situation in order to establish a sense of mastery, control, and self-efficacy.

Help the Patient Build a Network of Support with Professional Caregivers, Other Patients, Family, and Friends

The ability to communicate effectively with physicians and other health care professionals is often critical to the adaptation of the patient who has a chronic illness. Since the illness may span a lifetime and may require treatment from multiple specialists and health care agencies, the patient needs to develop communication skills. Patients must learn how to obtain timely and accurate information from their caregivers and simultaneously give health care professionals sufficient information that enables them to offer sound treatment guidance. An important focus of brief treatment is to improve the patient's skills by identifying conscious and unconscious barriers to effective communication and teaching needed abilities. For example, individuals may be so eager for others to see their value that they fail to discuss realistic limitations, such as their need for more time for rest. As a consequence, employers may misinterpret their absences as malingering. Avoidance of rehabilitation can also reflect patients' denial of their physical needs (Berkman 1996, Christ 1987).

Individuals' perceptions of having good social support has been repeatedly found to protect them from severe depressive symptoms (Penninx et al. 1998). However, social isolation is a risk for individuals with chronic illness. Their realistic dependency (and fear of it), limitations in their daily functioning, preexisting personality and life experiences, the social stigma attached to those who are "different," and the unrealistic social expectations that one should emerge from an illness unchanged often present barriers to retaining close supportive relationships (Christ 1987). Finding ways to expand social support networks and improving interactions with existing supports is an essential focus of treatment with the chronically ill.

Facilitate the Process of Reconstituting the Patient's Identity around the Realities of Illness

Reconstituting identity is an ongoing process that requires patients to grieve losses, but affirm remaining capacities and strengths as they forge a new sense of themselves, and integrate past and present with future expectations (Mathieson and Henderikus 1995). This process is a highly creative aspect of working with individuals with chronic illness. The clinician explores how the individual's previous way of managing stress may be helpful or unhelpful in the current situation. This is done because the patients' experiences before illness frame their view of themselves and their reactions to different kinds of losses. An individual who considered himself or herself to be an athlete will react more strongly to the loss of the ability to engage in sports than someone who found more gratification in sedentary activities. An individual who struggled with alcoholism or substance abuse may find it more difficult to control his behavior after being diagnosed with AIDS.

In addition to highlighting patients' strengths, the clinician encourages them to recognize areas in which they have achieved personal growth in the face of extraordinary stress. Existential and spiritual contemplation of the meaning of life, illness, death, suffering, redemption, and restoration often aid in the reconstitution of a valued identity after illness.

Facilitate Accurate and Ego-Enhancing Illness Appraisals and Attributions

Often erroneous and destructive beliefs about the illness and its causes and consequences need to be challenged. For example, patients may believe incorrectly that they caused their illness, that it is a punishment for sin, or that they are less valuable as human beings because of the illness.

They may think their life is over or that all opportunities are closed to them. Increasingly, research has found that the way individuals think about their illness affects how they feel about it and how well they adapt to it (Taylor 1983). Their level of optimism that treatments will be effective, and their belief in their ability to master the many physical and psychological challenges of illness and to maintain a sense of their worth seem to affect patients' ability to function effectively (McCubbin et al. 1998).

Implement Case Management Activities

Because of the complex and long-term nature of many chronic illnesses, there are often gaps in the continuity of patients' care (Francoeur et al. 1997). Effective case management links patients and families to a continuum of services, including rehabilitation, mental health, substance abuse, and self-help, financial, educational, and vocational organizations.

Managing a chronic illness can be a costly process. Individuals who have fewer resources have greater problems with out-of-pocket costs, with expensive procedures and equipment, and obtaining necessary personal assistance in many areas. Clinicians may assist patients in locating resources and teach them how to access them.

Monitor Concurrent Stresses

Research has shown that chronically ill individuals who struggle with other stresses in their lives as well face additional adaptive challenges (McCubbin et al. 1998, Nezu et al. 1999). Such stresses may include poverty, deaths in the family, other losses, and inability to find work or necessary benefits. Patients can experience a pileup of stressors, some of which may be secondary to or exacerbated by the chronic illness condition, while others have concurrent stresses unrelated to the illness. The clinician helps individuals and families recognize the level of stress they are experiencing and suggests ways they can mitigate its impact on them.

The most difficult aspect of developing a *DSM-IV* diagnosis for patients with a chronic illness is clarifying whether their behaviors, thoughts, and emotions are reactive to their illness, that is, are part of an adaptive process, or whether they represent more enduring psychopathology that needs to be treated separately from adaptation to the chronic illness. A history of patients' premorbid functioning can provide an important comparison in those situations where the illness occurred after early childhood. Understanding the full dimensions of the multiple stresses they are experiencing also helps to assess the adaptiveness of their responses. A response to a given situation may be more extreme than expected because of the particular meaning the illness has to the patient, the multiple stresses that have overwhelmed the individual's capacities to cope, or the exacerbation of preexisting psychological problems such as depression or substance abuse.

> John was 36 when his leukemia was treated with a bone marrow transplant. This treatment required that he remain in an isolation room for several weeks in order to protect him from infection as his immune system was compromised by total body irradiation. It was a condition of extreme stimulus deprivation, as everyone wore a mask and gown in the room and his activity was quite restricted. It was especially important that nothing be dropped on the floor, as that was the one part of the room that was not sterile. The clinician was called for a consultation because the patient had become combative with everyone, dropping food on the floor and using offensive language with nurses. The rest of the time he was curled up in a ball on his bed staring at the wall. The clinician was aware that John had spent seven years in prison before he was diagnosed with leukemia. She wondered if depression or posttraumatic stress might underlie his manipulative and antisocial behavior and might be emerging in the present situation.
>
> John told the clinician that he found the isolation room after treatment was like being in prison, only worse. In prison he knew the rules; he knew what to expect. Here he felt completely out of control, he did not know what would happen with his illness, and he

did not know how to express himself. Furthermore, his mother had been able to bring him food every week when he was in prison. Here he had to eat the very bland food that had been sterilized. As he spoke of his anger and frustration, his mood improved. The clinician reminded John that he had told her on admission that anger would be an indication that he was feeling highly stressed. He agreed this was now happening. The clinician then discussed with John other ways he could express his anger that would be less threatening to him physically and that would make it easier for staff to respond to him in a positive way. They identified several areas in which he did have choices as well as confronting behaviors that were unacceptable, such as dropping items on the floor or making sexual comments about the nurses. He was helped to recognize that he had more choices over his menu than he initially realized and that his family was able to bring him certain foods. Rather than acting on his feelings, John was encouraged to try to talk with staff members about his concerns and questions so that they could suggest alternatives. Also, they could help him feel more in control if they knew more about his concerns.

Within a day, John's mood had improved considerably and he gained control of his more provocative acting out. While he had shown symptoms of severe depression, it was clearly reactive to the situation in very idiosyncratic ways. Understanding his view of the treatment and helping him find ways to express himself and negotiate some sense of control within the parameters of this environmental reality enabled him to adapt in a more positive way. Although he never became the staff's favorite patient, his remaining time on the unit was less stressful and he was successfully discharged.

Adults with chronic illness (most notably individuals with AIDS) are at greater risk for experiencing depression, and they have a higher risk of suicide than healthy adults (Mancoske et al. 1995, Nezu et al. 1998). Individuals with severe mental illnesses also have a higher risk of having a chronic medical illness. Medical illnesses of the mentally ill may be underdiagnosed (Depression Guideline Panel 1993). These are particular risk factors associated with chronic illness that the clinician integrates into the ongoing assessment of the individual's functioning.

TREATMENT GOALS

Frequently brief treatment goals for individuals with chronic illness include the following:

Restore or maintain realistic levels of independence.
Increase knowledge of the impact of illness.
Restore previous levels of functioning in the individual and support network.
Assist patients in developing problem-solving skills.
Increase a sense of control and self-esteem.
Decrease depression and anxiety.
Encourage a more optimistic and hopeful attitude.
Limit negative thought patterns and encourage positive thinking.
Encourage the expansion and better utilization of support networks.
Support the ongoing development of a positive identity of self despite the illness.

The progress on each of the above goals can be used to evaluate the effectiveness of the treatment process. The following case illustrates the process of brief treatment with an individual who has a chronic illness.

CASE ILLUSTRATION

Beginning Phase: Engagement and Assessment

Jennifer was 25 years old when she came for her first appointment at a community mental health clinic. After two years in college, she was employed as an accountant with a large restaurant chain. She was currently living with another employee and her husband. Jennifer said she was having trouble sleeping, had lost twenty pounds within the past six months, and was feeling depressed and totally overwhelmed. The clinician noticed that she wore a brace on her leg. Jennifer explained that at the age of 16 she had been diagnosed with osteosarcoma, a cancer of the bone in her leg. They were able to save her leg from amputation by replacing the knee and part of the femur with a metal implant. Her attitude was matter-of-fact and she offered little elaboration, giving the impression she thought the illness experience was in the past and not relevant to her current situation.

The therapist asked about other symptoms of depression and specifically whether she had thoughts about hurting herself. Jennifer admitted feeling empty and hopeless. She had thought about giving up and taking her own life, but had no specific plan and did not intend to commit suicide. She said these thoughts scared her and were the major reason for her making this appointment. When asked if she had felt this way before, she said she had felt down when she first went away to college, but never this desperate and overwhelmed. She was also having difficulty concentrating at work, something she had never experienced before. She had had no previous therapy.

Jennifer had worked for the restaurant chain for five years, initially managing the accounts of four restaurants. Because she had done so well, she was promoted and placed in charge of the accounts of thirty restaurants. This required a move to a different state. Jennifer first lived with her older sister and her new husband, but they were having marital problems, blamed her for their troubles, and asked her to leave. She then moved in with her co-worker who was also her supervisor. Her co-worker was also having marital problems. Jennifer didn't like living there, but felt she had no alternatives.

The therapist asked Jennifer to tell her more about what was overwhelming her in her current situation. Jennifer said things had not gone well with her new job. In fact, two months ago she told her employers she could not continue in the new position, giving them no options or explanations. They were angry and unhappy with her decision and gave her per diem work, which reduced her salary. Her co-worker was also angry because she had recommended Jennifer for the promotion and felt Jennifer had let her down by quitting. Jennifer now felt she had no one in the company to talk to and that living with her co-worker had become unbearable. She would have to move in the next few months anyway because her co-worker was being transferred to California. She felt completely alone, overwhelmed, and wondered how she would get enough money to pay the security deposit for an apartment.

The clinician inquired more specifically about what Jennifer disliked about the job. She said she had found it difficult to manage even four restaurants while living near family and friends. "If I traveled as much as I would need to for this job, I could never make friends because I wouldn't have weekends to meet people. With all that traveling the pain in my leg was getting worse and worse." When asked to elaborate, Jennifer explained that every time she got in and out of a car it hurt. There was very little muscle left around the knee, as it was removed with the tumor. She was unable to straighten her leg completely, and sitting for long periods was very uncomfortable. The clinician asked if she had talked with the company about this. She said she had not because she was afraid they would consider her handicapped and not offer her other promotions.

The therapist asked if there was anyone else she felt she could talk to or who could help her with her situation, such as her parents. Jennifer said she felt her parents had been through so much with her cancer that she didn't want them to think they were going to have to worry about her for the rest of their lives. In addition, her father was very sick with asthma, a serious chronic condition he'd had for many years. He was now becoming severely disabled. She felt very close to her father and wanted to see him more, but did not want to burden him with her problems. She also did not want to burden her older sister, who was moving on with her life and beginning a new job, or her older brother. She felt that both had been negatively affected by her cancer diagnosis. She had not told her company about her father's condition either. She teared up as she talked about his illness, saying she missed him and worried about what would happen to him. The clinician asked how her mother was managing, and only then did Jennifer reveal that her parents had been divorced when she was 12 years old. Her mother had remarried and Jennifer was close to her stepfather, but her father had never remarried and he remained alone. The divorce was another topic Jennifer did not discuss easily.

The clinician confirmed that Jennifer was indeed depressed, and summarized that her depression seemed to be a reaction to the pileup of a number of difficult situations she was facing: the ongoing problems with her leg, her father's worsening illness, being in a new city far from family and friends, and difficulties at work. The clinician observed that Jennifer was clearly a bright and highly skilled young woman, that she had friends and people who cared about her and whom she cared about, but that right now she was having difficulty using her resources effectively. People had helped her in the past, but she was afraid to ask for help again. The clinician affirmed Jennifer's strength in making the appointment for an evaluation, a sign of her ability to actively problem solve and an important first step in that direction. She empathized with Jennifer by saying she could appreciate how difficult these last few months must have been for her. Because of Jennifer's depression, the world looked very bleak and she would have trouble making decisions that pleased her or even knowing what would please her.

The clinician proposed that they contract for twelve sessions to explore Jennifer's feelings about her job, living away from home, and about her difficulty in asking for help. Jennifer agreed, but with more resignation than enthusiasm. The therapist contracted for safety, obtaining agreement that Jennifer would not attempt suicide while they were meeting and, if she felt that way, she would call the therapist. She agreed to this and seemed relieved that the clinician had recognized the depth of her despair. The clinician said that she was concerned that Jennifer did not feel she had anyone here with whom she could talk. Jennifer then recalled that there was one woman at work she had lunch with on occasion. As a first step, the clinician encouraged her to do so again in the coming week. The clinician also offered an evaluation for medication for her depression. She said she thought Jennifer would begin to feel better as she was able to make some decisions about her situation that were right for her, and as she found ways to talk more openly with people. But medication would also help to lift her mood and enable her to feel better. Jennifer said she had had so much medication for the cancer and now for the pain in her leg that she did not want to take more. She was adamant about this, and seemed to feel good about asserting herself in making this decision.

The clinician was impressed with Jennifer's strengths, intelligence, history of effective work, and supportive family and friends. Most apparent was her difficulty in acknowledging the realistic limitations caused by the condition of her leg. Her underlying fear of vulnerability, dependence, and devaluation by others caused her to provide an inaccurate portrait of herself to people. As a consequence, they were unaware of her vulnerability and the origins of her stress, so they blamed her when she failed to respond to their requests. By trying to unrealistically please everyone else, she made things worse for herself. Her employers personalized her refusal to take the promotion as rejection or irresponsibility and became angry with her.

A critical issue for individuals with a disability is to maintain self-esteem, while acknowledging realistic dependency needs and accepting help when necessary. Fears of dependence are especially salient when the illness occurs during the separation phase of adolescence (Blos 1962, Masterson 1972).

Over the next two sessions the clinician focused on (1) understanding Jennifer's ambivalence about dependence and independence; (2) clarifying the history of her illness and reconstitution of identity; and (3) assuring that she was taking initial steps to secure housing, maintaining communication with family and friends, and solving urgent and immediate problems. Jennifer's symptoms of depression were carefully monitored by having her complete a standardized measure at each session. The clinician was assuring Jennifer's physical and psychological safety, while beginning to probe more deeply into her identity problems. Just identifying the causes of her depression gave her an increased sense of control and improved her mood. Solving some of her problems helped Jennifer feel more in control.

It became clear that Jennifer had been devastated by the loss of mobility and athletic ability as an adolescent, as she had been an outstanding athlete. Furthermore, she had never fully acknowledged this blow to her self-esteem. Rather, she became highly fearful of rejection and went out of her way to prove she was worthy and valuable.

Formulation Summary

Upon completion of the initial assessment, it is helpful for the clinician to write a formulation summary that provides an overview of the therapist's understanding of the case dynamics and the patient's strengths and vulnerabilities, and a preliminary organization of treatment priorities for the middle phase of treatment:

> This 25-year-old is a nine-year survivor of bone cancer who required a limb salvage procedure to prevent amputation, resulting in compromised ambulation. She now works for a large restaurant chain as an accountant. She presents with symptoms of major clinical depression—inability to concentrate, early morning wakening, anhedonia, loss of twenty pounds, and suicidal thoughts—for the past two months. The move to a different state for a job promotion with increased responsibility reactivated her fears of rejection and failure, initially experienced upon her diagnosis with cancer and reexperienced when she left home for college. Her inability to talk with her employers about her condition and the stress of her father's illness contributed to their misunderstanding her reasons for refusing the job and provoked their anger. Additional stresses include her lack of sufficient finances for housing, her rejection by her sister and her supervisor, her fear of burdening her parents, and her increasing social isolation. Jennifer also evidences difficulty accepting her disability, which results in lowered self-esteem when she cannot function physically in the way she and the

job require. Her need to prove her value to others has prevented her from developing a positive identity of her own, one that incorporates the reality of her disability and related realistic dependency needs. Rather, she is ambivalent about independence and fearful of failure. Fear of further burdening her parents and siblings more with her needs increases her social isolation.

Middle Phase of Integrated Short-Term Treatment

After the initial three sessions, Jennifer reported less frequent early morning wakening, a better appetite, and improvement in her sense of optimism and hopefulness. She continued to have lunch with another friend at work and discovered that this friend was looking for a roommate. Jennifer was planning to move in with her the following week and felt good that she had been able to solve one problem. The middle phase of her treatment occurred over a period of nine weeks and focused on Jennifer's ambivalence about dependence/independence and on the process of grieving losses and affirming remaining strengths.

The therapist brought up the difficulty Jennifer was experiencing in talking with her employers about the problems posed by her leg disability, and her fear of what they thought of her and how they would respond. The therapist wondered if Jennifer's reluctance had something to do with how difficult it was for her to accept the changes the illness had made in her life. This led Jennifer to review how her illness had begun and what it meant to her. She talked about how much she had loved athletic activities, how she had excelled in three different sports, and about her excitement when she was offered a college sports scholarship. As she spoke of this, it became clear to the clinician that Jennifer had never previously grieved the loss of this part of her identity. Jennifer cried as she reexperienced her anger and resentment at the loss of these specific attributes and dreams. She recalled stopping herself from expressing and from even feeling this anger, so as to protect her frightened and distraught parents. Jennifer restated that the hardest thing for her after the surgery was not the appearance of the leg but her inability to participate in athletics. Athletics was a source of social interaction and family pride, as well as personal gratification. An unfortunate consequence of her experience was that her siblings had also become angry with her because her illness had absorbed family time, attention, and money.

During the sessions Jennifer cried as she recalled not only her inability to participate in athletics, but also, and more intensely, her feelings of ineptness and defeat. She expressed her sadness, but needed encouragement to discuss her anger as well. She said she was angry a lot, but found it difficult to think about because she knew how much her family and friends were trying to help her. She believed she had caused considerable disruption in their lives. This guilt, inhibition of anger, and intense fear of rejection and abandonment added to the traumatic nature of the whole episode and had prevented her from grieving the loss of her healthy leg and the change in her life circumstances.

Jennifer managed to finish high school with a lot of support from her siblings and her friends. A second blow occurred when she went to college. There no one knew about her previous competence at sports, or valued her prior role as an athlete. She now had to think of new ways to meet people and to make decisions about whether and when to inform them about her illness. She still could not think of herself as disabled. After taking a few courses in physical therapy, which she had considered as a career, she realized that she could not physically do the tasks required for that profession. The competitive dating environment, without her valued athletic activities, was also experienced as overwhelming. She left school after two years, in large part because she believed she could not succeed there.

The individual with chronic illness must balance the process of grieving losses with that of affirming remaining strengths. The therapeutic challenge is to reactivate and support these processes, without encouraging extreme denial of losses, preoccupation with grief, or denial of remaining strengths. Having grieved her losses, some for the first time, Jennifer was able to accept the clinician's consistent emphasis on how well she had retained her academic abilities and a broad range of skills and relationships, even under adverse conditions. The value of her competitiveness and her ambition was also affirmed. This led Jennifer to think more about what she valued about herself, what she liked about herself, and what her dreams and interests were, and she began to consider alternative careers that she could manage physically but that might also be more personally gratifying.

Throughout this period the therapist found it difficult to encourage Jennifer to express negative feelings. Jennifer often lapsed into a sense of helplessness and hopelessness instead, and rejected the clinician's suggestions for opening the dialogue with a number of possible friends. At times she was passive and silent. When the clinician probed, Jennifer expressed irritation, acting as though the clinician was "making too big a deal" of her treatment. However, she did not miss any sessions. The clinician continued to interpret Jennifer's avoidance of problems as learned helplessness in the face of overwhelming trauma. The current situation was not beyond her ability to manage, and she could lessen her stress considerably by partializing her problems and solving them one at a time. In this way she began to gain some sense of mastery and a more optimistic outlook on her future capacity to cope.

The therapist specifically encouraged Jennifer to speak more openly with her employers about her situation. Finally she was able to talk with them, at first about her father's deteriorating physical illness and her wish to be geographically closer to him at this time, and only later about the more realistic limitations of her own physical disability. Her employers said they understood better her refusal of the job promotion, and encouraged Jennifer to explore an upcoming opening in this same restaurant chain near her home.

End Phase: Termination and Follow-Up

Treatment termination was complicated by Jennifer's plan to return to her family and friends in order to take the new company position that would be opening there. She didn't think the position was that good, since she would still be working per diem. However, her father's condition worsened and she felt desperate to see more of him and to know what was happening. She was feeling good about this decision, but was also beginning to think about other changes she might want to make.

Jennifer knew that some patients whose limb salvage had left them with severely compromised ambulation opted to have an amputation, which provided them greater mobility. She wondered about this possibility for herself. In addition, she had been told about a management job becoming available in a health club near her parents' home. She was excited about the possibility of working in a business that focused on sports and physical activity, something that felt familiar and more interesting to her than the restaurant business. If she could not be an athlete, she could manage athletic facilities and be around sports enthusiasts. She had begun to work out at a local gym to improve her upper body strength.

As to her concerns about dating, her interest in altruism, and meeting others in the same boat, Jennifer expressed a desire to work on establishing a more intimate dating relationship. In part this seemed to reflect a wish to continue the therapy beyond the contracted time. When the clinician commented on this, Jennifer said the brief treatment had been helpful, but she also wanted to move back to familiar friends and family. Also, she felt encouraged by a recent interaction she had with a new employee she met at a regional company conference who had her type of cancer. She went up to him and said, "I don't want to be intrusive, but I think I've had a similar illness to yours." The young man brightened and expressed amazement at how well she walked and at her ability to talk about her illness. He was still feeling awkward and reluctant to talk with anyone about his cancer. When they finished their discussion, he seemed in much better spirits and she determined that she was going to volunteer with the American Cancer Society when she got home to seek out other opportunities to talk with patients.

During termination, Jennifer missed one appointment, which was quite unusual for her. She said she forgot the appointment and that she had been having more difficulty concentrating, and some sleeping difficulties. The clinician asked her if she thought this might have something to do with ending treatment. Jennifer had not made the connection, but she said she was worried about how things were going to go in her new job. Treatment had helped her feel more confident, and she was wondering if she would be able to succeed without this kind of help. She talked about how she often associated change with failure, rejection, and abandonment. The clinician helped her to look at how independence and change had become associated in her mind with loss and failure—she was planning to go to college and then she was diagnosed with a life-threatening illness—rather than excitement and opportunity. She went away to college and her peers did not accept her in the way she had expected. She had come to expect failure, and rather than confront her fears, she tended to withdraw and give up. She had developed a phobic response that was not realistic in the face of her many strengths and abilities. The clinician emphasized that her reaction was understandable because of all she had been through. Jennifer said she had not thought of this before, but clearly she was aware of an increase in her fear of failure. The rest of the session was focused on the termination, and on how different her approach to this change was from previous ones. The clinician emphasized how Jennifer's more realistic appraisal of her assets and limitations resulted in more realistic goals, goals that had a better chance of satisfying her needs.

The clinician contracted with Jennifer to meet again in three months when she would be visiting her sister. If for some reason this did not work out, they could have a phone interview. Jennifer liked this plan. She identified her need to keep working on her fears of failure, her wish to become more active in helping other patients, and her desire to find a way to begin dating again. For the time being she thought she could work on them by herself, but welcomed the opportunity to review her progress in three months.

CONCLUSION

Brief treatment is responsive to managed care priorities and at the same time it is often the treatment of choice for individuals who have a chronic illness that they must adapt to over many years. It provides a legitimate protection and support during crises, but encourages continuation of independent functioning when the related problems have been resolved. At the same time, the therapist helps patients build and hone skills that strengthen their ability to respond to future crises. Brief treatment with individuals with chronic illness enables the clinician to be creative and inventive. While it can be challenging therapy, it often leaves the clinician awed by the strength and determination of the human spirit to overcome all odds.

REFERENCES

Berkman, B. (1996). The emerging health care world: implications for social work practice and education. *Social Work* 41(5):541–551.

Blos, P. (1962). *On Adolescence.* New York: Macmillan.

Christ, G. (1987). Social consequences of the cancer experience. *American Journal of Pediatric Hematology/Oncology* 9:84–88.

——— (1991). Principles of oncology social work. In *American Cancer Society Textbook of Clinical Oncology,* ed. A. Holieb, D. Fink, and G. Murphy, pp. 594–605. Atlanta, GA: American Cancer Society.

Christ, G., Lane, J., and Marcove, R. (1995). Psychosocial adaptation of long-term survivors of bone sarcoma. *Journal of Psychosocial Oncology* 13(4):1–22.

Christ, G., Sormanti, M., and Francoeur, R. (2000). Chronic illness and disability. In *Risk and Resilience in Vulnerable Populations,* ed. A. Gitterman, pp. 124–162. New York: Columbia University Press.

Corbin, J., and Strauss, A. (1988). *Unending Work and Care: Managing Chronic Illness at Home.* San Francisco: Jossey-Bass.

Depression Guideline Panel (1993). *Depression in Primary Care. Vol. 2. Treatment of Major Depression.* Rockville, MD: Agency for Health Care Policy and Research.

Dimond, M. (1984). Identifying the needs of the chronically ill. In *Community Health Care for Chronic Physical Illness: Issues and Models,* ed. S.

Milligan, pp. 1–14. Cleveland, OH: Case Western Reserve University.

D'Zurilla, T. J., and Goldfried, M. R. (1971). Problem-solving and behavior modification. *Journal of Abnormal Psychology* 78:107–126.

D'Zurilla, T. J., and Nezu, A. M. (1982). Social problem-solving in adults. In *Advances in Cognitive-Behavioral Research and Therapy*, ed. P. C. Kendal, pp. 202–274. New York: Academic Press.

Erikson, E. (1959). *Identity and the Life Cycle.* New York: International Universities Press.

Francoeur, R., Copley, C., and Miller, P. (1997). The challenge to meet the mental health and biopsychosocial needs of the poor: expanding roles for hospital social workers in a changing health care environment. *Social Work in Health Care* 26(2):1–13.

Germain, C., and Gitterman, A. (1980). *The Life Model of Social Work Practice.* New York: Columbia University Press.

Goldstein, E. G., and Noonan, M. (1999). *Short-Term Treatment and Social Work Practice: An Integrative Perspective.* New York: Free Press.

Gonzales, S., Steinglass, P., and Reiss, D. (1989). Putting the illness in its place: discussion groups for families with chronic medical illness. *Family Process* 28:69–87.

Gustafson, D., McTavish, F., Hawkins, R., et al. (1998). Computer support for elderly women with breast cancer: results of a population-based intervention (letter). *Journal of the American Medical Association* 280:15.

Gustafson, D., Wise, M., McTavish, F., et al. (1993). Development and pilot evaluation of a computer based support system for women with breast cancer. *Journal of Psychosocial Oncology* 11(4):69–93.

Hoffman, C., and Rice, D. (1996). Persons with chronic conditions: their prevalence and costs. *Journal of the American Medical Association* 276(18): 1473–1479.

Kerson, T. (1985). *Understanding Chronic Illness.* New York: Free Press.

Lapham, E. (1986). Chronic illness: overview and theory. In *The Impact of Chronic Illness on Psychosocial Stages of Human Development*, ed. E. Lapham and K. Shevlin, pp. 91–104. Washington, DC: National Center for Education in Maternal and Child Health.

Lazarus, R. S., and Folkman, S. (1984). *Stress, Appraisal, and Coping.* New York: Springer.

Loscalzo, M. J., and Brinzenhofeszoc, K. (1998). Brief counseling. In *The Textbook of Psycho-Oncology*, ed. E. Lapham and K. Shevlin, pp. 662–675. London: Oxford University Press.

Mancoske, R., Wadsworth, C., Dugas, D., and Hasney, J. (1995). Suicide risk among people living with AIDS. *Social Work* 40(6):783–787.

Masterson, J. (1972). *Treatment of the Borderline Adolescent: A Developmental Approach.* New York: Wiley Interscience.

Mathieson, C. M., and Henderikus, J. S. (1995). *Sociology of Health and Illness* 17(3):283–306.

McCubbin, H., Thompson, E., Thompson, A., and Fromer, G., eds. (1998). *Stress, Coping and Health in Families: Sense of Coherence and Resilience.* Thousand Oaks, CA: Sage.

Meyer, C., ed. (1983). *Clinical Social Work in the Eco-Systems Perspective.* New York: Columbia University Press.

Moynihan, R., Christ, G., and Gallo-Silver, L. (1988). AIDS and terminal illness. *Social Casework* 68:380–387.

Nezu, A., Nezu, C., Friedman, S., et al. (1998). *Helping Cancer Patients Cope: A Problem-Solving Approach.* Washington, DC: American Psychological Association.

Nezu, A., Nezu, C., Houts, P., et al. (1999). Relevance of problem solving therapy to psychosocial oncology. *Journal of Psychosocial Oncology*, 16:5–26.

Parad, H. J., and Parad, L. G., eds. (1990). *Crisis Intervention Book 2: The Practitioner's Sourcebook for Brief Therapy.* Milwaukee, WI: Family Service America.

Penninx, B., Tilburg, T., Boeke, J., et al. (1998). Effects of social support and personal coping resources on depressive symptoms: Different for various chronic diseases? *Health Psychology* 17(6):551–558.

Perlman, H. (1957). *Social Casework: A Problem-Solving Process.* Chicago: University of Chicago Press.

Pollin, L. (1994). *Taking Charge: Overcoming the Challenge of Long-Term Illness.* New York: Random House.

Rolland, J. (1994). *Families, Illness and Disability.* New York: Basic Books.

Rowland, J. (1989). Intrapersonal resources: coping. In *Handbook of Psychooncology,* ed. J. C. Holland and J. H. Rowland, pp. 44–57. New York: Oxford University Press.

Russell, L. (1993). The role of prevention in health reform. *New England Journal of Medicine* 329(5):352–354.

Sidell, N. (1997). Adult adjustment to chronic illness: a review of the literature. *Health and Social Work* 22(1):5–11.

Strauss, A., and Glaser, B. (1975). *Chronic Illness and the Quality of Life.* St. Louis, MO: C. V. Mosby.

Taylor, S. (1983). Adjustment to threatening life events: a theory of cognitive adaptation. *American Psychologist* 38:1161–1173.

Telch, C. F., and Telch, M. J. (1985). Psychological approaches for enhancing coping among cancer patients: a review. *Clinical Psychology Review* 5:325–344.

Volland, P., Berkman, B., Stein, G., and Baghy, A. (1999). *Social Work Education for Practice in Health Care.* New York: The New York Academy of Medicine.

CHAPTER TWELVE

The Treatment of Posttraumatic Conditions within the Framework of the ISTT Model

MAY BENATAR

THEORETICAL OVERVIEW AND TREATMENT PERSPECTIVE

The *Diagnostic and Statistical Manual of Mental Disorders*, fourth edition (*DSM-IV*)(APA 1994) category of posttraumatic stress disorder (PTSD) covers a wide range of clinical phenomena and patient populations. A surprisingly wide array of presenting problems can mask a posttraumatic response of either an acute or a chronic nature. Depression, anxiety, sleep and eating disorders, drug and alcohol problems, employment difficulties, sexual and other addictions, couple problems, and parent–child conflict may, after a careful history taking and psychosocial assessment, reveal themselves to be at least in part a posttraumatic stress response (Courtois 1988). As a result, patients in a variety of social work settings such as hospitals, clinics, family and children agencies, and drug treatment and rehabilitation settings may be either presenting or masking evidence of posttraumatic conditions. A veteran who is a recovering alcoholic in a rehab or drug treatment setting may begin to have nightmares and intrusive thoughts of his combat experience many years after battle. The mother of an adolescent daughter visiting a family service agency or meeting with a school guidance counselor about the sexual acting out of her daughter may be unaware that her anger and distress are, at least in part, related to dimly recollected sexual abuse experiences in her own childhood. A woman referred by her gynecologist to a mental health clinic for postpartum depression following the birth of her second child may unwittingly be reacting to a violent sexual assault suffered many years before.

Awareness of the indicators of PTSD and treatment protocols are important tools for the beginning practitioner as well as the seasoned clinician. Treatment for patients who struggle with the sequelae of trauma, particularly childhood trauma, requires the development of a therapeutic relationship of trust and consistency. It is generally a long-term treatment, the length in part determined by the difficulties associated with the patient's ability or inability to maintain a reasonable attachment to the therapist and to sustain a trusting relationship. The recovery of traumatic memories, processing the memories within the context of a reliable empathic relationship, and reconstructing meaning for the individuals whose assumptive world has been severely disrupted most often requires extensive time (Briere 1992, Courtois 1988, Davies and Frawley 1994).

Additionally, individuals who have sustained severe or even moderate trauma as children are often disabled in their capacity to attach in relationship. Minor disruptions in the treatment can be perceived and experienced as a repetition of early betrayals. It is the enactment and repair of these disruptions within the transference that provides the context for healing (Davies and Frawley 1994). This also takes time.

Patients present with a range of resources and requirements. Individuals grappling with posttraumatic conditions may be unable or unwilling to enter into a lengthy treatment. The realities of a managed care environment, an environment wherein the approved number of treatment visits range from twelve to twenty-five weekly sessions, require practitioners to be thoughtful, responsible, and creative in designing treatment approaches that are adequately responsive to a wide range of patients who may be diagnosed with PTSD. The model provided by the integrative short-term treatment (ISTT) approach (Goldstein and Noonan 1999) provides the flexibility appropriate for many individuals suffering from PTSD. Where PTSD is chronic and complex and part of a larger personality disturbance, a short-term approach will be of limited usefulness. A careful partializing of the patient's presenting concerns will be necessary.

Other models of short-term, or "shorter" treatment specific to posttraumatic stress are those of Mardi Horowitz (1997) and Yvonne Dolan (1991). While not claiming to be short-term, Dolan's solution-focused approach tends to be a less lengthy treatment than one in which transference and countertransference enactments are the focus of treatment. Dolan employs modifications of Eriksonian hypnotherapy techniques in a manner particularly useful to the survivor of psychological trauma. Horowitz's technique is cognitively oriented and applicable to individuals dealing with a stress response of short duration. Medication for the temporary reduction of symptoms is also a time-honored short-term approach and can be a useful adjunct to psychological treatment (Courtois 1988).

INCLUSION AND EXCLUSION CRITERIA

Trauma is defined very specifically in the *DSM-IV* as "experiencing, witnessing, or confronting an event that involved actual or threatened death or serious injury, or a threat to the physical integrity of self or others, and the response involved intense fear, helplessness, or horror" (APA 1994, p. 427). Clinical writers have emphasized the meaning of the traumatic event or events to the individual. McCann and Pearlman (1990) define psychological trauma as an experience that is "sudden, unexpected or non-normative, exceeding the individual's perceived ability to meet its demands, and disrupts the individual's frame of reference and other central psychological needs and related (cognitive) schemas" (p. 10). For these authors, an experience is traumatic insofar as the individual has experienced it as such, the effects of the trauma reverberating throughout the psychological system of the individual.

Several Axis I diagnoses overlap with that of PTSD and are often ascribed to individuals suffering from posttraumatic conditions. Depression, substance abuse, anxiety, somatoform, dissociative, impulse control, and schizophrenia/schizoaffective disorders are often ascribed to individuals who have sustained trauma and are dealing with its aftereffects (Courtois 1994).

As described in the *DSM-IV*, PTSD has two types of symptomatology: intrusive experiences or "hyperarousal," in which the traumatic event is persistently reexperienced in some form, and experiences of "numbing" or dissociation, in which the trauma is blocked from consciousness at the expense of functioning. Intrusive symptoms include flashbacks, recurrent nightmares, and distress, including physiological reactivity at exposure to any triggers that may symbolize some aspect of the traumatic event. Sleep disorders, outbursts of anger, and hypervigilance also indicate the intrusion of traumatic memory. Manifestations of numbing include withdrawal and estrangement from others, persistent avoidance of any stimuli that might be associated with the trauma, reports of a sense of detachment or depersonalization, memory gaps related to the trauma, restricted range of affect, and a sense of a foreshortened future. These symptoms may cycle. Intrusive symptomatology may either alternate with numbing or predominate in an individual's functioning. These disturbances lead to significant impairment in social, occupational, and interpersonal functioning.

The hallmarks of PTSD are two alternating, sometimes exclusive conditions that could be summarized as hyperarousal and numbing. Hyperarousal or intrusive symptoms refers to the vulnerability of being triggered by internal or external cues that are in any way related or symbolized by the traumatic event in question. Thus, the postpartum mother cited earlier may well have had PTSD symptoms triggered by the delivery of her child. She reexperienced the terror and humiliation of a long ago rape and became symptomatic.

A short list of symptoms and signs related to intrusive experience and behavior would include the following (Horowitz 1997):

- Hypervigilance including hypersensitivity to associated events
- Startle reactions
- Intrusive-repetitive thoughts, images, emotions, and behaviors (including flashbacks)
- Overgeneralization of associations (e.g., fears of all bald-headed men because perpetrator was bald)
- Difficulty concentrating
- Unmodulated intense emotional reactions including explosions of anger
- Sleep disturbances

The numbing response, also characteristic of PTSD, may alternate with arousal or exist on its own. Clinically "numbing" may present as the following (Horowitz 1997):

- Daze
- Selective inattention
- Amnesia, partial or complete
- Disavowal of the significance of stimuli (allowing one's child to remain alone in the presence of the perpetrator)
- Constriction of thought and/or feeling
- A sense of numbness or detachment
- Behavioral avoidance of triggering stimuli
- Sleep disturbances
- Withdrawal
- Inability to imagine a future for oneself

McCann and Pearlman (1990) note several posttraumatic reactions and patterns of responses not covered by the *DSM-IV* description. These include fear and anxiety, depression, decreased self-esteem, identity distortion, anger, guilt, and shame. Cognitive distortions are also noted by many authors (Briere 1992, Courtois 1988, 1994, McCann and Pearlman 1990).

As mentioned above, individuals with chronic PTSD whose trauma(s) occurred in childhood, such as physical and/or sexual abuse, have suffered a deformation in self-development, which makes the treatment process itself very difficult. In addition, difficulties regarding issues of attachment and trust, and the inability to tolerate the frustrations of the therapeutic frame and to symbolize the traumatic event verbally are all limitations on the efficacy of a short-term approach. In some cases ISTT and other short-term treatment models may have to be ruled out. Individuals with a dissociative disorder and Impulse Disorder on Axis I will receive only very limited help from a short-term approach. Suicidality is an obvious contraindication to a short-term approach.

On Axis II those patients meeting the criteria for borderline personality disorder or schizoid personality disorder will also receive limited benefit, due to the difficulty of sustaining a positive connection to the therapist required for the treatment. Although transference per se does not figure importantly in an ISTT approach, some relational connection is required. An individual presenting features of borderline personality may be unable to sustain the essential bond—the working relationship with the therapist as the treatment proceeds.

Medical conditions may be associated with PTSD (Axis III). Somatic conditions may indicate or symbolize subtle interactions between physical vulnerability and traumatic memory. These could include back and neck pain and arthritic conditions including fibromyalgia, ulcers, chronic fatigue syndrome, headaches, and dysmenorrhea. This is a suggestive, not an exhaustive, list. It is essential in this, as in any psychological treatment, that underlying medical conditions be properly diagnosed and treated by the patient's physician and not assumed to be symptomatic of trauma. Evaluating the role of Axis III conditions is an important part of the beginning assessment.

Axis IV, psychosocial and environmental problems, is particularly key for individuals suffering from PTSD. Working with the patient to modify and improve environmental conditions might be crucial for someone who is living with or working with traumatic triggers every day. Abuse survivors often relive their trauma by attaching to individuals who reenact the abuse with them. This is often the situation in cases where battered spouses find themselves unaccountably attached to their batterers.

Judith Lewis Herman (1992) and others have argued that the PTSD classification in the *DSM-IV* is appropriate to and descriptive of survivors of circumscribed traumatic events such as natural disasters, rape, and combat. Individuals who have emerged from situations of prolonged abuse, such as children who have been sexually and physically abused, have developed characteristic personality problems and "deformations of relatedness and identity" (Herman 1992, p. 119). Additionally they are vulnerable to repeated victimization by their perpetrators as well of that of others (Courtois 1988, 1994). "Complex posttraumatic stress disorder," as conceived by Herman, is not a single disorder, but an umbrella for a wide variety of conditions. Complex PTSD emphasizes the damage to the self-system of the individual who has had to survive under conditions of prolonged terror and abuse.

Unfortunately complex posttraumatic stress disorder, or disorder of extreme stress not otherwise specified (DESNOS), as it was called by the working group for the *DSM-IV*, was not included in the current manual. The description of the disorder is extremely useful in an assessment of posttraumatic conditions and should be used as an adjunct to the existing PTSD diagnosis.

Complex PTSD describes the effects on victims of prolonged captivity. This includes hostages, POWs, concentration camp survivors, and survivors of some cults. Herman includes those held hostage in domestic life, battered women, and survivors of childhood physical or sexual abuse. Herman describes alterations in affect regulation, consciousness, and self-perception or identity, as well as alterations in perceptions of the perpetrator, in systems of meaning including faith, and alterations in interpersonal relations. A fuller discussion of this proposed diagnostic category can be found in Herman's *Trauma and Recovery* (1992).

Diagnosing a patient's symptom presentation as PTSD is in and of itself an important treatment intervention. For the patient as well as the clinician, a plethora of confusing and distressing complaints and behavioral manifestations begin to cohere and take on meaning for the patient. Feelings of shame, stigma, a sense of badness or defectiveness, and despair can and will be mitigated by the comprehension that symptoms have meaning and a context and are consequent to historical experience.

TREATMENT GOALS

Trauma-focused treatment approaches, whether cognitive-behavioral (Briere 1992), psychoanalytic–object relational (Davies and Frawley 1994), self psychological (Ulman and Brothers 1988), an integration of the above (McCann and Pearlman 1990), or long- or short-term (Dolan 1991, Horowitz 1997), have several guiding treatment principles they all share. These principles comprise the heart of "trauma theory." Many of these core principles can and should be adapted to a short-term approach (some of this discussion refers specifically to the traumatic sequelae of child abuse):

1. Child abuse is not rare and is the most common antecedent to complex PTSD. Much of adult psychopathology can be understood to derive from these childhood abuse experiences.
2. *Adaptational focus.* A trauma-based approach emphasizes the survival value that patients' symptoms have had for them, and thereby conveys respect for the meaning of symptoms. Briere (1992) summarizes the message:

> You have spent much of your life struggling to survive what was done to you as a child. The solutions you've found for the fear, emptiness, and memories you carry represent the best you

could do in the face of the abuse you experienced. Although some others, perhaps even you, see your coping behaviors as sick or "dysfunctional," your actions have been the reverse: healthy accommodations to a toxic environment. Because you are not sick, therapy is not about a cure—it is about survival at a new level, about even better survival. Your job is to marshal your courage, to go back to the frightening thoughts and images of your childhood, and to update your experience of yourself and the world. My job, the easier of the two, is to engineer an environment where you can do this important work, and to provide in our sessions the safety and respect that you deserve. [p. 83]

Within a short-term paradigm, the regression suggested by "going back to the frightening thoughts and images" is probably not appropriate, but the message is nonetheless germane and is part of the treatment process. In a short-term treatment as outlined below, there will be less emphasis on the exploration of traumatic memory and more focus on containment strategies that are more effective for and less destructive of the individual. This may be the only focus of treatment: safeguarding the patient.

1. The mechanism of defense of *dissociation* is ubiquitous for individuals dealing with post-traumatic conditions. Dissociation is distinct from repression, a concept with which it is sometimes confused. Dissociation is a radical splitting of experience, affects, cognition, and parts of the self, and is understood in trauma theory to be a normal, expectable consequence of severe, repetititive abuse, particularly sexual abuse of the young child (Davies and Frawley 1994). Over time these splits may take on lives of their own and become coherent, very separate parts of the self, albeit secret, hidden. This is the case with dissociative identity disorder (DID). The patient may have no awareness of the existence of these

split-off sectors of experience. The phenomenology of dissociation is congruent with many manifestations of PTSD.

2. Early traumatic experiences are retrievable (even if initially unavailable in a symbolized form), and the retrieval and reintegration of them into the mainstream of self experience is central to psychological treatment. This principle is not realistically implementable within a short-term treatment.

3. *Phenomenological perspective* as described by Briere amounts to what social therapists have commonly referred to as "starting where the patient is." A phenomenological perspective emphasizes what particular symptoms mean to the patient and eschews an approach that privileges the therapist's viewpoint over the patient's. For instance the patient who cuts herself,[1] a distressing but not uncommon consequence of childhood abuse, particularly sexual abuse, may view her behavior as self-soothing rather than hostile acting out or suicidality. The clinician may have to accept the painful fact that interpretation or limit setting will not lead to cessation of this activity. Instead the clinician may have to settle for the goal of helping the patient understand the meaning of the behavior while encouraging and assisting her to search for alternative methods of self-soothing.

4. *Exploration vs. consolidation:* An important part of any assessment, long- or short-term, is the level of stability of the patient. This refers to the patient's attempts to deal with intrusion and/or numbing symptoms that are destabilizing: self-harming behaviors, a degree of dissociation that interferes with functioning and avoiding harm, and self-soothing behaviors that have a negative impact, such as substance abuse, withdrawal, oversleeping, and eating-disordered behavior. The treatment priority will be to stabilize the patient and help her utilize resources to maintain her stability.

---

1. When referring to sexual abuse, the female pronoun will be employed. To date both the research and clinical data indicate that women are overrepresented as victims of childhood sexual abuse (Briere 1992, Finkelhor et al. 1990).

Exploration refers to aspects of the treatment that involve uncovering of memories, making connections between traumatic events and symptoms, and making meaning of the trauma and its sequelae. Short-term treatment will of necessity focus more on consolidation, and less on exploration, although "meaning making" can and should be an important part of short-term work.

5. *Intensity control* is a ubiquitous feature of almost all forms of treatment using a trauma paradigm (Briere 1992, Courtois 1994). The nature of PTSD requires therapist and patient vigilance of the process. The patient can be triggered by the treatment setting, the treatment process, or the therapeutic relationship itself, and be flooded by feelings, images, and symptoms. Although not always fully avoidable, this experience tends to be counterproductive if not retraumatizing. A variety of techniques is utilitized in the service of safeguarding the treatment and the patient so that this either does not occur or is kept to a minimum.

Guided by the core trauma-treatment principles outlined above and the integrative short-term therapy (ISTT) model (Goldstein and Noonan 1999), the goals of short treatment with trauma survivors are

- *consolidation and stabilization,*
- *psychoeducation,* which involves cognitive restructuring with the patient,
- *a focus on solutions* to the patient's presenting concerns,
- increasing the patient's sense of *mastery* over internal states as well as reality situations.

Not compatible with a short-term approach are extensive processing of traumatic memory, alteration of self structure, and the grieving of losses associated with trauma. Patients may receive relief from a retelling of the trauma tale, and the clinician should always be open to this, but the repetitive review and processing necessary to loosen the grip of trauma will not be possible within this format.

CASE ILLUSTRATION: PHASES OF TREATMENT

Beginning Phase I (ISTT Components 1 to 3)

The first three components of the ISTT model are problem identification, biopsychosocial assessment, and engagement. The key to success in any short-term trauma-focused treatment is rapid assessment of problems presented and a careful appraisal of the patient's personal psychological and social resources. As noted above, a central tenet of trauma-focused treatment is the view that symptoms arise from the patient's conscious and unconscious attempts to adapt to the consequences of traumatic events. Eschewing a view of symptoms as evidence of defect and pathology, PTSD and attendant symptomatology are seen as adaptations gone awry—what enabled an individual to survive the trauma now hobbles their functioning. Briere (1992) articulates the philosophy of treatment that can be conveyed early in the assessment process and carried thoughout:

> Abuse focused therapy suggests that the patient is not mentally ill or suffering from a defect, but rather is an individual whose life has been shaped, in part, by ongoing adaptation to a toxic environment. Thus the goal of therapy is less the survivor's recovery than his or her continued growth and development—an approach that utilizes the survivor's already existing skills to move beyond his or her current level of adaptive functioning. [p. 82]

This perspective conveys to the patient, even as the history and beginning assessment and problem identification are being implemented by the therapist, that there is a hopeful, respectful way of viewing their problems. This shift in perspective from a pathological to an adaptational perspective, in and of itself, can have a dramatic and ameliorative impact.

Mrs. G., a 41-year-old married woman with three children ranging in age from 11 to 20, applied for service at a mental health clinic in her community several days after deciding that she had a problem with alcohol. At a recent office party she had to be escorted home after drinking all evening. She awoke in the morning with little memory of the party or its aftermath. She later learned that she had flirted in a bold and embarrassing manner with her husband's colleague.

Mrs. G. was humiliated and frightened by the loss of control and particularly the memory blackout. She presented herself for treatment, requesting support as she attempted to stop drinking. She conveyed her story and her complaints in an organized, almost matter-of-fact way. Her affect was flat and somewhat depressed.

Mrs. G. presented with symptoms in the "numbing" group. She drank four to five glasses of wine daily, sometimes more. She was dimly aware that she drank to quell upsetting feelings. She reported memory gaps, and complained of feelings of distance and detachment.

When questioned on her developmental history, she was somewhat vague, giving only the bare bones of her story. She did mention missing pieces, like "all of second grade." Additionally she reported feeling increasingly estranged from her husband, most noticeably in the last three years since the death of her father. Mrs. G.'s father died of illnesses related to advanced alcoholism. She cared for him in the last six months of his life, as her mother was unable or unwilling to do so.

Mrs. G. was humiliated by the episode at the office party and deeply ashamed of what she perceived as a growing problem with alcohol; she wondered if she was becoming an alcoholic like her father. She was also troubled by the deadness in her marriage, but perceived her husband as a good and loving man. She was scared for him, as a chronic weight problem threatened his health. She feared he would die while they were both still young.

Although in the first two sessions not many details of family history were available, Mrs. G. had said enough about alcoholism and violence in the family that a provisional diagnosis of PTSD could be made. Her use of alcohol as a "dampener," the report of increased feelings of detachment and depression, and the memory problems supported this diagnosis. Mrs. G. also mentioned, almost parenthetically, that her sister had died of breast cancer eighteen months earlier.

Mrs. G.'s feelings of shame and self-blame were so prominent in the first two sessions that the clinician was moved to present her with this provisional clinical perspective, that is, that many of her problems might well relate to valiant attempts to contend with and adapt to difficult childhood experiences. The therapist went on to explain that children dealing with alcoholism and violence in their families develop coping mechanisms that allow them to survive, mechanisms like dampening their feelings and keeping some distance from frightening situations. Only later do these coping mechanisms get in their way.

Mrs. G. had always viewed herself as having overcome and put into perspective the difficulties of her life. She was skeptical of this view of her problems; nonetheless, she seemed to relax ever so slightly. Rather than challenge the patient, the therapist agreed that Mrs. G. had dealt admirably with all that she had had to deal with.

These last comments reflect the beginning indications by the therapist of a therapeutic stance that will be carried throughout the treatment. While the twenty sessions allotted to Mrs. G. by her managed care plan would not allow for an in-depth exploration of memories and feelings associated with the father's violence and alcoholism, identifying some of the functions that drinking has played in her life will help her deal with affects and maybe memories that will emerge as she remains sober. The therapist has attempted to de-stigmatize the presenting symptoms by sharing her beginning diagnostic ideas as well as preparing the patient for what will need to be addressed in the future. The therapist has introduced an approach that emphasizes Mrs. G.'s abilities to adapt and her strengths, and seeks to understand the meaning of her behavior.

The therapist treating trauma will need to gauge as early as possible the patient's predominant method of self-soothing, her capacity for affect tolerance, how numbing and intrusive are her symptoms, and how the patient has coped with these manifestations before coming to treatment.

Several assessment instruments are available for streamlining the assessment process and providing a shortcut for the therapist. While these tools are useful, they are not meant to substitute for the interpersonal process of evaluation:

- Dissociative Experiences Scale (Bernstein and Putnam 1986)
- Dissociative Disorders Interview Schedule (Ross et al. 1989)
- McPearl Belief Scale (McCann and Pearlman 1990)
- Trauma Symptom Checklist TSC-33 (Briere and Runtz 1989)
- Trauma Symptom Inventory (Briere 1992).

McCann and Pearlman (1990) offer a very useful conceptual frame for assessing and treating posttraumatic conditions. They have synthesized and integrated principles of cognitive psychology and self psychology and applied it to the therapy of adult survivors of psychological trauma. The focus of constructivist self development theory (CSDT), their theoretical construct, is on identifying and strengthening "self capacities" and building on "ego resources." Self capacities refer to those that regulate and maintain self-esteem in the individual, and include the ability to (1) tolerate strong affects, (2) soothe the self, and (3) regulate self-loathing. Ego resources are those ego functions that relate to interactions with others, such as intelligence; initiative; awareness of psychological needs; the ability to introspect, to establish boundaries, to make self-protective judgments, and to strive for personal growth with appropriate regard for others; and empathy. CSDT also addresses the cognitive schemas and psychological needs of the individual as they have been disrupted by the trauma. Cognitive schemas are the beliefs of individuals about their world and themselves. A disrupted cognitive schema would be a belief that one's sexual abuse was a result of one's own coquettish behavior. Psychological needs include those that motivate an individual, such as the needs for safety, trust, power, autonomy, and intimacy.

McCann and Pearlman (1990) offer a very useful conceptual frame for assessing and treating the sequelae of psychological trauma. A short-term therapy approach can utilize selected aspects of CSDT. Restoring, or at least improving on, the self-capacities of the individual, and thus increasing self-regulation, and targeting selected cognitive schemas are realistic goals for short-term treatment. Although this is an activity for the beginning sessions, monitoring patients' methodology for dealing with their distress, and the distress that may be increased at times by the

process of treatment, speaks to the twin goals of mastery and consolidation.

In the second and third sessions the therapist sought to evaluate with Mrs.
G. how she had been using alcohol before resolving to stop drinking
altogether as well as other methodologies that she had found since
stopping. The therapist also sought to get a sense of Mrs. G.'s strengths
and social supports.

Mrs. G. had been trained as a nurse. However, she had not practiced
in over a dozen years, preferring instead to remain home with her three
children. The youngest, age 11, was diagnosed with attention-deficit/
hyperactivity disorder (ADHD), and Mrs. G. was virtually consumed
with the care of this child.

The therapist asked Mrs. G. when she drank and if she was aware
of what was going on when she did. Mrs. G. replied that she drank at the
end of the day as she prepared dinner. She also talked on the phone at this
time of day. She regaled her friends with the frustrations of the day,
particularly about her daughter who frequently was driving her crazy at
that hour. Now that she was not drinking, she was aware that she felt even
more harried. She continued to call her friends, but they were not always
able to spend the time with her that she needed. She also found herself
missing her sister terribly at this time of day. When her sister was alive,
they had talked almost every day in the hours before dinner. The therapist
now learned how close the sisters had been and what a blow her death
had been to Mrs. G. As she spoke of her sister, Mrs. G.'s eyes welled
with tears, but she quickly brushed them away and changed the subject
back to her daughter, Joanie, and how difficult she was to deal with. The
therapist noted (to herself) that Mrs. G. seemed to avoid the expression
of any strong feelings, particularly grief, and frequently changed the
subject.

The therapist asked what other methods worked for her when she was tense and just wanted to treat herself well. Mrs. G. could not think of much. She was very busy with the care of the house, the children, the laundry, the shopping, the cleaning, and her church work. The list was long. Perhaps she did too much; she was busy from morning to night. The therapist wondered if Mrs. G. included herself in the long list of people and things to take care of and suggested that she take some time before they met again to list at least five things that she liked to do that would involve taking care of herself, things that had a calming effect on her.

Here the therapist is introducing a number of new ideas:

1. There will be homework—between session assignments—that Mrs. G. can do without the therapist.
2. She needs to include herself on the list of things that need looking after.
3. Drinking and self-soothing are related.
4. The therapist has assessed a deficit in self-soothing: the patient uses alcohol and overfunctioning to quiet her distress. She has lost both alcohol and her sister and needs to find adequate substitutes.
5. The therapist is holding in abeyance until a later time the direct suggestion to begin attending AA meetings as she sees how difficult it is for the patient to take the time to do for herself. Although Mrs. G. perceives herself as having a drinking problem, she is not acknowledging "alcoholism" at this point.

When Mrs. G. returns with her list or she demonstrates that she is unable to even conceive of a list of self-care, the therapist will be in a position to begin setting a contract with Mrs. G., for example:

You have come to us at the clinic so that we can help you stay sober and still be able to deal effectively with your hectic life. From what I've heard so far, an important issue for you is that you carry a lot of responsibilities in your life. From what you tell me of your earlier life, you have been doing this from the time you were very young, and doing it remarkably well. Drinking has been your friend. It has kept you calm and able to smooth things over in your home, and has enabled you to keep your cool with your kids and not get too mad at your husband for endangering his health. It has helped you to stay home and not feel too bad about caring for others when you might want to do some things for yourself. It has also helped in the last year or more to ease the pain of the loss of your sister. But it's not such a great friend anymore. I suggest we apply ourselves to seeing what else might work for you in helping you do want you want to do, that is, feel okay. We might even have to consider that it is sometimes okay to not be so calm, to get angry, and to be sad. How does that sound to you?

The therapist might then outline some of the approaches they will utilize to address these issues.

Middle Phase
(ISTT Components 6 to 10):
Implementing Interventions, Maintaining and/or Altering the Focus, Monitoring Progress, Dealing with Obstacles, Managing the Therapist−Patient Relationship

In the middle phase, the therapist and Mrs. G. will apply themselves to improving her self-soothing capacities, and increasing her tolerance for strong feelings, which in her case are the anger that she feels with both her husband and daughter, and the sadness at the untimely loss of her sister. There are many interventions that can be drawn on in this phase. The case of Mrs. G. illustrates only a few.

Mrs. G. began to feel more as her sobriety continued. She remembered things she hadn't remembered before. Eleven-year-old Joanie often reminded her of her father in her destructiveness and outbursts at the dinner table and her total disregard for other people's feelings. Mrs. G. began to realize that the haze of predinner drinking had enabled her not to notice the resemblance, even physical, to her father, and not to remember. Inadvertently, she was promoting the similarity by not dealing with Joanie's outrageous behavior. The drinking made her passive. All of these insights, while useful to her, also made her anxious, and Mrs. G. feared she would start abusing alcohol again.

The therapist utilized many directive techniques with Mrs. G., learning early on that Mrs. G. enjoyed reading. Noting this woman's fine intelligence, the therapist suggested readings on alcoholism, particularly adult children of alcoholics, family dysfunction and its effects on the developing child, and even fiction that dealt with some of these issues. Homework assignments were frequently made that involved identifying triggers to her cravings and brainstorming alternative soothing techniques. The therapist also offered to see Mrs. G.'s husband to aid her in her work, but Mrs. G. declined.

The therapist frequently took the role of educator, teaching Mrs. G. the generic sequelae of trauma and applying them to her situation and the role of her trauma in her current life. The therapist talked about the role of dissociation and how alcohol can be understood as an aid to dissociation. It had helped her to disconnect from her pain.

The therapist made no effort to encourage Mrs. G. to remember what did not easily come to mind, but did prepare her for the possibility of the unbidden return of painful memories in the future.

Mrs. G. was a good student. She learned quickly to search and find alternatives, and improve her self-regulation. Eventually she did attend AA meetings and made very good use of the program. By week 12 of the treatment she had a sponsor in AA and was "working the program." AA substituted for alcohol and became the main source of self-esteem regulation. The treatment built on that. Less successful were interventions aimed at helping her tolerate more of her emotions. She still resisted dealing with her anger toward her husband and the grief work she needed to do on the loss of her sister. This would have to await a later time.

Twelve-step programs abound. These very thoughtful, well-structured, self-help programs are available for almost every conceivable mental health issue: alcoholism, family members of current or past alcoholics, and teen children of alcoholics; gamblers; overeaters; sex addicts; and individuals identified as co-dependent. Many members of twelve-step programs are dealing with posttraumatic conditions, both identified and unidentified. Meetings are available daily, all over the world, and provide members with support as needed, something a therapist, particular in a short-term treatment, cannot provide.

There is a plethora of techniques available to the short-term therapist. Listed below are a few, with suggestions for further exploration:

- *EMDR* (Eye Movement Desensitization and Reprocessing) (Shapiro 1995): For those trained in this technique, EMDR can be an effective adjunctive technique for processing trauma. However, it cannot be used without extensive training.
- *Hypnotic techniques*, including relaxation and guided visualizations: Some training is necessary to do hypnotherapy. However, a relaxation protocol and guided visualization, both techniques that can be taught to the patient and used for intensity control, are relatively easy to learn for both the therapist and the patient.
- *Journal writing* can be used to help the patient follow through and track the work of the treatment sessions, as well as do some work on her own. An excellent resource for structured journaling exercises for the trauma survivor is *The Way of the Journal* (Adams 1993). This workbook attends to the issue of dosing, for the patient who needs to avoid triggering intrusive symptoms.
- *Bibliotherapy*, or guided reading: The Sidran Foundation of Lutherville, MD maintains and distributes publications that address various aspects of trauma—for the survivor of trauma, their families, and their therapists.
- *Ericksonian techniques*: Dolan's *Resolving Sexual Abuse: Solution-Focused Therapy and Ericksonian Hypnosis for Adult Survivors* (1991) is a rich resource for interventions that can be easily adapted to any trauma survivor with or without specific training in Ericksonian hypnosis. One interesting technique employs the posttraumatic patient's en-

hanced ability to dissociate in the interest of containing intrusive symptoms, improving memory, or retrieving traumatic memory.

- *Group treatment* is a valuable adjunct to individual therapy, or alone for the individual who has had at least some individual work. Group treatment is generally more affordable than individual therapy, and therefore more sessions may be available to the patient working under managed care restraints.

Ending Phase
(Components 11 to 14):
Addressing Termination, Reviewing Progress and Identifying
Unresolved Issues, Resolving the Therapist–Patient Relationship,
Referral and Follow-Up

At the sixteenth session the therapist reminded Mrs. G. that, in addition to today, they had three more sessions to wrap up their work together. Mrs. G. gasped. Four months had passed quickly. Together they reviewed Mrs. G.'s progress. She had been sober for four and a half months, was well launched with AA, and was generally feeling better. Going to meetings had accelerated her awareness of the effects on her of growing up in a family where alcohol was an honorary member, and she and her sponsor were talking a lot about her father's abusiveness toward her mother and her younger sister, who had died almost two years ago. Mrs. G. had found journal writing the most useful of all the techniques they had employed to help her cope with stress, and recently Mrs. G. had joined a gym in hopes of adding that to her growing arsenal of stress reduction methods.

What was still problematic, they both agreed, was Mrs. G.'s avoidance of dealing with her husband and her anger with him over his health and eating habits. She was more aware now that her sister's death had heightened her anxiety, but what was less accessible was how avoidant Mrs. G. was of her own strong feelings. It was almost as if she started to be angry with her husband but she feared she would lose control, as her father so often did, and become abusive.

Another area, only barely touched on in the allotted time, was Mrs. G.'s style of parenting. With her daughter she was quite unable to set reasonable limits and was raising a clone of her explosive father. As both the therapist and Mrs. G. were aware that this situation would only get worse as Joanie approached adolescence, they agreed to spend the remaining time exploring how to improve Mrs. G.'s parenting skills. In some ways this seemed more accessible than the marital problem, or at least Mrs. G. seemed more motivated here.

Reviewing what techniques had been most useful to Mrs. G., the therapist and patient agreed that reading had been both effective and enjoyable and was something that would continue beyond the allotted sessions. Mrs. G. would go to the library or bookstore and review what was available on developing parenting skills. The therapist, on her part, would investigate self-help or leader-led parenting groups in the area.

The therapist recognized and discussed with Mrs. G. that much of her style with Joanie was trauma-based. Her parenting of the two older children, who were temperamentally more easygoing than Joanie, had been much more effective. Joanie's personality and appearance reminded Mrs. G. more of her father. Encouraging Mrs. G. to process additional memories of her father's explosiveness was not something Mrs. G. wanted to do, nor was it realistic within the framework of the twenty sessions. She could, however, seek to improve her management of Joanie within the context of knowing that her responses to Joanie were complicated and multidetermined.

Mrs. G. did not say much about how she felt about leaving the therapist, but she did worry aloud somewhat about possible relapse. The therapist inquired directly about this and Mrs. G. said that she had AA and she would continue her work with her sponsor, but requested of the therapist that they have a follow-up meeting in the future—something she could think about and look forward to in the following month. The therapist readily agreed that this was desirable and expressed both her genuine admiration and faith in Mrs. G. for her continued good work.

The ending phase can be challenging for both the therapist and the patient. The therapist may be all too aware of all that has not been accomplished, while the patient may be understandably anxious about coping without the help of the therapist.

In the case of Mrs. G., the patient expressed only minimal anxiety about ending. This was probably a result of both her disengaged style and her growing reliance on AA. The therapist felt somewhat let down by the patient's lack of affect about ending. She liked Mrs. G. and found herself regretting the termination of their work. She would miss her. One way to understand Mrs. G.'s lack of expressed feeling about the ending is as a variation of dissociation. Mrs. G. was often not in touch with her feelings; she disconnected and sometimes projected them, as she did with her daughter. The therapist may well have been experiencing both her own regret and the disavowed sadness of her patient. This understanding was certainly congruent with the patient's previous adaptations, and it helped the therapist to accept that this was the way the patient chose to leave. The therapist was able to observe in the ending sessions that the patient had internalized an object representation of the therapist, albeit unwittingly. Mrs. G. now employed concepts she had learned from the therapist and even the therapist's language. Referral was not indicated in this case, as Mrs. G. was well on her way with AA. Both looked forward to the follow-up interview one month after the last session.

CONCLUSION

Posttraumatic conditions present frequently in a disguised manner as depression, anxiety states, interpersonal problems, and addictions. An understanding of the clinical manifestations of PTSD and complex PTSD can enhance the therapist's ability to intervene quickly and with deeper understanding of the patient. Although short-term treatment of posttraumatic conditions may not address the developmental and personality deformations of the individual and allow for in-depth processing of traumatic memory and its meanings, many important tasks can be dealt with successfully. Goldstein and Noonan's (1999) ISTT model provides a balanced, structured, and dynamically informed approach for the individual suffering from posttraumatic stress and its clinical elaborations.

REFERENCES

Adams, K. (1993). *The Way of the Journal: A Journal Therapy Workbook for Healing.* Lutherville, MD: Sidran.

American Psychiatric Association. (1994). *Diagnostic and Statistical Manual of Mental Disorders,* 4th Edition. Washington, DC: Author.

Bernstein, E. M., and Putnam, F. W. (1986). Development, reliability, and validity of a dissociation scale. *Journal of Nervous Mental Disease* 174:727–735.

Briere, J. (1992). *Child Abuse Trauma: Theory and Treatment of the Lasting Effects.* Newbury Park, CA: Sage.

Briere, J., and Runtz, M. (1989). The trauma symptom checklist (TSC-33): early data on a new scale. *Journal of Interpersonal Violence* 4:151–163.

Courtois, C. (1988). *Healing the Incest Wound: Adult Survivors in Therapy.* New York: Norton.

——— (1994). *The treatment of complex post-traumatic conditions under health care restraints.* Workshop presented at the conference on treating complex conditions, Orange, NJ, February.

Davies, J., and Frawley, M. (1994). *Treating the Adult Survivor of Childhood Sexual Abuse: A Psychoanalytic Perspective.* New York: Basic Books.

Dolan, Y. (1991). *Resolving Sexual Abuse: Solution-Focused Therapy and Ericksonian Hypnosis for Adult Survivors.* New York: Norton.

Finkelhor, D., Hotaling, G., Lewis, I. A., and Smith, C. (1990). Sexual abuse in a national survey of adult men and women: prevalence, characteristics, and risk factors. *Child Abuse and Neglect* 14:19–28.

Goldstein, E. G., and Noonan, M. (1999). *Short-Term Treatment and Social Work Practice: An Integrative Perspective.* New York: Free Press.

Herman, J. L. (1992). *Trauma and Recovery: The Aftermath of Violence from Domestic Abuse to Political Terror.* New York: Basic Books.

Horowitz, M. (1997). *Stress Response Syndromes: PTSD, Grief and Adjustment Disorders.* Northvale, NJ: Jason Aronson.

McCann, L., and Pearlman, L. A. (1990). *Psychological Trauma and the Adult Survivor: Theory, Therapy, and Transformation.* New York: Brunner/ Mazel.

Ross, C., Heber, S., and Norton, G. R. (1989). Dissociative disorders interview schedule: a structured interview. *Dissociation* 2(3):169– 189.

Shapiro, F. (1995). *Eye Movement Desensitization and Reprocessing.* New York: Guilford.

Ulman, R., and Brothers, B. (1988). *The Shattered Self: A Psychoanalytic Study of Trauma.* Hillsdale, NJ: Analytic Press.

CHAPTER THIRTEEN

Treatment of the Borderline Personality Disorder Using the ISTT Model

MARYELLEN NOONAN

THEORETICAL OVERVIEW
AND TREATMENT PERSPECTIVE

The fourth edition of the *Diagnostic and Statistical Manual of Mental Disorders* (*DSM-IV*) (APA 1994) defines personality disorders as enduring subjective experiences and behaviors that deviate from normal cultural patterns, are rigidly pervasive, have an onset in adolescence or early adulthood, are stable through time, and lead to unhappiness, maladaptive behavior, and functional impairment. The self-defeating character traits associated with personality disorders are not only inflexible and of a long-standing nature, but more importantly are ego-syntonic; that is, the pathological nature of such traits is unconscious and such individuals steadfastly believe that others are responsible for their problems and sense of unhappiness. Consequently, those diagnosed with a personality disorder generally resist psychotherapeutic intervention (Kaplan and Sadock 1998).

The *DSM-IV* lists ten personality disorders clustered into three categories. Behavioral manifestion and symptomatology are the sole criteria for diagnosis. The descriptive approach was purposely chosen by the developers of the *DSM* to avoid disagreement over the etiology of personality disorders and to provide clinicians the freedom to determine and implement their own course of treatment (Marziali 1992). The first group of disorders is the paranoid, schizoid, and the schizotypal. Characteristically, these individuals appear strange, eccentric, and aloof. The second group of disorders includes the histrionic, narcissistic, and borderline, and such individuals appear dramatic, chaotic, and labile. The third group of disorders includes avoidant, dependent, obsessive-compulsive, and nonspecified personality disorders. These individuals are generally fearful and anxious (Kaplan and Sadock 1998). People often exhibit traits suggestive of a variety of personality disorders, however, they are usually diagnosed based on the characteristic that is most prominent and permeates their relation to self and others. The personality disorders are coded on Axis II, the inclusion of which was to ensure that enduring personality traits that might underlie Axis I conditions would be assessed independently (Blum and Pfohl 1998).

Each of the personality disorders presents with unique features and a distinct underlying psychic organization, and thus treatment goals and interventions will differ. This chapter focuses on the subgroup of border-line personality disorder (BPD), one of the most common personality disorders encountered by mental health professionals and one of the most difficult to treat (Goldstein 1990, Waldinger and Gunderson 1984). According to the *DSM-IV* the patient must exhibit at least five of the following criteria (clinical signs and symptoms) for the diagnosis of borderline:

1. A pattern of unstable and intense interpersonal relationships characterized by alternating between extremes of overidealization and devaluation
2. Impulsiveness in at least two areas that are potentially self-damaging

3. Affective instability
4. Inappropriately intense anger or lack of control of anger
5. Recurrent suicidal threats, gestures, or behavior, or self-mutilating behavior
6. Marked and persistent identity disturbances
7. Chronic feelings of emptiness
8. Frantic efforts to avoid real or imagined abandonment
9. Transient stress-related paranoid ideation or severe dissociative symptoms. [p. 654]

There is much controversy regarding the use of the borderline diagnosis. Those representing the feminist perspective suggest that gender bias is codified into the *DSM* and that characteristics of men are used as the criteria for health, while female traits are more likely to be considered unhealthy or pathological (Brown 1992). Women are also diagnosed with BPD three times more frequently than men, suggesting to some that the symptoms women present may be indicative of posttraumatic stress disorder rather than BPD (Hertz 1996, Layton 1995). The *DSM* has also been criticized as being culturally insensitive and biased in that what is considered the norm in one culture may, when taken out of context, be erroneously diagnosed as pathological in a different culture (Kaplan and Sadock 1998, Mendez-Villarrubia and LaBruzza 1994). However, in spite of these criticisms, BPD is generally accepted as a reliable *DSM-IV* diagnosis (Marziali 1992, Smith 1992, Waldinger and Gunderson 1984).

Etiology

There are varying postulates regarding the etiology of the borderline syndrome. The three principal ones are the psychodynamic, neurological, and early/childhood neglect/abuse perspectives (Marziali 1992). The principal representative of the psychodynamic perspective is Kernberg (1975), who, as a classical drive theorist, believes that BPD develops in those people who are constitutionally predisposed to high levels of aggression and experience conflictual relationships with caregivers. The confluence of these factors may result in unneutralized aggression and an inability to integrate positive and negative self and object representations. Such individuals are unable to tolerate ambivalent feelings, and, to protect the "good" images from the "bad" images, they employ primitive defenses such as splitting, projective identification, idealization, and devaluation. Other psychodynamic theorists, such as Buie and Adler (1982) and Gunderson (1984), contend that the borderline syndrome originates from environmental failures and deficits related to separation-individuation and that such individuals have failed to develop a stable self-identity.

The neurological perspective suggests that there is a connection between the effects of childhood brain dysfunction and the subsequent onset of the borderline syndrome particularly as relates to males (Akiskal et al. 1985, Andrulonis et al. 1981). For example, in a retrospective review of 91 charts, Andrulonis and colleagues (1982) found that 52 percent of males diagnosed as borderline had a history of epilepsy, head trauma, or encephalitis. They concluded that borderlines with minimal brain dysfunction are predominately male and considered their difficulties as constitutional.

Several studies have suggested that BPD is more frequent among family members of people diagnosed with the disorder (Pope et al. 1983), while other studies conclude that there is a high incidence of depression and mood disorders in the families of borderlines (Kaplan and Sadock 1998). Children reared in such environments seem more inclined to develop borderline symptomatology. Finally, some researchers believe that genes controlling the activity of neurotransmitters are likely to account for personality differences (Siever and Davis 1991).

The neglect/abuse perspective proposes that individuals who have a BPD diagnosis have suffered from persistent abuse and/or neglect as children, and some studies carried out within the last decade suggest a connection between these two factors. For example, Zanarini and colleagues (1989) used semistructured interviews to obtain family histories of adults with borderline, dysthymic, and antisocial diagnoses. A significantly higher percentage of borderlines reported being sexually, physically, or verbally abused during childhood. Paris and Frank (1989) explored patients' recollections of the quality of care they received as children. Borderlines and nonborderlines differed significantly in the degree of perceived maternal care. There is also growing evidence that sexual abuse in childhood is associated with psychological difficulties in adulthood. Briere and Zaidi (1989) reviewed the charts of 100 female patients seen for emergency psychiatric services and found that three times as many abused women than nonabused women were diagnosed with a personality disorder, and five times as many abused women received the diagnosis of borderline. Findings such as these are consistent with suggestions that a diagnosis of posttraumatic stress disorder might be more accurate for some patients who are diagnosed as borderline. At the very least it suggests that inquiries around abuse and neglect need to be made during the assessment phase.

Clinical Picture

Regardless of how one understands the causes of borderline personality disorder, there is general consensus as to the clinical picture: it is the patient's inability to tolerate ambivalence that is the hallmark of BPD and the primary reason for serious interpersonal conflicts characterized by unpredictability, instability, volatility, and impulsivity (Kaplan and Sadock 1998, Kernberg 1975, Linehan 1993, Marziali 1992). Such patients relate in an all-or-nothing manner, with no gray or in-between areas, and are unable to tolerate two opposing or seemingly contradictory feelings such as love and hate. They often make intense attachments to others whom they idealize and become dependent on. When they are disappointed in these relationships or their dependency needs are not met, they express intense rage and hostility. However, they are also terrified of being alone, often complain about feelings of emptiness and boredom, and, in an effort to avoid such feelings, frantically attempt to connect with others. This pattern of attachment and distancing is repeated frequently, giving an overall chaotic, unpredictable picture of functioning and a sense that they are always in a crisis (Goldstein 1990, Kaplan and Sadock 1998).

Individuals with BPD also tend to be impulse ridden, prone to enactment (acting on rather than talking about feelings), exhibit an inability to tolerate frustration, and, because painful affects are poorly tolerated, frequently engage in self-destructive acts, such as self-mutilation, sexual promiscuity, substance abuse, and violence. Rapid mood swings are also common in BPD. One minute these patients can seem optimistic, happy, and even euphoric, and in a seeming blink of an eye become enraged, disappointed, resentful, and vindictive. Likewise, borderline patients demonstrate what is known as identity diffusion, meaning there is no stable, secure sense of self. Due to this fragility these patients are at the mercy of their emotional states, the vagaries of life, and the behavior of others.

Finally, the volatility that characterizes the interpersonal relationships of borderline patients is repeated in the treatment situation, and as such taxes the commitment and patience of the treating clinician. Therapists must be alert and vigilant in the monitoring of their reactions and refrain from retaliating against such patients.

Adherents of the psychodynamic perspective also suggest that there are specific defenses associated with BPD, most notably splitting, projection, projective identification, and acting out (Kaplan and Sadock 1998, Kernberg 1975). In splitting, feelings toward others are divided into either all good or all bad. Patients are unable to tolerate ambivalence, and resolve such feelings by separating others into either all good or all bad. In projection, patients' unacknowledged feelings are attributed to others. These impulses, which cannot be tolerated, are perceived as emanating from others, and thus these patients frequently find fault, collect injustices, and are prejudiced against others. In projective identification, the unacceptable impulses (anger) are attributed to the other, and the patient then tries to induce the person to act out the warded-off impulse, which in turn makes the projector fearful and in need of controlling the other. In the therapeutic situation this often accounts for the therapist's anger and desire to retaliate against the patient. In acting out, the patient, again unable to tolerate strong feeling states, uses action rather then verbalization to express the unacceptable impulses. Such patients are unable to talk about what they are feeling and instead act it out, with no insight into the self-destructive or maladaptive behavior.

While the proponents of a cognitive-behavioral perspective may emphasize cognition and behavior over psychic structure and defenses, in fact, there are many similarities between the cognitive behavioral and psychodynamic approaches (Beck and Freeman 1990, Heller and North-cut 1996, Weston 1990, 1991). For example, a cognitive-behaviorally oriented clinician might use the term *cognitive distortion* in much the same way a psychodynamically oriented clinician might use the term *splitting*. The former term implies the patient's inaccurate perception of others, while the latter refers to the patient's affective state and the separating of good and bad self and object images. Additionally, some cognitive therapists identify what is termed attributional style (Weston 1991). Similar to projection, attributional style is people's attempt to make sense or meaning of their worlds by attributing causes to their own and others' thoughts, feelings, and behaviors. *Dysregulation* is a term used by cognitive therapists to denote "affective overload" (Weston 1991), a concept reminiscent of a psychodynamic clinician's description of the patient's inability to regulate or tolerate intense affect.

TREATMENT APPROACHES

Due to the constellation of symptoms and behaviors exhibited by patients with BPD, until recently most clinicians have favored long-term psycho-analytically oriented psychotherapy aimed at modifying the patient's personality structure (Marziali 1992). While some follow-up studies suggest that certain patients have benefited from this approach (McGlashan 1986, Waldinger and Gunderson 1984), there has been little research as to the effectiveness of any particular treatment for BPD. For example, follow-up studies show that 50 percent of borderline patients who begin psychodynamic psychotherapy drop out within the first six months of treatment, and of those who remain only 10 percent have moderately successful outcomes (Marziali 1992).

The most prominent psychodynamic treatment models are the conflict model and the deficit model. Clarkin and colleagues (1999) are proponents of the conflict model and have recently developed a structured approach termed *transference focused psychotherapy* (TFP). As its name suggests, the interventive process centers on the analysis of the transference. Its main goal is to bring a patient's unconscious conflicts to the surface, where they can be worked through in the context of the transference to the therapist. The approach is long term and sessions are held twice weekly.

Buie and Adler (1982) are proponents of the deficit model. This approach emphasizes the positive aspects of the transference and stresses the importance of the therapist's creating a safe holding environment in which the patient can express rage and anger. The eventual goal is to have the patient build up a strong evocative memory of the therapist as a base from which to develop positive self and object representations. As with the aforementioned approach, treatment is long term and is aimed at structural change.

Although cognitive-behavioral models generally are not associated with the treatment of BPD, the cognitive-behavioral approach of Linehan (1993)—dialectical behavioral therapy (DBT)—is currently receiving much attention. According to Linehan, the patient's inability to tolerate strong affective states, particularly negative affect, is a hallmark of BPD. In DBT the borderline patient is encouraged to tolerate the affect without resorting to maladaptive or self-destructive behaviors. A variety of cognitive and behavioral techniques are used within a problem-oriented framework to accomplish this goal. Techniques include behavioral skills training, contingency management, cognitive modification, and exposure to emotional cues. Patients are helped to learn new coping strategies to deal with emotional distress. In Linehan's approach the patient must be motivated to cease his or her self-destructive behavior. A contract is established, whereby the patient concurrently attends group and individual treatment, and missing four sessions in a row of either modality results in termination. The program is limited to one year.

Although many psychodynamic and cognitive-behavioral brief treatment models have been developed, with the exception of some preliminary work done by Winston and colleagues (1994), there are no specific short-term models developed for the treatment of BPD. In fact, most brief treatment models would tend to exclude patients diagnosed as borderline. For example, in their review of brief treatment models, Koss and Shiang (1994) found that many brief therapies are recommended primarily for patients who have a history of satisfactory social and psychological functioning, exhibit a good capacity to relate, and are highly motivated—characteristics not associated with BPD. Also, cognitive-behavioral approaches are generally found to be most appropriate for patients who present with a circumscribed behavioral problem and intact cognitive functioning. Koss and Shiang conclude, "Brief therapy has been found to be less effective for patients with more severe disorders such as those of personality, substance abuse, and psychosis" (p. 681).

Although research into the treatment of BPD, be it in terms of long- or short-term models, may seem less than encouraging, there is also some evidence that borderline patients can be helped by treatments that integrate a variety of strategies and techniques, and limit the goals of the treatment (Horowitz 1991, Marziali 1992, Koss and Shiang 1994). Borderline patients generally enter treatment before the age of 40 and they do so because they have occupational, marital, or other life stage problems (Kaplan and Sadock 1998), and even when these patients engage in intensive treatment with highly trained clinicians, improvement reflects a change in coping skills rather than structural changes in the personality (Waldinger and Gunderson 1984). As noted earlier, a high percentage of borderline patients terminate treatment within six months (Marziali 1992), and there is some evidence from practice research that in general short-term treatment is not less effective than long-term intervention (Koss and Shiang 1994). Thus, a brief treatment approach aimed at helping such patients develop coping skills that can enhance functioning and are specifically related to life cycle issues may be an effective means of addressing the syndrome.

Goldstein and Noonan (1999) developed a short-term framework, which forms the basis of this chapter. Integrative short-term treatment (ISTT) is broad based, applicable to a variety of patient problems, and, as its name implies, integrative in nature. Although primarily a here-and-now approach, it posits the existence of a psychic structure, recognizes defenses and the existence of unconscious conflict, limits the treatment goals, and utilizes psychodynamic, cognitive-behavioral, and problem-solving techniques and strategies. ISTT seems particularly well suited to working with some specific subcategories of BPD.

The ISTT model delineates the treatment situation into the beginning, middle, and termination phases. The framework is applicable for treatment of any length but was developed specifically for treatments of between eight and twenty-five sessions. The beginning phase includes problem identification, engagement, assessment, planning the intervention, and contracting. It is during the middle phase that the bulk of the treatment is carried out. This phase includes implementing the plan, monitoring progress, and dealing with and working through resistances. In the termination phase therapist and patient review the progress, identify unresolved issues, and, if indicated, make arrangements for follow-up and/or referral.

Delineating the treatment situation into phases and components can help to organize the therapist's thinking, provide structure for both therapist and patient, ensure that the treatment goals are kept in the forefront, and minimize the intense transference and countertransference reactions associated with BPD (Goldstein and Noonan 1999). Also it is in the specific use of techniques, the timing of interventions, and the handling of transference, countertransference, and resistance that the training and skill of the worker are most evident.

INCLUSION AND EXCLUSION CRITERIA

As previously noted, short-term psychotherapeutic work with borderlines must be carefully focused and generally limited to the stressful life event that brought them into treatment. The *DSM-IV* uses a descriptive approach, whereby symptoms and behaviors are used to make a diagnosis. But to be considered appropriate for ISTT, the patient must also present with an Axis IV environmental or psychosocial problem. This is consistent with ISTT both in terms of goals, which are limited, and the notion of partialization, the process by which problems are delineated into manageable segments with the therapist determining which aspects of the problem are most amenable to therapeutic intervention. Indicating the presence of an Axis IV difficulty makes it eminently clear that it is a specific problem area rather than the borderline syndrome itself that is the focus of the therapeutic intervention. However, this does not preclude the possibility that during the course of treatment certain aspects of the personality may in fact undergo change.

The *DSM-IV* (APA 1994) recognizes nine environmental or psychosocial problems in the Axis IV category:

1. Problems with the primary support group: examples include a death in the family, health problems, or a divorce.
2. Problems related to the social environment: examples include a life-cycle problem such as moving away from one's family, marriage, conflictual interpersonal relationships, isolation, or inadequate social support.
3. Educational problems: examples include conflict with teachers or classmates, and academic problems.
4. Occupational problems: examples include unemployment, threat of job loss, conflict with employer or co-workers.
5. Housing problems: examples include difficulties with landlord or neighbors, homelessness, inadequate housing, or unsafe neighborhood.

6. Economic problems: examples include poverty or inadequate finances.
7. Problems with access to health care services: examples include inadequate health care services or inadequate health insurance.
8. Problems with the legal or criminal system: examples include arrest, incarceration, or being the victim of a crime.
9. Other psychosocial or environmental problem: examples include natural disasters, and conflict with medical or mental health personnel or nonfamily caregivers. [p. 30]

Patients who are a danger to themselves or others would not be appropriate for the ISTT approach. Specifically, patients who have a history of suicidal ideation, gestures, attempts, and/or self-mutilation and are at risk to act out such behaviors during the treatment should be excluded, as should patients with a history of violence toward others, homicidal ideation, or presenting behaviors that are potentially harmful to others. Also, patients who are impulse ridden, as in the case of alcoholics or substance abusers, and are unable to respond to the structure of outpatient treatment should not be included. Finally, patients who, for over one year, exhibit multiple Axis IV problems may not be appropriate for short-term psychotherapy due to the multiplicity of problems and the ingrained nature of the pathology. These patients may require a more in-depth treatment aimed at modifying the personality such as Kernberg's (1975) expressive psychotherapy model and Buie and Adler's (1982) mixed model approach.

In summary, brief treatment for those diagnosed with BPD is ideally suited for those patients who present with discrete problems related to specific psychosocial or environmental difficulties and who have no history of severe acting-out behaviors toward the self or others.

TREATMENT GOALS

Individuals who present with BPD generally seek treatment at the behest of others or because they want to relieve their situation rather than alter anything about themselves. The primary therapeutic goal is to help patients resolve the Axis IV environmental or psychosocial problem that brought them into treatment. Therapists may also aid patients in reestablishing their previous level of functioning (Koss and Shiang 1994). The clinician seeks to help these patients develop some beginning insight into selective aspects of their functioning that are connected to the problem at hand, help patients modify these, and acquire more adaptive coping strategies and problem-solving techniques (Goldstein and Noonan 1999). To achieve these goals, it is necessary to focus on helping patients understand that some aspect of their thinking, feeling, or behaving is connected to their difficulties and that a characteristic or trait that was once adaptive may now be maladaptive and self-defeating. For example, patients who are generally aggressive, hostile, or controlling may have developed these traits as a form of protection from abusive caregivers. While these traits may have served them well in the past, they may in the present be dysfunctional. Finally, and most importantly, the therapist must help patients to recognize the benefits of modifying their behavior, as there would be no reason to relinquish a behavior if it did not result in some gain.

CASE ILLUSTRATION

Initial Phase

The initial phase of ISTT includes engagement; problem identification, including underlying issues that may be impacting on the problem; biopsychosocial assessment; and contracting. Each of these components occur simultaneously, but because borderline patients are generally resistant to psychotherapy, engagement is crucial. Empirical evidence suggests a direct association between the therapeutic alliance and positive treatment outcome (Kolden 1991), and an essential element in the formation of the alliance is patient collaboration (Allen et al. 1990). It is imperative that therapists "join" with patients in their understanding of what the problem situation is and who is causing their difficulties. The clinician empathizes with patients' experiences, while simultaneously attempting to help them recognize that although others may be responsible for what is happening, it is they themselves who are suffering. The therapist's capacity to relate to the patient's suffering is the first step toward the development of the therapeutic alliance.

Borderline patients tend to blame others for their difficulties, and thus are likely to be angry and resentful at the mere fact of being in a therapist's office. Due to problems in affect regulation, they may be highly agitated; given to illogical, distorted thinking; and unresponsive, even hostile, to the therapist's attempts at empathy. As Kaplan and Sadock (1998) suggest, borderline patients generally enter treatment at a time of crisis, which can create such a high level of anxiety that patients are unable to present a coherent description of their difficulties. The therapist in turn may experience the patient as bizarre and unmanageable, and feel overwhelmed and intimidated.

The recognition and handling of transference and countertransference manifestations in the beginning of treatment are also critical to the establishment and maintenance of the therapeutic alliance. For example, some borderline patients may begin treatment with volatile, primitive reactions to even the most benign of therapists. These patients may devalue or attempt to control the therapist, and the intensity of these transference reactions is likely to interfere with the establishment of the therapeutic alliance. Other borderline patients may defend against aggressive impulses through the use of splitting, denial, or idealization. In such cases the anger may be projected onto the therapist and result in the destruction of the therapeutic relationship. Although such transference manifestations generally are a part of all treatment situations, with borderline patients these reactions tend to be evident right from the outset.

The countertransference reactions to borderline patients, particularly in the initial phase, also can be intense, as therapists frequently feel bombarded, controlled, depleted, and hateful toward such patients. It often is easier for therapists to tolerate their own countertransference as the treatment unfolds, but to be the recipient of patients' primitive reactions so early in the treatment can be unsettling and unnerving. Such reactions often lead clinicians to thoughts of either getting rid of the patient or becoming indifferent toward the treatment as well as the patient. If therapists can acknowledge their feelings, and attempt to depersonalize their reactions by understanding that these feelings may be induced by patients and are reflective of their disorder, patient behaviors may be more tolerable (Noonan 1998).

Therapists need to be aware of early transference manifestations, and, if indicated, interpret them to their patients. Most important, therapists must not be seduced into replicating patients' early experiences. On a cautionary note, it is essential that before reaching this conclusion, therapists first consider and carefully examine if it is their interventions that may be inducing patients' reactions.

In addition to establishing the therapeutic alliance, the beginning phase is characterized by the therapist's attempts to diffuse patients' cognitive and affective overload (Linehan 1993), articulate some benefit that they can derive from the treatment, identify the problems to be worked on, determine strengths and liabilities, and establish a contract (Goldstein and Noonan 1999).

Ms. Longo, a 35-year-old, single woman, was referred to an outpatient mental health clinic by an acquaintance she had met in a local park. She entered the consulting room agitated and angry. As she paced back and forth, she spoke in a shrill voice stating that she didn't like sitting in the waiting room.

Ms. Longo: What if someone saw me here, how would I explain this? I don't belong here. She's the one who's crazy. All I need are some pills. I just need something to calm me down. Something so I can deal with this nut job. Are you a psychiatrist? Can you give me a prescription? That's all I need. Aren't you going to say anything?

Therapist (feeling bombarded and overwhelmed): I can see you're upset. Would you like to sit down?

Ms. Longo: No! I told you she's crazy. I'm not leaving my house. Let her go get a job. She never worked a fucking day in her life. She just wants me to take care of her. Yeah, I watch TV and go to the park. So what. What's it to her?

The patient went on in this disjointed manner for some minutes. Eventually, the therapist was able to piece together that Ms. Longo's mother, with whom she lived, had threatened to have her evicted from their apartment if she didn't get some psychiatric help. Ms. Longo had been unemployed for six months, her benefits were running out, and her mother accused her of being crazy because she wasn't looking for another job and spent her time either in the house watching TV or talking to strangers in the park.

Therapist: Maybe watching TV and going to the park are the only ways of dealing with your mother's nagging and criticism.

Ms. Longo: You got it! You really got it.

Therapist: It sounds like she's driving you crazy and you'd like her to stop badgering you.

Ms. Longo: Well, I do want to get to work. I want to get another job. But her nagging at me isn't helping.

Therapist: I can certainly understand that.

Ms. Longo (interrupting with much hostility): You never answered my question. Are you or aren't you a psychiatrist? I just want some pills to calm me down.

Therapist (calmly and clearly): I am not a psychiatrist. The clinic procedures require that we find out more about your situation and then you see the psychiatrist. If you receive medication here it is also necessary that you meet weekly with a therapist.

Ms. Longo (yelling and pacing): I can't believe it. Everyone is always giving me the runaround. Nobody cares about what I want. Nobody listens to me. I'm sick and tired of this bull.

The therapist did not interrupt but waited instead until the patient had ended her tirade.

Therapist: It sounds like a number of people have let you down and disappointed you. Although I'm not a psychiatrist, I do want to listen to your concerns. Unfortunately, if you need medication, this is the procedure we must follow. I can understand if you decide not to continue with our interview and decide to see a private psychiatrist. It's your choice. But I do want to try to help you if I can.

Ms. Longo: I'm already here. I might as well get my money's worth.

The therapist learned that Ms. Longo had worked as a bookkeeper with the same retail chain for the last sixteen years. The company was sold and her job had been eliminated. Although she loved her job, often worked late into the evening and weekends without compensation, and "adored" her boss, she disliked her co-workers, whom she described as nosy and always getting into her business. After losing her job she didn't know what to do. She had no siblings, no close friends, hated her mother, with whom she engaged in frequent shouting matches (her father was deceased six years), and had no hobbies or interests outside of her work. Ms. Longo was given a generous buyout package, but her money was almost gone, she missed working, and she felt lost and empty. Her anxiety and agitation began shortly after she was laid off. Her internist prescribed various medications, but when she insisted that he wasn't helping her, he referred her to a psychiatrist who dismissed her because she called him repeatedly, refused to take the medication as prescribed, and was disrupting his practice. He told her to go to a psychiatric emergency room and never call him again.

Ms. Longo: It's my nerves. If I could just get the right medication and get my nerves under control, everything would be all right.

Therapist: What medications did you try?

Ms. Longo (emptying pill vials onto the table): I tried all of these, nothing worked. The psychiatrist suggested some others that I hadn't tried but a friend I met in the park, he's the one who told me to come here, said they were for crazy people. I'm not crazy.

Therapist (exasperated): I thought that you did want a change in medication.

Ms. Longo: Don't get an attitude with me. You're just like everybody else. I can't believe it. Here I go again.

Therapist: I apologize if you thought I had an attitude, but maybe I misunderstood. I thought you wanted to see a psychiatrist for some medication.

Ms. Longo: I don't know what I want. I just want my old job back.

Therapist: That's understandable. You worked for sixteen years in a job you loved with a boss who understood and valued you. It sounds perfect. Anyone might feel nervous in your situation, having to look for a new position and needing to deal with new people. All of this would be hard for anyone. Maybe the anxious feelings you're having are about losing the job and being a little scared about looking for another one. Maybe we could try to understand this better, which might get your mother to stop badgering you and reduce some of your anxiety. You then may feel more able to look for another job.

The patient agreed to return and then pulled out her insurance policy. She didn't understand it. The worker read it and explained that the policy covered twenty-five sessions yearly. Ms. Longo indicated that since she didn't have to pay, she would return one more time, the following day. Before the worker could explain that the clinic wasn't set up that way, Ms. Longo began yelling.

Ms. Longo: I come here for help. I ask for a psychiatrist. You don't give me one. I agree to come back when I don't want to and then you tell me no. What the hell is going on here?

Therapist: I understand that this may seem confusing and maybe you're feeling like I'm purposely being difficult or frustrating you like other people, but I do want to be of help. I can give you an appointment in three days' time or in a week.

Ms. Longo (exiting the consulting room): Fine. I'll see you next week at the same time.

Establishing the therapeutic alliance remained in the forefront of sessions 2 through 5. The therapist explored Ms. Longo's anger and sadness regarding the elimination of her position, addressed any hint of conflict, frustration, or anger that she exhibited toward the therapist, and educated the patient as to the connection between her anxiety and the loss of her job and fears of seeking new employment. Finally, Ms. Longo was encouraged to be more aware of the thoughts and feelings (triggers) that preceded her anxiety and the therapist introduced new coping strategies.

Ms. Longo: I really loved that job. My boss was so wonderful. Nobody could be as great as he was. He always told me what great work I did. I got terrific evaluations from him.
Therapist: Why do you think that was?
Ms. Longo: I guess he liked me?
Therapist: You sound uncertain.
Ms. Longo (getting frustrated): Well, I don't know. What kind of questions are these?
Therapist: Let's stop for a minute. I can see that you're getting frustrated. Do you know what that's about?
Ms. Longo: I don't know. Maybe I don't know why he liked me.
Therapist: Maybe it's hard for you to really believe that someone could like you, and from all you've told me about what a good job you did I can certainly understand that he would like you and think very highly of you. It sounds like you got great evaluations because you did a great job. Maybe when you get anxious it would be helpful to keep these thoughts in mind and to remember that any employer would be fortunate to have you as an employee.

Although reluctant to speak of her early life, because she saw it as unrelated to her present difficulties, Ms. Longo related enough information that the therapist was able to gain some beginning understanding of the patient's intense conflicts with others and her need to feel in control. The patient was an only child in what she described as a dysfunctional household. Her parents had a conflictual marriage, her mother and father seemed to take their disappointment out on the patient, and in doing so were verbally abusive and highly critical of Ms. Longo. She recalled her mother as being particularly cruel, telling the patient she was "ugly, stupid, and would never amount to anything." Screaming and yelling was the order of the day and the patient could recall no happy times. Ms. Longo described herself as a willful, unruly child, who could only be disciplined by being locked in her room for hours at a time. Although angry with her parents, she also rationalized and defended their behavior, saying: "What else were they to do? I wasn't easy to live with."

Discussion

The patient presented as a classic BPD. Her interpersonal relationships were characterized by conflict and disappointment. She was impulse ridden and unable to tolerate frustration; had difficulty regulating her self-esteem; lacked a stable, cohesive sense of self; utilized the primitive defensives of projection and splitting; and demonstrated distortions in thinking and feeling.

Intense negative transference was evident from the outset and reflected the patient's relationship with her mother. Ms. Longo was hostile and belligerent because she viewed the therapist as being like her mother, that is, insensitive, controlling, critical, and nonresponsive to her needs and wishes. Also Ms. Longo maintained a hostile, dependent relationship with her mother, but was unable to form intimate relationships with others. She either impulsively ended relationships when others disappointed her or succeeded in getting others to reject her because of her demanding, dependent behavior. The therapist needed to provide an experience that was decidedly different from the one she had had with her mother, and rather than replicate the hostile interaction that characterized the mother–daughter relationship, the therapist remained calm, attentive, and nonargumentative. Most important, the therapist needed to explore and address the transference distortions as they arose because the patient's history, pattern of relating, and impulsivity suggested that to do otherwise would result in Ms. Longo abruptly ending the treatment or attempting to induce the therapist to reject her. The therapist also helped identify some benefit that Ms. Longo might obtain from the treatment, thereby responding to *her* needs and wishes. Additionally, the patient was presented with options, which allowed her to feel in control of the situation.

The patient also exhibited some real strengths: she had worked successfully and conscientiously at a job for many years, seemed motivated to return to work, and was of at least average intelligence. In that the patient presented with a discrete psychosocial problem, was not suicidal or homicidal, and was motivated to return to work, the therapist determined that Ms. Longo would be appropriate for ISTT.

The therapist knew it would not be possible to help Ms. Longo with all of her issues but the patient did want her mother to stop badgering her and she was somewhat motivated to resume working. The therapist believed that she needed to help Ms. Longo develop more impulse control and frustration tolerance, acquire new coping strategies and beginning insight into the nature of her difficulties, and relinquish some of her maladaptive ways of relating to herself and others. She also needed to provide her with a new and more positive object relationship.

Although tenuous, by the end of the fifth session therapist and patient had established a working alliance. Ms. Longo's anxiety had diminished somewhat, she felt calmer, and presented in a more appropriate, coherent manner. The therapist determined that it was now time to try to focus on helping Ms. Longo begin the process of job hunting or, more precisely, to examine her expectations and her inability to initiate a job search.

Middle Phase

Middle-phase work is composed of five interrelated components: (1) implementing the interventive plan, (2) maintaining the focus, (3) monitoring progress, (4) dealing with resistances, and (5) managing the therapeutic relationship (Goldstein and Noonan 1999). In the case of Ms. Longo, the middle phase began with the sixth session and continued through the twenty-second. Sessions were held either once or twice weekly, based on the patient's need. In the sixth session the therapist wondered aloud if Ms. Longo might want to begin to work on the issue of her job search.

Ms. Longo (angry and screeching): I was just getting to like you. Now you're pushing me and trying to make me do things. You're just like everybody else. Once you like them they take advantage of you. That's why I hate people. Why did I ever think you would be different?
Therapist (calm and confident): I can hear how angry and frustrated you are. Maybe you could try to help me to understand why you feel this way. I would never try to force you to do anything you didn't want to do. In fact, I'm only here to help you with what you want, not what I want.
Ms. Longo (in a calm tone): I know you're trying to help me. I just get this way sometimes. Like my father said, I was always unruly.

When the therapist explored what the patient meant by unruly, she learned that whenever Ms. Longo asserted her needs, wishes, or desires, she was either banished to her room for hours or severely criticized. Ms. Longo described her father as an isolated man who spent his leisure time in his room reading and her mother as an angry woman who spent much of her time watching TV. The therapist sensed that the parents wanted peace and quiet and to be left alone in their isolation.

As the patient described these family dynamics the nature of the transference became clearer. The parents, clearly depressed and unhappy, were unable to either recognize or respond to their daughter's needs. The father completely ignored his wife and daughter, and the mother projected her negative self-image and inadequacies onto her daughter while also displacing her anger at her husband onto Ms. Longo. Her mother was openly critical and demanding, and any expression of need, be it for attention or validation, was met with verbal abuse. Thus, in the transference the patient also viewed the therapist's responses as critical and demanding. In an effort to correct Ms. Longo's distortions, the therapist pointed out the legitimacy of her needs and interpreted the transference. The therapist also suggested that together they try to explore and understand what Ms. Longo was experiencing with the therapist rather than engaging in shouting matches that in her childhood at least ensured some interaction between mother and daughter. It was hoped that the use of such interventions would lead Ms. Longo to recognize that not everyone would respond to her as her parents had, thus opening up the possibility of new, more positive relationships. (Upon reflection and with the advantage of hindsight, it might also have been beneficial had the therapist directly interpreted Ms. Longo's attempts to engage the therapist in conflict as reflective of how she secured her mother's attention.)

Therapist: Maybe you were difficult for your parents because you had a mind of your own, and what they thought of as unruly was you just saying what you needed, and when you were unruly at least they were paying attention to you.

Ms. Longo: I spent hours by myself in my room watching TV. My mother only yelled at me to do chores and tell me I was lazy and ugly. My father would just yell at both of us to shut up and give him a little peace.

Therapist: Maybe you thought I was criticizing you when I brought up the topic of work. Instead of hearing that I want to help you with your work situation, you heard me say you're lazy for not getting a job.

Ms. Longo (nodding): Yes. I just fly off the handle.

Therapist: I understand. In the future maybe you could try to tell me if something I say upsets you or isn't clear. That way we could try to work it out.

The middle phase of treatment was difficult for both patient and therapist. Ms. Longo's job expectations were highly unrealistic. Although she had only basic bookkeeping skills, she "required" a private office, refused to work on a computer, and wanted to earn double her previous salary. The patient's insight was limited and she could not accept that her expectations were unrealistic and a form of resistance that reflected her sense of inadequacy and impaired self-esteem. The therapist felt frustrated and at an impasse with the patient's inflexibility and inability to consider other options such as computer training or lowering her salary requirements, and with no alternative, the therapist accepted where the patient was and together they searched the want ads.

Ms. Longo became frustrated in that the want ads did not specify the conditions that she insisted on. The therapist suggested that maybe she could at least try to secure interviews for positions that looked promising and then attempt to negotiate around her needs and priorities. The patient agreed to this, but due to her impulsiveness and inability to tolerate frustration, other aspects of the process were also problematic. For example, if she responded to an ad and was told the job was filled, she would slam down the phone, stating she didn't want the job anyway. If put on hold by an agency receptionist, she would hang up the phone, saying she had no patience to wait for these people. In these instances the therapist patiently explored Ms. Longo's reactions, corrected distortions, and suggested options for dealing with her frustrations.

Ms. Longo finally secured a job interview that went well enough that she was told she would be considered for the position. Unfortunately, she then called the company twice daily inquiring about the status of her application, to which they finally responded that the position had been filled. After reporting this to the therapist in the next session and expressing rage that the therapist had not helped her, Ms. Longo stormed out of the session and did not return for three weeks. The therapist left telephone voice messages that she was still committed to the patient, was leaving her session time open, and hoped that Ms. Longo would return.

Ms. Longo returned for the fourteenth session looking forlorn, defeated, and bedraggled. Her depression was evident.

Therapist: I can see that you're feeling discouraged and that you must be very disappointed that you didn't get the job. But you have to try to remember how hard you've been working both in here and in terms of getting a new job. You've really come a long way and should be pleased with your efforts.

Patient (crying for the first time): My mother just keeps screaming "You shouldn't have kept calling. You're crazy and it's your own fault. Nobody will ever give you a job."

Therapist: She certainly isn't helping the situation and we both know what she said isn't true.

Because of the patient's limited insight and sensitivity to criticism, the therapist suggested that Ms. Longo had continued to call the company only because she had wanted the job so badly. Ms. Longo responded that she probably would not have taken the job anyway, because the salary was too low. It took all the restraint that the therapist could muster not to lose her patience with Ms. Longo. Instead, the therapist suggested that maybe knowing that she might not accept the job made the disappointment a little easier for Ms. Longo to tolerate.

It is important to point out that during this phase of the treatment the therapist was vigilant about monitoring her predominately negative countertransference. Ms. Longo lacked insight into her problems and behavior, blamed others for her difficulties, and rejected the therapist's attempts at empathy or understanding. The therapist wanted to be helpful, was consistent in her acceptance of the patient, supplied Ms. Longo with concrete assistance, and provided a new and more positive object relationship. However, such efforts were frequently met with anger, devaluation, and dismissal, and resulted in the therapist's feeling used, abused, and at times virtually nonexistent, as though she functioned as a need-gratifying object rather than as a person in her own right. As a result, the therapist entertained fantasies of retaliating against the patient either by verbally abusing her or by terminating the treatment. Maybe then the patient would know that the therapist was also a person! Although painful and somewhat guilt provoking, the therapist acknowledged such feelings. Being able to admit to such sadistic fantasies led to an examination of these reactions and the recognition that what the therapist was feeling essentially replicated what Ms. Longo must have felt during her childhood. She did not exist as a separate person in the eyes of her parents but was only what they needed her to be, most notably the object of their disappointment, anger, and resentment. Ms. Longo communicated what her early experiences were like in the only way she could, that is, by inducing such feelings in the therapist. The therapist's recognition of what the patient had experienced and her need to replicate that experience, coupled with the therapist's acknowledgment of her sadistic fantasies, helped the therapist tolerate the patient's behavior rather than act out against her.

Over the next four sessions the therapist supported the patient's efforts to secure interviews and continued to help her develop strategies to control her impulses. For example, when Ms. Longo went for another interview, she agreed not to call about the status of her application. When she felt the urge to call, she was to distract herself with another activity and remind herself that appearing overly desirous of the job might make the future employer think she was desperate. Not calling actually gave her more control over the situation.

After a number of disappointments, Ms. Longo finally received a job offer, but it paid less than she wanted and required that she learn some basic computer skills, which the company would train her for. Ms. Longo was reluctant to accept the position, but was willing to at least discuss the positive and negatives. Her ambivalence about the position left her feeling anxious, overwhelmed, and needy. However, the therapist determined that it was her fear of being out of control that was most problematic but also something that the patient could actively work on. With the therapist's help, Ms. Longo realized that she was evaluating the job just as the employer was evaluating her, and she was not tied to the position just because she had accepted the offer. She now felt more in control and decided that she would try the job for a few days.

Although still upset about the salary, Ms. Longo thought that maybe she could use this job as a stepping stone. At least the job paid more than she had been earning. The therapist thought this was a very good way to look at the situation, at which point the patient voiced concerns about her lack of computer skills. While empathizing with how overwhelmed Ms. Longo felt about learning something new, the therapist suggested that she keep in mind that the person teaching her was not her critical mother but rather someone who was trying to help her learn a new skill. The patient was also encouraged to call the therapist if she felt overwhelmed and anxious and was given a list of times that the therapist would be available. The patient called four times daily over the next three days but maintained herself on the job.

Ms. Longo completed the first week of work but entered the next session angry and resentful, stating that she felt mistreated and thought that her supervisor was incompetent and unable to teach anybody anything. The therapist understood this as a transference reaction, whereby the patient was experiencing and reacting to the supervisor as though it were her mother and she defended against her feelings of vulnerability by blaming the supervisor. However, with exploration Ms. Longo was able to acknowledge that she felt frightened and inadequate, and feared that she would be fired. This was the first sign that the patient was developing some insight into her own thoughts and feelings and that she felt safe enough with the therapist to share her vulnerabilities. She continued to use projection but with support was able to recognize her own fears and anxieties.

The therapist feared that the second week of work might bring further disillusionment and new anxieties for the patient. They discussed difficulties that might arise and possible means for handling them. Also the therapist had Ms. Longo imagine how she might feel if problems developed, and reminded her that sometimes she had a tendency to overreact because of how her mother had treated her. The therapist encouraged Ms. Longo to think about what she was feeling and thinking and whether it was appropriate to the present situation before reacting immediately. The therapist hoped that this discussion would help contain the patient's impulse to either quit or become angry and argumentative, and further develop her capacity to distinguish her mother from others. Therapist and patient met twice during Ms. Longo's second week of work.

Termination Phase

The termination phase includes reviewing progress, and addressing termination and its implications, including resolving the patient–therapist relationship, and referral and/or follow-up.

Ms. Longo began the twenty-third session stating that she was feeling more comfortable at the job, particularly since her supervisor had complimented her conscientiousness and told her she was doing a good job. Ms. Longo also reported that she was keeping her distance from her co-workers but that no one seemed to mind. She found that learning the computer was continuing to cause her anxiety. The therapist was pleased for the patient, again reminded her of how much effort she had put into securing the position, and commended her for her persistence in light of how difficult the process had been. The therapist suggested that they could talk about what Ms. Longo might do to feel less anxious about learning the computer just as they had dealt with other things that made her feel nervous.

Therapist: Computers are complicated and there's a lot to learn. Can you think of any way to make it easier for you?

Ms. Longo: No. That's why I come to you.

Therapist: Well, you may not like this suggestion but there are many adult education classes for those of us who didn't grow up using computers.

Ms. Longo: I'm no kid. I'm not going to any school. Now you're talking stupid.

Therapist: I said I didn't think you'd like the suggestion, but why are you getting so upset?

Ms. Longo: I don't know but I knew what you would say. You'd say it was because I was afraid that I couldn't do it, but instead of being afraid I get mad.

Therapist: Well, you're right. That's exactly what I would say because we both know that sometimes when you get angry it's because you're afraid to let anybody see how you really feel. You believe that you can't do things and you're also worried that others will criticize or take advantage of you.

Ms. Longo: I know I'm not stupid but everyone always said I was.

Therapist: You certainly aren't stupid and look how well you're doing on the job. You've been complimented on your performance and your supervisor believes enough in your abilities to take the time to teach you the computer. And it was not everyone who said you were stupid.

Ms. Longo: That's true but I can't seem to remember it.

Therapist: We've worked hard together to help you recognize your very real abilities and to keep in mind that your parents' treatment of you had to do with them, not you. And yes, maybe when you were a child being angry was a good way to protect yourself, but as an adult it's often worked against you. Not everyone is going to put you down, take advantage of you, or criticize you.

The patient had only two remaining sessions. Due to the newness of her job and her need for continued support, Ms. Longo and the therapist agreed to meet every other week with the understanding that the patient could call at any time if she felt the need. The patient did not call nor did she come to the next scheduled appointment. When the therapist phoned to inquire what had happened, the patient said she wasn't coming in again. "The job is fine. I got what I wanted. There's no reason to come back." The therapist was shocked and angry. She had devoted much time and energy to this very difficult woman and was now being summarily dismissed. She was at a loss for what to say and ended by saying, "I hope everything works out well for you."

Considering the patient's behavior from a psychodynamic perspective can help to explain why Ms. Longo terminated in the way she did. She maintained a strong identification with her early caregivers, her aggression remained unneutralized, and she was unable to tolerate ambivalent feelings toward the therapist (Kernberg 1975). Although the therapist provided a new object relationship and a corrective emotional experience, Ms. Longo also had not separated either psychologically or physically from her parents, and thus she retreated back to what was familiar and safe

(Buie and Adler 1982). She had made progress in dealing with a discrete, circumscribed problem, but her internalized structure had not been modified.

With the help of her supervisor, the therapist accepted that the abrupt ending was probably the only way the patient could leave the treatment. Ms. Longo needed to control situations, dismiss others as she had felt dismissed, and could not tolerate dealing with the ambivalence she might be feeling about ending.

At the supervisor's direction the therapist waited two weeks and then called to see how Ms. Longo was faring. The patient seemed surprised and pleased that the therapist was still thinking about her, and reported that she was still on the job and liked the work itself, her boss seemed pleased with her performance, and her co-workers were keeping their distance. Things with her mother were back to "normal" now that she was working, but she was getting out of the house more and taking a computer course at the local high school. She even liked some of her classmates. The therapist concluded by saying she was happy that things were better and that if anything should come up again in the future Ms. Longo should not hesitate to call. She reminded Ms. Longo of how hard she had worked in her treatment and commented that it seemed to be paying off.

TECHNIQUES

In the initial phase of treatment, the therapist began with the patient's concerns, affording Ms. Longo control over the treatment situation, accepting her perception of the problem, and establishing some benefit that the patient might derive from the treatment (Goldstein and Noonan 1999). Patient and therapist established a common ground, or at least a beginning sense that they were working on the same goals and objectives, thus exemplifying the mutual, collaborative nature of the treatment (Allen et al. 1990). Additionally, the therapist identified triggers to Ms. Longo's anxiety, and suggested and role-played ways that the patient might better cope with her fears (Linehan 1993). The therapist also validated and mirrored the patient's strengths, tolerated her anger and hostility while remaining neutral and nondefensive, confronted and interpreted distortions, and offered support and guidance.

Once the patient's anxiety was more manageable, the middle-phase work began. The therapist maintained a high level of activity, focused on the patient's inability to return to work and the underlying issues impacting on this problem, and directed Ms. Longo's efforts toward exploring the problem area and developing problem-solving techniques (Goldstein and Noonan 1999). Although the therapist initially attempted to confront the patient's unrealistic expectations about a future position, it soon became clear that this would not be possible and that the therapist would need to accept where the patient was and work within this context. Also, the therapist continued to confront transference distortions by encouraging Ms. Longo to talk about what she was feeling rather than acting on it (Goldstein 1990), and the therapist continued to monitor her own countertransference reactions, so as to not retaliate. Additionally, the therapist role modeled more appropriate ways of managing frustration, interpreted the transference to the supervisor, validated the patient's beginning efforts at insight, offered guidance and suggestions, and continued to function as a benign good object (Goldstein and Noonan 1999). Most importantly, the therapist continued to reiterate the benefit to the patient of altering her characteristic ways of thinking, feeling, and behaving.

The termination phase included techniques that emphasized strengths and accomplishments and supported the patient's progress in developing impulse control and frustration tolerance (Goldstein and Noonan 1999). For example, the therapist explored anxieties that might arise during the patient's second week of work and suggested how Ms. Longo might deal with her fears and conflicts. The therapist also pointed out the connection between the patient's early life experiences and her difficulties in managing her thoughts, feelings, and behaviors. Although the therapist wanted to address the patient–therapist relationship, the patient prematurely terminated. With the help of her supervisor, the therapist gained some understanding of what might be driving the patient's behavior. The therapist concluded the treatment on a positive note, through both the follow-up telephone call and the offer of further treatment if the patient should ever so desire.

CONCLUSION

As the Longo case demonstrates, the treatment of borderline patients can be particularly difficult. When such patients seek treatment, it is generally for symptom relief, problem solving, or at the insistence of others—not for personality change (Kaplan and Sadock 1998). It is important that the focus of the work be directed toward the patient's specific psychosocial problem while also being flexible and responsive to the patient's needs. Underlying conflicts or difficulties are addressed only to the degree that they are interfering with the individual's ability to resolve the identified problem (Goldstein and Noonan 1999). Initially, it is important for the therapist to join with the patient's perception of the problem and identify some benefit that the patient can derive from being involved in psychotherapy. As the work progresses the therapist helps the patient develop new problem-solving skills and gain some understanding that altering characteristic ways of thinking, feeling, or behaving can be beneficial (Heller and Northcut 1996). The therapeutic relationship can be used to correct distortions and to model more adaptive behaviors. Often borderline patients need concrete advice and guidance in addition to the more widely accepted techniques of interpretation and insight development (Goldstein 1990). Finally, and most important, therapists must be alert to and able to manage the intense countertransference reactions that are associated with the borderline syndrome.

REFERENCES

Akiskal, H. S., Chen, S. E., Davis, G. C., et al. (1985). Borderline: an adjective in search of a noun. *Journal of Clinical Psychiatry* 46:41–48.

Allen, J. G., Gabbard, G. O., Newsom, G. W., and Coyne, L. (1990). Detecting patterns of change in patient's collaboration within individual psychotherapy sessions. *Psychotherapy* 27:522–530.

American Psychiatric Association. (1994). *Diagnostic and Statistical Manual of Mental Disorders*, 4th ed. Washington, DC: American Psychiatric Association.

Andrulonis, P. A., Glueck, B. C., Stoebel, C. F., et al. (1981). Organic brain dysfunction and the borderline syndrome. *Psychiatric Clinics of North America* 4:47–66.

Beck, A. T., and Freeman, A. (1990). *Cognitive Therapy of Personality Disorders.* New York: Guilford.

Blum, N., and Pfohl, B. (1998). Personality disorders. In *Advances in Mental Health Research: Implications for Practice*, ed. J. Williams and K. Ell, pp. 203–216. Washington, DC: NASW Press.

Briere, J., and Zaidi, L. Y. (1989). Sexual abuse histories and sequelae in female psychiatric room patients. *American Journal of Psychiatry* 146: 1602–1606.

Brown, L. (1992). A feminist critique of personality disorders. In *Personality and Psychopathology: Feminist Reappraisals*, ed. L. Brown and M. Ballou, pp. 206–228. New York: Guilford.

Buie, D. H., and Adler, G. (1982). The definitive treatment of the borderline personality. *International Journal of Psychoanalytic Psychotherapy* 9:51–87.

Clarkin, J. F., Yeomans, F. E., and Kernberg, O. F. (1999). *Psychotherapy for Borderline Personality.* New York: Wiley.

Goldstein, E. (1990). *Borderline Disorders: Clinical Models and Techniques.* New York: Guilford.

Goldstein, E., and Noonan, M. (1999). *Short-Term Treatment and Social Work Practice: An Integrative Perspective.* New York: Free Press.

Gunderson, J. G. (1984). *Borderline Personality Disorder.* Washington, DC: American Psychiatric Press.

Heller, N. R., and Northcut, T. B. (1996). Utilizing cognitive-behavioral techniques in psychodynamic practice with clients diagnosed as borderline. *Clinical Social Work Journal* 24:203–215.

Hertz, P. (1996). Borderline and narcissistic personality disorders. In *Inside Out and Outside In: Psychodynamic Clinical Theory and Practice in Contemporary Multicultural Contexts*, ed. J. Berzoff, L. Flanagan, and P. Hertz, pp. 299–364. Northvale, NJ: Jason Aronson.

Horowitz, M. (1991). Short-term dynamic therapy of stress response syndromes. In *Handbook of Short-Term Dynamic Psychotherapy*, ed. P. Crits-Christoph and J. P. Barber, pp. 166–199. New York: Basic Books.

Kaplan, H., and Sadock, B. (1998). *Synopsis of Psychiatry*. Baltimore, MD: Williams & Wilkins.

Kernberg, O. (1975). *Borderline Conditions and Pathological Narcissism*. New York: Jason Aronson.

Kolden, G. G. (1991). The generic model of psychotherapy: an empirical investigation of patterns of process and outcome relationships. *Psychotherapy Research* 1:62–73.

Koss, M. P., and Shiang, J. (1994). Research of brief psychotherapy. In *Handbook of Psychotherapy and Behavior Change*, ed. A. E. Bergin and S. L. Garfield, pp. 664–700. New York: Wiley.

Layton, M. (1995). Emerging from the shadows. *Family Networker* 19(3): 35–41.

Linehan, M. M. (1993). *Cognitive-Behavioral Treatment of Borderline Personality Disorder*. New York: Guilford.

Marziali, E. (1992). Borderline personality disorder: diagnosis, etiology, and treatment. *Smith College Studies in Social Work* 62(3):205–227.

McGlashan, T. H. (1986). The Chestnut Lodge follow-up study, III: Long-term outcomes of borderline personalities. *Archives of General Psychiatry* 43:20–30.

Mendez-Villarrubia, J. M., and LaBruzza, A. (1994). Issues in the assessment of Puerto Rican and other Hispanic clients, including *ataques de nervios*. In *Women of Color: Integrating Ethnic and Gender Identities in Psychotherapy*, ed. L. Comas-Diaz and B. Greene, pp. 141–176. New York: Guilford.

Noonan, M. (1998). Understanding the "difficult" patient from a dual person perspective. *Clinical Social Work Journal* 26(3):129–143.

Paris, J., and Frank, H. (1989). Perceptions of parental bonding in borderline patients. *American Journal of Psychiatry* 142:15–21.

Pope, H. G., Jonas, J., Hudson, J., et al. (1983). The validity of *DSM-III* borderline personality disorder. *Archives of General Psychiatry* 40:23–30.

Siever, L. J., and Davis, K. L. (1991). A psychobiological perspective on the personality disorders. *American Journal of Psychiatry* 4:1647–1648.

Smith, B. L. (1992). An interpersonal approach to the diagnosis of borderline personality disorder. In *Borderline Personality Disorder: Clinical and Empirical Perspectives*, ed. J. Clarkin, E. Marziali, and H. Munroe-Blu, pp. 161–195. New York: Guilford.

Waldinger, R., and Gunderson, J. G. (1984). Completed psychotherapies with borderline patients. *American Journal of Psychotherapy* 88:190–202.

Weston, D. (1990). Toward a revised theory of borderline object relations: contributions of empirical research. *International Journal of Psycho-Analysis* 71:661–693.

———— (1991). Cognitive behavioral interventions in the psychoanalytic psychotherapy of borderline personality disorders. *Clinical Psychology Review* 11:211–230.

Winston, A., Pollack, J., Samstag, L.W., et al. (1994). Brief psychotherapy of personality disorders. *American Journal of Psychiatry* 151:190–194.

Zanarini, M. C., Gunderson, J. G., Marino, M. F., et al. (1989). Childhood experiences of borderline patients. *Comprehensive Psychiatry* 30:149–156.

CHAPTER FOURTEEN

A Brief Treatment Approach to Bereavement

BARBARA T. DANE

THEORETICAL OVERVIEW
AND TREATMENT PERSPECTIVE

Grief, defined as a natural and normal response to loss (James and Cherry 1988), is a pervasive and fundamental aspect of the human experience central to clinical work. For each of the more than two million deaths that occur annually in the United States, bereaved family members and friends are all at risk of negative effects on their physical and mental health (Stroebe et al. 1993). The death of a loved one is complicated for mourners when it is a result of violence or suffering, often disproportionately experienced by persons of color who live in poverty-stricken urban neighborhoods (Polednak 1989, Schilling et al. 1992). As Stroebe and colleagues (1993) assert, "Survivors of such terrible losses are particularly vulnerable to long-term adverse effects and are in special need of care and support" (p. 3). Although not all persons who experience the death of a loved one require or seek psychotherapy, some individuals have great difficulty coping with bereavement. They may experience a sustained loss of social or occupational functioning, prolonged or severe depression, or intense anger, guilt, anxiety, or self-blame. Others may appear not to grieve at all but may still show maladaptive changes in their lives, including increased alcohol consumption, social withdrawal, irritability, or a studious neglect of any reminders of the deceased. Psychotherapy can be helpful for these individuals (Eells 1995).

Grieving individuals and families must confront their mourning within a death-denying culture. Given the centrality of grief as a universal response to loss, clinicians' awareness of short-term treatment interventions for grief disorders is essential and can provide bereaved patients with support aimed at assisting them in responding to the issues surrounding the loss. Recognition of the death by those who provide support and comfort is necessary to resolve and adapt to the loss; otherwise, mourners may have significant difficulty grieving and resolving their loss.

Clarification of the terms *grief, mourning,* and *bereavement* as used in this chapter, will help distinguish the application of these concepts in the clinical setting. Grief refers to the painful emotions and thoughts experienced in connection with the death of a significant other. Mourning is the developmental process of adapting to the loss of a loved one; it entails moving from a state of grieving to one of nongrieving. It is characterized by varying degrees of painful grief and a range of intense emotions such as of shock, panic, anxiety, sadness, and anger, among others. The mourning process involves the task of working through these feelings. The mourner must accept and resolve the loss and adapt to a changed life. Bereavement refers to the social, cultural, and interpersonal status of an individual who has lost someone important (Piper et al. 1992).

Freud (1917) presented the first psychodynamic model of grief. According to Freud, the grieving individual is unable to immediately relinquish the tie to the deceased and thus maintains it through a process of identification. The bereaved directs psychic energy inward, internalizing an image of the deceased in order to maintain the relationship. With the passage of time and the expenditure of considerable psychic energy, the individual gradually relinquishes the strong tie to the deceased and is able to initiate new love relationships. Abnormal or unresolved mourning occurs when the individual is unable to accomplish the task of disengagement from the deceased. A key obstruction occurs when the relationship to the deceased is characterized by ambivalence. The bereaved might have loved the deceased but also might have unconsciously directed feelings of anger or hatred toward that person. The death catalyzes feelings of guilt as individuals irrationally blame themselves for the loss.

Bowlby (1980), a British psychiatrist and psychoanalyst, studied human separation and loss and developed his well-known theory of attachment. He rejected Freud's emphasis on psychic energy, stressing instead the bereaved's attachment to the deceased. According to Bowlby, striving to recover the lost person is more significant in grief than is the redirection of psychic energy inward through identification with the deceased. He identified four main phases of grief. Initially, the bereaved "protests" the loss, then begins an agitated search for the deceased. When the search fails, as it inevitably will, despair and depression set in. Eventually, the bereaved forms new interpersonal attachments.

Life-Cycle Loss

Loss is experienced at all stages of the individual and family life cycle. It is understood and resolved in differing ways, dependent on a variety of factors such as personality, age and life stage, social support, previous loss experiences, and circumstances related to the loss. The nature of the loss and its symbolic meaning to the mourner, whether expected or unexpected, normative or non-normative, are important factors contributing to the loss experience (Walsh and McGoldrick 1991). Rando (1984, 1986) categorized loss as physical or psychosocial. Physical losses are tangible losses, including persons or objects evident to others—as, for example, the death of a loved one or the loss of cherished belongings. Psychosocial losses are symbolic, intangible losses not necessarily evident to others.

The timing of the loss in the life cycle and the opportunity to prepare for a loss are significant factors affecting the experience. An expected, normative loss is the death of one's parents, inasmuch as children generally outlive their parents. The normative timing of such a loss is during one's adult years. If the death occurs earlier in the life cycle, it is viewed as a non-normative loss because it occurs unexpectedly relative to time. Prolonged mourning responses may follow such an untimely death. Survivor guilt is often present in this kind of loss (Walsh and McGoldrick 1991).

The role status of the deceased member is an important dynamic in adaptation to the loss. The more pivotal the role of the deceased within the family unit, the more difficult the adjustment the surviving family members will experience. Both the functions of the deceased's role in the family and the level of emotional dependence on that family member will influence the reactions to the loss (Herz 1980). If the roles assigned to the deceased were pivotal to the family's functioning, reorganization of the family system will be more difficult. Vess and colleagues (1985) suggest that "child-present" families will experience more stress than "child-absent" families because child-rearing demands and economic issues will tax the family system. Every loss causes a degree of disruption and pain, but the more profound the loss is, the more intense are the disruption and the affective reaction. Further, every significant loss is experienced as a loss of oneself and as an end (O'Connor 1984). As a result, loss threatens our sense of survival, always causing some disruption in our lives.

Grief reactions following a child's death are prolonged and complicated for both the parents and the surviving children. Since parents are consumed with their own grief, the surviving children are often overlooked and their needs go unmet. Surviving children gain a new status, that of a survivor, which can impose a significant hardship for them. Krell and Rabkin (1979) noted a number of maladaptive reactions seen in families following a child's death. A surviving child may try to replace the dead sibling, taking on special attributes of the deceased. "The absent child thus remains in some sense alive, a misbegotten restoration protecting the family from having to fully face their loss" (p. 473). This can impede the child's own sense of identity as she or he tries to represent not one but two children to the parents. Such children may become "precious children," bound to the parents who have become vigilant and overprotective. Or they may be "haunted children," who collude in the family's conspiracy of silence, where little is ever said about the deceased child. Family members may suppress details of their child's death and their feelings about the loss when significant guilt and shame are present. These family interaction patterns impede the psychosocial development of the surviving children and the mourning experience for the entire family.

Marital relations are also affected and strained following a child's death. Each partner has had a different relationship with the child and, most likely, their methods for coping with the loss will also differ. Gender differences appear to account for the typically greater emotional expressiveness shown by mothers than by fathers over the loss of a child (Bohannon 1990, Rando 1986). Rando (1986) suggests that spouses are out of sync with one another.

Grief Reactions

Horowitz (1986) coined the term *stress response syndrome* to label a set of intrusive and "omissive" experiences associated with psychological trauma. Intrusions are images, thoughts, or emotions that encroach on an individual's conscious experience. In grief, intrusions may take the form of intensely disturbing images of the deceased as endangered and calling out for help, or as physically damaged. The bereaved may also experience transient auditory hallucinations of the deceased, such as hearing their name called. Additional intrusive phenomena may include self-blame, guilt, mental replaying of events related to the death, unexpected outbursts of anger or tears, ruminations about what one might have done differently to help the deceased, and misperceiving others as the deceased. Omissions are symptoms indicating deflections of normal conscious awareness, which include emotional numbness, forgetfulness (including forgetting parts of the relationship with the deceased), distractibility, depersonalization or derealization experiences, depressed mood, poor concentration, and confusion.

There is no consensus as to the symptom patterns that distinguish grief disorders from normal grief (Middleton et al. 1993). In large part, this lack is due to the high degree of variability in individuals' responses to bereavement. In a review of the empirical literature, Wortman and Silver (1989) found that many individuals do not experience intense distress following a loss and do not develop symptoms later in life. In fact, following a loss, individuals who have fewer and less intense symptoms show the best adaptation months and years later (Parkes and Weiss 1983, Vachon et al. 1982).

Due to the range and intensity of emotions experienced by the bereaved, grief reactions are both physically and psychologically taxing. Rando (1984) suggests "grief is work," with physical and emotional strain. She describes the psychological reactions to grief and proposes three phases: avoidance, confrontation, and reestablishment.

Considerable variability as to the length of a grief response has run an interesting gamut over the last fifty years. Early theorists and researchers assumed that the bereaved could just adjust to a loss in a matter of a few weeks or months (Engel 1961, Lindemann 1944). More recent research, however, shows that depression, anxiety, and rumination about the loss can extend for years. Vachon and her colleagues (1982) classified 38 percent of widows as highly distressed one year after the death of their spouse; 26 percent remained so after two years. Similarly, Parkes and Weiss (1983) found that 40 percent of their sample of widows and widowers were moderately to severely anxious two to four years after the loss. In a long-term study of adaptation to major life stressors, including bereavement, Tait and Silver (1989) reported that more than half of their sample continued to ruminate about losses that had occurred decades earlier. Forty percent still searched for the meaning of the death.

Most researchers and clinicians agree that deviant forms of grief exist. For example, Parkes and Weiss (1983) identified chronic, delayed, and inhibited grief. Chronic grief is characterized by intense distress beginning just after the news of the death and extending for a long period of time, perhaps years. Delayed grief, which Parkes (1991) considers relatively rare, is a pattern in which the emotional upheaval of grief begins after a period of apparent emotional quiescence. Inhibited grief, also rare, is characterized by the absence of intense emotions accompanied by other signs of maladjustment, such as intense overactivity, somatic symptoms, lengthy social withdrawal, and/or depression without a sense of a loss. As noted earlier, many individuals who show few signs of distress immediately after a loss continue to function well years later. Therefore, clinicians should not precipitously conclude that a patient with a recent loss is repressing grief if painful affects are not experienced. Instead of psychopathology, these responses may indicate resilience to stress.

The major conclusion to be drawn from the above review is that responses to bereavement are highly individualized and variable, and that some individuals do respond maladaptively to loss, sometimes for extended periods of time and at great cost to their well-being and to that of others. To help clinicians identify the latter group, two symptom clusters are suggested: depressive and psychological trauma. Depressive symptoms include guilt, dejected mood, loss of interest in one's usual activities, irritability, poor concentration, crying spells, and low energy. Positive self-esteem may be left intact more often in bereavement than in depression (Freud 1917). Symptoms of trauma include the psychological intrusions and omissions cited earlier as characteristic of a stress response syndrome. An additional symptom often observed in bereaved individuals is the emergence of identification processes. It is noteworthy that bereaved individuals may initially present with complaints of anxiety or depression that they do not connect to their loss. During the initial session it may become apparent to the clinician that these symptoms are related to loss.

There is no diagnosis of grief disorder in the *DSM-IV*, although bereavement is listed as an Axis V code. Most individuals will meet diagnostic criteria for one or more of the Axis I diagnoses: adjustment disorder, major depressive disorder, and posttraumatic stress disorder, depending on the circumstances of the death and the individual's response to it.

As stated earlier, many people suffering from the death of a loved one do not request psychotherapy. When clinicians assess a patient and observe that internal obstacles to mourning are present, psychotherapy should be considered. Time-limited treatment models such as those of Dolan (1991), Mann (1973), Sifneos (1979), Davanloo (1978), and Malan (1976), encompassing both the traditional emphasis on the unconscious and conflictual components and use of interpretation and object relationships, may be particularly appropriate for symptom manifestations related to grief. Goldstein and Noonan's (1999) integrative short-term treatment (ISTT) provides depth and flexibility for treating many patients experiencing grief over the death of a loved one. In all these treatments, patients are provided with the opportunity to reexperience loss and examine how they and others attempt to respond to it.

Short-term therapies, ranging from twelve to twenty-five weekly sessions or other time variations, are here to stay for a number of economic and conceptual reasons. Although it is not a panacea, the objectives of symptom relief and a greater tolerance of ambivalent feelings toward the deceased are within the framework of short-term work.

INCLUSION/EXCLUSION CRITERIA

Most bereaved individuals with adequate motivation and verbal skills to express their thoughts and feelings are appropriate for short-term treatment. Exclusion criteria include individuals with psychotic or dementing disorders and those with primary substance abuse or dependence disorders. Suicidal, severely depressed, and psychotic patients may need to be hospitalized if they represent an imminent danger to themselves or others. If treated on an outpatient basis, they are offered a psychopharmacological intervention and are seen for individual supportive sessions until they no longer constitute a danger. Whereas these sessions need only last ten to fifteen minutes each, for some patients they need to be conducted on a daily basis. Those with substance abuse disorders may be appropriate for treatment when the abuse pattern has been controlled. Many individuals with grief disorders use small or moderate amounts of alcohol or non-prescription mood-altering substances in an attempt to self-medicate for the intrusive symptoms of grief. Such patterns need not, in themselves, exclude the individual from treatment but might be explored during therapy. For those patients with current substance abuse problems, a referral to AA can be suggested. After the symptoms that make these patients unsuitable have been counteracted, they can be reconsidered for treatment.

Individuals with prominent personality disorders may do best in ongoing work. Those with borderline or narcissistic personality disorders, in particular, are generally not appropriate for brief treatment. Individuals who are experiencing an uncomplicated mourning process can be offered support and problem-solving strategies through individual crisis intervention sessions. They may also be referred to community agencies. For example, if the death was due to sudden infant death syndrome (SIDS), the patient is offered a referral to a SIDS support group; if the death was due to acquired immune deficiency syndrome (AIDS), the patient is referred to the AIDS Network, which offers support groups for survivors.

TREATMENT GOALS

Clinicians who initially assess patients attempt to understand the meaning of the patient's complaints. By the time the patient appears, symptomatology is usually well developed. If the patient's history reveals significant losses, a pathological grief process may be suspected. More is needed, however, to make an accurate assessment of the problem and recommend appropriate treatment. A knowledge of risk factors and indicators that are independent of symptomatology is required.

Worden (1982) translates the processes of mourning into four tasks that can serve as guides to short-term work with the bereaved. The first task is to accept the reality of the loss and entails coming to believe that reunion with the deceased is impossible. Worden relates the accomplishment of this task to Bowlby's (1980) initial stage of protest and open expression of angry striving to retrieve the lost object. Thus, Worden agrees with Bowlby that an initial denial of the fact, meaning, or irreversibility of the loss is normal and that only if this stage of not believing becomes protracted is the process pathologic.

The second task of mourning, according to Worden, is to experience the pain associated with the loss. Again, consistent with Bowlby, Worden posits that the open expression of sadness and anger is a normal part of mourning, whereas the avoidance of the pain predisposes the mourner to pathologic grief. "Sooner or later, some of those who avoid all conscious grieving, break down usually with some form of depression" (Bowlby 1980, as cited in Worden 1982, p. 14).

Worden's third task of mourning is to adjust to an environment in which the deceased is missing. When mourners fail to accomplish this task, they do not adapt to the loss. Rather, they promote their own helplessness. "Many survivors resent having to develop new skills and to take on roles themselves that were formerly performed by their spouses" (Worden 1982, pp. 14–15). Tahka (1984) emphasizes the mourner's inability to perform the functions for him- or herself. Worden suggests that the mourner is unwilling to do so because of resentment.

The fourth task is to withdraw emotional energy and reinvest it in another relationship. This task is almost identical to Freud's (1917) characterization of the normal mourning process as "one of withdrawal of the libido from this [lost] object and transference of it to a new one" (p. 249). The failure to accomplish this task is reflected in the mourner "holding on to the past attachment rather than going onto and forming new ones" (Worden 1982, p. 16). Worden traces this failure to an avoidance of new relationships based on the wish to avoid a repetition of the pain if another loss occurs. He also finds that guilt and disloyalty to the memory of the deceased contribute to the avoidance of new relationships. Although Worden acknowledges the difficulties of the four tasks of mourning, especially the fourth one, he emphasizes that they can be successfully accomplished and that they are part of normal mourning.

Within a short-term treatment paradigm, various treatment methods have been described. Cognitive "regrief" (Melges and De Maso 1980) emphasizes guided imagery for reliving, revising, and revisiting scenes of loss, for example, the funeral. Ramsey and DeGroot (1984) have used the behavioral techniques of flooding and prolonged exposure to stimuli associated with the loss. Volkan (1985) has used an approach that includes identifying linking objects. This approach includes reminders that link the person to the deceased, such as emotionally reliving the circumstances of the death and visiting the grave site. The interpretive part of Raphael's (1983) approach and the approaches of Melges and De Maso, Ramsey and DeGroot, and Volkan constitute brief therapy because they are aimed at identifying and removing obstacles to the mourning process.

Family Intervention

When working with families who have young children, family drawings can be a valuable tool in treatment (Schumacher 1984). Asking the family to draw a picture of the family before and after the death can enhance an understanding of the impact of the death on the family unit. This technique can be particularly useful for children, since their drawings often communicate alliances and feelings among family members. Sessions with parents may allow the unfolding of toxic issues and help the therapist gain an understanding of the parents' perception of the children's adaptation to the loss and the degree of shame and guilt that the parents may be experiencing. Normalizing such feelings of guilt for the parents can be useful, since they often view it as pathological (Miles and Demi 1991–1992).

Sessions with the children can provide an opportunity to explore feelings that children fear may upset their parents. It is important to allow siblings the opportunity to explore guilt they may experience in surviving a sibling's death. Exploring fantasies about causing the sibling's death and fears about their own mortality is important. Using therapeutic play activities for children under age 11 can permit the child to enact and ultimately to resolve ambivalent feelings experienced toward the deceased family member (Minuchin et al. 1992).

Rituals give the family a shared activity where open emotional expression and support are encouraged, permitting the family members to acknowledge their loss publicly (Imber-Black 1991). They are particularly useful on holidays and anniversaries of the death or birth of the deceased family member. "Besides helping to resolve contradictions, face anxiety, and strong emotions, rituals support transitions" (Imber-Black et al. 1988, p. 19).

Issues that can be adapted to short-term treatment associated with both initial and transitional stages are described by Horowitz and colleagues (1984) in their time-limited psychodynamic approach. The objective is to identify and resolve conflicts (obstacles) related to the mourning process and maladaptive relationship patterns. Themes activated by the loss are explored by means of catharsis, confrontation of current resistances, and interpretation of defensive styles, warded-off ideas, and repressed emotions. An individual therapy method that was developed to treat depression, including that which is part of an abnormal grief reaction, is the interpersonal therapy of Klerman and colleagues (1984). This approach is focused and time limited. It attends to current symptoms and their interpersonal context and attempts to free the patient from a maladaptive attachment to the lost person. In contrast to psychodynamic therapy, it does not focus on internal unconscious components of the intrapsychic conflict. Another individual therapy method for pathologic grief is outlined by Worden (1982). Its goal is to identify and resolve the conflicts of separation that preclude the completion of mourning tasks. Worden advocates a variety of techniques to serve this purpose, including the Gestalt "empty chair" method, role-playing psychodrama, focusing on "linking objects," and more traditional forms of interpretation.

Worden (1982) outlines techniques associated with grief interventions, where the goal is helping people who are experiencing normal grief reactions to complete the various tasks of mourning within a short-term model. The Widow-to-Widow Program of Phyllis Silverman (1969) is similar in purpose. One of a number of well-organized self-help and mutual help programs, Silverman's contribution is based on the assumption that someone who has experienced and adapted well to loss is potentially an ideal caregiver for the bereaved. The program has followed a public health, preventive approach. Recently (three to six weeks) but not immediately bereaved widows are personally contacted by another widow with an offer of assistance and friendship. Help in finding a job, sorting out finances, and rearing children is commonly provided. The program grew from an initial pilot project in the Boston area to a national and international network. Like the therapy approaches earlier described, this treatment approach advocates individual rather than group contacts at the initial stage. The widows are regarded as nonreceptive to group counseling until several months after their losses. This conclusion was also reached by Vachon and her colleagues (1982).

In practice, short-term intervention with bereaved persons involves the use of specific personal and behavioral change methods over a short period of time, with the focus of positive change in the patient's current life. Short-term treatment with bereaved person using the ISTT model (Goldstein and Noonan 1999) includes clinical interventions that are directed toward a range of methods and interventive techniques during the beginning, middle, and ending phases. In fulfilling these activities, the clinician becomes in many ways an educator; he or she is also an expert problem solver (Nezu 1989) guiding patients in systematic ways of coping with grief.

CASE ILLUSTRATION: PHASES OF TREATMENT

Beginning Phase: Sessions 1 to 5

Bowlby (1980) and Parkes (1971) both state that mourning is finished when a person completes the final mourning phase of restitution. It is impossible to set a definitive date. One benchmark of a completed grief reaction is when the person is able to think of the deceased without pain. There is always a sense of sadness when you think about the deceased person you have loved. Grieving, however, begins to dissipate the intensity and the wrenching quality of the sadness.

To help the survivors grieve the death of a loved one, four overall goals need to be considered:

1. Increase the reality of the loss.
2. Help the patient deal with both expressed and latent affect.
3. Help the patient overcome various impediments to readjustment after the death.
4. Encourage the patient to make a healthy emotional withdrawal from the deceased and to feel comfortable reinvesting that emotion in other relationships (Worden 1982).

Within a short-term treatment paradigm utilizing the ISTT framework, a careful but quick assessment of the client's personal, psychological, social, and spiritual/religion resources is undertaken. Assessing symptoms, both conscious and unconscious, that the patient uses to adapt to the loss gives the therapist a way to view the presenting problem. The first phase of treatment begins to focus on the relationship to the inner representation of the deceased as central to the working through of loss. This phase may include the following aspects: (1) who the person was; (2) the nature of the attachment; (3) the mode of death; (4) the historical antecedents; (5) personality variables; and (6) social, religious, spiritual, and cultural norms. Encouraging the person to talk about the death, how it happened, who told them about it, where they were, and if there was a funeral or service, is an intervention geared to engagement and problem identification. Many people need these aspects of the experience of loss in their minds before they come to full awareness of what has happened. "Giving sorrow words" throughout the treatment process is cathartic and helps the therapist do a holistic biopsychosocial spiritual assessment. The focus on adaptation to the loss, as well as expressing a range of feelings of anxiety, guilt, helplessness, and anger, can have a restorative effect (Wells 1994). Implicit in the short-term helping process is the belief that change is not likely to ensue from a concentrated focus on a single, significant problem in living. In this case, it is coping with the death of a spouse.

Mrs. Maxton is a 67-year-old widow with two adult sons, Paul, 32, and Seth, 27. Both sons are married and the elder son has a 6-year-old son, Andrew. Mrs. Maxton was referred by the American Cancer Society for fifteen sessions under a grant sponsored by the organization. An active member of their fund-raising endeavors, Mrs. Maxton became withdrawn and tearful, and experienced moments of uncontrollable crying when she would come bimonthly to volunteer at the agency. Her husband died about nine months ago after prostate surgery. The director of patient services knew Mrs. Maxton and told her about their therapy program of which she had some awareness. She responded positively to the director's interest. Within a week Mrs. Maxton called me and we arranged a mutually convenient appointment.

Mrs. Maxton was a well-groomed, petite woman who peered over her eyeglasses. She walked with an unsteady gait and conveyed an apparent unease as she related her anger toward the medical staff for their callous treatment of her husband. During the first four sessions, Mrs. Maxton cried uncontrollably. She had moments of sobbing and some-times gasped for air as she recalled the last three months before her husband's death. She felt like she was on a roller coaster. She had experienced her husband as a tender, kind, loving, and generous man. She conveyed their relationship in an idyllic way. I chose not to challenge her idealization at this time. Although 72 years of age, Mr. Maxton worked as a stockbroker and was described as healthy. He retired six months prior to his death. The first three months were described by Mrs. Maxton as a flurry of activities. They had numerous retirement parties to attend for her husband. Her favorite was when her grandson made a speech about the love he felt for his grandparents, in particular for "Poppi." Three weeks in Europe combined with a cruise had been a way to begin another chapter in their lives.

Mrs. Maxton spoke of her yearning to be with her husband and her dreams of their retirement years during the initial three to four sessions. As she revealed these wishes, hopes, and memories, she interjected her anger at her husband's physician for not monitoring him more closely the last few days postsurgery. She repeatedly asked me if I thought she would get over this deep resentment she had toward Dr. Wilson. I acknowledged her strong feelings of hurt and disappointment, and suggested they were not inappropriate, and we could listen to them together. She was unaware that her anger kept her from feeling the deep pain of her loss and her anger toward her husband for leaving her alone. The tenor of the sessions changed markedly when we explored the significance of her anger, increasing her emotional readiness to work on other early relationships.

Mrs. Maxton reported in the fifth session that her mother had died when she was 17 years of age. Her younger sister and she had become closer after her mother's death. She never felt close to her mother and does not remember having the feelings she presently experiences since the death of her husband. There was a vagueness around the mourning of her mother's death and father's, which occurred twelve years later when she was 29. She had no memory of sitting shiva for either parent. This was striking, as Mrs. Maxton is a religious person who attends synagogue and observes the Jewish holidays.

I explored her relationship with her parents, both of whom died of cancer. She remembered them suffering for a number of years and feels guilty that she was relieved when they died. She remembered traveling hours back and forth every Sunday to visit her father while her husband entertained the children in the backyard of her parents' home so the noise would not upset her father. The clinician explored her memories and feelings surrounding her parents' deaths and wondered how she coped. In stark contrast to her present loss, she conveyed a detachment indicating some unresolved mourning. I wondered if she ever thought about her parents' illness and death and if she talked to anyone about the experience. She felt she did not want to burden her husband and children, or her sister, whom she sees infrequently. When they do have an annual family reunion, "that's the last thing I want to discuss."

This unresolved mourning is a critical aspect of work. Although some awareness of past and present is essential to facilitate mourning in brief treatment, in-depth exploration of the primary objects is countertherapeutic. However, working with Mrs. Maxton's present intense anger was helpful in relieving her earlier guilt and giving her permission to feel the anger. Referring patients to a widow-to-widow group can be helpful.

Middle Phase: Sessions 6 to 11

Mrs. Maxton freely talked about her loneliness and feelings of abandonment. "Why did God have to take Murray so fast? Who do I turn to now?" she repeated.

Her initial rage at the medical system abated as she explored her naïveté in writing checks and reviewing her monthly bank statements. "I don't know why Murray kept me in the dark." This seemed to be the first mild anger that Mrs. Maxton expressed toward her husband. I acknowledged her feeling of anger at him and she gave me a deep penetrating look. "Only because I like you and feel okay with you can I show you the dark side of me."

This seemed to be a turning point in the treatment. The next few weeks, Mrs. Maxton revealed her husband's emotional and verbal assaults toward her in their married life. Her entire posture changed from appearing hunched and small to sitting up tall in the chair, using lots of hand gestures. It was like a valve was released and permission was given to do a life review.

Mrs. M.: I could never say anything to Murray when he asked what I did all day.

Therapist: Sounds like your feelings were hurt. Did you have any thoughts about what you would like to say?

Mrs. M.: "You think you're high and mighty because you make so much money. Who washes your dirty shirt collars and stained underwear?"

Therapist: If Murray was sitting in here now, what would he say?

Mrs. M.: Nothing. He would be shocked that his little lady had a voice. Sometimes I wonder why I'm crying. I should feel relieved. No more sarcastic remarks, no more dirty clothes to wash, no more superficial dinner parties to attend and put on a mask. But you know, I miss him. He had a wonderful sense of humor that could get me out of my bad mood. He was very much like my father. As angry as my sister and I could be, he had a way to make us laugh.

For the first time, Mrs. Maxton connected her father and her husband.

Therapist: It seems Mr. Maxton and your father had something in common.

Mrs. M.: I never thought about it. But, you know, I missed my father's sense of humor when he died. He was wonderful with my sons. They never had a chance to know him. I always felt bad that Murray and the boys only know him through me.

Therapist: What more would you have liked your sons and Murray to know about him?

Mrs. M.: I think I gave them a negative picture. Right now, you got me wondering if I did that purposefully, so I wouldn't have to miss all the wonderful parts of him that I loved so much. (Long pause.) Do you think (crying) I acted the same way about my mother? You know, I rarely tell anyone about the quilt she made me. I have it on the bed in the guest room. In a way, she's always with me.

I encouraged Mrs. Maxton to talk about objects (Volkan 1972). This invitation can be helpful in facilitating the mourning in a concrete way to discuss linking objects to the deceased.

Ending Phase: Sessions 12 to 15

During this time, the patient is helped to

1. acknowledge the finality of the loss,
2. deal with the fantasy of ending the grief process,
3. say a final good-bye (Worden 1982).

To adjust to widowhood, besides working on grief the patient may need to evaluate her or his personal situation; identify the roles and functions previously assumed by the spouse; and assess educational, occupational, and social skills in order that they and their family can survive. One of the major problems in adjusting to widowhood stems from having to shoulder responsibilities alone.

In this ending phase the clinician and patient have an opportunity to review their relationship and the progress made, and initiate a referral to a support group to sustain the gains and discuss follow-up plans.

Mrs. Maxton began her twelfth session by asking if she was unusual in feeling so sad and if other women have had similar experiences. After some acknowledgment, reflection, and support of her feeling different, I encouraged her to think about joining a widow-to-widow group. There was one close to her home. This would provide her with a regular social context, an opportunity to be with people undergoing a similar experience, and something new that may sustain her after termination. Research findings suggest that self-help and professional services are means of reducing the impact of psychiatric and psychosomatic disorders resulting from bereavement (Parkes and Weiss 1983).

Groups (Leiberman and Videka-Sherman 1986, Lund et al. 1985, Yalom and Vinogradow 1988) and widow-to-widow programs (Silverman 1969) have been found helpful for the bereaved. Through these groups, individuals who have had similar bereavement experiences can share feelings and problems, and can encourage one another to regain control in living by evaluating options and alternatives represented in the lives of others.

During today's session, I reminded Mrs. Maxton that we would be ending treatment in three weeks. She cried and said she liked me and felt attached to me, but remembered that the American Cancer Society gave only fifteen sessions, saying, "I guess I'm in better shape now." We reviewed what was different over the past two months and what we could do over the next three sessions. Mrs. Maxton felt she wanted to prepare herself for the unveiling of her husband's headstone, which would take place after we terminated. Her worry was she would become depressed again and feel alone.

Over the next two sessions we discussed ways and people that Mrs. Maxton could reach out to for emotional support. We also arranged a telephone contact after termination as a check-in if needed.

At the thirteenth session, Mrs. Maxton announced that she was in touch with the widow-to-widow group and would go to the first meeting in two days. She felt the woman she spoke to on the phone was a lot like herself; her husband had died fifteen months ago. "Although I know a lot of women whose husbands died, it just seemed different—it felt so helpful."

What was still problematic was the estrangement she felt toward her sister. She realized it created tension and anxiety when they met for their annual get-together, and felt she wanted to do something different this time when they met. She explained, "I think I've been avoiding very strong feelings. I remember the day you listened to my anger toward Murray. I hope I can do a rehearsal with you for my sister."

Mrs. Maxton spent the remainder of the session role playing her upcoming meeting with her sister, both at their annual get-together and at the unveiling of the headstone. Although negative feelings emerged now and then, we agreed to focus on gaining strength to cope with Murray's death and her feelings of loneliness. Her sons and grandson are strong supports who she feels are both available and receptive. It seems she has a positive relationship with her sons, and together they reminisce about their father.

During the last session, Mrs. Maxton spent time talking about her positive feelings for me. She also conveyed that I was the daughter she longed to have. She gave me a decorative vase as a remembrance of life and that she is a survivor who will go on. I acknowledged her strength and courage, and supported her involvement in the widow-to-widow group.

For Mrs. Maxton, short-term treatment supported improved personal functioning in the face of grieving the death of her husband. Unlike for some widows, financial issues were not a problem, but how to navigate unknown emotional terrain was overwhelming. Within the constraints of fifteen weeks, Mrs. Maxton's motivation and clearly focused treatment goals propelled change. During this time, focus on mastery over internal and external stressors enhanced emotional growth. Some resolution of separation-individuation began and will continue over time. The use of reflection, support, and confrontation of resistance helped to enhance the patient's ego strength. Achievement of a positive outcome improves self-esteem and brings pleasure. Although no homework assignments were given to this patient, many times they serve both conscious and unconscious purposes. Anxieties that surface in the course of doing an assignment must be mastered to complete it, and the experience of dealing with these anxieties is helpful when discussed in treatment. In this treatment solution, transference was an important aspect of the therapeutic relationship that supported the resolution of separation by encouraging growth.

No treatment can ignore the relationship that forms between therapist and patient. The death of a loved one is so painful and devastating that the bereaved are often convinced they will never recover. As the treatment progressed with Mrs. Maxton, aspects of the significance of parental losses and the significance of the therapist emerged in the relationship. To varying degrees, Mrs. Maxton's experience of the therapist as supportive and helpful assisted her to return to a productive life after treatment. Rubin (1998) notes that in cases of shorter duration, it is most appropriate to focus on the relationship to the deceased as the benchmark for the change process.

CONCLUSION

Recent clinical theorists believe that time limitations can support a patient's motivation for therapeutic gain, and that well-focused and clearly limited treatment goals propel change. In the case of bereaved persons, the further resolution of a separation-individuation conflict is a viable treatment goal.

Although most death experiences are characterized by some degree of pain, the experience can also result in growth opportunities. Typical reactions to loss result in dejection, withdrawal, and lack of interest in one's world for a period following the loss. In the classic psychoanalytic perspective, the work of mourning is completed bit by bit, and resolution of the loss occurs only after the bereaved individual successfully withdraws the libidinal energy attached to the loved object. Paul and Grasser (1991) proposed that treatment can provide a "corrective mourning experience" (p. 96). Within a brief treatment paradigm, this approach can activate the mourning by encouraging the mourner to reminisce, express feelings, and empathize with other family members. In a family it can influence the communication to forge a new level of emotional closeness. Another critical aspect of grief resolution requires the bereaved to divert the emotional energy focused on the deceased and begin to invest in new relationships. The principle of short-term intervention allows mourners the opportunity to experience and express a range of uncomfortable emotions and feelings evoked by the loved one's death. An important aspect of brief treatment is the termination phase, since it represents a loss of the therapist and the therapeutic relationship.

In bereavement work, utilizing a short-term approach may be more useful in viewing the deceased as the dominant relational figure. In this way, the effort that is often devoted to the analysis of the transference may be more effectively deflected toward the relationship with the deceased. Many of the transference observations and interpretations normally focused on the therapist may have greater meaning and potential for patient change when they are directed toward the bereaved's relationship with the deceased. When issues of loss and bereavement are central to the work with patients, this relationship may constitute the bulk of treatment work. No treatment can ignore the therapeutic relationship that forms between patient and therapist. In work with the bereaved, however, the therapeutic relationship may function as an environment for work on the relationship to the deceased, rather than as a derivative of the relationship to the deceased (Rubin 1998).

The emotional experience of the therapist, which is neglected or set aside in working with the bereaved, can be a valuable source for achieving an understanding of important aspects the treatment (via the real relationship and the countertransferential reactions that develop). In ways that may be strikingly similar to the disregard of all else in order to remain focused on the deceased, the therapist may be ignored, and the real relationship and the transferential aspects are denied or relegated to inferior status. The further development of this experience by the therapist may be most helpful if it assists the therapist in understanding the nature, and not just the dominance, of the representation of the deceased. The implications that the deceased has for the functioning and internal self-image of the bereaved are as important as the therapist's becoming attuned to the reactions of others in the interpersonal environment of the bereaved (Klass et al. 1996). Listening to the description of the deceased, as well as appreciating that the bereaved may be unavailable to discuss anything but the loss, provides information for the therapist. These same experiences, however, also serve as a source of tension and frustration for the therapist.

When one considers the impact of bereavement years following the loss, it is well to keep in mind that both recovery and resolution range across the continuum, varying in degrees of adjustment, coping, and continued relationship to the representations of the deceased, which are neither fixed nor static. In many ways, the continuing relationship to the deceased is similar to the relationships we have with the living. The greater the degree of comfort and openness that characterizes the connection to memories and thoughts of a particular relationship, the greater the likelihood that the relationship is not a focus of conflict or difficulty requiring intervention. Changes in the relationship to the deceased will continue across the life cycle. The presence of flexibility and resilience in the internal object world are important features of the individual's ability to deal with the ebb and flow of a life course (Rubin 1998).

REFERENCES

Bohannon, J. (1990). Grief responses of spouses following the death of a child: a longitudinal study. *Omega* 22:109–121.

Bowlby, J. (1980). *Attachment and Loss, Vol. 3: Loss, Sadness, and Depression.* New York: Basic Books.

Davanloo, H. (1978). *Basic Principles and Techniques in Short-Term Dynamic Psychotherapy.* New York: Spectrum.

Dolan, Y. (1991). *Resolving Sexual Abuse: Solution-Focused Therapy and Eriksonian Hypnosis for Adult Survivors.* New York: Norton.

Eells, T. D. (1995). Relational therapy for grief disorder. In *Dynamic Therapies for Psychiatric Disorders,* ed. J. P. Barber and P. Crits-Christoph, pp. 386–416. New York: Basic Books.

Engel, G. L. (1961). Is grief a disease? *Psychosomatic Medicine* 23:18–22.

Freud, S. (1917). Mourning and melancholia. *Standard Edition* 14:243–258.

Goldstein, E. G., and Noonan, M. (1999). *Short-Term Treatment and Social Work Practice: An Integrative Perspective.* New York: Free Press.

Herz, F. (1980). The impact of death and serious illness on the family life cycle. In *The Family Life Cycle: A Framework for Family Therapy,* ed. M. McGoldrick and E. Carter, pp. 223–240. New York: Gardner.

Horowitz, M. (1986). *Stress Response Syndromes,* 2nd ed. Northvale, NJ: Jason Aronson.

Horowitz, M. J., Marmar, C., Weiss, D. S., et al. (1984). Brief psychotherapy of bereavement reactions: the relationship of process to outcome. *Archives of General Psychiatry* 41:438–445.

Imber-Black, E. (1991). Rituals and the healing process. In *Living Beyond Loss: Death in the Family,* ed. F. Walsh and M. McGoldrick, pp. 207–223. New York: Norton.

Imber-Black, E., Roberts, J., and Whiting, R. (1988). *Rituals in Families and Family Therapy.* New York: Norton.

James, J. W., and Cherry, F. (1988). *The Grief Recovery Handbook: A Step by Step Program for Moving beyond Loss.* New York: Harper & Row.

Klass, D., Silverman, P. R., and Nickman, S. L., eds. (1996). *Continuing Bonds: New Understanding of Grief.* Washington, DC: Taylor and Francis.

Klerman, G. L., Weisman, M. M., Rounsaville, B. J., and Chevron, E. S. (1984). *Short-Term Dynamic Psychotherapy.* New York: Jason Aronson.

Krell, R., and Rabkin, L. (1979). The effects of sibling death on the surviving child: a family perspective. *Family Process* 10:471–479.

Leiberman, M. A., and Videka-Sherman, L. (1986). The impact of self-help groups on the mental health of widows and widowers. *American Journal of Orthopsychiatry* 56:435–449.

Lindemann, E. (1944). Symptomatology and management of acute grief. *American Journal of Orthopsychiatry* 101:141–148.

Lund, D. A., Dimond, M., and Juretich, M. (1985). Bereavement support groups for the elderly: characterization of potential participants. *Death Studies* 9:309–321.

Malan, D. H. (1976). *The Frontier of Brief Psychotherapy.* New York: Plenum.

Mann, J. (1973). *Time-Limited Psychotherapy.* Cambridge, MA: Harvard University Press.

Melges, F. T., and De Maso, D. R. (1980). Grief resolution therapy: reliving, reusing, and revisiting. *American Journal of Psychotherapy* 34: 51–61.

Middleton, W., Raphael, B., Martinek, N., and Misso, V. (1993). Pathological grief reactions. In *Handbook of Bereavement: Theory, Research, and Intervention*, ed. M. S. Stroebe, W. Stroebe, and R. O. Hanson, pp. 44–61. New York: Cambridge University Press.

Miles, M. S., and Demi, A. (1991–1992). A comparison of guilt in bereaved parents whose children died by suicide, accident or chronic illness. *Omega* 24(3):203–215.

Minuchin, S., Rosman, B. L., and Baker, L., eds. (1992). *Psychosomatic Families.* Cambridge, MA: Harvard University Press.

Nezu, A. M. (1989). *Problem Solving Therapy for Depression.* New York: Wiley.

O'Connor, N. (1984). *Letting Go with Love: The Grieving Process.* Apache Junction, AZ: La Mariposa.

Parkes, C. M. (1971). The first year of bereavement: a longitudinal study of the reaction of London wives to the death of their husbands. *Psychiatry* 33:444–467.

——— (1991). Attachment, bonding and psychiatric problems after bereavement in adult life. In *Attachment Across the Life Cycle*, ed. C. M.

Parker, J. Stevenson-Hinde, and P. Morris, pp. 268–297. London: Tavistock.

Parkes, C. M., and Weiss, R. S. (1983). *Recovery from Bereavement.* New York: Basic Books.

Paul, N., and Grosser, G. (1991). Operational mourning and its role in conjoint family therapy. In *Living beyond Loss,* ed. F. Walsh and M. McGoldrick, pp. 93–103. New York: Norton.

Piper, W. E., Mc Callum, M., and Hassan, F. A., eds. (1992). *Adaptation to Loss through Short-Term Psychotherapy.* New York: Guilford.

Polednak, A. P. (1989). *Racial and Ethnic Differences in Disease.* New York: Oxford University Press.

Ramsey, R., and DeGroot, W. (1984). A further look at bereavement: abnormal grief and its therapy. *Psychology in Practice* 2:49–65.

Rando, T. (1984). *Grief, Dying and Death: Clinical Interventions for Caregivers.* Champaign, IL: Research Press.

——— (1986). *Parental Loss of a Child.* Champaign, IL: Research Press.

Raphael, B. (1983). *The Anatomy of Bereavement.* New York: Basic Books.

Rubin, S. (1998). Case study: reconsidering the transference paradigm in treatment with the bereaved. *American Journal of Psychotherapy* 52(2): 215–228.

Schilling, R. F., El-Bassel, N., Serrano, Y., and Wallace, B. (1992). SIDS preventive strategies for Latino and African-American substance abusers. *Journal of Psychology of Addictive Behavior* 13:29–41.

Schumacher, J. (1984). Helping children cope with a sibling's death. In *Death and Grief in the Family,* ed. J. Hansen, pp. 82–94. Rockville, MD: Aspen.

Sifneos, P. (1979). *Short-Term Psychotherapy and Emotional Crisis.* Cambridge, MA: Harvard University Press.

Silverman, P. (1969). The widow-to-widow program: an experiment in preventive intervention. *Mental Hygiene* 53:333–337.

Stroebe, M. S., Stroebe, W., and Hansson, R. O., eds. (1993). *Handbook of Bereavement: Theory, Research and Intervention.* Cambridge, MA: Cambridge University Press.

Tahka, V. (1984). Dealing with object loss. *Scandanavian Psychoanalytic Review* 7:13–33.

Tait, R., and Silver, R. C. (1989). Coming to terms with major negative life events. In *Unintended Thought*, ed. J. S. Uleman and J. A. Bargh, pp. 351–382. New York: Guilford.

Vachon, M. L. S., Rogers, J., Lyall, W. A. L., et al. (1982). Predictors and correlates of adaptation to conjugal bereavement. *American Journal of Psychiatry* 139:998–1002.

Vess, J., Moreland, J., and Schwebel, A. (1985). Understanding family role reallocation following a death: a theoretical framework. *Omega* 19(2):116–127.

Volkan, J. (1985). Complicated mourning. *Annual of Psychoanalysis* 12: 323–348.

Volkan, V. D. (1972). The linking of objects of pathological mourners. *Archives of General Psychiatry* 27:215–221.

Walsh, F., and McGoldrick, M. (1991). Loss and the family: a systemic perspective. In *Living Beyond Loss: Death in the Family*, ed. F. Walsh and M. McGoldrick, pp. 1–29. New York: Norton.

Wells, R. A. (1994). *Planned Short-Term Treatment*. New York: Free Press.

Worden, J. W. (1982). *Grief Counseling and Grief Therapy: A Handbook for the Mental Health Practitioner*. New York: Springer.

——— (1991). *Grief Counseling and Grief Therapy*, 2nd ed. New York: Springer.

Wortman, C., and Silver, R. (1989). The myths of coping with loss. *Journal of Consulting and Clinical Psychology* 57(3):349–357.

Yalom, J. D., and Vinogradov, S. (1988). Bereavement groups: techniques and themes. *International Journal of Group Psychotherapy* 38:419–446.

INDEX